THE AUT

KT-149-763

Walter Allen was born in Aston, Birmingham, in 1911. The youngest of four sons of a silversmith, he grew up in a working-class community and won a scholarship to King Edward's Grammar School, Aston (although he felt his real education took place in the city's Public Reference Library). In 1929 he went to Birmingham University to read English, where he made friends with Louis MacNeice and Henry Reed, the latter having been at the same school. On graduating he worked as a freelance journalist and broadcaster, for the *Birmingham Post*, the *Gazette* and BBC Midland, and later for the London weeklies. His literary acquaintance ranged from W. H. Auden and E. M. Forster to the regional writers John Hampson, Walter Brierley, Peter Chamberlain and Leslie Halward, with whom he was linked in the so-called Birmingham Group in the mid-Thirties. Allen's first two novels, *Innocence is Drowned* and *Dead Men Over All*, appeared in 1938 and 1940, and in 1938 he moved to London to read scripts for MGM, where one of his co-readers was Olivia Manning.

After the war, Walter Allen and his wife Peggy (whom he married in 1944) lived in Edgbaston, before settling in London. He contributed to *Time and Tide* and *Penguin New Writing* and reviewed widely, notably for the *New Statesman*, where he later became literary editor. In the Fifties he was also well known for his weekly radio programme 'Talking of Books', his highly influential study *The English Novel* (1952) and the acclaimed *All in a Lifetime* (1959), also in Hogarth. *Tradition and Dream* was published in 1966, and in 1967 Allen gave up literary journalism to become the first Professor of English Studies at the New University of Ulster. Between 1955 and 1975 he also spent several periods as a visiting professor to American universities. His own account of this full literary life is given in *As I Walked Down New Grub Street* (1981). He has now retired and lives in London.

TRADITION AND DREAM

The English and American Novel
from the Twenties to Our Time

Walter Allen

New Afterword by
the Author

THE HOGARTH PRESS
LONDON

Published in 1986 by
The Hogarth Press
Chatto & Windus Ltd
40 William IV Street, London WC2N 4DF

First published in Great Britain by J. M. Dent & Sons Ltd 1964
Copyright © Walter Allen 1964, 1986

All rights reserved. No part of this publication may be reproduced, stored in a
retrieval system, or transmitted in any form, or by any means, electronic,
mechanical, photocopying, recording or otherwise, without the prior
permission of the publisher.

British Library Cataloguing in Publication Data

Allen, Walter
Tradition and dream: the English and American novel from
the twenties to our time.
1. English fiction – 20th century – History and criticism
I. Title
823'.009   PR881

ISBN 0 7012 0692 6

Printed in Finland by
Werner Söderström Oy

CONTENTS

AUTHOR'S PREFACE

THIS IS a sequel to my book *The English Novel*. That ended as this begins: with a consideration of Joyce, Virginia Woolf and Lawrence. There is, therefore, some repetition, though I have taken the opportunity to incorporate what second thoughts I have had about those writers. Roughly, the book covers the period from 1920 to 1960, though I have not dealt with novelists whose first works were published after 1955.

In order to set limits to a field that often seemed, while I was writing, to be dauntingly vast, I have ignored historical fiction and short stories generally, except when they appeared to throw light on an author's novels; and I have confined myself to the novel in English as written in the United States and the United Kingdom only. This may not be logical: I can only plead necessity.

I am acutely conscious of many omissions. Readers will decide for themselves which are wilful and which the result of ignorance. If I had considered all the British and American novelists during the forty years whom I admire or who seem worthy of note for one reason or another, this book would either have been twice as long as it is or a catalogue of names and titles.

ACKNOWLEDGMENTS

THE author and publisher are grateful to the following for permission to quote copyright passages from the books named:

W. H. Allen & Co. for *Classics and Commercials* by Edmund Wilson; Edward Arnold (Publishers) Ltd for *A Passage to India* by E. M. Forster; Basic Books Inc. for *Summer in Williamsburg, Homage to Blenholt*, and *Low Company* by Daniel Fuchs; G. Bell & Sons Ltd for *The American Novel and its Tradition* by Richard Chase; The Bodley Head Ltd for *The Great Gatsby* (*The Bodley Head Scott Fitzgerald*, Vol. I), *This Side of Paradise* and *The Rich Boy* (*The Bodley Head Scott Fitzgerald*, Vol. III); Miss Sonia Brownell for review by George Orwell in 'The New Yorker' of *The Heart of the Matter* by Graham Greene.

Jonathan Cape Ltd for *Four Countries, Museum Pieces*, and *Sado* by William Plomer, *The Death of the Heart* and *The Heat of the Day* by Elizabeth Bowen, *Winesburg, Ohio* by Sherwood Anderson, *All the Conspirators* by Christopher Isherwood, and *The Retreat* by P. H. Newby; Jonathan Cape Ltd and the Executors of the Authors' Estates for *Under the Volcano* by Malcolm Lowry, *In Our Time, The Sun also Rises*, and *A Farewell to Arms* by Ernest Hemingway, and *Main Street* and *Babbitt* by Sinclair Lewis; Chatto & Windus Ltd for *High Wind in Jamaica* and *In Hazard* by Richard Hughes, *Lady into Fox* by David Garnett, *The Great Tradition* by F. R. Leavis, *The Classical Temper* by S. L. Goldberg, *After Many A Summer* by Aldous Huxley, *Mr Tasker's Gods* by T. F. Powys, *Intruder in the Dust, The Sound and the Fury, Light in August*, and *Absalom, Absalom!* by William Faulkner, *Nothing Like Leather* and 'A Plymouth Brother' from *The Living Novel* by V. S. Pritchett; Chatto & Windus Ltd and the proprietors, Alfred A. Knopf Inc., for *A Long Day's Dying* by Frederick Buechner; City Lights Books, San Francisco, for *Bottom Dogs* by Edward Dahlberg; Wm Collins Sons & Co. Ltd for *The Life and Death of Harriet Frean* by May Sinclair, and *H. M. Pulham, Esquire* by John P. Marquand; Constable & Co. Ltd for *None Shall Look Back* by Caroline Gordon, *Manhattan Transfer* by John Dos Passos, and *A True Story* by Stephen Hudson; The Cresset Press for *The Heart is a Lonely Hunter, The Member of the Wedding, The Ballad of the Sad Café*, and *Clock Without Hands* by Carson McCullers.

J. M. Dent & Sons Ltd for *Quite Early One Morning* by Dylan Thomas, and *Living* by Henry Green; André Deutsch Ltd for *The Literary Situation* by Malcolm Cowley, *The Naked and the Dead* by Norman Mailer, *The Dharma Bums* by Jack Kerouac, and *Therefore be Bold* by Herbert Gold; Gerald Duckworth & Co. Ltd for *The Flower Beneath the Foot* and *Concerning the Eccentricities of Cardinal Pirelli* by Ronald Firbank; Eyre & Spottiswoode Ltd for *Men and Wives* by Ivy Compton-Burnett, *The End of an Old Song* by J. D. Scott, and *The Fathers* by Allen Tate; Faber & Faber Ltd for 'In Memory of Sigmund Freud' from *Another Time* by W. H. Auden, and *Clea* and *Balthazar* by Lawrence

Durrell; John Farquharson Ltd on behalf of the Estate of the late Henry James for *Hawthorne* by Henry James; James T. Farrell, for his *Studs Lonigan*.

William Gerhardi for his *Resurrection*; Victor Gollancz Ltd for *I Like It Here* by Kingsley Amis; Victor Gollancz Ltd and the proprietors, Random House Inc., for *The Invisible Man* by Ralph Ellison; Hamish Hamilton Ltd for *Lie Down in Darkness* by William Styron and *The Mirror in the Roadway* by Frank O'Connor; Hamish Hamilton Ltd and Houghton Mifflin Company, Boston, for *My Antonia* by Willa Cather; Hamish Hamilton Ltd and Alfred A. Knopf Inc., New York, for *A Lost Lady* by Willa Cather; Harcourt, Brace & World Inc. for *Barren Ground* by Ellen Glasgow; Harper & Row, Publishers, Incorporated, for *The Grandmothers* by Glenway Wescott and *Native Son* by Richard Wright; William Heinemann Ltd for *Look Homeward, Angel* and *Of Time and the River* by Thomas Wolfe, *In Dubious Battle* and *The Grapes of Wrath* by John Steinbeck, *The Spoilt City* by Olivia Manning, *Other Voices, Other Rooms* by Truman Capote, *Brighton Rock* by Graham Greene, and *Afternoon Men* and *A Question of Up-bringing* by Anthony Powell; The Hogarth Press for *Loving* by Henry Green and *Mr Norris Changes Trains* by Christopher Isherwood.

Jarrolds Publishers (London) Ltd for *Sunset Song* and *Grey Granite* by Lewis Grassic Gibbon; Michael Joseph Ltd for *Call it Sleep* by Henry Roth, *To Be a Pilgrim* by Joyce Cary, and *Notes of a Native Son* by James Baldwin; John Lehmann Ltd for *U.S.A.—The Big Money* and *U.S.A.—The 42nd Parallel* by John Dos Passos and *The Sheltering Sky* by Paul Bowles; Longmans, Green & Co. Ltd for *The Cabala* and *Heaven's my Destination* by Thornton Wilder, *The Just and the Unjust* by James Gould Cozzens, and *The Violent Bear It Away* by Flannery O'Connor; Macdonald & Co. (Publishers) Ltd for *A Glastonbury Romance* by John Cowper Powys; Macmillan & Co. Ltd for *The Masters* and *The Light and the Dark* by C. P. Snow, *Young People* by William Cooper, and *The Last Resort* by Pamela Hansford Johnson; Methuen & Co. Ltd for *The Revenge for Love* and *Self Condemned* by Wyndham Lewis, and *Lions and Shadows* by Christopher Isherwood.

Oxford University Press Inc., New York, for *Form and Fable in American Fiction* by Daniel G. Hoffman; Laurence Pollinger Ltd and the Estate of the late Mrs Frieda Lawrence for *Sons and Lovers*, *The Collected Letters of D. H. Lawrence*, *Aaron's Rod*, *The Rainbow*, and *Women in Love* by D. H. Lawrence, published by William Heinemann Ltd; Princeton University Press for *Radical Innocence* by Ihab Hassan; Putnam & Co. Ltd for *The Shrimp and the Anemone* and *The Sixth Heaven* by L. P. Hartley, and *Strange Glory* by L. H. Myers; Martin Secker & Warburg Ltd for *Miss Lonelyhearts* and *The Day of the Locust* by Nathanael West, *The Liberal Imagination* and *The Middle of the Journey* by Lionel Trilling, *Love and Death in the American Novel* by Leslie A. Fiedler, *Hurry On Down* by John Wain, and *The Gallery* by John Horne Burns; The Society of Authors and the author for *The Echoing Grove* by Rosamond Lehmann, published by Collins; Neville Spearman and the author for *Wise Blood* by Flannery O'Connor.

University of North Carolina Press for *The Fugitives: a Critical Account* by John Bradbury; Evelyn Waugh for his *Brideshead Revisited*, *Vile Bodies*, *Unconditional Surrender*, and *Decline and Fall*, published by Chapman & Hall

Ltd; George Weidenfeld & Nicholson Ltd for *Dangling Man*, *The Victim*, *The Adventures of Augie March*, *Seize the Day*, and *Henderson the Rain King* by Saul Bellow, and *Cards of Identity* by Nigel Dennis; Rebecca West for her *The Thinking Reed*; Leonard Woolf and The Hogarth Press Ltd for *Between the Acts* and *The Common Reader* by Virginia Woolf; Mrs Anne Wyndham Lewis for *Men Without Art* by Wyndham Lewis; the owner of the copyright for *The Romantic Comedians* by Ellen Glasgow, published by Doubleday & Company Inc.

Some passages in this book have appeared, generally in a rather different form, in *The Times Literary Supplement*, *The New Statesman*, *New Writing*, *Encounter*, and *The London Magazine*, to the editors of which I gratefully make the usual acknowledgments.

Every effort has been made to trace the owners of copyright material quoted in this book. Should any material have been included inadvertently without the permission of the owner of the copyright, acknowledgment will be made in any future edition.

INTRODUCTION

THE FACT that English novels and American are written in a common language often blinds us to the differences between them. In individual instances, of course, these differences may be so slight as to be almost indistinguishable. Is Henry James an American novelist or an English? The commonsense answer is that he is both; his novels belong to both literatures. Even so, the English reader tends to forget that James was an American before he was English and that Hawthorne was his literary ancestor no less than George Eliot. And when one turns from individual novels to the body of what seem representative novels of both countries then broad and well-defined differences between them are immediately apparent, differences that reflect differences in historical experience and in the national character history produces.

These differences are not recent in origin. They were just as strongly marked in nineteenth-century fiction as they are in that of today. Indeed, to set the great English Victorian novels side by side with the great Americans of the same period is to be aware almost of a difference in kind. If there was no American Dickens, Thackeray, George Eliot or Trollope, there was equally no English Hawthorne or Melville. The divergence is radical, and light is thrown upon it by F. R. Leavis's note on *Wuthering Heights* in *The Great Tradition*:

> I have said nothing about *Wuthering Heights* because that astonishing work seems to me a kind of sport ... Emily Brontë broke completely, and in the most challenging way, both with the Scott tradition that imposed on the novelist a romantic resolution of his themes, and with the tradition coming down from the eighteenth century that demanded a plane-mirror reflection of the surface of 'real' life.

Leavis is right: in terms of the English novel as the overwhelming mass of its finest examples compels us to conceive it, *Wuthering Heights* is a sport—a freak. But suppose, writes the American critic Richard Chase in *The American Novel and Its Tradition*, suppose it were discovered that *Wuthering Heights* was written by an American of New England Calvinist or Southern Presbyterian background. The novel would be astonishing and unique no matter who wrote it or where. But if it were an American novel it would not be a sport: it has too close an affinity with too many American novels, and among them some of the best.

Mr Chase goes on to list some of these—they include *The Scarlet Letter* and *The Blithedale Romance*, *Moby Dick*, *Huckleberry Finn*, *The Red Badge of Courage*, *As I Lay Dying* and *The Sun Also Rises* (*Fiesta*)—remarking that 'all are eccentric, in their differing ways, to a tradition of which, let us say, *Middlemarch* is a standard representative. Not one of them has any close kinship with the massive, temperate, moralistic rendering of life and thought we associate with Mr Leavis's "great tradition".'

From the very beginning, American novelists themselves have been aware of their divergence from the English tradition. Awareness was forced upon them by the nature of the society in which they lived as compared with that of Britain. Almost a century and a half ago Fenimore Cooper complained of the American scene:

> There is scarcely any ore which contributes to the wealth of the author, that is found, here, in veins as rich as in Europe. There are no annals for the historian; no follies (beyond the most vulgar and commonplace) for the satirist; no manners for the dramatist; no obscure fictions for the writer of romance; no gross and hardy offences against decorum for the moralist; nor any of the rich artificial auxiliaries of poetry.

Hawthorne took up the complaint thirty years later and was at pains to persuade his readers that his books were not novels but romances. Novels, he said, were 'presumed to aim at a very minute fidelity, not merely to the possible, but to the probable and ordinary course of man's experience'; and his reason for not writing novels was that the attendant circumstances necessary for the novel did not exist in the United States.

After the passage of a further thirty years we find Henry James, in his critical biography of Hawthorne, expanding the indictment of the shortcomings of American society from the novelist's point of view:

> One might enumerate the items of high civilization, as it exists in

other countries, which are absent from the texture of American life, until it should be a wonder to know what was left. No State, in the European sense of the word, and indeed barely a specific national name. No sovereign, no court, no personal loyalty, no aristocracy, no church, no clergy, no army, no diplomatic service, no country gentlemen, no palaces, no castles, nor manors, nor old country houses, no parsonages, nor thatched cottages, nor ivied ruins; no great universities nor public schools —no Oxford, nor Eton, nor Harrow; no literature, no novels, no museums, no pictures, no political society, no sporting class —no Epsom nor Ascot! Some such list as that might be drawn up of the absent things in American life—especially in the American life of forty years ago, the effect of which, upon an English or French imagination, would probably as a general thing be appalling. The natural remark, in the light of such an indictment, would be that if these things are left out, everything is left out.

Everything? Not at all, exclaimed James's friend and fellow-novelist William Dean Howells: there remained 'simply the whole of human life'. One sympathizes with Howells's democratic fervour, but, from the point of view of the novel, he was wrong and James, soaked as he was in the fiction of Balzac and Dickens, Flaubert, Turgenev and George Eliot, was right. The great theme of the European novel, and perhaps especially of the English novel, has been man's life in society; more precisely, the education of men and women, in the sense of their learning to distinguish, through their inescapable involvement in society, the true from the false both in themselves and in the world about them; and this applies no less to the fiction of a rebel like D. H. Lawrence, whose work is as much about society as about sex, than to that of Jane Austen.

The kind of society that was the natural soil for the growth of the English novel not only did not exist in the United States of a hundred and fifty years ago; by the definition of the United States itself it could not. The items of high civilization listed by James in conscious and humorous exaggeration were precisely those elements of European society the first Americans had left Europe to escape. 'If the nineteenth century', Lewis Mumford has written, 'found us more raw and rude, it was not because we had settled in a new territory; it was rather because our minds were not buoyed up by all those memorials of a great past that floated over the surface of Europe. The American was thus a stripped European; and the colonization of America can, with justice, be called the dispersion of Europe—a movement carried out by people incapable of sharing or continuing its past. It was to America that the outcast Europeans turned, without a Moses to guide them, to wander in the wilderness; and here they have remained in exile, not without an occasional glimpse, perhaps, of the promised land.'

The promised land, the American Dream, whatever it was to be, was to be as unlike the Europe that had been renounced as possible. Its nature had been stated as early as 1782 by Hector de Crèvecœur in his famous essay, 'What is an American?'. American society, Crèvecœur writes,

> is not composed, as in Europe, of great lords who possess every-thing, and of a herd of people who have nothing. Here are no aristocratical families, no courts, no kings, no bishops, no ecclesiastical dominion, no invisible power giving to a few a very visible one; no great manufacturers employing thousands, no great refinements of luxury. The rich and the poor are not so far removed from each other as they are in Europe. . . . We are all animated with the spirit of an industry which is unfettered and unrestrained, because each person works for himself . . . We have no princes for whom we toil, starve, and bleed; we are the most perfect society now existing in the world. Here man is free as he ought to be. . . .

And Crèvecœur ends his catalogue of the virtues of American life, which is quite strikingly similar to James's list of its deficiencies sixty years later, by announcing, 'The American is a new man'.

In a sense, the classic American was a man who had opted out of society in anything but the simplest form. For many Americans, the repudiation of Europe and the past was tantamount to a repudiation of all external restraint upon the individual. To society the American opposed—himself. In a way, this is the point of the great novel that has been so potent a shaping factor in the American myth, *The Adventures of Huckleberry Finn*, with its concluding sentences: 'I reckon I got to light out for the Territory ahead of the rest, because Aunt Sally she's going to adopt me and sivilize me, and I can't stand it. I been there before.'

The classic American novels have dealt not so much with the lives of men in society as with the life of solitary man, man alone and wrestling with himself. Thus Hawthorne dramatized his own tortured, ambiguous relationship with his Puritan ancestors and with his consciousness of sin. Melville, in *Moby Dick*, dramatized his sense of the evil that stems from man's overweening pride, his refusal to recognize limits. Whitman's line, 'I was the man, I suffer'd, I was there', echoes through much of the best American fiction, of past and present alike. The emphasis is on the individual, whether Crane's hero in *The Red Badge of Courage* or the boy Nick in the early stories of Hemingway, on the individual human being alone, testing life. And there are times when the individual becomes more than an individual and seems to contain all human life within himself, to become Man, as in the Walt of Walt Whitman's *Song of Myself* or the heroes of Thomas Wolfe's novels. Continually, there is the opting out of society. In our time, the great example of this is Hemingway. From a European point of view, it must seem a weakness in him, the fundamental weakness, that after his early stories he could not take in or come to terms with the American life of his day; but seen in the tradition of American writing it appears rather differently: he was lighting out for the Territory, seeking the promised land that seems to be an essential part of the American Dream.

Such solitary heroes dominate American fiction. They appear, by contrast with the heroes of English novels, often to belong to a different order of experience and conception. Abstracted, alienated from the society of their times, surrounded as it were by an envelope of emptiness, they seem somewhat larger than life, at any rate than life as rendered in the broadly realistic English novel in which the crowd of men and women depicted must bring the central figures down to a level approximating to their own. They have, these American heroes, an epic, mythic quality; and the point may be made merely by a roll-call of characteristic American heroes: Cooper's Natty Bumppo, Hawthorne's Hester Prynne, Melville's Ishmael and Ahab, Twain's Huck Finn, Fitzgerald's Gatsby, Wolfe's Eugene Gant, Faulkner's Sutpen and Joe Christmas, Salinger's Holden Caulfield, Bellow's Henderson. They are characters not in process of discovering the nature of society and of themselves in and through society but are, on the contrary, characters profoundly alienated from society. One may here contrast Holden Caulfield in Salinger's *The Catcher in the Rye* with a roughly contemporaneous English hero, Kingsley Amis's Jim Dixon, in *Lucky Jim*. Each is at odds with the society in which he finds himself, but Dixon much more superficially so. In the end, one knows, he will find the society to which he can adapt himself; but for Caulfield adaptation, any adaptation, will be self-mutilation. One might say that society and the characteristic American hero are irreconcilably opposed.

These heroes strike one as being, in a sense, figures of dream, projections even of a national unconscious, and the novels as being really interior dramas in which the author works out, often violently—the violence frequently being as much evidenced by the texture of the prose as by the action delineated—the causes and the consequences of what Henry James called, in a famous phrase, the complex fate of being an American. By that, James meant the continuously ambivalent relationship of the American to the Old World, with its fluctuations, often rapidly alternating, of rejection and over-valuation of Europe. But there are other factors making for the complexity of the fate. The conditions of frontier life, which dominated American behaviour for several generations and which are still a powerful shaping force in the way Americans see themselves, are among them. Another is what Richard Chase has called 'The Manichaean quality of New England Puritanism'. 'As apprehended by the literary imagination', Chase writes, 'New England Puritanism, with its grand metaphors of election and damnation, its opposition of the kingdom of light and the kingdom of darkness, its eternal and autonomous contraries of good and evil—seems to have recaptured the Manichaean sensibility. The American imagination, like the New England Puritan mind itself, seems less interested in redemption than in the melodrama of the eternal struggle of good and evil, less interested in incarnation and reconciliation than in alienation and disorder.'

All these deep-seated historical factors have contributed to the sense of individual isolation that seems central to the American experience. It is out of this sense of isolation and the sense of alienation that goes with it that the American novel and its characteristic mode of expression spring.

The mode of expression is allegory and symbolism, which, though different in effect, are closely related, almost at times to the degree of Siamese twinship. Indeed, symbolism seems to be the specifically American way of apprehending and rendering experience in literature. It is not the English way. And allegory and symbolism are ingrained in the American sensibility for good reasons: they are part of the heritage of Puritanism. Daniel G. Hoffman, in his *Form and Fable in American*

Fiction, has shown how Hawthorne, with Melville, depended 'upon the single mode of literary expression sanctioned by his inherited culture: allegory'. Professor Hoffman goes on:

> As the faith which had sustained Puritan allegory withered or was transformed, as the supernatural certainties to which allegory anchored the things of this world became dubious or obscure, the mode yet persisted and lent itself to new uses. The imaginations of Hawthorne and Melville were both committed to allegorical premises and sceptical of allegorical truths. Allegory was designed for the elucidation of certainty; they used it in the service of search and scepticism, and, at times, of comedic affirmation of human values. In the process they transformed allegorism into a symbolic method.

This bent towards symbolism was further strengthened in the nineteenth century by another derivative of Puritanism, the Transcendentalism of Emerson, with his doctrine:

1. Words are signs of natural facts.
2. Particular natural facts are symbols of particular spiritual facts.
3. Nature is a symbol of spirit.

And behind all this is the inevitable tendency of the interior drama of the solitary human being to body itself forth in symbolic terms. For it is not as though American fiction was symbolist only at one stage in its development: it has remained so right up to the present time, in Faulkner, in whose work symbolism and allegory are often confused, in Carson McCullers, in much younger novelists like Flannery O'Connor.

But there is another abiding factor in the American novel: a constant preoccupation with the meaning of being an American. It is only in work written in times of extreme national peril that one finds anything in the English novel comparable to this: Joyce Cary's *To be a Pilgrim* comes to mind as an instance. Generally, Englishness, what it means to be an Englishman, is not a subject of the English novel. No Englishman could have written, or made his hero say, as Joyce does Dedalus in *Portrait of the Artist as a Young Man*: 'Welcome, O life! I go to encounter for the millionth time the reality of experience and to forge in the smithy of my soul the uncreated conscience of my race.' The conscience of the English was created not by one man but by a multitude living in many centuries. But historically it has been the great task

of the American poets and novelists to do exactly what Stephen
Dedalus boasted he would do; and after almost two centuries of
national independence they continue to do so. It is as though the
American were not simply, as Crèvecœur said, a new man but also a
self-created man. In every generation it seems that the American, by
virtue of his being an American, with all that that entails, must come
to terms with his Americanness and seek to define it. In the last
analysis, the theme of many of the best American novels is America
itself. The obvious instance, perhaps, is *The Great Gatsby*. Fitzgerald's novel is an exposure of the quality of life at a certain place at a
certain point in time; but, as we see in the last pages, it is also something more, and the 'something more' is exactly what we would not
expect to find in any English novel.

The interpretation and the emphasis shift, of course, from generation
to generation. When the theme was James's he sought to define it by
contrasting his American heroes and more particularly his American
heroines with the Europeans they encountered in their pilgrimages to
the Old World. In our own day, not entirely owing to the genius of
Faulkner, it often seems to have narrowed down to the consideration
of what it means to be a Southerner.

But there is something else. *The Great Gatsby* ends with these
words:

> Gatsby believed in the green light, the orgastic future that
> year by year recedes before us. It eluded us then, but that's no
> matter—tomorrow we will run faster, stretch out our arms
> farther . . . And one fine morning—
> So we beat on, boats against the current, borne back ceaselessly
> into the past.

The green light at the end of Daisy Buchanan's dock, the orgastic
future, are Fitzgerald's images of the American Dream that lures and
recedes. The Dream, which is still one of the most potent myths in the
American mind, is impossible of realization because impossible of anything like accurate definition: its only blue-print is each man's private
dream. Nevertheless, the lure of the Dream and the feeling that it has
been betrayed have been central to much American fiction since the
earliest days. It is fundamental to Cooper's Natty Bumppo novels and
it accounts in large measure for the especial bitterness and violence of
many American Radical novels from Frank Norris's and Dreiser's to

Norman Mailer's. These novels are critical in attitude; it is as though the novelist has come to his subject—America or some aspect of America—with a pattern in his mind of what life in America should be which he has to set against the actualities of American life in order to judge them.

Dreiser is an almost perfect example of another apparently abiding characteristic of the American novelist, what Professor John McCormick, in his *Catastrophe and Imagination: An Interpretation of the Recent English and American Novel*, calls 'the American writer's paradox of traditionless tradition'. It seems worth noting here that the notion of literary tradition scarcely existed in English literary theory until it was introduced round about 1917 by two young American poets, T. S. Eliot and Ezra Pound, and for them the works that made up the tradition were drawn from all the literatures of the civilized world.

Plainly, Professor McCormick's 'paradox' is akin to W. H. Auden's idea that 'every American poet feels that the whole responsibility for contemporary poetry has fallen upon his shoulders, that he is a literary aristocracy of one', committed as it were to a wholly new start for poetry. We are back with the twin themes of American isolation and alienation. It is an historical fact that American novelists have tended to live as solitaries as English novelists have not. One recalls Hawthorne's twelve years of seclusion in Salem, Melville's obscurity in the New York Customs and, in our time, Faulkner's long periods of inaccessibility in Oxford, Mississippi. No doubt too much can be made of this, but the contrast between the American literary scene and the gregariousness of English literary life, concentrated as it is almost entirely in London, is violent. The isolation in which many American writers live must seem to an Englishman deliberate and wilful. It is as though the literary life itself has become a microcosm of the society the novelist is opting out of.

Isolation has both advantages and disadvantages for a writer. Nothing so strongly nourishes ambition as the feeling that one is different from one's fellows and alone; and when a man has no peers to measure himself against anything may seem possible to him. But if a man is to continue to write and to remain alone the severest self-criticism is called for if he is not to lapse into indiscipline and eccentricity. Faulkner, genius as he is, is a case in point. Indeed, there are times when one feels that without the genius he would be nothing. His genius pulls him through, but all the same there is much truth in Edmund Wilson's criticism:

> ... the weaknesses of Faulkner ... have their origin in the anti-quated community he inhabits, for they result from his not having mastered—I speak of the design of his books as wholes as well as that of his sentences and paragraphs—the discipline of the Joyces, Prousts and Conrads ... The technique of the modern novel, with its ideal of technical efficiency, its specializa-tion of means for ends, has grown up in the industrial age, and it has, after all, a good deal in common with the other manifesta-tions of that age. In practising it so far from such cities as produced the Flauberts, Joyces and Jameses, Faulkner's pro-vinciality, stubbornly cherished and turned into an asset, inevi-tably tempts him to be slipshod and has apparently made it impossible for him to acquire complete expertness in an art that demands of the artist the closest attention and care.

There is, of course, another obvious difference between the Ameri-can novel and the English. If the great theme of American fiction has been the exploration of what it means to be an American, expressed often in solitary heroes with a whole world to roam over, the great overriding preoccupation of English fiction throughout its history has been class. Class turns up everywhere in the English novel, and in all ages. It is in Gissing and Wells and Lawrence and Orwell no less than in Jane Austen and Thackeray and Meredith. The snobberies and the aspirations inseparable from the notion of social class have been a source of comedy in English fiction from Fanny Burney to L. P. Hartley and Anthony Powell. Though it would be absurd to deny the existence of a class system in the United States, it is, for the majority of Americans at any rate, largely a concealed thing. Americans are certainly much less aware of class than are the English, who, as the whole world knows, are obsessed with it to a degree almost pathological.

Perhaps the differences between the two fictions could be summed up in this way. It may still be possible for a young novelist in the United States to dream of writing the Great American Novel: nothing comparable is permitted to an Englishman. Behind him lie two and a half centuries of English novels, and their pressure is all but inescapable except by writers of genius. Whether he likes it or not, whether he is conscious of it or not, the English novelist is born into a tradition of fiction. It is not a narrow one; and since the novel is anyway an international form, the English novelist may derive in part from traditions of the novel as they exist outside England; he may draw on Dostoevsky or Proust or Joyce, to say nothing of the nineteenth-century French. Nevertheless, while the native English tradition is extraordinarily capable of assimilating foreign modes, it subtly changes them even as it absorbs them. Arnold Bennett, for instance, came to the writing of fiction in considerable ignorance of what had been done in the English novel but with a pretty good knowledge of the French and Russian, and in *The Old Wives' Tale* was working in conscious rivalry with Maupassant. His aim, in a sense, was to write a French masterpiece in English. But when we read his novel today it is certainly not its French affinities that strike us but its incurable Englishness. Whatever Bennett himself may have thought, *The Old Wives' Tale* shows that he had much more in common with Dickens and Wells than with Maupassant.

The power of the great English novelists has been such as to impose upon the English, writers and readers alike, certain ways of looking at and interpreting experience that have become almost conventional. It is as though Fielding, Jane Austen, Peacock, Dickens, Trollope, George Eliot, even Gissing, have become gigantic invisible presences that compel the English to observe and assess certain combinations of characters and situation through their eyes; or it is as though, in given circumstances, the English tend to play parts and speak lines allotted to them by these invisible presences. From this form of tyranny of the past the American novelist is free.

All the same, the English novelist gains much from the tradition of which he is, willy-nilly, a part. He can see himself as a member of a body of craftsmen whose existence goes relatively far back in time. Given reasonable powers of self-criticism, he will know what he is likely to be able to accomplish in relation to his forbears. Or he may react violently against one or more of them. He will scarcely be able to escape awareness of them, which means that his attitude towards the novel will tend to be literary, with all that that implies both positively and negatively. He will probably be much less self-conscious about his writing than his American colleagues, and probably more sure of himself since he will know his limitations. Yet the very existence of the broad tradition of the novel in which he works, dominated as it is by a dozen or so exceedingly powerful figures, of whom the lesser figures will generally seem in some sense derivatives, may blinker and inhibit him more than he is ever likely to know.

The American novelist, on the other hand, will probably be more ambitious and more daring; and also, perhaps, more crude, relatively unconcerned with or impatient of style in the narrow sense of elegance of expression and of subtlety of psychological analysis, of what Thomas Wolfe dismissed as the 'European and fancy'. If the gap between ambition and talent is marked, he will seem much more pretentious.

Individual novelists on both sides of the Atlantic will continue, as in the past, to make nonsense of these generalizations; and changes in historical and social circumstances may completely destroy their validity. Indeed, when one looks at what has been happening in the fiction of the two countries during the past five years, one is aware of changes that, if enduring, may well be of great significance. The period has seen, almost for the first time in Britain, the appearance of a quite sizable body of fiction that can fairly be called working-class; Alan Sillitoe, David Storey and Keith Waterhouse are probably the best-known of those contributing to it. While in the United States it now seems as though the dominance of the South in the novel has largely passed to Jewish writers, through the best of whose work, the novels of Saul Bellow and Bernard Malamud in particular, a recognizably new note has come into American fiction, not the less American for being unmistakably Jewish.

THE TWENTIES: BRITISH

[I]

AFTER THE first world war, the age that had ended in July 1914 seemed as remote as the far side of the moon. The war split the landscape of time like an enormous natural catastrophe, obliterating long-established boundaries, blowing sky-high landmarks that for years had been taken for granted. It lay like an unbridgeable chasm between the present and the past, so that present and past seemed almost laughably different in kind. It set a gulf between the young who had fought it and the old who had stayed at home. What had seemed certainties, all the assumptions nurtured in Britain by a hundred years of virtual peace, during which wars were fought either by foreigners or, if the British were involved, by small professional armies on the peripheries of empire, were exposed as illusions. The war had speeded up social change as it had never been speeded up before. It emancipated women; it emancipated the working-class. It made the motor car and the aeroplane commonplace. It affected everything and everybody. Nothing was as it was before.

Its effects are plain enough to see in the literature of the twenties; neither *The Waste Land* nor, at a lower level, the novels of Aldous Huxley seem thinkable before 1914. Yet, as one looks harder, at English writing at any rate, for historical circumstances were different in the United States, doubts rise in the mind. When we think we see the war as lying athwart twentieth-century English writing, dividing it neatly into contrasted parts, what we are really seeing, I suspect, is the shadow of the war across it, not the actual historical event. The division it seems to make is as much artificial as not. Its effect is to make more glaring facts that would have been the same in any case; that the Edwardians who survived into the twenties and sometimes well beyond, Conrad, Kipling, Wells, Bennett, Galsworthy, had done their best work before 1914; and that, one writer apart, and he bringing up the dusty rear, the novelists Henry James named in his famous *Times*

Literary Supplement essay, 'The Younger Generation' (1914), did little in the end that was significant. The war is not to be blamed because James's prophecies went wrong. What was apparent, in the years after the war, was that a new generation had arrived, a generation very different from that of the novelists who had dominated fiction during the pre-war years of the century. It would have arrived in any case.

Wyndham Lewis, who belonged to it, called it 'The Men of 1914'. Reasonably enough, he reserved the title for himself and his friends Joyce, Pound and Eliot; it seems just as reasonable now to extend it to include Lawrence, Virginia Woolf and Dorothy Richardson. These men and women of 1914, all of whom began to publish in the years immediately before the war or while the war was on, shared little except their seriousness as writers. But one thing they did have in common: however the experience of the war affected them, and of them all only Lewis was a combatant, all were formed before the war broke out. They were products of an earlier age; all would have understood, though each might have interpreted it differently, what Virginia Woolf meant when she said: 'On or about December 1910 human nature changed.'

December 1910 was the date of the opening in London of the Post-Impressionist Exhibition, organized by Virginia Woolf's friends Roger Fry and Desmond MacCarthy, which introduced Van Gogh, Gauguin, Cézanne, Matisse and Picasso among others to the British public. But the Post-Impressionist Exhibition was only one of a constellation of significant events that cluster around Virginia Woolf's date. Diaghilev's Russian Ballet, which combined modern music with modern painting, paid its first visit to London in 1911. Chekhov's stories were translated into English in 1909 and Dostoevsky's novels, already well known in their French versions, in 1912. The twelve volumes of Frazer's *The Golden Bough* appeared between 1911 and 1915, though the first two volumes had been known since 1890. Most important of all, perhaps, since, as Auden has written,

> To us he is no more a person
> Now but a whole climate of opinion,

Freud had lectured with Jung on psychoanalysis in America in 1909; *The Interpretation of Dreams* appeared in English four years later.

These events provided the inescapable environment of ideas for the sort of people the Men of 1914 were—young, immensely intelligent, conscious of their talent, consciously repudiating the generation that had gone before them. All break up the accepted realistic surface of things and emphasize, at the expense of the rational and mechanical, of the scientific in its simpler manifestations, the irrational, the unconscious, the mythical. Reality lies in a hitherto unsuspected labyrinthine complexity beneath the surface of things; and to be content with the surface of things is, these events seem severally to argue, to be content with unreality.

Indeed, this is precisely the burden of Virginia Woolf's attack on the Edwardian novelists. In her essay, 'The Modern Novel', in *The Common Reader*, she writes:

> The writer seems constrained, not by his own free will but by some powerful and unscrupulous tyrant who has him in thrall, to provide a plot, to provide comedy, tragedy, love interest, and an air of probability embalming the whole so impeccable that if all his figures were to come to life they would find themselves dressed down to the last button of their coats in the fashion of the hour. The tyrant is obeyed; the novel is done to a turn. But sometimes, more and more often as time goes by, we suspect a momentary doubt, a spasm of rebellion, as the pages fill themselves in the customary way. Is life like this? Must novels be like this?
>
> Look within and life, it seems, is very far from being 'like this'. Examine for a moment an ordinary day. The mind receives a myriad impressions—trivial, fantastic, evanescent, or engraved with the sharpness of steel. From all sides they come, an incessant shower of innumerable atoms; and as they fall, as they shape themselves into the life of Monday or Tuesday, the accent falls differently from of old; the moment of importance came not here but there; so that, if a writer were a free man and not a slave, if he could base his work upon his own feeling and not upon convention, there would be no plot, no comedy, no tragedy, no love interest or catastrophe in the accepted sense, and perhaps not a single button sewn on as the Bond Street tailors would have it. Life is not a series of gig-lamps symmetrically arranged; life is a luminous halo, a semi-transparent envelope surrounding us from the beginning of consciousness to the end.

The last paragraph echoes closely both in its point of view and in its language the passage in William James's *Principles of Psychology* in which the phrase, 'stream of consciousness', is first used. James's book had appeared in 1890: Virginia Woolf was writing in 1920, and her criticism of 'the form of fiction most in vogue' anticipates the kind of novel she was, for the most part, to write herself from the publication of *Jacob's Room* (1922) onwards. But when she wrote her essay she had certainly read the parts of James Joyce's *Ulysses* which had been published in the *Little Review* and which in many respects fulfilled her requirements of the novel; and what is interesting now is the affinity between her view of what was wanted in fiction and Joyce's.

The *Stephen Hero* fragment—it runs to 220 pages in the British paperback edition—is all that remains of an early version of Joyce's first novel *Portrait of the Artist as a Young Man*. We know that, as Joyce wrote it, though he seems never to have finished it, it amounted to 150,000 words. *Portrait of the Artist* is not very much longer than the fragment, and a comparison between the two works throws invaluable light on Joyce's artistic methods. *Stephen Hero* strikes one as an extract from a very good realistic novel of its time. Stephen Dedalus, the young Joyce himself, is the central character; but he is merely one among many, all of whom are presented objectively, that is, for the time they are present on the page they have as much validity as Stephen himself.

The essential difference between the two versions is that in the *Portrait* there is really only one character, Stephen himself, and the whole action takes place in his consciousness. Indeed, his consciousness *is* the novel; the other characters—his father and mother, brothesr and sisters, professors, priests, fellow-students—are 'there' only insofar as they impinge upon his mind. Whatever reality they have they have through Stephen. This undoubtedly makes for a vagueness at the edges of the novel, as it were, or rather, at the edges of Stephen's consciousness. The girl to whom he is attracted is, in the *Portrait*, known only by her initials, E. C., and we know little more about her than her initials; she is as nearly anonymous, and faceless, as a character can be, as too is the girl Stephen watches on the beach and who provides him with the epiphany that determines him to be an artist. All the same, we accept them as forces acting upon him, because of the intensity of his mind as Joyce reveals it.

Inevitably, because Stephen is the whole world of the *Portrait* and everything in the novel exists merely as attributes of him, as the raw materials of his sensations, reveries, reflections, the fuel of his ambitions, he appears in the later version as a much more arrogant figure than in the earlier. He is in every way intensified. And this was necessary if Joyce was to succeed in convincing us of the truth and reality of a character who must utter such a sentence as: 'Welcome, O life! I go to encounter for the millionth time the reality of experience and to forge in the smithy of my soul the uncreated conscience of my race.' The announcement is appalling in its arrogance and presumption; but this is not how we react towards it while reading the novel. We accept it; and that this should be so is the index of Joyce's triumph. It is gained by unsparing concentration on Stephen's mind and its development from those first sentences of baby talk or, rather, of the equivalents of baby thought with which the novel opens. Stephen so much dominates his world as we read that he appears indeed as a sort of Lucifer; he becomes truly Dedalus, the master-craftsman who in his daring and ambition partook of the Promethean.

Joyce imposes this image of Stephen upon us in spite of all the evidence, liberally exhibited, of Stephen's immaturity. The verse he writes, though exactly right for a very young poet at the turn of the century, is pretty thin stuff; and much of the prose, including the prose in which some of the epiphanies are registered, strikes one now as tired and deliquescent Pater. But all this is part of Stephen's growth; what Joyce is giving us is precisely a portrait of the artist *as a young man*, and the tension between his ambition and what, in the novel, he has actually achieved, is constant. All of which is to say that the *Portrait* is, as it were, the novel as dramatic poem. Joyce himself is quite outside it. In this sense, it is a masterpiece of objectivity; Joyce has become the artist as Stephen describes him: 'like the God of creation', who 'remains within or behind or beyond or above his handiwork, invisible, refined out of existence, indifferent, paring his finger-nails'.

Daedalus in the classical myth constructed the Minoan labyrinth: Joyce as Daedalus went on from the *Portrait* to construct the labyrinths of *Ulysses* and *Finnegans Wake*. They are the most extraordinary works in modern English—and having written those words, one sees that they imply a reservation. More perhaps than any writer who has ever lived, Joyce lived almost entirely in a world of words, and, very often, of words as sounds, divorced, that is, from meaning. And every word reminded him of other words: his mind seems to have worked entirely by verbal association. The result, as soon as one is aware of it, can be trivializing.

In 1907 Joyce published a small volume of verse, *Chamber Music*. The poems in this collection are derivations from the Elizabethan song-writers and the poets of the nineties, strongly reminiscent of those Stephen is writing in *Portrait of the Artist*. There is a catch in these poems, or in some of them. The title of the volume is the clue. It is a pun. It describes the surface of the poems, which is elegant, delicate, elusive; but a 'chamber' is also an English euphemism for chamber-pot, and the chamber music these poems evoke is the music of urination in a chamber-pot. Professor William York Tyndall has said: 'For Joyce, the lutanist of love, as for Yeats, love had pitched his mansion in the place of excrement.' No real comparison is possible between Joyce and Yeats. Yeats's poems, like Swift's before him, spring out of his contemplation of the human condition; they come out of life and refer back to life; but Joyce's are based on a pun, and the principle of the pun is that the single sound stands for two or more entirely disparate things.

All this is relevant to *Ulysses* because similar mechanisms are at work there, but made enormously complex by Joyce's positively medieval addiction to allegory. For Joyce it was impossible for any one thing to mean that one thing and nothing more. In one of the most famous sentences of *Ulysses*—it is our first introduction to the character—we are told that 'Mr Leopold Bloom ate with relish the inner organs of beasts and fowls'. He therefore has kidneys for breakfast. The detail is a perfectly proper piece of naturalistic detail. But this is not the reason for Joyce's deciding that Bloom should have kidneys for breakfast. It was dictated by the very structure of the work. Each episode of the book is related to an organ of the body, and in the Old Testament the kidney is associated with the heart as the seat of the emotions.

In *The Classical Temper*, the best single study I know of *Ulysses*, S. L. Goldberg lists five main interpretations of the work: that it is 'only a naturalistic Irish Comedy, the apotheosis of the bar-room joke'; that it expresses 'complete, cosmic indifference to all moral values, reducing all experience to ultimate meaninglessness either by its implicit nihilism or, what is much the same thing, its implicit relativity'; that it expresses 'some important body of mystical, esoteric or metaphysical belief'; that it is 'a pessimistic rejection of modern life, an encyclopaedic satire on "the immense panorama of futility and anarchy which is contemporary history"'; that it is 'an optimistic acceptance of life as it is, whether in a spirit of humorous relaxation, or tense tragic awareness, or quasi-mythic abstraction'. Finding each view in turn 'true but limited', Goldberg concludes:

> What meaning is truly realized in it, what value it has, lies in its *dramatic* presentation and ordering of experience, and nowhere else. In short, it is not 'Romance', not a joke, not a spiritual guide, not even an encyclopaedia of social disintegration or a recreation of Myth or a symbolist poem; it is a novel, and what is of permanent interest about it is what always interests us with the novel: its imaginative illumination of the moral—and ultimately, spiritual—experience of representative human beings.

Though it follows from this that many things in *Ulysses* will appear to be aberrations, errors of judgment or aesthetic tact, for example the parodies of the development of English prose in 'The Oxen of the Sun' episode which are supposed, according to the principle of onto-genesis repeating phylogenesis, to represent the development of the child in the womb, Mr Goldberg's conclusions seem to me just; and it is worth remembering that when Pound, who was close to Joyce throughout the writing of the novel, reviewed *Ulysses* in *The Dial* in 1922, he accepted it as a naturalistic novel after Flaubert.

In many ways, *Ulysses* fulfils Virginia Woolf's dream: 'If a writer were a free man and not a slave, if he could base his work upon his own feeling and not upon convention, there would be no plot, no comedy, no tragedy, no love interest or catastrophe in the accepted sense . . .' We have the single day in Dublin in June, 1904, the progress through the city and the day of Stephen Dedalus, lately returned from Paris, and of Leopold Bloom, and their slow coming together; Dedalus, the arrogant, poverty-stricken artist and intellectual in spiritual exile from his country and family, seeking a father; Bloom, the Jewish advertising-space salesman, *l'homme moyen sensuel*, much cuckolded, by virtue of being a Jew also an exile, seeking a son. As the day goes on, they move steadily nearer each other, sometimes passing, always meshed in a constantly enlarging net of associations, and finally meeting, coming together in a kind of recognition. The difficulties facing Virginia Woolf's writer, who is a free man and not a slave, are of course obvious, and the greatest of these is the overwhelming problem of imposing some sort of order on chaos when conventional notions of story and plot are disdained. Joyce solves the problem for himself by paralleling the progress of his characters with that of the characters of the *Odyssey*, so that Bloom as a modern Ulysses re-enacts in a single day the twenty years' journey of Homer's hero, meeting Stephen, his son Telemachus, and returning at night to his wife Penelope, Marion Bloom. By basing his story on Homer, Joyce is attempting to express the universal in the particular; Bloom, Marion Bloom and Stephen become modern versions of archetypal figures—and for good measure Joyce makes them versions not of classical archetypes only. Thus Bloom is not only Ulysses, he is the Wandering Jew; Stephen not only Telemachus but Shakespeare and perhaps even Christ; and Marion not only Penelope but the Magna Mater, Gea Tellus, the female principle.

Nevertheless, when the literary archaeologists have finally deciphered the much-scored palimpsest that is *Ulysses*, taken as a novel, it must still stand or fall by Joyce's delineation of the actual. *Ulysses* is an intensely local novel; for Joyce's purpose it has to be; and it must be the most documented novel in any language. No place, and no single day, have ever been re-created in such detail; and the re-creation is never that of a museum piece. Joyce's Dublin is the element in which his characters live; it surrounds them, flows around and through them; they are aware of it all the time on the periphery of their consciousness. And of the three main characters two, Bloom and his wife, we know more completely, perhaps, than any others in fiction and certainly more intimately. We know them at stool; we know them in the fantasies of their sexual lives. And we know all three of them wholly from the inside. As in the *Portrait*, in *Ulysses* Joyce has refined himself out of existence. The dramatic method in fiction can go no further than it does in *Ulysses*. Bloom, Marion and Stephen think and feel in utterly different terms; for each of them Joyce perfects a separate style, as contrasted as the characters.

The basis of all these styles is the technical method known as stream-of-consciousness or interior monologue. Joyce did not invent it himself. The method is essentially one of free-association. In the *Dictionary of World Literary Terms* I find this suggestive passage from John Donne illustrating its basis in reality. Donne complained that his prayers were disturbed by 'a memory of yesterday's pleasures, a fear of tomorrow's dangers, a straw under my knee, an anything, a nothing, a fancy, a Chimera in my braine'. The method reproduces, or rather, suggests the ordinary working of the mind, the constant flow of sense-impressions involuntarily registered and of apparently irrelevant associations which is never totally inhibited even when thinking is at its most logical and purposive. No doubt stream-of-consciousness in the twentieth century is related to the psychological discoveries of the time, especially Jung's invention of free-association tests as a tool in psychotherapy. But it is worth noting that an earlier associative psychology, Locke's at the end of the seventeenth century, had also achieved its literary monument in fiction, in Sterne's *Tristram Shandy*, which depends entirely on a technique very close to stream-of-consciousness.

Joyce uses stream-of-consciousness most thoroughly in his treatment of Marion Bloom. She enters the novel as a character in her own person only at the end; and her thoughts, poured out pell mell in rich associative profusion, form its tremendous climax. She is, significantly, in bed at night, relaxed and drowsy after sex, on the verge of sleep; in a state, in other words, in which conscious control over the mind's working has all but gone; so that the flow of her thoughts, her memories of love, her erotic reveries and her speculations about Bloom and Stephen, can proceed in spate, uninhibited, unchecked, unpunctuated. The circumstances in which we meet Marion Bloom make a full revelation of her mind possible. But what is revealed is not of a very high level of interest. She emerges as undifferentiated female almost to the point of being purely animal; so that if, as some critics have claimed, she expresses Joyce's affirmation of life, one can only say that the life affirmed is not more than life at the level of rut and reproduction.

With Bloom, it is different. Joyce suggests rather than fully records the stream of consciousness. Bloom's mind is infinitely richer than Marion's. As he walks through the city, stray thoughts flicker through his mind like fishes, thoughts suggested by whatever business he is about, by whatever catches his eye in the streets, by the smells that assail his nostrils; but all the while, surfacing from time to time to consciousness through association with these sense-impressions, below the scum and froth of his mind are certain permanent preoccupations: the void in his life because of his son's death as a child, his father's suicide, his humiliation as a cuckold, his sense of being an outsider as a Jew. It is these that give him his real moral stature. He is certainly the most universal figure in modern fiction. *L'homme moyen sensuel* and also the 'little man' of a later generation, vulgar, half-educated but unfailingly curious, nursing his 'dirty little secret' of sex, essentially unheroic, indeed the anti-hero and yet capable of moral courage, he is also kind and expansive, and in his naïvety there is even a sort of innocence. He is comic, but also a figure of great pathos: a creation of Shakespearean amplitude comparable in achievement to Falstaff.

With his Hamlet, Stephen, Joyce seems to me much less successful. He is the Stephen of the *Portrait* a little older, returned from Paris; yet, tortured by a vast ambition still unrealized, struck with remorse for his behaviour towards his mother, the repudiator of his family, his country and his religion, he seems curiously smaller than his earlier avatar. 'Oh, an impossible person', is Buck Mulligan's comment on him in the first pages of the novel; and so, drawn with unsparing detachment, he is. The reason seems plain. He is, in *Ulysses*, one man among many, not the commanding centre of a novel. Lost among a multitude, himself lost and derided, he no longer partakes of the brightness of Lucifer but has dwindled, as Wyndham Lewis said, to the likeness of a stage poet.

His mode of thought is completely distinct from Bloom's; 'stream-of-consciousness' is scarcely the word for it. When we are within his mind we are aware of a much greater degree of awareness, control and purpose. He thinks in highly intellectual terms, in learned, latinate words, in a vocabulary derived from a vast and often comparatively remote reading; he figures his remorse, for instance, in the Middle English phrase, 'agenbite of inwit'. The words Joyce puts into his mind are much more a notation of the way his mind works than an attempt literally to transcribe his thoughts.

Joyce places an order on the flux of Bloom's day by his parallels with Homer. He varies the surface of the day and its events not only through styles of thought and feeling appropriate to each of his three main characters but also through an astonishing range of literary virtuosity in the rendering of the separate episodes of the novel. The parodies of the growth of language in the 'Oxen of the Sun' episode set in the lying-in hospital have already been mentioned. Another is the 'Nausicaa' episode, in which Nausicaa appears as the adolescent girl Gerty MacDowell, whose exhibitionism moves Bloom to masturbation: her fantasy of love is presented not directly, in any form of stream-of-consciousness, but as pastiche of the cheapest kind of romantic fiction, with the heroines of which Gerty identifies herself. Another is the Nighttown episode, in which Stephen and Bloom meet in a brothel, which is cast in the form of an Expressionist play. Though this extreme variety of method certainly adds to the difficulty of seeing *Ulysses* as a whole it makes for continuous interest in the work. More than any other novel, *Ulysses* has the quality Flaubert sought when he desired 'to give verse-rhythm to prose, yet to leave it prose and very much prose, and to write about ordinary life as histories and epics are written'. Joyce bodies forth the very feel and texture of specific scenes and atmospheres, as, for example, the evocation of early morning at the very beginning of the novel. And every sentence of description is as right, as inevitable, as a line of classical poetry. We do not identify ourselves with Joyce's characters. They exist in their own profoundly felt world, a world of great density and solidity. It is this world that gives the novel its real unity, for through the shared experiences of the scene it links character organically with character.

It is, admittedly, a limited world. Joyce's Dublin, as has often been pointed out, is a city in which no work is done, a city whose inhabitants continually pass and re-pass one another without making contact, a city of solitaries, one sign of which, of course, is Joyce's use of the stream-of-consciousness technique itself, for it is essentially the technique for rendering man-alone. Though it is probably the most highly integrated novel technically ever written, *Ulysses* is an epic of disintegration. Yet it is the most stupendous attempt to see life whole in fiction in our century; and in the end it is a great affirmation of life, not of undifferentiated biological life as represented by Marion, but of the moral life, the life of man suffering, falling, struggling to rise and to seek the good, which is embodied in Leopold Bloom. *Ulysses* stands or falls by Bloom.

'*Ulysses*', wrote Pound in his *Dial* review in 1922, 'is, presumably, as unrepeatable as *Tristram Shandy*; I mean you cannot duplicate it; you can't take it as a "model", as you could take *Bovary*; but it does complete something begun in *Bouvard*; and it does add definitely to the international store of literary technique.' It is unrepeatable, it cannot be duplicated, because its author, like Sterne, was a man of extreme idiosyncrasy. To write 'like Joyce' it would be necessary to be Joyce; which is why the more or less close imitations of *Ulysses* that were written in the twenties now appear still-born—Conrad Aiken's *Blue Voyage* for example. But that, as Pound said, *Ulysses* added to the international store of literary technique is surely unquestionable. In this respect Joyce has been one of the great fertilizers of art, one of the great shapers of the form art has taken in our time, comparable to

Eliot in poetry, Picasso in painting and Stravinsky in music. If one wants instances of the direct influence of Joyce, instances of work that could not have been written if *Ulysses* had not been already there to be drawn on as example and inspiration, one need only refer to Dos Passos's *U.S.A.*, the novels of Faulkner as a whole, Farrell's *Studs Lonigan* trilogy and Henry Roth's *Call It Sleep*. For novelists who came to consciousness of their craft in the twenties and early thirties Joyce was part of the climate of their time and therefore inescapable, a major fact of their art that had to be reckoned with, even though in some instances the recognition took the form of a complete rejection of his work. If today, in English fiction particularly, his influence seems largely to have vanished it is because the world view of which he was part has also largely vanished. When the temper of the age changes and the world-view shifts, his influence will assert itself again.

But one can say this of the Joyce of *Ulysses* only. *Finnegans Wake* seems to me quite inaccessible to the kind of criticism one brings to novels. Joyce addressed it, as he said himself, to 'that ideal reader suffering from an ideal insomnia': in our time, the only reader likely to have the time and resources to give it the attention Joyce demanded is the professional scholar, and in fact *Finnegans Wake* has become almost wholly a scholar's book. This is not to say that it is by any means completely closed to the general reader; the scholars have seen to that with such books as Joseph Campbell's and Henry Morton Robinson's *A Skeleton Key to Finnegans Wake*. The works of exegesis now existing are many, and even without them the general reader may find it a fascinating book to dip into for its richly comic word-play, which is continuous, and for its incidental poetry. It is obviously one of the great eccentric masterpieces of literature, but we need a name for the kind of masterpiece it is. It is not, if the word has meaning at all, a novel.

Finnegans Wake is a work without beginning or end, or rather, it is circular: in it, we are outside time altogether, in the world of sleep and dream. The sleeper is a Dublin saloon-keeper, H. C. Earwicker, together with his wife and his two sons. Whether the dreamer is Earwicker or Joyce himself it seems impossible to tell, which indicates part of the essential difficulty of the book, its intrinsic ambiguity. Earwicker is not only a Dublin saloon-keeper, he is also Everybody—his initials stand for Here Comes Everybody—and his metamorphoses are legion. The action of the book, in so far as one can speak of action in a world in which past, present and future have been merged into one, takes in all history. This is conveyed in one way by the language in which the book is written, which is English certainly, but an English on to whose vocabulary words from many languages have been superimposed, so that one moves, as it were, in a world of multiple puns, the end of which should be greatly to enrich meaning. It does not invariably result in this, and often the act of reading *Finnegans Wake* brings to mind Frank O'Connor's revealing anecdote about visiting Joyce in Paris. There was a picture of Cork in the hallway.

> I could not detect what the frame was made of. 'What is it?' I asked. 'Cork', he replied. 'Yes', I said, 'I know it's Cork, but what's the frame?' 'Cork', he replied with a smile. 'I had the greatest difficulty in finding a French frame-maker who would make it.'

O'Connor quotes this as an example of what he calls Joyce's 'associative mania', and it is here that the real difficulty of making a judgment of *Finnegans Wake* resides.

In his chapter on Joyce in *The Pelican Guide to English Literature*, Dr Arnold Kettle writes: 'What, one is constantly brought up against the question, is relevant to what?' Kettle takes as an example the passage in which Earwicker is copulating with his wife. It abounds with images from the game of cricket. 'What,' Kettle asks, 'apart from some purely verbal fun, do they give or add to the passage?' He concludes:

> Indeed so visually irrelevant do these cricketing images seem that one would be tempted to assume that Joyce had never seen a cricket match in his life and had merely collected the terms from a study of Wisden. Judged by a normally acceptable standard I do not see how the conclusion can be avoided that this group of images is arbitrary and unsuccessful; but the snag about making such a judgment is that one has in the end no means of knowing what Joyce is *basically* trying to do. The ambiguities do not, as in a speech in Shakespeare, enrich and modify the meaning; they are the book itself . . . Always in the later Joyce there is hovering in the air the suspicion that words have *in themselves* some mystic significance. Because of Joyce's refusal to commit himself to the proposition that dream is less real than reality he ends up, it sometimes seems, with the implication that nothing is real except words.

This seems to me true; and it is why it is impossible to discuss *Finnegans Wake* as a novel. It refers to nothing except itself. And, extraordinary as it is as a *tour de force*, it is, one believes, *Ulysses*, rooted in the actual and the specific, that will remain as the enduring influence on the general reader and the general writer alike.

[2]

ONE WOULDN'T prophesy with any such confidence a revived influence of, or interest in, the novels of Dorothy Richardson, whose sequence of twelve novels, beginning in 1915 and ending in 1935, together compose a single work, *Pilgrimage*. Remarkable as it is, once having read it, one feels little wish to return to it.

The weakness is that one's interest is much more in the method than what the method reveals. The first volumes are fascinating in the freshness with which they suggest the day-to-day flux of a very intelligent girl's moods and sensibility to the world outside her and the people who dwell in it. We share Miriam's individual re-creation of her world from moment to moment. But when she returns to England from her school in Germany and is disappointed in love, against a background of the advanced thought of the day, it is another matter. Miriam's momentary perceptions are often delightful: her aspirations are dull even in their worthiness; and by the end of the twelfth volume one is left feeling that for Dorothy Richardson the external world exists merely to provide so much fodder for the voracious sensibility of her character.

In *A Portrait of the Artist*, which in any case is a relatively short novel, there is a lyrical intensity and a narrow focus of concentration quite beyond anything Dorothy Richardson was capable of; and in *Ulysses* there is, quite apart from the structure derived from the Homeric parallels and the variety that comes from the variety of styles, the drama stemming, however slowly, from the presence of three towering characters. With *Pilgrimage*, it is impossible to speak of structure or form at all. The interest is limited almost wholly to the psychological, to the revelation of a woman's life through stream-of-consciousness. But unfortunately for this interest, Miss Richardson's notion of psychology is nineteenth-century, pre-Freud. There are whole areas of a woman's experience—every woman's experience—Miriam is never allowed to be conscious of. The bodily functions do not exist for her; in this respect, she is at one with the most conventional Victorian heroine of fiction. And the stream-of-consciousness technique makes us the more aware of this. It is unfair, but it is next to impossible now not to think that Dorothy Richardson cheated.

This cannot be said of May Sinclair. A student of psychology and philosophy—it was she who, reviewing *Pilgrimage* in 1918, first borrowed the term 'stream of consciousness' from William James—she must have been among the earliest English novelists to have been aware of the work of Freud. Neither *Mary Olivier: A Life* (1919) nor *The Life and Death of Harriet Frean* (1922) could have been written without a knowledge of psychoanalysis. Both describe the upbringing of young women during the second half of the Victorian age. The general attitude towards the age, at any rate as seen in the middle-class family, is akin to Samuel Butler's in *The Way of All Flesh*, though the modern reader may also see in them foreshadowings of the matter, though not the manner, of the fiction of Ivy Compton-Burnett.

Mary Olivier relates the life of the heroine from 1865 to middle age in 1900. It is a life of self-sacrifice, though of conscious self-sacrifice; Mary knows the mechanism of the trap in which she is caught, for she is a ferociously intelligent young woman. She is the youngest of a family of four children, the others being boys, who are imprisoned in an Oedipal situation. The mother and the eldest son, Mark, are locked in a relationship so close as to be almost incestuous, while the father is consumed with jealousy of Mark in particular and of the other sons only to a lesser degree. In the end he takes refuge in compulsive drinking, and all the sons in turn are defeated and destroyed by the family situation, the reality of which is disguised by the forms and trappings of evangelical religion. Mary herself, whose role it is to be the helpmeet of her mother and who cannot marry because her mother 'needs' her, despite the boredom of her external life and the consciousness that she is being wasted, manages to live in an inner freedom and in spiritual intransigence as a self-proclaimed atheist, a reader of Spinoza, Plato and Kant, Darwin, Haeckel, Ribot and Maudesley. This contrast between the conventional, convention-ridden, culturally poverty-stricken surroundings, whether Essex or Yorkshire, and the richness of Mary's interior life, which finally finds expression in poetry and in translating the Greek poets, is finely conveyed. In her honesty, her refusal to make concessions to sentimentality, May Sinclair appears in this novel as perhaps the female counterpart in our fiction of Gissing.

Especially interesting now is May Sinclair's technique. Throughout the novel we are placed as it were in Mary's consciousness, but there is no stream-of-consciousness as such. Her thoughts are reported for the most part in *oratio obliqua*, usually in the second person: 'Jenny didn't believe that a big girl, nine next birthday, could really be afraid of funerals. She thought you were only trying to be tiresome. She said you could stop thinking about funerals well enough if you wanted.' At the same time, though not going anywhere as far as Joyce in *Portrait of the Artist*, May Sinclair very ably renders the increasing complexity of the mind from the simple terms of childhood.

Fine as *Mary Olivier* is, May Sinclair's masterpiece is probably *The Life and Death of Harriet Frean*, again a story of waste and frustrations and self-sacrifice. It is a very short novel, and from this much of its distinction derives. Not a word is superfluous. Witness the opening paragraphs of the novel:

> '"Pussycat, Pussycat, where have you been?"
> "I've been to London, to see the Queen."
> "Pussycat, Pussycat, what did you there?"
> "I caught a little mouse under the chair."'
>
> Her mother said it three times. And each time the Baby Harriet laughed. The sound of her laugh was so funny that she laughed again at that; she kept on laughing, with shriller and shriller squeals.
> 'I wonder why she thinks it's funny,' her mother said.
> Her father considered it. 'I don't know. The cat perhaps. The cat the Queen. But no; that isn't funny.'
> 'She sees something in it we don't see, bless her,' said her mother.
> Each kissed her in turn, and the Baby Harriet stopped laughing suddenly.

The novel is conducted throughout in short episodes of that kind, episodes that carry their own irony. Harriet Frean's complacent self-sacrifice, which is not so pure or disinterested as she conceives it, together with the misery it works in the lives of the others, of the man who loved her and of his wife, who retreats from his hatred of her into conversion hysteria, is beautifully rendered. Again, one thinks of Gissing, of *The Odd Women*; but this is a profounder book, and part of the profundity is a consequence of the extreme sharpness of focus in which Harriet Frean's life—by implication a whole way of nine-teenth-century life—is caught.

[3]

VIRGINIA WOOLF'S essay on modern fiction was written before she had realized in her novels the ideas adumbrated in it, but from 1919 onwards the task she set herself in fiction was to impose signifi-cance on the flux, to snare the significant, the transcending moment (obviously akin to the Joycean epiphany) as it flies. Transience is the very stuff of her material. What happens on the surface is relatively unimportant. In *Mrs Dalloway*, a fashionable lady gives a party, a man who has been in love with her comes back from India, a young man suffering from war neurosis commits suicide. But this is enough to enable Virginia Woolf to show us life as in a state of constant creation, changing endlessly from moment to moment, like a fountain, the moment being the individual drop of water of the fountain. The characters are abnormally aware of the moment as it passes, and this awareness gives it a remarkable complexity, for it is compounded not only of the character's mood at the instant of apprehension but also of a most delicate sensuous, though not always a fully conscious, appre-hension of the physical world in which the character moves. At the same time, the moment apprehended is bound to and recapitulates through the link of association moments of similar experience in the past. Virginia Woolf is constantly doing on a small scale what Proust did in *À la Recherche du Temps Perdu*.

But Mrs Woolf is no less close to Joyce. Indeed, *Mrs Dalloway* in some ways is a tiny *Ulysses* in its method of organization. It covers an even shorter span of time than *Ulysses*, and as Dublin in Joyce's novel is caught, reflected and refracted through the consciousness of the characters moving through it, so is London in Virginia Woolf's. It is a very small area of London, compared with Dickens's or even Henry James's, but it is solidly there. Again, as in *Ulysses*, individual characters are brought into relationship with others by shared experiences, of seeing, for instance, a motor-car in which the Queen may be sitting as it goes through Mayfair, of gazing at an aeroplane sky-writing, even of being vaguely aware of Big Ben striking the hours through the day. So is created the illusion of many lives lived simultaneously in a specific time at a specific place.

Virginia Woolf is admittedly a novelist of very narrow limits. Her range of characters is small. They belong not only to a certain class, the upper middle-class intelligentsia, but also to a certain temperament. They tend to think and feel alike, to be the aesthetes of one set of sensations. They are distinguished by a discriminating intelligence and an acute self-consciousness which together weave a close sieve through which, no doubt, much of the common experience of life will not pass. From time to time also, the exercise of sensibility, one cannot help feeling, becomes an end in itself. Nor are the moments of revelation and illumination always illuminative in any real sense. Sometimes they don't amount to much more than a series of short, sharp feminine gasps of ecstasy, an impression intensified by Virginia Woolf's use of the semi-colon where the comma is ordinarily used.

Yet within her limits Virginia Woolf is a highly original and most accomplished artist. She never repeats herself, even though her theme is a constant one, the search for a pattern of meaning in the flux of myriad impressions. In *To the Lighthouse* (1927), apart from the beautifully suggested relationship between Mrs Ramsey and her husband and children, a powerful unifying factor is the lighthouse itself, which becomes a symbol carrying many meanings. In the second part of the novel, an interlude between the two periods of the action, time itself is evoked; rather as in the later novel, *The Waves* (1931), the soliloquies of the characters are set in the context of nine passages descriptive of the sun's progress over the sea from first light to night.

Not all of these devices making for unity are successful. Virginia Woolf is often seen as a poet who used the medium of prose. She is in fact at her weakest where she is most consciously the poet; and the celebration of time in *To the Lighthouse*, like the interludes in *The*

Waves, suffers from the usual faults of prose-poetry. It seems over-written and pretentious. In any case, to juxtapose characters with the passage of time is not necessarily to integrate them. What unity there is is imposed from outside; and unity and significance are much more satisfactorily realized in the episode, towards the end of *To the Light-house*, in which Lily Briscoe suddenly completes the painting she had begun years before at the beginning of the novel. Almost by chance, her vision, which among other things is her vision of Mrs Ramsay, now dead, and of all that has happened in the Ramsays' house, is set down.

The fact that her characters are highly articulate and quite abnor-mally self-aware means that stream-of-consciousness as found in Joyce when he is rendering Bloom or Marion Bloom is scarcely possible in Virginia Woolf's fiction. What she uses is a very deft adaptation of it, which suggests rather than quite realizes it. There is a rendering, vivid almost to the point of the hallucinatory, of the scene and bustle of everyday living refracted through the consciousness of the character, together with the very strong sense, below it, of a mind engaged in perpetual soliloquy, obsessed with a question that is always the same. We deduce the continuous existence of the soliloquy from the moments when suddenly it breaks through the surface of everyday living. In *The Waves* soliloquy breaks clean through altogether, and we are presented with a set of six characters, three men and three women taken up at selected points in their lives beginning with child-hood, whose sole end is, as it were, to soliloquize. The actions they perform in everyday life have to be inferred from their soliloquies. The soliloquy becomes what might be called a poetic equivalent, even a symbol, of what is thought and felt obsessively. Of course the solilo-quies do trace a pattern of events, of a lifetime's relationships between the six characters; so that one has in the end a series of dramatic monologues, though, since the characters have been so far abstracted from the day-to-day flux of living, the drama is exceedingly tenuous as compared with Joyce's in *Ulysses*.

Virginia Woolf's most successful novel seems to me her last, *Between the Acts* (1941). The glancing, significant image that reveals and sums up the moment of revelation here takes the place of her former attempts in the direction of stream-of-consciousness. It is seen at the very beginning of the book, which is set in a country house, inhabited by old Mr Oliver and his sister Mrs Swithin, Mr Oliver's son and Isa his daughter-in-law and their children. Isa is perhaps in love with, certainly attracted to, a neighbouring farmer. Old Mr Oliver quotes two lines from Byron:

> Isa raised her head. The words made two rings, perfect rings, that floated them, herself and Haines, like two swans down stream. But his snow-white breast was circled with a tangle of dirty duck-weed; and she too, in her webbed feet was entangled, by her husband, the stockbroker.

All Virginia Woolf's preoccupations come together in this novel, which recapitulates, as it were in capsule form, in the setting of a summer day in an English country house just before the war, the course of human history, racial no less than national. She sets out to show us the continuity of life, man as the inheritor of all the past. She does it with a beautiful lightness and indirection. The background of the history of life is contained in the imaginative flights of old Mrs Swithin reading her Wellsian outline of history.

In this novel, more than in any of her others, Virginia Woolf glances at rather than stresses the themes that preoccupy her; the light of a darting, whimsical humour plays over them. Mrs Swithin's vision of evolution is the ultimate background of the book; the nearer background is the history of England, realized in a pageant—a brilliant parody of any village pageant—enacted by the villagers. It is all kept deliberately light. It has to be; otherwise it would be too heavy a burden for the fragile structure of the plot. Isa and her husband must be reconciled; and so the book ends with the human as it were taking in the animal, the personal relations of man and wife seen in the shadow of evolutionary development:

> The old people had gone up to bed. Giles crumpled the newspaper and turned out the light. Left alone for the first time that day, they were silent. Alone, enmity was bared; also love. Before they slept, they must fight; after they had fought, they would embrace. From that embrace another life might be born. But first they must fight, as the dog fights with the vixen, in the heart of darkness, in the fields of night.
> Isa let her sewing drop. The great hooded chairs had become enormous. And Giles, too. And Isa, too, against the window. The window was all sky without colour. The house had lost its shelter. It was night before roads were made, or houses. It was

night that dwellers in caves had watched from some high place among rocks.

Then the curtain rose. They spoke.

But there is also that other abiding obsession of Virginia Woolf's, of art as the unifying principle of life. Art is represented by the pageant, and the pageant-mistress, Miss Le Trobe, is the eternal artist. That she is a comic figure, almost a figure of fun, just as the pageant itself is mainly an exercise in doggerel, makes no difference. For the other characters of the novel the pageant is just an entertainment; for Miss La Torbe it is an act of creation:

> Hadn't she, for twenty-five minutes, made them see? A vision imparted was relief from agony ... for one moment ... for one moment. She heard the breeze rustle in the branches. She saw Giles Oliver with his back to the audience. Also Cobbet of Cobbs Corner. She hadn't made them see. It was a failure, another damned failure! As usual. Her vision escaped her. And turning, she strode to the actors, undressing, down in the hollow, where butterflies feasted upon swords of silver paper; where the dish-cloths in the shadow made pools of yellow.

Miss La Trobe, indeed, is Virginia Woolf's burlesque of herself as artist, and through her she states the truth about the artist and his unceasing endeavour to make his audience see which Eliot expresses in *East Coker*: 'Every attempt is a wholly new start, and a different kind of failure.'

[4]

JOYCE WAS A European writer, the heir both of the French natur-alists and the symbolists: Lawrence was incurably English, much closer in spirit and in his view of the novel to George Eliot than to Flaubert. As much as Fielding or George Eliot, he is the novelist as moralist—or the moralist as novelist. He was much else besides: one of the best short-story writers in English, a poet, a writer of brilliant travel books, and a literary critic. He was, inevitably in so romantic a writer, who was as it were transcribing the serial story of his life, very uneven; and though in all his novels there is not one, with the possible exception of his second, *The Trespasser*, that does not contain passages blazing with his genius, his greatness as a novelist rests ultimately on three books, *Sons and Lovers*, *The Rainbow* and *Women in Love*. Of these the two latter are the more important.

In form, *Sons and Lovers* is a traditional autobiographical novel, comparable with Bennett's *Clayhanger*. In this respect, it is very much of its time—1913. Yet, when one compares it with *Clayhanger*, there can be no question which now has the greater impact. Bennett is detached; he contemplates his characters from a height; he records a completed action. Lawrence is much closer to his characters, much more passionately engaged with them; and we are brought into immediate, intimate relation with them through the sheer urgency of his writing. Without recourse to anything like stream-of-consciousness, he takes us right inside his characters; we apprehend them instantaneously through the force of his intuition. He captures, it seems, the moment of life itself, both in men and women and in the physical world of nature. There is a delighted, immediate, non-intellectual response to everything that lives. It was precisely this quality that distinguished Lawrence's father, the Morel of the novel. Unlike him, Lawrence was never a miner, but he had what one feels was essentially a miner's response to the world of nature; as though daily he had emerged from the darkness of the pit and daily seen the world new-born.

The struggle between his father and his mother lies at the heart of *Sons and Lovers*. His father was a miner, practically illiterate, often drunk, but possessed of an extraordinarily vivid apprehension of natural life and living; while his mother, of a somewhat higher social class, was intellectual, spiritual, refined, high-minded, 'cut out', as he was to write years later, 'to play a superior role in the god-damned bourgeoisie'. The meeting between them is beautifully described in the first chapter:

> . . . the dusky, golden softness of this man's sensuous flame of life, that flowed off his flesh like the flame from a candle, not baffled and gripped into incandescence by thought and spirit as her life was, seemed to her something wonderful, beyond her.

But their marriage was unhappy, and something was killed in the father. The children were caught up in the clash between them, and in *Sons and Lovers*, try to be fair as he may, Lawrence is on his mother's side.

Later, he was to change sides, and it is the anticipation of this in his first novel, *The White Peacock*, that gives the book its interest today. On the face of it, in this novel, the work of an extremely clever young man steeped in Meredith and George Eliot, Lawrence sidesteps the problem of his father by leaving him out. Lawrence's spokesman, the narrator, Cyril, is a middle-class young man, whose father is scarcely present at all: he dies half-way through the book, a bad lot who has deserted his wife and children. Even so, it was not so easy for Lawrence to kill his father: before the end of the novel Cyril is standing almost in the relation of a son to the gamekeeper, Annable, 'a man of one idea— that all civilization was the painted fungus of rottenness. He hated any sign of culture'. Annable has been a clergyman married to a peer's daughter who went 'souly' on him. And the white peacock of the title, fouling the tombstones in the abandoned churchyard, is, for Annable, 'the very soul of a lady ... a woman to the end, I tell you, all vanity and screech and defilement'; in other words, the angel of destruction, as she was to remain for Lawrence for many years. In *The White Peacock* Annable is defeated by the high-born lady: almost twenty years later, as Mellors, the gamekeeper of *Lady Chatterley's Lover*, he gets his own back on her. But until *The Plumed Serpent* the situation—the destruction of instinctive man by the spiritual woman—is fundamental to Lawrence; and among the avatars of Annable's peeress-wife are Miriam in *Sons and Lovers*, Hermione Roddice in *Women in Love*, and Aaron's wife in *Aaron's Rod*.

Annable, of course, is a highly sophisticated version of Lawrence's father. Lawrence was anti-intellectual, but he had to intellectualize his anti-intellectuality if he was to communicate his vision. For it *was* a vision. He expressed it negatively in his essay on Poe in *Studies in Classic North American Literature*: 'These terribly conscious birds, like Poe and his Ligeia, deny the very life that is in them; they want to turn it all into talk, into knowing. And so life, which will *not* be known, leaves them.' Life, which will *not* be known: the concept goes to the heart of Lawrence. Life, which for Lawrence was essentially a mystery, was not to be apprehended or explained in terms of reason and logic— that was the way to kill it. It could be experienced only by direct intuition, transmitted only by touch; and the value of people, for

Lawrence, consisted in how far mystery resided in them, how far they were conscious of mystery both in themselves and in others. Since the mystery was killed by the analysing, scientific intellect, it obviously flourished most strongly where the analysing, scientific intellect was least powerful, at the instinctual levels of life, in sexual relationships, in the experience of death, in the impulsive, non-rational existence of animals and nature.

He had to a quite extraordinary degree the faculty Jung calls primitive thinking and feeling. 'The ancients', according to Jung, 'had, if one may so express it, an almost exclusively biological appreciation of their fellow men.' It is much the same sort of appreciation that Lawrence was continually seeking. This primitivism enabled him to explore, as no one else has done in modern literature, what are still relatively 'unknown modes of being'. To express these in fiction Lawrence had to dispense with character as it is normally conceived. As he wrote to Edward Garnett while engaged upon *The Rainbow*:

> I have a different attitude to my characters . . . I don't care what the woman feels . . . That presumes an ego to feel with. I only care for what the woman is . . . You mustn't look in my novel for the old stable ego of character. There is another ego, according to whose action the individual is unrecognizable, and passes through, as it were, allotropic states which it needs a deeper sense than any we've been used to exercise, to discover—states of the same radically unchanged element. (Like as diamond and carbon are the same pure single element of carbon. The ordinary novelist would trace the history of the diamond—but I say, 'Diamond, what! This is carbon!' And my diamond might be coal or soot, and my theme is carbon.)

What interested him, then, in his characters is not primarily the social man, though he did not neglect him, but that part of man that is submerged and never seen, the unconscious, to which he preaches something like passivity on the part of the conscious. This accounts for the difficulty we experience on first reading Lawrence. We deduce emotion from gesture. But Lawrence's problem was to express emotion, feelings, as they exist far below the surface of gesture. He cannot, of course, dispense with gesture altogether, but gesture as normally understood is not enough for his purposes. A simple instance of his method may be seen in his description of the pocket-picking in *Aaron's Rod*:

As he was going home, suddenly, just as he was passing the Bargello, he stopped. He stopped, and put his hand to his breast-pocket. His letter-case was gone. He had been robbed. It was as if lightning ran through him at that moment, as if a fluid light-ning ran down his limbs, through the sluice of his knees, and out of his feet, leaving him standing there almost unconscious. For a moment unconscious and superconscious he stood there. He had been robbed. They had put their hand to his breast and robbed him.

In a sense, one often feels that Lawrence's characters are always 'unconscious and superconscious'. What is lacking, deliberately, is the middle term. But the convention must be accepted, as the conventions of any artist must be; and granted the problem, the remarkable thing is not that Lawrence sometimes fails to solve it but how often he succeeds, at any rate in his two greatest novels, *The Rainbow* and *Women in Love*.

Neither is easy to describe. On the face of it, *The Rainbow* is a chronicle novel relating the history of three generations of the Brang-wens, a family of farming stock living in the Erewash Valley in Derbyshire from the middle years of the nineteenth century to the beginning of the twentieth. It abounds in superb passages of broad realism in the nineteenth-century English tradition of the novel: one is reminded everywhere of Lawrence's kinship with George Eliot and Hardy. To illustrate this, one can instance the account of the wedding of the second Brangwen generation, of Anna and her cousin Will, or almost the whole last part of the book, which describes Ursula Brang-wen's experiences as a pupil teacher in a slum school in Nottingham and her career as a student at the University College. The novel is as saturated in the actual as Bennett's *The Old Wives' Tale*, and as a social novel it takes in not only the life of the countryside but also that of the industrial city and of industrialism; there is nothing in the book more powerful than Lawrence's description, seen through Ursula, of the colliery of which her uncle Tom is manager. The novel describes an England changing through three generations from the rural to the urban, and this density of scene, the detail by which the social fabric of life is realized, is the sheet-anchor of the novel.

But Lawrence's first interest is not in writing anything so simple as the conventional social novel. What he was after has been excellently put by Eliseo Vivas, in his *D. H. Lawrence. The Failure and the Triumph of Art*, of all the many books on Lawrence's novels the most perceptive as well as the most provocative: '. . . in *The Rainbow* Lawrence sought to present in language the felt quality of experience; he tried to convey by means of language the ebb and flow of the affective life, particularly the felt quality of erotic passion and of religious emotion—or at least of what he took to be religious emotion.' And this is made plain in the superb opening paragraphs of the novel, describing the traditional life of the Brangwens, farmers in the Erewash Valley, whose lives are scarcely to be distinguished from the seasonal life of the earth they cultivate and the beasts they tend. But within this life subjugated to nature there is a rift:

> It was enough for the men, that the earth heaved and opened its furrow to them, that the wind blew to dry the wet wheat, and set the young ears of corn wheeling freshly round about; it was enough that they helped the cow in labour, or ferreted the rats from under the barn, or broke the back of a rabbit with a sharp knock of the hand. So much warmth and generating and pain and death did they know in their blood, earth and sky and beast and green plants, so much exchange and interchange they had with these, that they lived full and surcharged, their senses full fed, their faces always turned to the heat of the blood, staring into the sun, dazed with looking towards the source of generation, unable to turn round.
>
> But the woman wanted another form of life than this, something that was not blood-intimacy. Her house faced away from the farm-buildings and fields, looked out to the road and the village with church and Hall and the world beyond. She stood to see the far-off world of cities and governments and the active scope of man, the magic land to her, where secrets were made known and desires fulfilled. She faced outwards to where men moved dominant and creative, having turned their back on the pulsing heat of creation, and with this behind them, were set out to discover what was beyond, to enlarge their own scope and range and freedom; whereas the Brangwen men faced inwards to the teeming life of creation, which poured unresolved through their veins.

The rift is that between Mr and Mrs Morel in *Sons and Lovers* expressed in much more generalized terms, so that it becomes almost a universal law of the polarity of the sexes.

How does Lawrence succeed in conveying the quality of this felt experience of what he called 'the immediate and instant self'? Through an imaginative act that Vivas calls 'the constitutive symbol', which is a symbol 'whose referend cannot be fully exhausted by explication, because that to which it refers is symbolized not only *through* it but *in* it'. The concept is obviously related to Jung's definition of the symbol in the psychological sense: 'In so far as a symbol is a living thing, it is the expression of a thing not to be characterized in any other or better way. The symbol is alive in so far as it is pregnant with meaning.'

The constitutive symbol is essentially poetic in its working. Out of many possible examples one may instance the scene in the final chapter of *The Rainbow*, in which Ursula encounters the horses on the common. Have the horses an objective existence? Are they projections of her unconscious? The passage cannot be reduced to any one prose meaning; it is 'the formulation of a relatively unknown thing'. Another example—this time from *Women in Love*—is the extraordinarily compelling scene, compelling partly because of its obscurity, in which Birkin throws stones into the pool to shatter the image of the moon, an episode to which, in *Aspects of the Novel*, E. M. Forster, stumbling for a phrase to define its dark magic, applies the word 'prophetic'.

It is the successful use of the constitutive symbol that makes Lawrence the great poetic novelist he is. It enabled him to render the felt experience of the immediate, instant self as it had never been before, and it is his achievement here that makes his criticism of modern industrial society viable. Lawrence was concerned with quality of experience, with the depth of the individual human being's response to experience. He believed that both the quality of experience of human beings and their capacity for experience had become impoverished by the very nature of modern society, by the nature of modern work. This is, perhaps, clearer in *Women in Love* than in *The Rainbow*. *Women in Love* is conceived dramatically, as the earlier novel is not, in a series of short episodes in which the characters come together and clash; it moves, enormously more than *The Rainbow*, through dialogue. It is the story of two pairs of lovers, Ursula Brangwen of *The Rainbow*, now a school teacher, and Rupert Birkin, Ursula's sister Gudrun, also a teacher, and Gerald Crich, Birkin's best friend, a mine-owner.

If *Women in Love* is a more difficult novel than *The Rainbow* it is so because of the presence in it of Birkin, who is a persona for Lawrence himself. Fiction for Lawrence was, in his own words, a 'thought-adventure', and with *Women in Love* we are in the presence, as it were, of the act of thinking itself, thinking that has not reached its conclusion. Birkin-Lawrence is seeking, but what he is seeking is never very clear and indeed cannot be, because he cannot know himself what it is till he has found it. Again Vivas's analysis of the novel is perceptive and enlightening. Vivas suggests: 'In *Women in Love*, religion, as ordinarily understood, does not enter: man's relation to God is not part of the substance of the novel; but Lawrence poses the problem of human destiny in view of the fact that his characters cannot believe in God, so that religion, by its failure, defines the central problem of the novel.' This of course was the central problem for Lawrence himself throughout his life: how to maintain and preserve the sacramental quality of life in a world in which God is dead. Obviously, the problem can admit only of tentative solutions. But at least Lawrence, who, as Father Martin Jarrett-Kerr, CR, has said, was 'an astonishing diagnostician of life. His sensitive nose could smell death a mile away', could show us those areas of modern life where no hope lay, which were fatal to the spirit.

Looked at from this point of view, *Women in Love* is almost a picaresque novel, a *Pilgrim's Progress* in which various ways of life are tried by Birkin and Gerald and found wanting. There is the experience of Bohemian life among the artists in London. There is the whole brilliant chapter exposing the emptiness of the intellectual life, centred in Hermione Roddice's country house in Derbyshire. There is, too, the figure of Gerald Crich, who, as the images that cluster about him proclaim, is a figure of death. He is also a representation of social man at his most modern, the production engineer, the expert in efficiency for efficiency's sake. As a mine-owner, his father had existed in an almost feudal, patriarchal relation to his miners. Gerald is very different; for him all that matters is production; and, Lawrence suggests, his very ruthlessness is the mirror-image of a changed state in the miners themselves;

> Gerald was their high priest, he represented the religion they really felt. His father was forgotten already. There was a new world, a new order, strict, terrible, inhuman, but satisfying in its very destructiveness. The men were satisfied to belong to the great and wonderful machine, even whilst it destroyed them. It was what they wanted. It was the highest that man had produced, the most wonderful and superhuman. They were exalted by belonging to this great and superhuman system which was

beyond feeling or reason, something really godlike. Their hearts died within them, but their souls were satisfied. It was what they wanted. Otherwise Gerald could never have done what he did. He was just ahead of them in giving them what they wanted, this participation in a great and perfect system that subjected life to pure mathematical principles. It was a sort of freedom, the sort they really wanted. It was the first great step in undoing, the first great phase of chaos, the substitution of the mechanical principle for the organic, the destruction of the organic purpose, the organic unity, and the subordination of every organic unit to the great mechanical purpose. It was pure organic disintegration and pure mechanical organization. This is the first and finest state of chaos.

It is also the state of death; and Lawrence underlines this both by the inadequacy of Crich's attitude towards sex and by the manner of his death, climbing in the Alps and panic-stricken, falling in the snow.

This indictment of industrialism as the final blasphemy against life Lawrence took up again, with much less art, in *Lady Chatterley's Lover*. By comparison with *Women in Love*, it exists at the level of a tract, for all the passion with which it is written.

[5]

LAWRENCE, Mrs Woolf and Joyce were all in their turn targets for the satire of Wyndham Lewis. Lewis was both painter and writer, and as a painter, he was the founder before the first world war of the vorticist movement, the English counterpart of cubism and futurism. He was one of the master-draughtsmen of his time and also one of its finest art critics. In addition to this, besides his fiction, he was a most formidable critic of ideas, in books like *The Art of Being Ruled*, *Time and Western Man*, *Paleface* and *The Writer and the Absolute*. He took over and made his own the doctrines of French neo-classicism, together with the authoritarianism in politics that went with them. Yet his concern for political ideas, his interest in the nature of society, were always subsidiary to his passion for art, were indeed an offshoot of it;

and perhaps he most clearly stated his position in a late book, *The Demon of Progress in the Arts*: 'The only thing that is not absurd is what is found when the earth conditions are stable and peaceful enough to allow of the production of such great classical works as those of Leonardo, Michelangelo, Van Eyck, El Greco.'

For Lewis, art and satire were almost interchangeable terms. In a famous passage he wrote:

> The *external* approach to things (relying on the evidence of the *eye* rather than of the more emotional organs of sense) can make of the 'grotesque' a healthy and attractive companion . . . Dogmatically, then, I am for the Great Without, for the method of *external* approach.

This is obviously a position at the opposite extreme to that of Lawrence and Joyce. For Lewis, the absolute essential of art, whether plastic or literary, was a ferocious accuracy in the rendering of the forms of things. One says 'things' because in practice his external approach to human beings led to their being seen as things. In this he is akin to Smollett, whose conception of character-drawing was also derived very consciously from painting. Behind Smollett stood Hogarth; he tried to render his characters as he believed Hogarth would have painted them. Lewis got his method of drawing character from painters much less familiar, from his own practice as a painter and, generally, from the whole movement in painting since the turn of the century. Here is an example from *The Revenge for Love* (1937), in which Lewis describes a Spanish peasant girl:

> She was walking very slowly: she was walking with the orthodox majesty of the women of those unspoilt districts—their skulls flattened with heavy pitchers—with a hieratic hip-roll that bore her away no quicker than a tortoise showing off its speed at the mating season . . . She and Don Alvaro were the only people in sight. Don Alvaro spat and waited for a few more revolutions of the hips to bring this slowly-ploughing traditional vessel of Old Spain (built to accommodate, in capacious quarters, the fiery man-child below, and at the same time, several pints of water upon top—incubator and caryatid at once) to the tramlined thoroughfare for which it was headed. At the corner this slowly trampling contraption turned, on its own centre, with a sultry swirl of the skirt, and started to walk back.

As with Smollett, an intimidating eye for externals combines with a ferocious wit to dehumanize the object seized upon, to turn it precisely into an object, a monstrous zoological specimen or an equally monstrous creaking mechanism, often into both together. Lewis's prose at its best is as exciting as any written in English this century; whether it is a natural prose for a novelist is another matter. Because of the very intensity of his visual perceptions, it is, as it were, prose in slow motion, and one is aware sometimes of a lack of synchronization between the rhythms of the novels as wholes and those of the sentences, paragraphs and chapters that compose them.

At the same time, Lewis's prose is the perfect vehicle for the rendering of his intellectual perceptions—and here one uses the word 'intellectual' almost in a double sense, for Lewis was an intellectual whose work was based on a cluster of deeply pondered ideas which were for him a permanent measuring rod for the phenomena of the world about him. It was this that made him a very formidable satirist indeed, both in *The Apes of God*, a satire on dilettantism in art and literature in London in the twenties, on art as a fashionable racket, and in his mighty unfinished work *The Human Age*, which in its final stages goes beyond satire to become what may very well be the most remarkable piece of imaginative writing in English of the past two decades, magnificent and dreadful, in the strictest and purest sense of the word, as Swift in the last pages of *Gulliver's Travels* is dreadful. These two books seem to me the most sustained *tours de force* in English since *Ulysses*, but in my view they go so far beyond the bounds of what one normally thinks of as novels as to fall outside present consideration.

There remains to Lewis a sizable body of fiction that can be considered strictly as novels, the most important being his first, *Tarr* (1918), *The Revenge for Love*, and *Self Condemned* (1954). *Tarr* shows Lewis's style at its most powerful and intransigent: 'There is *literally* nothing', one of his earlier critics, Hugh Gordon Porteus, has remarked, 'that is not translated into hard, external, visible images.' Set in the Paris of the artists before the first world war, it is highly intellectual comedy on the themes of art versus life and of Teutonic romanticism. Lewis himself noted that the title should have been *Kreisler*, not *Tarr*, since it is Kreisler, the German artist without talent, who is the central character of the novel. Tarr is something of a self-portrait, the intellectual artist coming to terms with art and with sex. As a character he throws considerable light on the young Lewis; but it is Kreisler who runs away with the book, as a ferociously comic rendering of the German mind in its inordinate romanticism. When the novel appeared it was compared widely to Dostoevsky, and Lewis was admittedly under Dostoevsky's influence when he wrote it. But now the novel reads as though it were Dostoevsky rewritten by a latter-day Ben Jonson, for Kreisler is interpreted throughout in terms of a savage comedy that, in a way, exalts its subject even as it destroys it.

Superficially, *The Revenge for Love* is much more like a novel as the confirmed novel-reader expects it to be than the earlier work; but only superficially. It is a political satire, or rather, a satire on political naivety. Its theme is the difference between political reality, which for Lewis means the pursuit of power, and political illusions. The action takes place in Spain and in London just before the outbreak of the Spanish Civil War, the central character, Percy Hardcaster, being a Communist, a professional revolutionary round whom are clustered a mixed bunch of intellectuals and artists, fellow-travellers who are blinded to the reality by their sentimental illusions. As a result, two of them lose their lives.

The title Lewis originally chose for the novel was *False Bottoms*, and the image of the false bottom runs through the novel. The book opens with the discovery by a prison warder that the bottom of a Spanish girl's basket is false; and so on. Indeed, from the beginning Lewis seems to suggest that falsity and the acquiescence in falsity are the general human condition and that human beings live as shams in a world of shams. This falsity is dramatized in a superb comic account of an art factory that produces fake Van Goghs. And the penalty for failure to acquiesce, to play the universal game of make-believe? Death or betrayal—or both. Such is the fate of the three characters who are unable to acquiesce—Percy Hardcaster, the professional revolutionary, a 'serious' man as Lewis himself was serious, Margot, who is as it were made serious by love, and her husband Victor. It is the presence of these characters, of Hardcaster and Margot especially, that lifts the novel far above the sheerly satirical, for in the end the satirical vision of man has become a tragic vision of man.

Lewis's are novels of ideas rather than of characters; his characters are largely embodiments of points of view, ways of life; they are intellectually conceived, intellectually controlled. The exception is *Self Condemned*, which, written late in life, was his last major novel. It is the most moving of Lewis's novels, because here he is very largely presenting a full-length portrait of one character which is obviously close to a self-portrait, firmly and classically controlled, rendered with complete objectivity. The note of personal anguish sounds through it all the same, the deeper and the more affecting because of the control; and the author's judgment on himself may perhaps be seen in the punning title of the novel.

In *Self Condemned*, the satire is purely incidental: Lewis is essaying tragedy. His tragic hero, Professor René Harding, half-French (as Lewis was half-American), is an historian who resigns his university chair in the months before the war because he no longer believes in the kind of history he has taught and who emigrates with his wife to Canada, as Lewis himself did, when the second world war breaks out. Like his creator, Harding is a man in revolt against the cataclysmic insanity of modern war and, rather than go on living in a society pledged to it, opts out of it—into life in an hotel in the Canadian city of Momaco. The description of the hotel and its inhabitants forms the middle section of the novel; by implication, it is a description of Canada and, beyond that, perhaps of mankind in its unregenerate state. One of Lewis's most powerful pieces of writing, at once terrifying and comic, this section of the novel is dominated by images of ice and fire. In the end, the hotel is burnt down, and Harding emerges from it to resume authorship and become a professor again—but 'the Gods cannot strike *twice* and the man survive'. His wife commits suicide, Harding has a breakdown and comes out of it as the shell of himself, a man driven by 'the pressure of his own will-to-success, of the most vulgar type'. Success comes to him, and he moves to one of the great American universities; 'and the Faculty had no idea that it was a glacial shell of a man who had come to live among them, mainly because they were themselves unfilled with anything more than a little academic stuffing'.

[6]

TWO NOVELISTS, Ford Madox Ford and E. M. Forster, whose early novels had been published well before the first world war, added significantly to their reputations in the twenties. Ford's finest novel is probably *The Good Soldier* (1915), as formally perfect a novel as any in English and an amazingly subtle account, by one of them, of the lives of four people who appear to live in harmony and friendship, whose 'intimacy was like a minuet', for more than ten years. *The Good Soldier* sprang out of Ford's own sufferings. So, too, did the four novels that compose the Tietjens sequence, *Some Do Not*, *No More Parades*, *A Man Could Stand Up* and *Last Post*, which appeared between 1924 and 1928.

Of the genesis of these novels he wrote: 'I needed someone, some character, in lasting tribulation—with a permanent shackle and ball on his leg . . . A physical defect it could not be, for if I wrote about that character he would have to go into the trenches. It would be something of a moral order, and something inscrutable.' In fact, Ford had been rendering just such a character on and off since 1905, when he wrote *The Benefactor*, in which the character appears as George Moffatt. In *The Good Soldier* the character turns up as Ashburnham. Together with Tietjens, they define the essential Ford character: the English gentleman—Ford sometimes calls him the Tory—for whom money exists only in order that others may be helped, who neither explains his actions nor apologizes for them, who follows his code without question and with full knowledge of the consequences, which are inevitably that his motives will be misunderstood and that he will be betrayed by those whom he has befriended. He suffers, but does so in silence. He is the man in the impossible position, impossible because it can be resolved only at the cost of his honour, the one thing he will never allow himself to lose.

The first sentence of *Some Do Not* indicates the world Ford is re-creating: 'The two young men—they were of the English public official class—sat in the perfectly appointed railway carriage.' The world is that of the ruling class of Edwardian England, a world already breaking up: one of the young men in the railway carriage is there through brains not birth, a lower middle-class careerist from Leith. But for the most part, Ford's characters are of that world by birth, cabinet ministers, permanent under-secretaries, generals, right-wing journalists; and they are there not out of interest, inclination or the desire for fame or wealth, but simply from duty. So one theme of these novels is duty, the observance of the code that says without argument, 'It isn't done'.

That, of course, is a variant of the title of the first novel in the sequence, *Some Do Not*. Tietjens's lasting tribulation, his shackle and ball, is his wife, a wanton, whose child may not be his, who deserts him, whom he takes back, who throughout his life does her best to ruin him and indeed does so in the eyes of the world. He will not divorce her because a gentleman does not divorce his wife; she cannot divorce him because she is a Catholic. He is in love with Valentine Wannup, the daughter of his father's oldest friend; he will not tell her so because he is married. But loving him, she becomes yet another means by which his wife Sylvia can persecute him, for Sylvia is possessed by a lust to ruin him. Tietjens suffers all her attempts passively, with a sort of Christian stoicism. Partly through her intrigues, partly through his integrity which will not, for example, permit him to fake official statistics in the Government interest, his career as a civil servant comes to an early end. In the war he is no more successful as a soldier: beloved of his men, he suffers the final ignominy of being put in charge of prisoners behind the line.

To depict a positively good man is the most difficult task a novelist can set himself. Does Ford succeed with Tietjens? In the last analysis, I think not. The tribulations are piled on too heavily. So many make us suspicious, just as a psychiatrist raises his eyebrows in the presence of a man who is knocked down by motor-cars too often. Tietjens's role in the four novels is always to be the victim of the booby-traps set by his wife or by fate. He is, and has to be, a static character, ending as he began, the Tory Christian. In the end, one feels he is a little too good to be convincing, and it is difficult not to see him a sentimental creation.

Yet Ford's marvellous technical adroitness goes a long way towards blinding us to the fact that Tietjens is a fixed character. In the four novels he is examined and exposed from every possible angle; we see him through the eyes of his wife, of his careerist friend Macmaster, of his brother the permanent under-secretary, his godfather and commanding officer, General Campion, of the woman who loves him, of his fellow officers and of the men serving under him. And the whole is presented with the utmost compression. Ford rarely indulges in direct narration; everything is elusive, elliptical, for the story progresses always through the thoughts of the character that is engaging his attention at the moment. And though Tietjens may be too good to be true, such a character was essential to the work Ford was aiming at, the subject of which was to be nothing less than 'the public events of a decade'. Tietjens is the fixed point round which the flux eddies, his integrity the criterion of that of the other characters and of the decade itself.

Of E. M. Forster's five novels, four appeared between 1905 and 1910, the fifth, *A Passage to India*, in 1924. In *Mr Bennett and Mrs Brown*, Virginia Woolf associated Forster with Lawrence, Joyce and herself as one of the novelists writing in reaction against the novel as understood by the Edwardians. This is true neither as fact nor in implication. Technically, Forster is a very old-fashioned novelist; so far as he is concerned, neither the French Naturalists nor James might have written. His plots, that of *A Passage to India* excepted, are as improbable and as melodramatic as any in Victorian fiction; and in his own person of the omniscient narrator, he comments on his characters, interprets their motives and actions, moralizes on them, bids us admire or detest. As with Fielding and Thackeray, his novels are triumphs of a personal attitude expressed in a special tone of voice; and it is the tone of voice, the style, which gives his novels their unity and almost persuades us to ignore the improbable violence of the earlier ones and the discontinuities of his attitude.

But what is his attitude? It is more complex and ambiguous than may at first appear. Fundamental to his public attitude has been his faith in the holiness of the heart's affections and in personal relations, rational discourse and disinterestedness, qualities associated with the good life as conceived through his experiences of Cambridge University as a young man. When we turn to the novels, however, we see that things are not so simple. The rational surface is deceptive. Time and again an ominous note is struck which anticipates Mrs Moore's intuition in *A Passage to India*, where in the Marabar Caves the echo murmurs to her:

> 'Pathos, piety, courage—they exist, but are identical, and so is filth. Everything exists, nothing has value.' If one had spoken vileness in that place, or quoted lofty poetry, the comment would have been the same—'ou-boum'.

For Forster, then, beneath the surface of things there is a nullity, a void. Fundamentally, Forster is a tragic humanist for whom man justi-fies himself by his self-awareness and by the fruits of his imagination, by the arts, especially, perhaps, music. Forster is the advocate of balance, of the whole man; but man is rarely balanced and few are whole. The criticism of lack of balance, lack of wholeness, is the impulse behind his first four novels, *Where Angels Fear to Tread*, *The Longest Journey*, *A Room with a View* and *Howards End*.

These novels are a mingling of social comedy and poetry: the social comedy, even remembering Meredith, is the best we have had since Jane Austen, but the poetry doesn't work. This is strikingly apparent in *Howards End*, Forster's most ambitious novel and the most explicit as a statement of his values. 'Only connect' is the motto of the book: 'Only connect the passion and the prose.' In some sense at least, *Howards End* is a symbolic novel about the state of England at the time of writing; but none of the characters in it is quite large enough, quite fitting, to illustrate the general thesis. We are aware when reading the novel that something devised and not wholly corresponding to life as we know it is being forced upon us.

'Only connect' might also be the motto of *A Passage to India*, an incomparably more successful novel. The very subject of India, with its clash of race, religion and colour, compelled Forster to interpret his values in terms of a concrete historical situation. The complicated plots of the earlier novels had to go; instead, within the brilliantly described world of conventional Anglo-Indian relations, we have the attempts, fumbling yet moving, of English and Indian—on the one hand Mrs Moore, Adela Quested, Fielding, on the other Dr Aziz—to make contact as human beings. They fail—the mysterious happening in the Marabar Caves, with its upshot in the trial of Aziz for the attempted rape of Adela, seems to represent a perverseness in the very nature of things. The attempts at contact have served only to exacerbate the Anglo-Indian situation. And yet . . .

The 'and yet' indicates the ambiguity at the heart not only of the novel but of Forster's view of life. India, he has written, is not a mystery, it is a muddle; herein it is very much like life itself as Forster sees it. The novel exists on two planes and has a different meaning according to the plane we concentrate on. There is the plane of realism, and here Forster's great gifts of satire and sympathy, humour and understanding, come together as never before: all his previous criticisms of the 'undeveloped heart' are summed up in his descriptions of the behaviour of the English at Chandrapore; all his sympathy with those who seek reality, who feel the necessity to connect, are implicit in his presentation and analysis of Mrs Moore, Adela, Fielding and Aziz; while his humour and understanding are beautifully embodied in the evocations of Hinduism and its ceremonies. On this level, *A Passage to India* is a superb realistic novel, and its conclusion, with Aziz and Fielding meeting while out riding in a native state years after Aziz's trial, is what the facts of the novel dictate:

> 'Why can't we be friends now?' said the other, holding him affectionately. 'It's what I want. It's what you want.'
> But the horses didn't want it—they swerved apart; the earth didn't want it, sending up rocks through which riders must pass single file; the temples, the tank, the jail, the palace, the birds, the carrion, the Guest House, that came into view as they issued from the gap and saw Mau beneath: they didn't want it, they said in their hundred voices: 'No, not yet', and the sky said: 'No, not there.'

But on the other plane this conclusion is contradicted. Reconciliation *is* possible; and it comes about through the figure of Mrs Moore, the old lady on whom India has so strange an effect and who becomes, after she leaves India to die on the voyage home, almost a local goddess. She is not presented to us as an especially remarkable old lady; but she has her moments of perception, she expresses Forster's own awareness of the nature of things; and when at the trial Adela suddenly perceives reality and knows that whatever did happen in the Caves—and what did we never know—it is, as it were, through Mrs Moore's eyes that she sees. And it is significant that when Fielding reappears, in the last part of the novel, it is as the husband of her daughter.

Mrs Moore seems to me successful as a symbol. What she means cannot be paraphrased, though one may make many guesses about her significance. She is among other things a Magna Mater figure, older than English and Indian and the strife between them. She broods over the novel; not benignly, anything but that, but as a symbol of acceptance, of unconscious life that goes on heedless of the disputes of the passing moment. Mrs Moore, one feels, will be there when England and India alike are forgotten.

[7]

THE TWENTIES was a period in English fiction bristling with remarkable talents. None was more remarkable, in the simplest sense of the word, than that of Ronald Firbank (1886–1926). Writing on Firbank, E. M. Forster has observed that 'to break a butterfly, or even a beetle, upon a wheel is a delicate task'; and any criticism of Firbank's novels—*Caprice* (1917), *Valmouth* (1919), *The Flower beneath the Foot* (1923), *Prancing Nigger* (1925), *Concerning the Eccentricities of Cardinal Pirelli* (1926), *The Artificial Princess* (1934)—is almost bound to appear an act of clumsiness. Wealthy, homosexual, a Roman Catholic, he has affinities with Beckford in *Vathek* and with Aubrey Beardsley in his Venusburg fragment *Under the Hill*. Decadent, frivolous, trivial—the adjectives come hopping off the typewriter—Firbank creates an artificial world, but, whatever its locale, it is always the same world; and to illustrate it one novel is probably as good as another. I will take *The Flower beneath the Foot* as the example.

It is set in the imaginary country of Pisuerga, at the Court of St James. The main strand of the book is the liaison between Laura de Nazianzi, a lady of the Court, and the heir-apparent, His Weariness Prince Youssef. But a marriage is arranged between the Prince and Princess Elsie, daughter of King Geo and Queen Glory of England. Laura retires heart-broken to the Convent of the Flaming Hood, to become in the course of time a saint. Other strands cross this main one: the efforts of Madame Wetme to be presented at Court, Queen Thleeanhouee's attachment to Lady Something, the wife of the British Ambassador; an archaeological expedition to the ruins of Chedorlahomor, 'a *faubourg* of Sodom'.

Firbank's quality can best be demonstrated by quotation:

'Let us go away by and by, my dear gazelle', she exclaimed with a primitive smile, 'and remove our corsets and talk.'

Or:

'Go to the window, Willie', the Queen exhorted her Consort, fixing an eye on the last trouser button that adorned his long, straggling legs.
The King, who had the air of a tired pastry-cook, sat down.
'We feel', he said, 'today, we've had our fill of stares.'

'One little bow, Willie', the Queen entreated, 'that wouldn't
kill you.'

'We'd give perfect worlds', the King went on, 'to go, by
Ourselves, to bed . . .

'Whenever I go out', the King complained, 'I get an impression of raised hats.'

It was seldom King William of Pisuerga spoke in the singular
tense, and Doctor Babcock looked perturbed.

'Raised hats, sir?' he murmured in impressive tones.

'Nude heads, doctor.'

Frivolous, flippant, outrageously affected, written, it seems, *épater
la bourgeoisie*, though in fact all we know of him suggests that the
author himself might have stepped out of one of his own novels,
Firbank's novels proceed mainly by dialogue. The normal structure of
the novel has been abandoned, as though Firbank found it boring and
therefore left it out. On the surface what seems to be created is a *fin-de-
siècle* homosexual aesthete's artificial paradise; yet, as one reads, one
discovers it is not quite this. It is not paradise. There is suffering, there
are misunderstandings, even tragedy. They are made to appear absurd,
or they take place between chapters; which is merely another way of
saying that Firbank was quite aware of what he could and could not do.
But they are there all the same, and their effects ripple through the
gossamer tissue of the novels. In a brilliant analysis of Firbank, A.
Alvarez has noted that one of Firbank's ingredients is 'a sense of
ominous unease'.

It is significant that this sense of ominous unease achieves its most
direct expression—direct, that is, for Firbank—in his most outrageously irreverent and most explicitly perverse novel, *Concerning the
Eccentricities of Cardinal Pirelli*, which ends with the Cardinal, 'dispossessed of everything but his fabulous mitre . . . nude and elementary
now as Adam himself', chasing a choirboy round his cathedral and
dropping dead in the pursuit 'before a painting of old Dominic
Theotocopuli, the Greek, showing the splendour of Christ's martyrdom':

> Now that the ache of life, with its fevers, passions, doubts, its
> routine, vulgarity, and boredom, was over, his serene, unclouded
> face was a marvelment to behold. Very great distinction and
> sweetness was visible there, together with much nobility, and
> love, all magnified and commingled.

Firbank called one of his earliest and least successful works *A Study in Temperament*. The title describes all his novels. However we may react to the temperament, the novels are its complete expression. Its nature makes Firbank, at first sight, a marginal figure in the history of recent fiction; yet, when we look closer and look at him in the context of his time, of the nineties in which he grew up and the decade from 1916 to 1926 in which he wrote most of his novels, we realize that he is not so marginal after all. One can find parallels and affinity, too, between his work and much contemporary writing, in particular, perhaps, the poems of Edith Sitwell and E. E. Cummings. Firbank, too, in his own intensely mannered, muted way is the clown with the broken heart.

His novels, like much of the writing of his period, remind us that the twenties were considerably nearer in time to the nineties than we are now to the twenties; but if his immediate ancestors were the men of the nineties his mode of expression was strictly contemporary, the literary equivalent of much of what we find in the Russian Ballet, in cubist painting and in the music of composers like *Les Six*. And for a novelist at first glimpse so marginal, his influence has been considerable. It can be seen during his lifetime on his slightly older contemporary, the American Carl Van Vechten, the title of whose *The Tattooed Countess* is far from being the only Firbankian thing about it. What Evelyn Waugh and Anthony Powell, both self-confessed admirers of Firbank, learnt from him is evident in their early novels, particularly *Decline and Fall* and *Vile Bodies* and *Afternoon Men*. It was a technique, or parts of a technique, certainly not a manner; a way of suppressing description and allowing dialogue to convey character and also largely to carry a novel forward.

Firbank helps to define the literary atmosphere of the later war years and of the early twenties. So too does Norman Douglas, whose *South Wind* (1917) provided a pattern a number of later novelists were to follow. It re-established the conversation-novel in the manner of Peacock but placed it in a Mediterranean setting, the effect of which on Anglo-Saxon characters was to thaw inhibitions and release hitherto repressed desires. It was a form that Aldous Huxley was to follow on occasion. The twenties and Huxley are inseparable; he helped to create its atmosphere and also the change of atmosphere in which the decade ended. He is, of course, a much more complex personality than Firbank and his interests and sympathies are wider than Douglas's;

and he has developed in ways that could scarcely have been guessed when his first works appeared. What excited one in his novels thirty years ago, one now realizes, were the ideas they contained, ideas expressed with a wit that then seemed incomparable. His novels were, so to speak, the machinery by which he projected his ideas. As novels, they now appear very much do-it-yourself jobs copied from altogether superior models.

Mr Propter, the exponent of Huxley's own beliefs in *After Many a Summer*, notes

> the weariness, to an adult mind, of all those merely descriptive plays and novels which critics expected one to admire . . . Just a huge collection of facts about lust and greed, fear and ambition, duty and affection: just facts, and imaginary facts at that, with no co-ordinating philosophy superior to common sense and the local system of conventions, no principle of arrangement more rational than simple aesthetic expediency . . . If you considered them dispassionately, nothing could be more silly and squalid than the themes of *Phèdre*, or *Othello*, or *Wuthering Heights*, or *Agamemnon*.

But Huxley has not always believed this; as his first novels, *Chrome Yellow* (1920) and *Antic Hay* (1923), show. They remain almost as fresh as when they were written, *Chrome Yellow* especially: gay and charming as well as witty, it is Huxley in the manner of Peacock, a delightful conversation novel. Intermittently, *Antic Hay* is more brilliant; it is also darker; already the well-known Huxleyan dichotomies are apparent. In the next novel, *Those Barren Leaves* (1925), the cloven hoof of the serious Huxley, the Huxley who is often hard put to it to distinguish between seriousness and solemnity, is plainly visible. And with the emergence of the seriousness—and the solemnity —there is a coarsening.

This is evident in more ways than one. First, technically. There was a period when it seemed that though not in any real sense interested in extending the bounds of fiction, Huxley was determined to appear as though he was. So *Point Counterpoint* (1928) borrows heavily from Gide's *Les faux-monnayeurs*; while *Eyeless in Gaza* (1936) plays tricks with chronological time in a manner reminiscent of Christopher Isherwood in *The Memorial*. Then the characters become caricatures, lath-and-paper dummies with gramophones in the bellies, existing as it were in a perpetual brains-trust session, indulging more and more in what are in fact detachable essays. Moreover, they are repeated from novel to novel: the heartless vamp, the would-be diabolist, the seeker of sensation for sensation's sake, the research worker who is a child at everything outside the narrow field of his research, the earnest young man who confuses literature with life, the artist-without-talent who bawls of his own genius, the introverted writer who, faced with the meaninglessness of life, is in search of meaning. And the caricatures are drawn from literature and from life indiscriminately. Thus, in *Point Counterpoint*, Rampion is no doubt D. H. Lawrence, Burlap Middleton Murry and Philip Quarles Huxley himself; but Spandrell is just as plainly an attempt to place Baudelaire in the London of the twenties. This last is instructive. The psychological motivation of Spandrell is precisely that of Baudelaire as seen by the psychoanalysts, even to Spandrell's having a stepfather who is a general. The hidden springs of action are similar; but Baudelaire was the greatest poet of his time, whereas Spandrell remains simply an example of one particular neurosis, a textbook example.

What Huxley is attempting here could not be more serious. He is presenting a vision of contemporary life in which all human activities, except one, are at the best valueless and self-thwarting, while most will lead to agony of mind in those who indulge in them and suffering for all who have anything to do with them. Yet the characters are presented in terms of a mechanistic philosophy which determines their every action. In *Eyeless in Gaza* one character alone is shown as being free, or achieving freedom. He is Anthony Beavis, a version of the author himself; and that he should be shown as capable of choice is significant. We may see others as wholly conditioned beings, but we always consider that we ourselves have some measure of freedom. What Huxley has claimed for himself he denies to his characters.

'As a man sows, so shall he reap.' It is a favourite quotation of Mr Propter's, in *After Many a Summer* (1939), and it is the moral of Huxley's later fiction. It is the theme of many great works of fiction, but what we are conscious of in Huxley is not the degradation which is the consequence of wrong choice but only of the jigging of puppets. The drama the puppets play out is horrifying enough, but we are unaffected because it is not played out in terms of flesh and blood. If it were, it would be unbearable. As it is, in the novels that follow *Point Counterpoint*, one can scarcely help feeling that Huxley himself is indulging in sensation for sensation's sake; in *Eyeless in Gaza*, for example, with its gratuitous horrors such as a dog dropped from an aeroplane to burst beside naked lovers and a young woman seduced for a bet by her fiancé's best friend, with the fiancé's consequent suicide; and, almost in desperation, as it were, forcing meaning into a world he has shown to be devoid of meaning, Huxley's own retreat into mysticism. The horrors are merely the illustrations of a number of intellectual propositions; they provide the action among the essays, as it were. It was not really difficult, having chosen such illustrations of action, to show that all action ends in evil and that the only thing to do is to refuse to act at all.

From the beginning—one sees it in the early poems—Huxley has been agonizingly aware of the terrible contrast, the irreconcilable conflict within himself, between the idealization of art and the physiological, animal realities of human existence, the fact that, to hark back to an early poem, lovers among other things sweat. The conflict has continued throughout his work, apparently insoluble, reaching its climax perhaps—though *Ape and Essence*, published eight years later, falls little short of it—in *After Many a Summer*, where the consequences of the quest for an elixir of life are depicted in the spectacle of a man and woman who, at two hundred years old, have retrogressed into apes, savaging each other in a stinking cage. Here Huxley comes very near to literary coprophilia.

Since *Ape and Essence*, Huxley has written only three novels. The mystical reality he now accepts is intractable to dramatization in fiction. Perhaps his best work was always to be found in his essays and in the superb biography, *Grey Eminence*, which contains, among much else, the finest of his incursions into fantasy since *Chrome Yellow*.

[8]

FANTASY was an abiding interest of the novelists of the twenties. David Garnett's *Lady into Fox* appeared in 1922, to be followed by *A Man in the Zoo* in 1925 and *The Sailor's Return* in 1925. *Lady into Fox* remains a brilliant *tour de force*.

... the sudden changing of Mrs Tebrick into a vixen is an established fact which we may attempt to account for as we will. Certainly it is in the explanation of the fact, and the reconciling of it with our general notions that we shall find most difficulty, and not in accepting for true a story which is so fully proved, and that by no witness but by a dozen, all respectable, and with no possibility of collusion between them.

In fact, Garnett does not attempt to explain the strange event which occurred in the first days of 1880, he merely narrates it as a true story, telling it in a style a little archaic, a little mannered, suggestive of Defoe's *A True Relation of the Apparition of One Mrs Veal*. A triumph, if you like, of artificiality, it is also a triumph of story-telling: reading, we find ourselves caught up immediately in what Coleridge called 'that willing suspension of disbelief for the moment, that constitutes poetic faith'. *Lady into Fox*, *A Man in the Zoo* and *The Sailor's Return* are delightful *divertissements*, and that is how we should take them. With them we might include Sylvia Townsend Warner's tale of witchcraft, *Lolly Willowes* (1926), and John Collier's *His Monkey Wife* (1930).

In *Go She Must* (1927) and *No Love* (1929), David Garnett moves much closer to the naturalistic novel of character and situation. The prose of *Go She Must* remains faintly old-fashioned, echoing with biblical turns of phrase and with suggestions of the eighteenth century, which, together with the remoteness of the main scene, the village of Dry Coulter, near the Fens, create an effect of timelessness. It comes as a surprise to realize, when the heroine Anne moves to Paris, that we are in the twentieth century. The two scenes do not fit well together, and the whole novel seems to me to be over-distanced and in consequence to lose its full impact. It exists, perhaps, rather as a collection of pictures than as a fully realized novel; but the pictures are extraordinarily fine and memorable, especially those that begin and end the novel, of the world under snow in the first chapter and of the Rev. Mr Dunnock gently mad in the last, with his house turned into an enormous nesting-place for swallows: '"Angels", said Mr Dunnock, putting a finger to his lips. "They are angels".'

No Love is fully realized. The prose is as pure and formal as ever, but much more contemporary; one no longer has the impression that the characters are figures in a tapestry: one feels they have their own independent life.

In this novel Garnett shows two contrasted ways of life lived in close proximity. There are the Lydiates, Roger Lydiate being an Anglican clergyman who has lost his faith and resigned his orders, his wife Alice the daughter of a famous scientist and notorious freethinker. They may stand for the world of high-minded Victorian rationalism, the forbears of the Bloomsbury Group to which Garnett himself belonged. Opposed to them are the Kelties, a naval family who share their island off the south of England. In general terms, the contrast is between the permissive and the authoritarian, and it achieves its full dramatization in the relations between the sons of the two families, Benedict Lydiate and Simon Keltie, who are forced by sheer proximity into a friendship that would, one feels, be otherwise impossible, so little have they in common. The character of Simon is brilliantly drawn, the striving neurotic impelled by pride and an inherited sense of family duty, unable to give or to accept love, imprisoned within himself and, for all his intelligence and his self-knowledge, doomed, as we realize in the last pages, to repeat the same pattern of behaviour towards his son as his father did to him. No less good, it seems to me, is the delineation of his wife Cynthia, who leaves him after an affair during the war with Benedict while he was on leave from sea; a delineation tender, sympathetic and very touching.

But there is something else to *No Love*. After a time one realizes—with some surprise, so unemphatic is Garnett's manner—that in this novel Garnett has become the novelist as historian of his own times. To say that the action of the novel moves against the panorama of English history from Queen Victoria's diamond jubilee until 1926 would be to put it altogether too crudely. The characters are not figures against a background; historical events enter into their lives naturally and condition them; they are part of their very being, inescapable, even when rendered in comic terms as in Admiral Keltie's life-long love-affair with the Japanese.

T. F. Powys's fiction has some resemblance, admittedly superficial, to Garnett's. For many years now, Powys's reputation has been in the powerful keeping of F. R. Leavis; and to admire Powys is *de rigueur* for Leavis's disciples. I think they greatly over-estimate him. There is a passage in an essay of Dylan Thomas's, obviously aimed at Powys, which causes them particular indignation:

Everyone, in this sophisticatedly contrived bucolic morality, has his or her obsession: Minnie Wurzel wants only the vicar; the Vicar, the Reverend Nut, wants only the ghost of William

Cowper to come into his brown study and read him 'The Task'; the Sexton wants worms; worms want the vicar. Lambkins, on those impossible hills, frolic, gambol, and are sheepish under the all-seeing eye of Uncle Teapot, the Celestial Tinker. Cruel farmers persecute old cowherds called Crumpet, who talk, all day long, to cows; cows, tired of vaccine-talk in which they can have no part, gore, in a female manner, the aged relatives of cruel farmers; it is all very cosy in Upper Story . . .

No doubt it was naughty of Thomas thus to satirize Powys, the more so since *Under Milk Wood* is not without its debts to him. Yet the implied criticism seems to me just: Powys's stories *are* sophisticatedly contrived bucolic moralities.

Mr Tasker's Gods (1924) may be taken as typical of Powys's novels. Mr Tasker is a farmer; his gods are his pigs, to which he feeds the corpse of his father, a rapist. At one point in the story Mr Tasker acquires a dog:

> With the dog under the seat, Mr Tasker drove into his yard. He let down the back of his cart and kicked out the dog, chain and all. Daisy Tasker, aged five years, was watching her father's return, and was standing near. In a moment the enraged beast sprang upon her and mauled her face. Mr Tasker pulled his prize away and conveyed it to a tub, where, at his leisure, he tied it up. Meanwhile, his little girl, covered with blood, half mad with terror, lay screaming. She was at last carried in, and fainted. Mr Tasker went out to milk his cows.
> After milking, Mr Tasker, much against his will, sent for the doctor.
> 'You know what people will say, if she dies', he told his wife.

Powys's novels, as Edwin Muir says, 'derive their power from an extreme simplification of life which seems to lay bare the forms of good and evil. When this happens life becomes something very like a night-mare filled with simple symbolical figures'. Mr Tasker is one of these, a moral monster, but so simplified, in my view, as to be without any kind of moral interest. Powys's is a monotonous vision of crude evil and ineffective namby-pamby good persecuted by wickedness almost to madness; and as a representation of the latter Powys never achieved any figure as fine as Garnett's Mr Dunnock in *Go She Must*. Nor does it seem to me that Powys's style, highly praised as it generally is, bears much examination. It is, certainly, extremely skilful; yet its archaism, with its reminiscences of the Authorized Version, Bunyan and Jane Austen, tends still further to remove Powys's moralities from the actual world by reference to which the moralities must be judged. At times, Powys's style becomes intolerably arch and coy, especially where sex is concerned. Powys's world is as artificial, as abstracted from common reality, as Firbank's; it seems to me much less entertaining.

One exception must be made: *Mr Weston's Good Wine*, the novel on which Powys's reputation will ultimately rest. This is a brilliant allegory, in which God appears to the village of Folly Down and its inhabitants with his good wine of death. But delightful as it is, and thoroughly worked out as it is, almost indeed as a version of the Last Judgment, I still find an impassable gap between myself and those who invoke *The Tempest* and *The Pilgrim's Progress* when discussing it.

The novels of John Cowper Powys likewise divide critical opinion. Whereas T. F. may be said to be a miniaturist—his best work is probably in his short stories, and his novels are never long—J. C. is very much the opposite: *A Glastonbury Romance*, for instance, is scarcely shorter than *War and Peace*. Its length is justified by the enormity of Powys's ambition; his vision of man is apocalyptic. It is this that makes him so extraordinarily difficult to get to grips with. It seems to me possible to recognize J. C. Powys's genius and at the same time to be thoroughly dissatisfied with what he has made of it. Being interested in man only in his relation to the universe and to universals, he has set him in a vast mythology of natural forces so alien to the temper of the age as to be impossible for many people to take seriously.

Any of his characters can be the meeting-point of forces both near and incredibly remote. The whole universe, for Powys, is a sentient thing, stones, sun, the furthest planets; all are engaged, it seems, in a ceaseless struggle between good and evil for which the individual human soul forms a convenient battle-ground; so that there is a continuous intensely living relationship between men and nature in all its aspects. Indeed, all nature exists in a state of constant vibration; and the thoughts of a man in Glastonbury literally touch the stars. All Powys's characters are possessed by immense natural and supernatural forces—though the distinction between them is often difficult to see—which they not only do not understand but to which understanding in the normal sense is irrelevant. Here is a comparatively simple instance from *A Glastonbury Romance*:

Cordelia reached the nearest of her great oaks—whether Viking or Druid—in what seemed to her so short a time that she felt as if she had been spirited there in the teeth of these western gusts. She came upon the oaks from the top of the eastern hedge-bank, for she had come, on her wild approach, recklessly across the country. Here on the top of this hedge-bank she rested, clutching a sweet-scented hazel-branch with one hand and a bitter-scented elder-branch with the other. The wind rose about her as she stood there, in wilder and wilder gusts. And then Cordelia, gazing directly into the wide-flung branches of the biggest of the two giant trees, was aware of something else upon the wind. Those enormous branches seemed to have begun an orchestral monotone, composed of the notes of many instruments gathered up into one. It was a cumulative and rustling sigh that came to the woman's ears, as if a group of sorrowful Titans had lifted up their united voices in one lamentable dirge over the downfall of their race. It kept beginning afresh, this solemn moan upon the air—a moan which always mounted to a certain pitch and then sank down. Sometimes, such were the vagaries of the wind, before this portentous requiem started afresh, there was a singular humming and droning in those huge branches, as if the tree wished to utter a private secret of its own to Cordelia's ears, before it recommenced its official chant. Yes! the peculiarity of this humming sound was that it shivered and shook with a special intonation for the woman standing upon the bank! And Cordelia knew well what that message was. The great tree was telling the hillside that there was rain upon the wind; but it was telling Cordelia something else! Then all was absolutely still; and in that stillness, a stillness like the terrible stillness of uttermost strain in travail, there came the first cry of birth, the fall of a single drop of rain. That first drop was followed by another and that again by another. Cordelia did not hear them in the same place. One drop would fall upon the roadway beneath her; one upon a dead burdock leaf; one upon a faded hart's tongue fern of last year's growth. Then the sound of the falling drops would be drowned in a reawakening of that orchestral dirge. Then the wind would die down over all the upland, and once more an absolute stillness would descend; and in the stillness again— only now in an increased number—the big raindrops would splash to earth, one falling upon a dead leaf, one upon a naked stone, one upon a knot of close-grown twigs, one upon Cordelia's bare forehead. Her feeling at that moment was that some deep psychic chain had been broken in her inmost being.

Hola—hola! She could not restrain herself from giving vent to a wild cry of exultant delight as the first bursting deluge followed these premonitory drops . . .

J. C. Powys's imaginative power can scarcely be questioned; and as an example of his genius working at length one might choose the scene in *A Glastonbury Romance* in which Philip Crow seduces Persephone Spear in the caves of Wookey Hole beside the subterranean river. Yet in my experience such passages impress more deeply in isolation than when read in their context; for Powys's romantic prose, which is always rhetorical, written as it were with all stops out, very easily becomes inflated rant, in which meaning is lost in a tempestuous roar of words. Conscious control, structure, selection seem to disappear altogether, and at such times Powys's characters, at best giant puppets set in fixed stances, resembling embodied single passions—of Faustian or Promethean ambition, of sado-masochism seeking to sublimate itself in imitations of the Crucifixion, of homosexuality and the like— go down destroyed in the storm and stress that they evoke and that is the form as well as the accompaniment of their being.

Admirers of Powys see him as comparable in manner and achievement to Melville. I do not think the comparison can be justified. Melville's symbolism is sustained by a perfectly comprehensible fable, whereas Powys's fiction suffers all the time from the lack of acceptable plausible stories out of which the symbolism can naturally rise. Powys's most successful fictions seem to me such novels as *Owen Glendower* (1940) and *Porius* (1951), novels set in Wales in the middle ages and at the time of King Arthur respectively, so far removed from present actualities, in other words, that the reference to reality is scarcely relevant.

[9]

WILLIAM GERHARDI's first novel, *Futility*, published in 1922, was sub-titled 'A Novel on Russian Themes'. It is a comedy of the

Russian Revolution as seen by a young British officer, largely Russian in upbringing, on the staff of the Army of Intervention and the honorary member, as it were, of a large, feckless Russian family, ever growing by accretions of friends, relations and servants, that accompanies him in exile across Siberia to Vladivostock. It is a comedy of futility, of the futility of intervention and of the various 'White' attempts at counter-revolution, and also of the efforts of the Bursanov family to get possession of and retain their largely imaginary fortunes. Looked at in the light of what has happened in Russia since the Revolution, *Futility*, one can scarcely help thinking, must have reinforced in a gratifying way Western stereotypes of the Russian character then popular, notions of 'typical' Russian behaviour as derived from nineteenth-century Russian fiction. One could say of Gerhardi's characters as he himself says of Chekhov's: 'It seems as though they had all been born on the line of demarcation between comedy and tragedy—in a kind of No Man's Land.'

This is just as true of the characters of his next novel, *The Polyglots* (1925), though they are not necessarily Russians but members of a Belgian family long resident in Russia to whom the narrator, a young British officer very similar in origins and character to the hero in *Futility*, is related and with whom he lives, as a member of a British military mission, in Harbin. In both novels the nature of the comedy is defined by the tone of the prose in which they are written. It is highly personal, light and glancing, often lyrical but always self-deflating, verging sometimes on the edge of sentimentality but never quite toppling over. It has close affinities with the prose of Sterne, and, as with Sterne's, one feels that it 'is but a different name for conversation'. It pins down unerringly absurdity and contradiction—of characters and aspirations and situations—but does so without malice; the narrator is as conscious of his own absurdity as of that of the other characters; the comic, we are made to feel, is the other face of the tragic, and absurdity is at the heart of things.

These two novels are delightful and original comedy, not in any way satirical but exercises in pure humour. They are a triumph of tone, and from time to time, not so much in asides as in the very texture of the writing, they hint at other worlds beyond the scenes described, carry with them insinuations of immortality. *Futility* and *The Polyglots* remain for me by far the best of Gerhardi's fiction, though they set the pattern for the later work. The narrator of both novels appears as a novelist, and we realize that what we are reading is the novel as it were in the course of writing. It is a dangerous device that succeeds much less well in Gerhardi's later books.

The most ambitious of these is *Resurrection* (1934), which Gerhardi himself calls an autobiographical novel. Certainly the hero and narrator is a novelist who has shared Gerhardi's strange upbringing as an English boy in Petrograd, and many of the experiences related in the novel can be set side by side with the author's experiences as told in his autobiography, *Memoirs of a Polyglot*. Again we are reading a novel that is about the writing of a novel, a novel to be called *Resurrection*. At the beginning of the book, the author reflects, of the novel he is writing: 'In the present I am held in a vice by the future. But if I strive to live in the future I am held in a vice by the images of the past. However much I twist and turn, I am doomed to live in the past. Only in death can I redeem the present—be free to roam in it at will.' These words may be taken as an adumbration of the theme of the novel being written; but a little later, while resting before a fashionable ball, the hero undergoes something like a mystical experience; he wakes up to find himself detached from his body, free of the bounds of space and time. He returns to his body, goes to the ball and spends his time there largely in discussing the implications of his experience, which is intimately related to the novel he is writing, with friends he meets there. In his flat afterwards he undergoes a repetition of the experience and finds himself in purgatory.

All this is fascinating, an account, one is persuaded, of a genuine experience in which the narrator finds himself suddenly liberated, to use his own images, from the hound Habit and the bitch Anxiety that dog his heels. The metaphysical implications of the experience are subtly argued, related to the findings of J. W. Dunne's influential *Experiment with Time* and to Proust's theories of memory and time; indeed, Proust's image of the vases that contain the fragrance of past years, which is many times invoked in the novel, provides the clue to Gerhardi's findings.

Exciting as a thought-adventure, *Resurrection* is much less satisfying as a novel. While engaged in the theme that is nearest to him Gerhardi writes with a passionate and lyrical eloquence, but this is often contradicted by the tone in which the rest of the novel is couched. By contrast with that of *Futility* and *The Polyglots*, it is self-conscious in the bad sense, is too knowing, too showy, almost as though the fashionable world which is the milieu of the novel is being accepted at newspaper gossip-writers' valuation, an impression reinforced by the presence of thinly-disguised characters from actual life. Lord Otter-cove, for example, who turns up frequently in Gerhardi's later fiction, is and can only be Lord Beaverbrook. There is, in these later novels of Gerhardi's, a continual seepage as it were from Gerhardi's private life that affects one as a vulgarity, a sort of button-holing intimacy with the reader that is distasteful because on the verge of exhibitionism. In *Futility* and *The Polyglots* the balance between the Gerhardi-like narrator and the other characters existed in a perfect equilibrium; the narrator was the ideal mediator between them and us. In *Resurrection* and the earlier novels, *My Sinful Earth* and *Pending Heaven*, the narrator tends to blot out the other characters, to parade himself in the foreground. There is insufficient objectivity, insufficient dramatization, too much the sense that what we are being given is a thinly-disguised transcript from life.

[10]

STEPHEN HUDSON wrote half a dozen novels of real distinction dealing with the life experience of Richard Kurt. Three of these, *Richard Kurt, Prince Hempseed* and *Elinor Colhouse*, he collected into a single work, *A True Story*, in 1930, adding to it in a later edition. Hudson's theme is that of estrangement; but Kurt's estrangement exists on two levels. There is the psychological estrangement:

> As he sat in that self-same spot, with incredible vividness his life unrolled itself, step by step and link by link; his brief child-hood, his schooldays, his youth, his marriage and his mother's death . . . And through it all loomed the sombre figure of his father, ever standing between him and his mother, robbing him of his birthright of happiness . . .

Then there is estrangement at the level of sublimation. At eighteen Kurt notes:

> When I was small, Nanny Clifford and Fräulein Schwind always said I was discontented. It was true, I am discontented

and I am afraid I always shall be because whether I'm right or wrong, I know I want something different in every way from what I've got or ever can get. Looking back, I can see that I was always like that. Certainly there are things I liked that other people liked, some books, some games, riding, hunting, rowing, swimming, but only one side of me liked them, not the whole of me. There was always an inside me that wanted something besides entirely different, something that couldn't be explained or done and that wasn't known to me by any particular name, and that I seemed to have had some time or other and that all sorts of things reminded me of, like the scent of a flower or the rustle of leaves or a broad sunbeam or the glistening of a calm sea when the sun sets. Looking back on my life, I see it like a river separated almost from its source into two streams which keep getting wider apart. And I see that everything I have done all my life, everything I have to do, has widened that angle and that everything always will widen it. And yet I don't think it ought to be widened. There ought to be some way or other of making these two streams meet again but I don't think I shall ever discover it or if I do, only after many, many years, and by then it may be too late.

Viewed simply as a study of the Oedipus complex working like a doom through a man's life, there is no parallel to *A True Story* in our fiction except *Sons and Lovers*, though the difference between them is profound. Lawrence takes sides in the triangular warfare; Hudson gives the impression of being wholly outside his material, of being completely objective. True, we are presented only with Kurt's point of view, but it would not be possible to identify him with his creator. Above all, Kurt's mother, unlike Paul Morel's, is inaccessible; he is rejected by her. Then there is the great technical difference between the two novels. *Sons and Lovers* is a chronicle-novel; *A True Story*, as the first pages show, is post-Joyce. No less great is the difference between the milieus of the two novels. Richard Kurt is the son of an Anglo-Austrian financier, and his frustrations are worked out against a background of the worlds of fashion and finance in Europe and America during the nineties and the first decade of the present century.

Hudson avoids the *longueurs* of the chronicle-novel by taking up and concentrating upon his hero's life at certain points; and he writes always with great economy. The first part of the book, no more than ninety pages, covers Kurt's life from early infancy to the age of eighteen and is told in the first person, growth being indicated by growth in the narrator's complexity of language and sentence-structure. Through young Kurt's expanding consciousness, we see his family, the relationship between his parents, his experiences at his public school and at crammers abroad and in England. The second part of the book, though twice as long as the first, covers a single year, Kurt at nineteen. I know nothing quite like it in either English or American fiction, for in it Kurt describes his life in a rapidly growing Middle West town, where he works in the office of his American uncle, the president of a railroad. It is an astonishingly detailed picture of life in all its violence, corruption and vulgarity in an American city during the 'Gilded Age', written from the point of view of someone coming into it from European civilization.

The third part, told in the third person, relates how Kurt, still a youth, is trapped into marriage by Elinor Colhouse, a cold, beautiful, ambitious American girl looking for a rich European husband. Brilliant in itself, this section is a flaw in the work as a whole, for Elinor is presented with such bitter irony that one feels Hudson has loaded the dice against her. Her beauty apart, Elinor has no redeeming qualities; her behaviour widens the estrangement between Kurt and his father; and in the fourth part of the book alienation between her and Kurt is almost complete. Despite its excellence, the sharp vignettes of cosmo-politan society, the beauty of the descriptions of the Italian landscape, this section seems to me over-long; and with Kurt frustrated at every turn, he becomes the passive character to whom things happen.

In the last part of the book, he overcomes his frustrations, liberates himself from Elinor through Myrtle, who becomes his second wife. Myrtle remains shadowy; deliberately so. Hudson deals with her in a later novel bearing her name. We never see her directly, only through the impressions she makes on others, on a nurse, governess, elder sister, and an assortment of young men who fall in love with her. She is a symbol, of beauty, serenity, wisdom, of that 'something that couldn't be explained' Kurt has always been looking for. But as a character Myrtle scarcely emerges at all.

A True Story cannot be considered a success as a whole. From the way in which Hudson published the book it seems clear that his method of composition was one of accretion; and *A True Story* suffers from this. The separate parts are admirably written and designed, but one is aware of a lack of proportion between them. Then Kurt is hardly a powerful enough character to carry the novel. He has intimations of other worlds, but he cannot express them. He ought, it seems clear, to be either a poet or a mystic, for the intimations are such as can be conveyed only in the language of poetry or mysticism. One is saying, of course, that Hudson himself should have been a poet.

Something like this must be said of another highly serious, intelligent and sensitive novelist, L. H. Myers. *The Root and the Flower* (1935) is a novel of great distinction. Its sequel, *The Pool of Vishnu* (1940), is less satisfying; but together, under the title *The Near and the Far*, they make up Myers's main achievement, though two much shorter novels remain interesting; *The Clio* (1925), a conversation-novel set in 'probably the most expensive steam yacht in the world' sailing up the Amazon, and *Strange Glory* (1936), the most explicit of Myers's fiction and therefore a useful approach to his work.

Myers was as much against his age as Lawrence. Fundamental to his vision of life was a mystical experience he had had as a young man. Time and again he attempted to express it in fiction, in the character of the hermit Wentworth, in *Strange Glory*, and in the Guru in *The Pool of Vishnu*. Wentworth, who has made and lost four fortunes before becoming a hermit, sums it up as follows:

'For the first time in my life I saw Man through the eyes of God. I saw the exquisite beauty that springs—and can only spring—from the relation between creature and Creator. To Man is given the privilege of worship—that I have known and felt for a long time. But tonight I saw Man as he stands in the vision of compassionate God. Raised very little above the beasts of the field, feeble in mind, sickly in body, oppressed by circumstances, blind of spirit; blackly and inescapably overshadowed by old age, disease and death, Man yet *struggles hard.* Consider the standards that he sets himself—his ideals of courage, of generosity, of endurance! Consider not only Man's disinterested devotion to truth, but his passion for nobility, his restless search after greatness. Consider that unconquerable fastidiousness which forces him to toil, always to toil, in order to bring the poor flesh-bound, witless creature that he is a little nearer to what he wishes to be.'

It was this vision and its implications ('You see', says the Guru, in *The Pool of Vishnu*, 'for one thing, I believe in the essential goodness of human nature.') which sets Myers apart from and against the majority of his contemporaries. Any way of life, any philosophy, that denied the essential goodness of human nature for him was evil. To his first novel, *The Orrissers*, Myers affixed as an epigraph Bacon's words from the *Novum Organum*: 'Four species of Illusions beset the human mind, to which (for distinction's sake) we have assigned names: calling the first, Illusions of the Tribe; the second, Illusions of the Den; the third, Illusions of the Market; the fourth, Illusions of the Schools.' It is the nature and influence of these illusions that Myers investigates in *The Near and the Far*.

The action is set in the India of Akbar. Myers's interest is not at all primarily in sixteenth-century India. It is rather that in that India of Akbar, the meeting place of Christianity, Buddhism, Islam and Hinduism, the scene of ossified civilizations and vigorous undirected new life, of intrigue and power politics, Myers found in microcosm all the illusions that 'intercept and corrupt the light of nature' and beset the human mind. He shows us a young prince, Jali, being subjected in turn to the influence of all the possible illusions, which are embodied sometimes in individual characters, sometimes in the organization of society itself, and having them revealed in their true shape and colour by the Guru, who functions as a sort of psychoanalyst on the grand scale and is the spokesman for Myers's own beliefs. These, as the Guru says in his great debate with Mobarek, 'amount to nothing more than that every man has the right to be treated as a person'. Nothing more —but the implications are revolutionary. Jali is shown as having perpetually to choose between becoming a person and succumbing to a type; for Myers, acquiescence in a type is akin to the Jungian notion of persona-identification.

Perhaps the most insidious of the illusions that tempt Jali are those represented by the statesman Mobarek on the one hand and on the other by Prince Daniyal. Mobarek wishes to establish in India the idea of the Church, 'by means of which man can satisfy—in the religious sphere—his desire for order, his respect for tradition, his craving for continuity', a view which for Myers was no less evil than the aestheticism and irresponsibility of Daniyal's Pleasaunce of the Arts.

The Root and the Flower and *The Pool of Vishnu* are absorbing novels of ideas, and the ideas are of the greatest importance. They are admirably expressed, but one feels that they were there before the characters, which scarcely live outside the ideas they express. Myers wrote well but his language is never quite adequate to the beauty of the thought he wishes to convey. Everything is a little too faint. This is especially so of *The Pool of Vishnu*, written at a time when Myers had become impatient of art as merely another illusion. As he says in his preface, 'I have made little attempt to conceal my ethical preoccupations'—or their immediate sources. His intuitions were his own, but he seemed to be constantly seeking philosophical and psychological authority for them; and in *The Pool of Vishnu* the philosophy and psychology appear too nakedly. Much too often, one can as it were translate back into the original Buber or Jung. Which means that the character that emerges most strongly and clearly is the Guru, the expository and impassioned voice of Myers himself.

Hudson and Myers can be regarded only with great respect and admiration; yet their comparative failure and its nature are made plain if one sets beside them Richard Hughes. His first novel, *A High Wind in Jamaica* (1928), is one of the classic novels of childhood and a completely original work. The originality consists in the stance Hughes adopts towards the children whose adventures he relates. Hughes shows us his children from the outside. He does, certainly, by an effort of will and imagination, interpret their modes of thinking and feeling for us; but what we are in effect given is a natural history of children, with Hughes the observing, recording, interpreting natural-ist. The parallel with the field naturalist or animal psychologist can be carried further. Hughes shows his children, Emily Bas-Thornton and her brothers and sisters, in as it were experimental conditions. The novel opens with a brilliant description of the life of the children on a plantation in Jamaica in the eighteen-sixties; then the children, on a voyage to England, become the prisoners of pirates. The pirates are rendered no more conventionally than the children; they are curiously reluctant pirates, the last, half-hearted remnants of a dying race. They are in some ways more at the mercy of the children than the children are of them. Yet the terrors, the casual violence, are real enough. We see the children as they are in their day-to-day behaviour, and then as they react and accept the interpretations of their experience as made by the horrified adults who rescue them. The irony that results reaches its climax in the trial of the pirates.

At the centre of it all is Emily, the child on the verge of girlhood, a child—and therefore, according to Hughes, mad—when captured by the pirates but by the time of her rescue troubled by the premonitions

of womanhood. She is rendered, one feels, exactly, and her essential
being is unparaphrasable; rendered partly by a process of indirection,
by a kind of symbolism that often has reference to the strange life of
animals, as in the chapter that describes the children's reception on the
steamer that takes them off the pirate ship. She goes to sleep that night
in unaccustomed comfort, with a baby alligator for company:

> In search of greater warmth, the creature high-stepped warily
> up the bed towards her face. About six inches away, it paused,
> and they looked each other in the eye, these two children.
>
> The eye of an alligator is large, protruding, and of a brilliant
> yellow, with a slit pupil like a cat's. A cat's eye, to the casual
> observer, is expressionless: though with attention one can
> distinguish in it many changes of emotion. But the eye of an
> alligator is infinitely more stony, and brilliant—reptilian.
>
> What possible meaning could Emily find in such an eye? Yet
> she lay there, and stared, and stared: and the alligator stared too.
> If there had been an observer it might have given him a shiver to
> see them so—well, eye to eye like that.
>
> Presently the beast opened his mouth and hissed again gently.
> Emily lifted a finger and began to rub the corner of his jaw. The
> hiss changed to a sound almost like a purr. A thin, filmy lid first
> covered his eye from the front backwards, then the outer lid
> closed up from below.
>
> Suddenly he opened his eye again, and snapped on her finger:
> then turned and wormed his way into the neck of her nightgown,
> and crawled down inside, cool and rough against her skin, till he
> found a place to rest. It is surprising that she could stand it, as she
> did, without flinching.
>
> Alligators are utterly untamable.

It is passages like this, together with Hughes's superb evocations of
tropical landscape and of the sea, which seem almost insolent in their
casualness and apparent lack of effort, that give the novel its strange
hallucinated quality, which is also a quality of what one might call
domesticated bizarreness. Much of the time one feels in the presence of
fantasy; and yet it is not fantasy; the children, the pirates, are all too
real for that.

Hughes's second novel, *In Hazard*, appeared in 1938. Very different
from *A High Wind in Jamaica* though it is, it is no less remarkable.
Unlike *A High Wind*, *In Hazard* has to stand up to comparison: with

Conrad, especially with *Typhoon*. It is a story about a steamer, the *Archimedes*, and the behaviour of her officers and crew in a hurricane where no hurricane should be. It has a freshness, an immediacy, I no longer find in *Typhoon*, a freshness that comes from the deceptive ease and casualness of the prose. There are no heroics, simply Hughes telling a heroic story; and the prevailing note of the narrative is struck in the first sentences: 'Amongst the people I have met, one of those who stand out most vividly in my memory is a certain Mr Ramsay MacDonald. He was a chief engineer: and a distant cousin, he said, of Mr J. Ramsay MacDonald, the statesman. He resembled his "cousin" very closely indeed; and it astonished me at first to see what appeared to be my Prime Minister, in a suit of overalls, crawling out of a piece of dismantled machinery with an air of real authority and knowledge and decision.' Despite the remarkable nature of the events described, the tone throughout is brisk, conversational, matter-of-fact. The effect of the tone is reinforced by what seems Hughes's extraordinary know-ledge of steamers in all their aspects.

There is throughout the novel a Defoe-like quality which provides the book with its special ambience. It is within this that the real subject of the novel has its being, the effects on those subjected to them of the stresses of an extraordinary situation. Their responses to these stresses are at once ordinary and as it were extra-ordinary. They are surprised into a knowledge of themselves, surprised perhaps into the revelation of their true qualities. Thus one officer, Rabb, 'an efficient and popular officer; a clean-living man', fails; fear breaks him. Another, Mr Buxton, realizes for the first time in twenty-five years why he had gone to sea: because he liked virtue, in the 'Roman rather than its Victorian sense'. As for the Captain:

Happy, happy, happy. Duwch, Captain Edwardes was happy as a sand-boy! Had he known, at the beginning, what was coming, would he have been happy and confident like this all through? Perhaps not. Perhaps no one could have borne that foreknowledge. But passing instead from each known moment only to the unknown moment ahead, his happiness had carried him along.

He had a million or so pounds' worth of ship and cargo to handle: and eighty men's lives. And very little chance but that he would lose them. It was the hugeness of the responsibility which made his heart so light.

It is such paradoxes and ironies of human behaviour that Hughes reveals in his re-creation of men at work, for that is what the novel is. It is of course a special kind of work. The officers of the *Archimedes* had been trained in sail. 'Why', asks Hughes, 'waste the man's time in learning a useless and outmoded technique?'

The answer is a matter of Virtue, really. For an inclination towards virtue (such as sent Mr Buxton to sea) is not enough in itself; it must be trained, like any other aptitude. Now there is a fundamental difference in kind between the everyday work of a sailing-vessel and the everyday work of a steamer. The latter does not essentially differ from a shore job: it is only occasionally, rarely, that emergencies arise in Steam. But every common action in the working of a sailing-vessel, all the time, partakes of something of the nature of an emergency. Everything must be done with your whole heart, and a little more than your whole strength. Thus is a natural aptitude for virtue increased by everyday practice. For changing a jib in a stiff breeze is a microcosm, as it were, of saving the ship in a storm.

So the theme is virtue in the Roman sense. Yet this is to oversimplify, for towards the end of the novel another, disconcerting element enters. It is feared that the Chinese crew may mutiny, and a young Chinese, Ao Ling, is arrested and put in irons. He is arrested on a completely false surmise, but he is also—and this is fact—wanted by the Hong Kong police as a bandit. He is indeed a Communist agitator, which is what in the context bandit means, aboard the *Archimedes* with forged papers. Hughes tells his story with considerable sympathy: Ao Ling may perhaps represent another variant of virtue. It scarcely matters. What is important is the extra dimension into which the novel suddenly soars when Ao Ling is projected into the action. The juxtaposition is, as I say, disconcerting but—one can see it now—curiously prophetic. It has led to the novel's being interpreted as a symbolic rendering of the downfall of the British Empire. I doubt whether it can be construed in any such precise terms. It is the juxtaposition itself that is disturbing and in the end imaginatively satisfying.

The long novel Hughes is currently writing is to be called *The Human Predicament*. One section of it has appeared, *The Fox in the Attic* (1961). It is not a self-contained part of a larger whole, as the separate novels of Powell's *The Music of Time* sequence are, for instance. All one can say of it, therefore, is that it is an exceedingly brilliant fragment which cannot yet provide answers to the questions it raises in the mind. The whole work is to be, the words are Hughes's, an 'historical novel of my own times'. In *The Fox in the Attic*, we are in 1923, with, as the bewildered, innocent, uncomprehending observer of what is narrated, Augustine Penry-Herbert, a young Welsh squire just down from Oxford. Withdrawn, haunted by the war which he has narrowly missed, oppressed by the sense of belonging to a generation different from any that has gone before, full of the large, vaguely liberal notions of the early twenties, he sets out to discover for himself the 'New Germany' of the Weimar Republic. He stays in the castle of a remote cousin, a Bavarian count whose family at once recapitulates the old Germany and contains within it the seeds of a new, more disastrous one. Ignorantly, absurdly, he plunges into love with his cousin Mitzi, unaware that she knows nothing of his love, is almost blind and is destined to be a nun; unaware, too, of the dreaming and the scheming going on all about him and above him. Wolff, for example, whose existence he does not suspect, a boy younger than himself but a veteran of the civil wars in the Baltic provinces, hides in the attics above him. Hitler and Ludendorff mount their farcical *putsch* in Munich—it is difficult to believe Hughes was not there—and, afterwards, Hitler, so much less important than Captain Goering and Captain Roehm, skulks half-crazed in the Hanfstaengls' country cottage. It is all completely convincing, and perhaps it is the sure sign of Hughes's talents as a novelist that the historical personages, Hitler above all, are as completely convincing within the framework of the novel as the fictitious characters. And the homelier Welsh and English scenes are as convincing as the German. At the moment, one may feel that Augustine is too much swamped by events, too innocent and too passive; but three-quarters of the novel are yet to come. If they are as good as the quarter we have it is difficult to see how the whole can fail to be the great English novel of the sixties.

Rebecca West is one of the most brilliant journalists of our time, which, no doubt, is why her novels are few. Her first, *The Return of the Soldier* (1918) and *The Judge* (1922), show, as much as May Sinclair's fiction of roughly the same time, the early impact of Freud on English novelists. Indeed, *The Return of the Soldier* now reads like a dramatization of a case-history, and *The Judge* as a too overt illustration of the Oedipus complex. All the same, Ellen Melville, in *The Judge*, is a striking character of a kind one has come to associate with her creator.

She is as passionate and as sure of herself as a Brontë heroine and consciously a woman who is the intellectual equal of men. And she has her being against a superbly rendered background of Edinburgh.

Rebecca West is romantic in the way that James and Conrad were romantic. She chooses her characters from the exceptional, not the ordinary, with minds at once large and clear-thinking and ambitions that are lofty; and these characters are heightened by her prose, which is richer in texture, more coloured and sustained in imagery than contemporary prose normally is. Already in these early novels she has a passionate apprehension of the necessity and beauty of order, the fruit of self-discipline and knowledge, and an equally vivid apprehension that order is in constant danger from the forces of violence and disintegration. In her later fiction, she seems to equate order with the female principle, the forces of destruction with the male.

This comes out strongly in *The Thinking Reed* (1936), the story of an American girl, Isabelle, married to a very rich French industrialist. Isabelle discovers that men 'do not belong to the same race as woman'. She discovers, too, the extreme danger in which the very rich live simply because they are very rich. Her husband, Marc, she reflects, 'was wise in his head and his body, but because of this exemption from criticism, this ability to evade the consequences of any action, he was without discipline, he was without the appropriate reverence for reality. He might get a little drunk tonight, he might say foolish and dangerous things. There was no safety where there were riches'. Isabelle herself feels corrupted by riches and the moral isolation in which they place those who possess them. She realizes she is defenceless against herself and others except for 'an insatiable craving for goodness'.

These strands in Miss West's thinking come together in her work in progress, of which one volume, *The Fountain Overflows* (1957) has so far appeared. Set for the most part in South London, it relates from the vantage-point of fifty years later, through the consciousness of Rose, the youngest of them, the fortunes of the Aubreys, a family whose members, a mother, three daughters and a son, know themselves to be set apart from the rest of the world. For them, music is the real world and the world of school, for instance, merely a necessary irrelevance. They are set apart, too, by the fecklessness of their father, who stands for the forces of destruction. Piers Aubrey is a masterly creation: a brilliant journalist and pamphleteer, he is in the ordinary traffic of life an impossible person and before the novel ends has abandoned his family to poverty and a life of frustration.

The impression the novel makes, however, is certainly not one of poverty and frustration. On the contrary, the solidarity and the glow of family life are beautifully described; and throughout, equally beautifully evoked, there is music as the symbol of the serenity of order that Rebecca West opposes to the destructive impulse.

THE TWENTIES: AMERICAN

[1]

'THE WORLD broke in two in 1922 or thereabouts', said Willa Cather; and the bestseller lists of the time provide an interesting commentary on her remark. From 1920 to 1923 they were dominated, in Britain and the United States alike, by two novelists, A. S. M. Hutchinson and Sinclair Lewis. Neither now seems of much literary merit; by any standard Hutchinson was an appallingly bad writer, and just why *If Winter Comes* and *One Increasing Purpose* achieved their enormous success was a mystery much debated even while they were achieving it. Lewis is another matter; his badness is of a different order altogether. His biographer, Mark Schorer, indicates its nature when he writes: 'He was one of the worst writers in modern American literature, but without his writing one cannot imagine modern American literature. This is because, without his writing, we can hardly imagine ourselves.'

The interesting thing now, though, is that they should have conquered and divided the reading public of the English-speaking world at the same time. Did the millions who wept over the tribulations of Mark Sabre, one wonders, also throb in sympathy with the aspirations of Carol Kennicott, or were they a different set of millions? For no two contemporaries—there were only six years' difference between them in age—could have existed in sharper contrast. Hutchinson's appeal, one guesses, was to the bewildered middle-aged of the middle classes, for whom the aftermath of war manifested itself as a breakdown of traditional values, in what seemed moral anarchy, and in the disturbing spectacle of young women and the working class no longer knowing their place. Faced with phenomena that could be labelled largely and loosely as Bolshevik, Hutchinson was clearly as bewildered as his readers. What strikes one now about his novels is how very old-fashioned they were even for their day. Wells might never have written; and by contrast with Hutchinson Sinclair Lewis appears very much as an American version of Wells. One can't, of course, press the parallel too far: Wells was the immeasurably better writer, his range wider, his imagination and insight deeper; but Lewis certainly saw himself in some sense as the English novelist's disciple and shared some at any rate of his interests, even to the extent of presenting science as the great force making for human liberation, in *Martin Arrowsmith*.

Sinclair Lewis was born in the small town of Sauk Center, Minnesota, in 1885, only seven years after the stage coach ceased to be the town's single link with the outside world. The place and the date are significant. By the time Lewis came to boyhood the Middle West—the old prairie lands between the Ohio River and the Rocky Mountains—had been settled by successive waves of immigrants, Germans, Bohemians, Swedes, Norwegians, following the founding fathers, who were mainly from New England; a whole vast new region had come into existence to counterbalance New England, the North-East states and the South, and by and large its people felt no allegiance either to New York or to New or old England. The days of the literary supremacy of Boston and New England had ended before the nineteenth century ended, and within a matter of years that of New York, which had taken Boston's place as the intellectual centre of things, was being challenged by Chicago, the Mid-West metropolis. Lewis was merely one of a whole generation of novelists who emerged from the farmlands and cities of the prairie states; Dreiser, Sherwood Anderson and Willa Cather, somewhat older than Lewis, had come out of Indiana, Ohio and Nebraska respectively; Scott Fitzgerald, Hemingway and Glenway Wescott, somewhat younger, were products of Minnesota, Illinois and Wisconsin. During the second and third decades of this century the Middle West, it might be said, came of age and into its own.

Naturally, the attitudes of these novelists to the environments in which they had spent their formative years differed enormously, but however they reacted against them they could not escape them. Lewis, who had gone East to Yale as a young man and then on to New York into publishing, had written a number of novels before his first significant work, *Main Street*, appeared in 1920. The point of view from which it is written is made plain in the epigraph:

This is America—a town of a few thousand, in a region of wheat and corn and dairies and little groves.

The town is, in our tale, called 'Gopher Prairie, Minnesota'.

But its Main Street is the continuation of Main Streets every-where . . .

Main Street is the climax of civilization. That this Ford car might stand in front of the Bon Ton Store, Hannibal invaded Rome and Erasmus wrote in Oxford cloisters. What Ole Jensen the grocer says to Ezra Stowbody the banker is the new law for London, Prague, and the unprofitable isles of the sea; what-soever Ezra does not know and sanction, that thing is heresy, worthless for knowing and wicked to consider.

Our railway station is the final aspiration of architecture. Sam Clark's annual hardware turnover is the envy of the four counties which constitute God's Country. In the sensitive art of the Rose-bud Movie Palace there is a Message, and humor strictly moral.

Such is our comfortable tradition and sure faith. Would he not betray himself an alien cynic who should otherwise portray Main Street, or distress the citizens by speculating whether there may not be other faiths?

The impulse, in other words, is satirical: Lewis is out to destroy by ridicule the provincialism and smug self-complacency of small-town values. The target is that implicit in President Warren Harding's declaration of 1922: 'If I could plant a Rotary Club in every city and hamlet in this country I could then rest assured that our ideals of free-dom would be safe and civilization would progress'; and the basis of attack is closely akin to that of Mencken's *American Mercury* which, in its onslaughts on what Mencken called the 'booboisie', pilloried American philistinism monthly in its famous feature, 'Americana'.

In fact, as an attack on anything *Main Street* now seems pretty ineffective, partly for reasons which may be discerned from the epigraph itself. The writing is much too slack and imprecise for its purpose. One can point to the awkward inversions and lazy rhythms, the almost stock invocations of Hannibal and Erasmus as symbols of the past and of high civilization, the poeticism of 'the unprofitable isles of the sea'. It is all too easy, and as prose is no better than an undistinguished piece of journalism or advertising copy. But there are other reasons for *Main Street*'s present ineffectiveness. They are bound up with Lewis's delineation of his heroine, Carol Kennicott:

A breeze which had crossed a thousand miles of wheat-lands bellied her taffeta skirt in a line so graceful, so full of animation and moving beauty, that the heart of a chance watcher on the

lower road tightened to wistfulness over her quality of suspended
freedom. She lifted her arms, she leaned back against the wind,
her skirt dipped and flared, a lock blew wild. A girl on a hilltop;
credulous, plastic, young; drinking the air as she longed to drink
life. The eternal aching comedy of expectant youth.

It is Carol Milford, fleeing for an hour from Blodgett College.

The days of pioneering, of lassies in sunbonnets, and bears
killed with axes in piney clearings, are deader now than Camelot;
and a rebellious girl is the spirit of that bewildered empire called
the American Middlewest.

That is our introduction to Carol, set in the conventional pose of a
young girl in an advertisement and described in prose of equal banality.
Carol becomes a librarian in St Paul and dreams of bringing beauty to
the raw towns of the Middle West. She marries a man considerably
older than herself, Will Kennicott, a doctor in the small town of
Gopher Prairie, the town that for him, unimaginative and easily satisfied, contains 'the best people on earth. And keen . . . They don't make
'em any more appreciative and so on'. Wooing her, he invites her to
'make the town—well—make it artistic. It's mighty pretty, but I'll
admit we aren't any too darn artistic'. But can she make it more
artistic? Can she change the inhabitants of Gopher Prairie, Sam Clark
from the hardware store, Harry Haydock and his wife Juanita, of the
Bon Ton, Dave Dyer the druggist, Jack Elder of the Minniemashie
House, Luke Dawson the richest man in town, Nat Hicks the tailor,
Professor George Edwin Mott, the superintendent of schools, Ezra
Stowbody, president of the Ionic Bank? Of course not. They are
perfectly happy as they are, and prepared to put up with her and her
attempts to brighten their lives until they think she is patronizing them;
and then she is cold-shouldered. Unfortunately, her attempts to
brighten their lives—redecorating her house according to taste current
in St Paul and Chicago, giving romp-and-fancy-dress parties—strike
one as pretty feeble, more feeble than they seem to have appeared to
Lewis.

There might be comedy in all this, the efforts of a young woman
from the outside to impose her taste on a self-sufficient community,
but there is in fact almost nothing that can be called comedy; for Carol
is the expression of the values, such as they are, that Lewis opposes to
those of Gopher Prairie, which are *a priori* inferior.

In the end one sees that Lewis knows no more what to do about

Gopher Prairie and its inhabitants than does Carol herself. Lewis's attitude towards Gopher Prairie was essentially ambiguous, perhaps because Gopher Prairie itself was based on Sauk Center, which, after all, was home. Our interest in *Main Street* is now mainly historical, and it is not easy to account for its phenomenal world-wide success in its day. For the world outside the United States it exposed for the first time the new America, the America of the Middle West, narrow, puritan, prohibitionist. It also in a curious way represented the entry of American literature into world literature, almost, one might say, of America itself into the consciousness of the world. It seems fantastic now that when *Babbitt* appeared in 1922, the English edition should have had appended to it a glossary of American slang. It was through Lewis more than any other writer that Europe discovered the modern United States; in this respect he established the image of his country for the rest of the world, precisely as Fenimore Cooper had done a century before.

And perhaps Gopher Prairie was almost as much a revelation to readers in New England and New York, where, as the saying is, they think the Indians begin at Buffalo, as it was to European readers. There is something else, too. In *Main Street*, as indeed in the work of Dreiser and Anderson, one sees American writing catching up with European. In Europe, Ibsen's Nora had slammed the door behind her as early as 1879. The slamming, muffled it must be admitted, is not heard in American writing until Carol Kennicott leaves her husband and Gopher Prairie in *Main Street*.

Lewis's most significant novel remains *Babbitt*, and in my experience even as late as 1955 college students in Iowa found no difficulty in accepting it as a fair representation of Middle West city life and values. In fact, Lewis's attitude towards those values is just as ambivalent as it was towards those of Gopher Prairie. The very name of Lewis's imaginary city of Zenith, in the imaginary state of Winnemac, indicates the close relation between the novel and *Main Street*. The ironical place-name, with its implication that there can be nothing higher or better than Babbitt's city, is the counterpart of the ironical epigraph to the earlier novel. But the satire, as in *Main Street*, is intermittent; Lewis is much more than half in love with what he is satirizing. He is no Dickens excoriating a commercial civilization through the persons of Podsnap and the Veneerings. Babbitt is always more than the stereotype of the small business man he has given his name to.

Just as he was an Elk, a Booster, and a member of the Chamber of Commerce, just as the priests of the Presbyterian Church determined his every religious belief and the senators who controlled the Republican party decided in little smoky rooms in Washington what he should think about disarmament, tariff, and Germany, so did the large national advertisers fix the surface of his life, fix what he believed to be his individuality. These standard advertised wares—toothpastes, socks, tyres, cameras, instantaneous hot-water heaters—were his symbols and proofs of excellence; at first the signs, then the substitutes, for joy and passion and wisdom.

That is only part of him. His individuality is elsewhere, and what *Babbitt* records are the timid rebellions of its hero against the pressures of conformity. They do not amount to much: a camping holiday in Maine with Paul Riesling, a tar-roofing salesman who had once dreamt of being a violinist, a clandestine affair with a vaguely Bohemian lady, a flirtation with Radical politics, which leads to a temporary ostracism by his friends. He comes to heel quickly enough every time, and with something like relief. His interior life is poverty-stricken; emotionally, he has scarcely reached adolescence.

And this surely is the point about the American society of the time that Lewis is making through his representative figure; it is here that the criticism lies. So we see him on the second page of the novel, waking in the sleeping-porch of his house on Floral Heights:

He was not fat but he was exceedingly well fed; his cheeks were pads, and the unroughened hand which lay helpless upon the khaki-coloured blanket was slightly puffy. He seemed prosperous, extremely married and unromantic; and altogether unromantic appeared this sleeping-porch, which looked on one sizeable elm, two respectable grass-plots, a cement drive, and a corrugated iron garage. Yet Babbitt was again dreaming of the fairy child, a dream more romantic than scarlet pagodas by a silver sea.

For years the fairy child had come to him. When others saw but George Babbitt, she discerned gallant youth. She waited for him, in the darkness beyond mysterious groves. When at last he could slip away from the crowded house he darted to her. His wife, his clamouring friends, sought to follow, but he escaped, the girl fleet beside him, and they crouched together on a shadowy hillside. She was so slim, so white, so eager! She cried

that he was gay and valiant, that she would wait for him, that
they would sail——
Rumble and bang of the milk-truck.
Babbitt moaned, turned over, struggled back toward his
dream. He could see only her face now, beyond misty waters. . . .

It is all incredibly thin, the most pathetically inhibited of fantasies. But
the point is made: this is the best you can get in the culture whose
zenith is Zenith, Winnemac. And the point is not invalidated by the
suspicion that the fantasy is not only Babbitt's but Lewis's. Lewis is
presenting Babbitt's fantasy not satirically but in dead seriousness; in
content and style it is closely akin to the keepsake-album verse he
wrote as a young man. The fantasy is, one feels, not merely the best
Babbitt can achieve, it is the best Lewis can.

It is the thinness of the fantasy, the poverty of the inner life, which
really exposes the threadbare quality of life in Zenith. If you have the
one, the novel remorselessly insists, not only in character and fable but
also in the very texture of the writing, then you must have the other;
you must have Chum Frink and Vergil Gunch and Willis Ijams and the
Rev. Dr Drew and Sheldon Smeeth of the Y.M.C.A., the whole parade
of Boosters whom Lewis mimics and caricatures with such relish.
Lewis, it is plain, enjoyed himself enormously in writing *Babbitt*. It is
still often horribly funny, the account, for example, of Babbitt's
attendance and performance at the annual convention at Monarch of
the State Association of Real Estate Boards. But one cannot quite call
it satire. It is rendered with an innocent exuberance that suggests that
if Babbitt could write he would write like Lewis. Lewis was to say,
years after writing the novel, 'I wrote *Babbitt* not out of hatred for
him but out of love'; and one believes him. Certainly he was to write
nothing as good again, for powerful as they are in their very different
ways, *Elmer Gantry* and *The Man Who Knew Coolidge* present
incredible monsters, while in *Dodsworth* he goes over wholeheartedly
to the side of the Babbitts in much the same way as Galsworthy went
over to the Forsytes in *A Modern Comedy*.

[2]

A RATHER older novelist also concerned with the emergence of the Middle West and, again like Lewis, ambiguous in her attitudes towards it, though she is the finer artist and the better writer, is Willa Cather. She was born in 1873 in the part of Virginia where her family had lived since the late eighteenth century, but at the age of nine was taken to Nebraska, where her father had bought a ranch. This move from the long-established pattern of life of Virginia to a prairie state not yet fenced and only recently abandoned by the Indian and the buffalo was the great formative experience of her life, one to which, in one way and another, she returned throughout her career as a novelist.

Her neighbours as a child were Bohemian, Scandinavian and German immigrants. Her attitude towards them is shown beautifully in her novel *My Antonia*, which appeared in 1918. It purports to be the recollections written in middle life of Jim Burden, a successful New York lawyer, unhappily married, of his childhood in Nebraska. He had been taken there, like his creator, at the age of ten from Virginia to live with his grandparents, and had arrived at the same time as the Shimerdas, an immigrant Czech family, whose daughter Antonia, slightly older than himself, had become his friend, constant companion, pupil in English lessons and protector. She is the centre of his memories.

The Nebraska scene is rendered with an intense but disciplined lyricism:

> All the years that have passed have not dimmed my memory of that first glorious autumn. The new country lay open before me: there were no fences in those days, and I could choose my own way over the grass uplands, trusting the pony to get me home again. Sometimes I followed the sunflower-bordered roads. Fuchs told me that the sunflowers were introduced into that country by the Mormons; that at the time of the persecution when they left Missouri and struck out into the wilderness to find a place where they could worship God in their own way, the members of the first exploring party, crossing the plains to Utah, scattered sunflower seed as they went. The next summer, when the long trains of wagons came through with all the women and children, they had the sunflower trail to follow. I believe that

botanists do not confirm Fuchs's story, but insist that the sunflower was native to those plains. Nevertheless, that legend has stuck in my mind, and sunflower-bordered roads always seem to me the roads to freedom.

With a similar elegiac gravity Burden recalls the Shimerdas' battle for existence, the fecklessness of the mother, the bitter suicide of the father, a man, the boy realizes even as a boy, from an older and richer culture, the courage and gaiety of Antonia, the goodness of his own grandparents and their practical Christianity.

When he is thirteen the Burdens move to town, to Black Hawk, and Antonia becomes a maid in the house of their neighbours the Harlings. There follows an extremely vivid evocation of small-town life in a still largely pioneer state. But now it is not so much Antonia who is the centre of Burden's memories but the 'hired girls', the daughters of central European immigrants who have come to town to go into service. Already the town is seen as in some sense corrupting; vitality belongs to the country, the frontier. Narrowness has closed in. The hired immigrant girls may almost be said to represent life as opposed to death, and it is with one of them, Lena Lingard, that young Burden has his first affair when a student at the state university.

Years later, Burden, a successful lawyer, travelling east from San Francisco, breaks his journey in Nebraska and seeks Antonia out. She is married now, a farmer's wife with many children. He spends the night with her and her family:

Antonia had always been one to leave images in the mind that did not fade—that grew stronger with time. In my memory there was a succession of such pictures, fixed there like the old woodcuts of one's first primer: Antonia kicking her bare legs against the sides of my pony when we came home in triumph with our snake; Antonia in her black shawl and fur cap, as she stood by her father's grave in the snowstorm; Antonia coming in with her work-team along the evening skyline. She lent herself to immemorial human attitudes which we recognize by instinct as universal and true. I had not been mistaken. She was a battered woman now, not a lovely girl; but she still had that something which fires the imagination, could still stop one's breath for a moment by a look or gesture that somehow revealed the meaning in common things. She had only to stand in the orchard, to put her hand on a little crab tree and look up at the apples, to make you feel the goodness of planting and tending and harvesting at last. All the strong things of her heart came out in her body, that had been so tireless in serving generous emotions.

It was no wonder that her sons stood tall and straight. She was a rich mine of life, like the founders of early races.

Willa Cather presents Antonia without sentimentality. She becomes the touchstone of what is good and what is most life-enhancing. The novel is her story primarily, not Burden's; but it is his, too, by implication. We learn next to nothing of his unhappy marriage. He has escaped the small town and been successful in the great city; but the prairie of his boyhood is a symbol almost of paradise, of Eden, and when we recall the words he speaks to Antonia before going up to Harvard: 'Do you know, Antonia, since I've been away, I think of you more often than of anyone else in this part of the world. I'd have liked to have you for a sweetheart, or a wife, or my mother or my sister—anything that a woman can be to a man. The idea of you is a part of my mind; you influence my likes and dislikes, all my tastes, hundreds of times when I don't realize it. You really are a part of me'; we realize that he is the victim of a Fall. She is the lost paradise, the lost mother.

My Antonia is a pastoral, and Willa Cather's intention in writing it is made quite plain. Burden remembers himself as a student at the state university:

I propped my book open and stared listlessly at the page of the Georgics where tomorrow's lesson began. It opened with the melancholy reflection that, in the lives of mortals, the best days are the first to flee. '*Optima dies . . . prima fugit.*' I turned back to the beginning of the third book, which we had read in class that morning. '*Primus ego in patriam mecum . . . deducam Musas*': 'for I shall be the first, if I live, to bring the Muse into my country.' Cleric had explained to us that 'patria' here meant, not a nation or even a province, but the little rural neighbourhood on the Mincio where the poet was born. This was not a boast, but a hope, at once bold and devoutly humble, that he might bring the Muse (but lately come to Italy from her cloudy Grecian mountains), not to the capital, the *palatia Romana*, but to his own little 'country'; to his father's fields . . .

The personal application is obvious, but equally important is the quotation '*Optima dies . . . prima fugit*', the best days are the first to flee. Increasingly this was to be the burden of Willa Cather's art.

It is implicit in *A Lost Lady*, which appeared in 1923. The novel begins: 'Thirty or forty years ago, in one of those gray towns along the Burlington railroad, which are so much grayer today than they were then, there was a house well known from Omaha to Denver for its hospitality and a certain charm of atmosphere.' It is the house, just outside Sweet Water, a small Nebraska town, of Captain Forrester, a veteran of the Civil War and of the building of the railways across the plains, and his wife. She is twenty-five years younger than he. He had rescued her in a climbing accident in California; courage and endurance had been demanded from, and displayed by, both; and they had married.

> . . . in the eyes of the admiring middle-aged men who visited there, whatever Mrs Forrester chose to do was 'lady-like' because she did it. They could not imagine her in any dress or situation in which she would not be charming. Captain Forrester himself, a man of few words, told Judge Pommeroy that he had never seen her look more captivating than on the day when she was chased by the new bull in the pasture. She had forgotten about the bull and gone into the meadow to gather wild flowers. He heard her scream, and as he ran puffing down the hill, she was scudding along the edge of the marshes like a hare, beside herself with laughter, and stubbornly clinging to the crimson parasol that had made all the trouble.

But Mrs Forrester has other admirers beside middle-aged railway tycoons; among them Niel Herbert, the nephew of Judge Pommeroy, Captain Forrester's lawyer. When the novel begins Niel is twelve years old. He may be regarded as the centre of consciousness of the novel; it is through him that we realize the gradual declension of Mrs Forrester, the increasing moral corruption arising out of the desperate boredom she feels behind her façade of gaiety and charm during her elderly husband's long years as an invalid. Niel discovers that she is having an affair with a wealthy friend of the Captain's; and then, when Niel returns from the East, where he has been studying architecture, he finds her in the hands of a loutish, vulgar lawyer, Ivy Peters, who has bought part of the Captain's estate, for the Captain has ruined himself by accepting moral responsibility for the affairs of a bankrupt bank with which he was associated. After the Captain's death, Mrs

Forrester leaves Sweet Water, disappears, and is last heard of as the wife of a very rich Englishman in the Argentine.

Miss Cather's attitude is quite explicitly expressed in Niel Herbert's reflections after meeting Ivy Peters in the train:

> After Ivy had gone on into the smoker, Niel sat looking out at the windings of the Sweet Water and playing with his idea. The Old West had been settled by dreamers, great-hearted adventurers who were unpractical to the point of magnificence; a courteous brotherhood, strong in attack but weak in defence, who could conquer but could not hold. Now all the vast territory they had won was to be at the mercy of men like Ivy Peters, who had never dared anything, never risked anything. They would drink up the mirage, dispel the morning freshness, root out the great brooding spirit of freedom, the generous, easy life of the great land-holders. The space, the colour, the princely carelessness of the pioneer they would destroy and cut up into profitable bits, as the match factory splinters the primeval forest. All the way from the Missouri to the mountains this generation of shrewd young men, trained to petty economies by hard times, would do exactly what Ivy Peters had done when he drained the Forrester Marsh.

In no novel is the symbolism more patent. Captain Forrester is the incarnate figure of the courteous brotherhood of the great-hearted dreamers who made the Old West; Ivy Peters is the new man, a petty, calculating exploiter, symbolic of the small-town spirit and commercial values; while Mrs Forrester, the lost lady, is as it were the West itself, lost in the sense of being no more and lost, too, in the sense of having been corrupted, of having fallen. It must be admitted that Miss Cather loads the dice as carefully as any professional gambler of the Old Frontier. When we first meet Ivy Peters in the early pages of the novel he is shown as a loutish youth who knocks down woodpeckers with a catapult, blinds them and turns them loose again. And one very much doubts whether the men who opened up the West, decimating the buffalo-herds and driving out the Indians as they did so, were quite the paragons of chivalry Willa Cather presents. One knows, as a matter of historical fact, that they were not; and if one wants what seems to be a truthful picture in fiction of the opening up of the West one must go to a much later novel, Michael Straight's *Carrington*.

But Willa Cather was in love with a dream of the American past and obsessed with a hatred of the American present. The love reached its finest expression in her novel *Death Comes for the Archbishop*, published in 1927, a novel of considerable beauty which describes the missionary enterprises of two Roman Catholic priests, Jean Marie Latour, Vicar Apostolic of New Mexico and Bishop of Agathonica *in partibus*, and Father Joseph Vaillant, in New Mexico in the eighteen-fifties. They are missionaries in a feudal, pastoral world, preaching to the descendants of the Spanish settlers and to the Pueblo Indians. It is, perhaps, a little too pastoral, a little too Arcadian; one feels that the rawness and crudity of what must have been the reality have been dissolved in the grave cadences of Willa Cather's classical prose. But by implication the hatred of the present is there as well, though now it has become a hatred of the industrial North, even, one might say, of Anglo-Saxon America. Even the crimes and violence of the Indians are shown as products of a sort of innocence.

[3]

Both Lewis and Willa Cather have been seen as leaders of 'the revolt from the village', as Carl Van Doren described Edgar Lee Masters's *Spoon River Anthology*; but their significance goes far beyond that, as does Sherwood Anderson's. Anderson is probably much underrated at present in the United States. Admittedly, his work is uneven, his later fiction, *Dark Laughter*, for instance, now seeming pretty silly even when not overshadowed by the writings of a man greater than himself, D. H. Lawrence. His reputation must stand or fall by *Winesburg, Ohio*, and that remains a remarkable work deeply rooted, one feels, in American experience. In that book, which appeared in 1919, he found himself and what he had to say, and he found himself through four writers. The example of Masters's *The Spoon River Anthology*, a series of free-verse poems in epitaph-form revealing the secret lives of more than two hundred people buried in the cemetery of a small Mid-West town, and baring, as Irving Howe has said, 'the hidden lesions of the American psyche', gave him the clue to his subject-matter. Turgenev, whose *A Sportsman's Sketches* he called 'the sweetest thing in literature', set him his ideal of writing; and the influence of Mark Twain and Gertrude Stein enabled him to attain it, one by the example of *Huckleberry Finn*, with its incomparable rendering of vernacular speech, the other by making him see how to break up the texture of conventional literary prose in order to express direct intuition. And perhaps a fifth influence should be added: the King James Bible, not for its contents but for its rhythms. Through these influences he learnt to write a prose freer, more idiomatic, more lyrical, less 'literary', than anyone had written since Mark Twain.

Winesburg, Ohio is a collection of short stories that very nearly becomes a novel, for, apart from the unity conferred upon it by the setting, most of the stories impinge upon young George Willard, the son of the town's hotel-proprietor and reporter on the *Winesburg Eagle*. He is, one might say, the young Anderson; significantly, his ambition is to be a writer, and one feels all the time that *Winesburg, Ohio* is the book he is destined to write. The prefatory story—it is not part of the Winesburg sequence—gives a rough clue to Anderson's intention. It is a fantasy called 'The Book of the Grotesque', which is an account of an unpublished book. It is certainly not to be taken literally as a description of the theories behind *Winesburg, Ohio*. All the same, Anderson *is* dealing with grotesques; *Winesburg, Ohio* is a parade of grotesques. His theme is estrangement and alienation; his characters are fixed, as it were, in postures of estrangement and alienation from which in vain they attempt to break away, generally through some effort to communicate with, confess to, George Willard, whom they see rather as a priest, certainly as a free spirit still uncommitted, pliable and plastic. They are all intolerably isolated characters, prisoners of their grotesqueness.

The archetypal story is 'Queer', which is the story of young Elmer Cowley, the son of an unsuccessful shopkeeper who differs from his son in not realizing that he is queer, whereas Elmer has been brought to the point of consciousness where he vows, 'I will not be queer—one to be looked at and listened to. I'll be like other people. I'll show that George Willard. He'll find out, I'll show him!' And he does attempt to show George, fetching him from the newspaper office at night to do so. (The significant moments of these stories, the attempts at communication, almost invariably take place at night, in the darkness, at the time when alienation is at its completest and is most aware of itself.) He fails, he has no words with which to communicate; he can only shout, 'Oh, you go on back', and plunge deeper into the night and into misery. Then an idea strikes him: he can lose his queerness simply by running away, catching the midnight freight train and in Cleveland losing himself in the crowds there. 'He would get work in some shop and become friends with the other workmen. Gradually he would become like other men and would be indistinguishable. Then he could talk and laugh. He would no longer be queer and would make friends. Life would begin to have warmth and meaning for him as it had for others.' He steals twenty dollars from his father's savings and goes to the railway station, sending Willard a message to join him there. Again he has no words with which to talk to Willard; he is tongue-tied.

Elmer Cowley danced with fury beside the groaning train in the darkness on the station platform. Lights leaped into the air and bobbed up and down before his eyes. Taking the two ten-dollar bills from his pocket, he thrust them into George Willard's hand. 'Take them', he cried. 'I don't want them. Give them to father. I stole them.' With a snarl of rage he turned and his long arms began to flay the air. Like one struggling for release from hands that held him he struck out, hitting George Willard blow after blow on the breast, the neck, the mouth. The young reporter rolled over on the platform half unconscious, stunned by the terrific force of the blows. Springing aboard the passing train and running over the tops of cars, Elmer sprang down to a flat car and lying on his face looked back. Pride surged up in him. 'I showed him', he cried. 'I guess I showed him. I ain't so queer. I guess I showed him I ain't so queer.'

'Queer' is the simplest and perhaps the most poignant story in the book, if only because of the very smallness of Elmer's ambitions. The characters in the other stories are much more complex, at any rate by implication, though always shown in a single frozen posture of distortion with a wild despairing effort to break loose in the confessional box of night to the priest-figure of George Willard. So across the pages of *Winesburg, Ohio* pass drunks, homosexuals, women-haters, voyeurs, frigid women, religious maniacs. There are triumphs; frustration is not universal; sublimation is occasionally achieved. Against the fate of Wing Biddlebaum, in the story 'Hands', the dedicated school teacher who is run out of town for what can be called a wholly innocent homosexuality, may be set the triumph of the Rev. Curtis Hartman, in 'The

Strength of God'. Hartman, the pastor of the Presbyterian Church of
Winesburg, is obsessed by carnal desire for Kate Swift, the school
teacher, into whose bedroom he can look from a room in the bell tower
of his church. The better to watch her, he breaks a hole in the stained
glass window. Night after night the minister struggles against his sin;
until there comes the night when he sees her naked on her bed, weep-
ing; she rises to pray: 'In the lamplight her figure, slim and strong,
looked like the figure of the boy in the presence of the Christ on the
leaded window.' Hartman rushes into the street and bursts in upon
George Willard in the *Eagle* office:

> 'I have found the light,' he cried. 'After ten years in this town,
> God has manifested himself to me in the body of a woman.' His
> voice dropped and he began to whisper. 'I did not understand,'
> he said. 'What I took to be a trial of my soul was only a prepara-
> tion for a new and more beautiful fervour of the spirit. God has
> appeared to me in the person of Kate Swift, the school teacher,
> kneeling naked on a bed. Do you know Kate Swift? Although
> she may not be aware of it, she is an instrument of God, bearing
> the message of God.'

Irving Howe, in his essay 'The Book of the Grotesque', the best
short study of Anderson, notes that at various times *Winesburg, Ohio*
'has been banished to such categories as the revolt against the village,
the rejection of middle-class morality, the proclamation of sexual freedom, and the rise of cultural primitivism'. None of these categories was
entirely irrelevant to the book, but it is now clear that Anderson goes
far beyond any of them. His criticism is fundamental; it is not a
criticism of society but of life. Anderson is describing the condition of
man as he sees it. And though his characters in *Winesburg, Ohio* are in a
sense the defeated, distorted by alienation, they are shown all the time
as being better than and preferable to their fellow-citizens who
acquiesce and accept, who are 'normal'. Distortion, one might say, is
almost a sign of grace; at any rate, a sign that the possibility of grace
has been recognized. Equally clearly, the book is not to be read as a
piece of realistic fiction. It is a rendering of the night-side of life; 'a
landscape', as Howe says, 'in which ghosts fumble erratically and
romance is reduced to mere fugitive brushings at night; a landscape
eerie with the cracked echoes of village queers rambling in their lonely
eccentricity'. *Winesburg, Ohio*, in fact, is a microcosm not of the world
perhaps but certainly of the United States as Anderson saw it. In his

time he was generally related, with good reason, to contemporaries like Dreiser, Lewis and Hemingway; now, one sees that his deeper affinities were with a later writer like Carson McCullers, who explores the twin themes of human alienation and incommunicableness not through grotesques but through freaks.

[4]

ANDERSON DEDICATED his collection of stories *Horses and Men* to Theodore Dreiser, a novelist who is almost certainly greatly underrated by his countrymen at the present time. Not that it is difficult to see why. His writings strike one as a triumph of honesty, and very little else. It is questionable whether he ever wrote a single sentence capable of giving pleasure in itself; and so rebarbative is his use of words, his grammar, his syntax, that a sustained reading of his finest book, *An American Tragedy*, the last half of which is written almost throughout with present participles usurping the function of verbs, is as lacerating to the sensibility as the continuous grinding of pneumatic drills. Yet in the end something has come through which perhaps needed that uncouth mode of expression in order to do so. The something is the impress of a mind powerfully moved by its sense of the human situation in a certain place at a certain time. In the end, one has to agree with Mencken: 'Dreiser can feel, and, feeling, he can move. The others are very skilful with words.'

The first thing that strikes the reader about the world Dreiser describes—and it is true of it whether it is the Philadelphia of a century ago in *The Financier* or the Kansas City and Lycurgus, N.Y., of *An American Tragedy*—is its sheer poverty, its spiritual poverty; in all but material comfort, its inhabitants exist on the subsistence level, the only relationships between them the cash nexus and biological urges. Dreiser's originality lies in the fact that he was the first American novelist to depict this aspect of American life. He knew it from the inside; it was the world which, in 1871, as the son of a German immigrant and his Czech-American wife with a family too large for them adequately to support, he was born into. He was brought up, too, not in the Middle West countryside of Willa Cather, Anderson and Lewis, but in the raw, immigrant-packed mill towns of Indiana. Before him, although there are obvious exceptions like Norris and Sinclair, American novelists had conceived it their duty, in Howells's famous phrase, to 'concern themselves with the more smiling aspects of life, which are the more American'. Dreiser, with his worm's eye view of the American dream and the American struggle, changed all that.

Dreiser, brought up in miserable poverty, one of a family in which it was common form for the daughters to 'go wrong' and the sons to go to jail, came to writing, and largely to reading, as a newspaper reporter, and the intellectual influences on him seem to have been few but intense. His notion of fiction he acquired from Balzac; Herbert Spencer gave him a philosophy, and the example of Thomas Hardy, who shared a similar philosophy, reinforced it. 'As I see him the utterly infinitesimal individual weaves among the mysteries a floss-like and wholly meaningless course—if course it be. In short I catch no meaning from all I have seen, and pass quite as I came, confused and dismayed.' Mutability, he believed, was at the heart of things, and his deepest feeling was one of compassion: 'I am crying for life', says a character in his last novel, *The Stoic*.

It is this painful, almost agonized fidelity to the grain of life as he saw and experienced it that is Dreiser's great virtue as a writer. It shines through his first novel, *Sister Carrie* (1900). Carrie Meeber, poor as Dreiser's sisters had been, goes to Chicago to find work, is picked up by a salesman Charles Drouet, and during a time of unemployment becomes his mistress. She leaves him for his friend George Hurstwood, the manager of a bar. He is a married man and causes Carrie to elope with him by a subterfuge; nor does he tell her that he has stolen the contents of his employer's safe. In New York, Hurstwood opens a bar; but from then on the novel traces the rise of Carrie, who draws apart from him to become a successful musical comedy actress, and the degeneration of Hurstwood through unemployment to final suicide.

Sister Carrie was suppressed on the grounds of immorality, the immorality consisting, apparently, in the fact that the heroine does not suffer from the consequences of her sin, but, instead, prospers. Actually Carrie is nothing like so convincing as Hurstwood, whose fall is rendered in impressive and remorseless detail. He is not a bad man— indeed, such concepts are foreign to Dreiser's way of thinking; he is simply the victim of chance. In a sense, he even steals by chance; for while there is no question about his wish to steal, the opportunity to do so comes about entirely by accident. In a way, even, the act of theft is forced upon him. Having removed the money from the safe and been surprised at the amount, he rebels against the impulse to steal; but the door of the safe swings shut as he is about to return the notes.

Jennie Gerhardt appeared in 1911. Again the theme is the fallen woman; again there is a complete absence of the poetic justice the times demanded. Jennie herself is a successful creation precisely as Carrie is not, and mainly because she is seen as almost entirely non-intellectual; she possesses, in Dreiser's words, 'a largeness of feeling not altogether squared with intellect'; and Dreiser conveys his regard for her when he comments: 'Virtue is that quality of generosity which offers itself willingly for another's service, and, being this, it is held by society to be nearly worthless.' She is presented, in her willing submission to others, to life and to nature, as a good woman.

In *The Financier* and *The Titan* Dreiser deals with a subject that had always fascinated him, the rise of the great American millionaires of the second half of the nineteenth century. Frank Cowperwood, the son of a Philadelphia bank clerk, grows up in that city in the years before the Civil War. *The Financier*—and Cowperwood—are set between two images derived from natural history. As a boy, Cowperwood sees a lobster devour a squid and realizes, 'Things live on each other—that was it'. At the end of the novel, released from jail after serving a sentence for larceny and about to seek a new fortune in Chicago, he is compared by Dreiser to the black grouper fish, which survives 'because of its very remarkable ability to adapt itself to conditions'. Dreiser sees the black grouper, and therefore Cowperwood, 'as the constructive genius of nature, which is not beatific'. Dreiser, that is, is morally neutral towards Cowperwood, who is presented almost as a magnificent animal for whom ends always justify means and who triumphs and deserves to triumph because of his superior vitality and ruthlessness, which are seen as much the same thing. Indeed, animal imagery runs throughout *The Financier*. Cowperwood and his mistress Aileen are compared to two leopards who run together 'temperamentally'; members of the stock exchange are seen as 'a lot of gulls . . . hungry and anxious to snap up any unwary fish'. At the same time, Dreiser presses parallels between Cowperwood and the merchant princes of the Italian renaissance; Cowperwood is presented as obsessed with magnificence.

Something in Dreiser's imagination responded to the spectacle of finance-capitalism at its most ruthless, the more so, no doubt, because it seemed to him to represent the working of the natural law. The result was the most impressive novel he wrote, apart from *An American Tragedy*; a most solid and vivid reconstruction in terms of actual events of the developments of American capitalism in the second half of the nineteenth century.

The Titan is much less good, mainly because of Dreiser's obvious difficulty in maintaining interest in Cowperwood. Dreiser piles on the comparisons with his hero, who is seen sometimes as Hannibal at the gates of Rome, sometimes as a great Elizabethan. But though the description of the financial world of Chicago in the seventies and eighties is well enough done, the difficulty of imaginatively presenting a being commensurate with the financial struggles depicted remains. All we get, as it were, is more and more of the same thing; the novel is repetitive and static.

For all its faults, Dreiser's greatest novel is unquestionably *An American Tragedy*. In outline, the work is simplicity itself. Clyde Griffiths, the son of street evangelists in Kansas City, dreams of a life of luxury and becomes a bellboy in an hotel. He has to leave Kansas City because of his innocent involvement in a motor accident, and in New York, where he works in a club, he meets his uncle Samuel Griffiths, owner of a collar factory in Lycurgus, New York. Admitting some obligation towards the youth, Griffiths gives him a job in his factory, where Clyde seduces a workgirl, Roberta Alden, gets her pregnant, and then realizes he has the chance of marrying Sondra Finchley, a wealthy girl of the town. He decides to murder Roberta and takes her rowing on a lonely lake, only to find that he lacks the courage to kill her. But the boat overturns and Roberta is drowned. After a long trial, in which his innocence or guilt becomes a political issue, he is sent to the electric chair.

Twin questions immediately pose themselves: Can the novel really justify its title of tragedy, and, in what way is the tragedy specifically American? Certainly the novel is no tragedy by any accepted standards, whether classical or in the way that *Tess* or *Jude the Obscure* may be considered tragedy. Clyde Griffiths is, almost by definition, Wyndham Lewis's dumb ox, the passive victim of circumstances. Dreiser himself says that he was a 'soul that was not destined to grow up'. He is selfish —this Dreiser insists upon—and weak, incapable even, whatever his wishes may be, of any decisive action. Objectively he seems scarcely to deserve our pity. 'Why don't they kill the God-damned bastard and be done with him?' asks a spectator in the court-room; and this emotional response to a creature who is characterized by 'the most feeble and blundering incapacity' is understandable. Clyde Griffiths is everything a tragic hero is not, and Dreiser meant him to be.

Yet Dreiser's pity for him is at once so vast and so deep that this is not how we react towards Clyde while we are reading the novel. Dreiser does not sentimentalize him at all; indeed, his pity is impersonal. And this is important, for its effect is to make us accept Clyde as something of a universal figure. This, Dreiser seems to be telling us, is the truth about man, will-less man, forever the victim of circumstances. The tragedy, if tragedy there is, lies in the implicit contrast between what a man expects of life, what he is born and brought up to expect, and what he gets. Whether intended or not, the title rings with a terrible irony. This, in effect, Dreiser is telling us, is what tragedy truly amounts to in the American world; and so large and noble is his brooding tragic sense, which can be so fired by an insignificant figure like Clyde Griffiths, that we are almost convinced, at any rate to the point of rephrasing Wilfred Owen and saying the tragedy is in the pity.

But what of the specifically American content of the tragedy? It lay, Dreiser seemed to believe, in the contrast between the promise of America, and indeed of its material pride and luxury, and the poverty in which so many millions of its people lived. And the poverty was not merely a material poverty: it was a poverty of values, a poverty of the spirit. This Dreiser brings out brilliantly; in the opening scenes with the reluctant boy tagging behind his evangelist parents preaching the goodness of God and themselves caught in perpetual want; in Clyde's identification of himself with the hotel in Kansas City, the symbol of success in America; in the sudden terror he feels when catching a glimpse of the poverty in which Roberta lives.

Dreiser faced the facts of American life more squarely, grappled with their implications more resolutely, than any other novelist of the first two decades of the century, in the Hardyesque mood of 'If a way to the better there be, it exacts a full look at the worst'. This is why he remains a founding father of the modern American novel, one of its permanent points of reference and, in the first two decades of the century, a period during which little of significance was happening in the American novel, a heroic figure, a solitary giant. There were other novelists of moment of course: Willa Cather, Anderson, Ellen Glasgow with her realistic studies of the South, Edith Wharton, both in her tragic novel of New England rural life, *Ethan Frome*, and her Jamesian investigations into the effects of great wealth on moral values and personality; but all these, fine as they were, were peripheral to the central facts of American experience. Dreiser alone had ambitions comparable to those of the important European novelists of the day; he alone seemed of their company.

[5]

THE COMPARATIVE sterility in American fiction during the first twenty years of the century is not easily explicable and is made the more mysterious by the fact that by 1912 a renascence of American poetry had become evident in the work of poets like Sandburg, Robinson, Vachel Lindsay and Lee Masters and, a little later, in that of younger men, Pound, Eliot, Conrad Aiken, Wallace Stevens, to say nothing of Robert Frost, who was different again. The other arts, painting especially, were almost as lively. But very little of this found expression in the novel until the young men returned from the war, even if the war meant only, as it did for many, a few months in the Army far away from the front in Flanders. The war, for the United States even more than for Britain, was the great precipitant; and in the American novel this means first of all F. Scott Fitzgerald, who both in his writings and his life seems to epitomize the Jazz Age, 'the ten-year period', as he said, 'that, as if reluctant to die outmoded on its bed, leapt to a spectacular death in October, 1929'.

Fitzgerald was a Middle-Westerner, born in 1896 at St Paul, Minnesota. His first novel, *This Side of Paradise*, begun at Princeton, was published in 1920 and was immediately successful. A volume of short stories, *Flappers and Philosophers*, a second novel, *The Beautiful and Damned*, and another book of stories, *Tales of the Jazz Age*, followed. *The Great Gatsby* appeared in 1925 and *All the Sad Young Men* a year later. And then the Jazz Age was over, and it seemed that Fitzgerald's career was over, too. In a sense, everything he wrote afterwards, apart from the pot-boiling short stories, was in the nature of obituaries and post-mortems upon himself. As he had been a symbol of the Jazz Age, so he might stand as a symbol of the crash that followed. He died in 1940, aged 44, a man who lived in the last twilight decade of his short life at the heroic pitch of desperation.

This Side of Paradise was the work of a very young man and reads like it. But it is still very readable. 'Why then the world's my oyster' was the epigraph Disraeli prefixed to *Vivian Grey*, and in Fitzgerald's novel as in his what we take away from the book is not so much an impression of the world as a sense of the author's ambition. It is a dream of adolescent youth at its most naïve, and the more touching because of the extreme cleverness that marks the book. It is the work, in other words, of a young man in love with literature and as yet unable to distinguish between literature and life.

All the same, the authentic note of the post-war generation, which Richard Hughes in *The Fox in the Attic* expresses in the question his hero puts to himself: 'how was it so great a gulf divided his own from every previous generation, so that they seemed like different species?' is there, struck particularly in the last paragraphs of the novel as Amory broods over the towers and spires of Princeton in the night:

> Here was a new generation, shouting the old cries, learning the old creeds, through a revery of long days and nights; destined finally to go out into that dirty grey turmoil to follow love and pride; a new generation dedicated more than the last to the fear of poverty and the worship of success; grown up to find all Gods dead, all wars fought, all faiths in man shaken. . . .

The importance of Fitzgerald's Mid-Western origins can hardly be overestimated, for they help to define the nature of his romanticism. Fitzgerald was the outsider who, even while imaginatively and romantically identifying himself with the object of his desires, was sceptical of its value or of its capacity to endure. The very rich fascinated Fitzgerald; they attracted him and repelled him at one and the same time. They are the corrupt and the corrupters, and they are insidious because they represent all the attraction of experience for the innocent.

Fitzgerald achieved one perfect dramatization of this, and by doing so achieved even more. *The Great Gatsby* sums up, with extraordinary economy, an epoch: here is the Jazz Age, but the Jazz Age as part of the fabric of American history. It is also, as the narrator Nick Carro-way says, 'a story of the West, after all—Tom and Gatsby, Daisy and Jordan and I, were all Westerners, and perhaps we possessed some deficiency in common which made us subtly unadaptable to Eastern life'. To these men and women from Chicago and Louisville and Minnesota, New York stands in the same relation as did Europe to James's New Englanders. At the centre of the novel is the fabulous figure of Gatsby, the man from nowhere—or more precisely, Minne-sota—who has made himself whatever the glazed eyes of his multitude of guests want him to be, an Oggsford man, a former German spy, Hindenburg's cousin, a murderer, a bootlegger.

How brilliantly Fitzgerald sets the scene of East Egg and West Egg, on Long Island, the valley of ashes half way to New York and the eyes of Dr T. J. Eckleburg that surmount it. 'The eyes of Doctor T. J. Eckleburg are blue and gigantic—their retinas are a yard high. They look out of no face, but, instead, from a pair of enormous yellow spectacles which pass over a non-existent nose.' In this valley of ashes we are in the valley of desolation, the valley of the shadow of death; and it is precisely here that the incident occurs on which the whole action of the novel hinges, the irony of Gatsby's—or rather Daisy's— killing of Tom Buchanan's mistress as she dashes out of the filling station to stop what she assumes to be Tom's car. And it is then, too, that Doctor T. J. Eckleburg's spectacles come into their own, when the demented widower, who had only recently discovered his wife's infidelity, reports to his neighbour what he had said to her:

> 'I spoke to her', he muttered, after a long silence. 'I told her she might fool me but she couldn't fool God. I took her to the window'—with an effort he got up and walked to the rear window and leaned with his face pressed against it—'and I said "God knows what you've been doing, everything you've been doing. You may fool me, but you can't fool God!"'
> Standing behind him, Michaelis saw with a shock that he was looking into the eyes of Doctor T. J. Eckleburg, which had just emerged pale and enormous, from the dissolving night.
> 'God sees everything', repeated Wilson.

The action of the novel is suddenly seen *sub specie aeternitatis*. Doctor T. J. Eckleburg's eyes have become the symbols of Fitzgerald's values.

With what brilliant comedy too, through the three-page list of names, Fitzgerald renders the nature of Gatsby's social success. The names are all plausible, only slightly burlesqued and never invariably so, and their owners sufficiently documented in passing to establish them:

> . . . Of theatrical people there were Gus Waize and Horace O'Donavan and Lester Myer and George Duckweed and Francis Bull. Also from New York were the Chromes and the Backhyssens and the Dennickers and Russel Betty and the Corrigans and the Kellehers and the Dewars and the Scullys and S. W. Belcher and the Smirkes and the young Quinns, divorced now, and Henry L. Palmetto, who killed himself by jumping in front of a subway train in Times Square . . .

Gatsby's social success is dubious in the extreme, but that does not matter to him; for he has amassed his wealth as a bootlegger and set himself up as a Long Island Trimalchio with the single end of manœuvring a meeting with Daisy Buchanan, the girl, now married and living on the other side of the bay, he had fallen in love with five years before and whom he still loves. He had met her 'by a colossal accident'. In peacetime it would never have been possible, but there he was, a young officer in Louisville, temporarily a gentleman. 'She was the first "nice" girl he had ever known . . . and Gatsby was overwhelmingly aware of the youth and mystery that wealth imprisons and preserves, of the freshness of many clothes, and of Daisy, gleaming like silver, safe and proud above the hot struggles of the poor.' He goes off to the war, does well, gets his majority, wins decorations—and does in fact go to Oxford for a time. But Daisy, tired of waiting for him, marries the rich Yale athlete Tom Buchanan, whom Fitzgerald draws as what would later be called a Fascist type. Then Gatsby begins his long siege of Daisy, though the word is wrong for his single-minded chivalrous devotion. Through Carroway he meets Daisy again:

> 'I wouldn't ask too much of her', I ventured. 'You can't repeat the past.'
> 'Can't repeat the past?' he cried incredulously. 'Why of course you can.'

Such is his fantastic, preposterous dream; and it ends in disaster, with Gatsby shot dead by the husband of Tom Buchanan's mistress.

But the good end is made by Gatsby, not the Buchanans, of whom Carroway says:

> They were careless people, Tom and Daisy—they smashed up things and creatures and then retreated back into their money or their vast carelessness, or whatever it was that kept them together, and let other people clear up the mess they had made ...

Gatsby is a remarkable conception, convincing because we see him through the eyes of Carroway. Carroway is not taken in; the attraction and the criticism of what is found attractive are simultaneous. Thus, in what is a key passage to the novel, he says:

> Jay Gatz—that was really, or legally, his name. He had changed it at the age of seventeen ... I suppose he'd had the name ready for a long time, even then. His parents were shiftless and unsuccessful farm people—his imagination had never really accepted them as his parents at all. The truth was that Jay Gatsby of West Egg, Long Island, sprang from his Platonic conception of himself. He was a son of God—a phrase which, if it means anything, means just that—and he must be about His Father's business, the service of a vast, vulgar, and meretricious beauty. So he invented just the sort of Jay Gatsby that a seventeen-year-old boy would be likely to invent, and to this conception he was faithful to the end.

The criticism could not be plainer: Fitzgerald is thoroughly aware of the vulgarity and adolescent nature of Gatsby's ambitions. But just as significant is the point made when Fitzgerald describes Gatsby as sprung 'from the Platonic idea of himself'. As Lionel Trilling has said: 'Gatsby, divided between power and dream, comes inevitably to stand for America itself. Ours is the only nation that prides itself upon a dream and gives its name to one ... Clearly it is Fitzgerald's intention that our mind should turn to the thought of the nation that has sprung from its "Platonic conception" of itself.' And this becomes quite explicit in the last paragraphs of the novel.

What had seemed to be a novel of American manners at a particular point in history and a study of the romantic mind at a certain time and place is revealed to be a novel about the nature of being an American, and Gatsby becomes the symbol almost of the United States itself at one moment in its history.

The Great Gatsby, in the last analysis, is about the specific nature of

American experience: *Tender is the Night* (1934) is about Fitzgerald. The generalization is, of course, too sweeping, but all the same *Tender is the Night* is one of those constantly beguiling, imperfect works of art that we read both for the light it throws on its author and in the light of its author's life. Not that the novel is autobiographical in any literal sense. It is, however, an exploration of emotional and spiritual bankruptcy akin to that suffered by Fitzgerald himself. Despite the complex form of the novel, the plot is very simple. Dick Diver, a young psychiatrist, comes to Zürich in 1917 to continue his studies. Among his patients is a very rich American girl Nicole Warren, whose schizophrenia is the product of an incestuous relation with her father. She falls in love with Dick in the usual course of transference and he marries her, out of pity for her helplessness. He is caught by her dependence on him, for she continues throughout the novel to have periodic bouts of insanity. Unwittingly, he is corrupted by the luxury native to her. His scientific ambitions fall away, dissipated in the exercise of that social charm which he himself calls a mere 'trick of the heart'. He is safe so long as Nicole is dependent on him but as she recovers corruption becomes degeneration. He drinks too much; he becomes socially impossible; and when Nicole's recovery manifests itself as a return to the selfishness characteristic of her family he is finished. Divorced, Diver returns to America, to small-town practice as a doctor in New York State. He has, the curt final paragraphs imply, been dismissed.

Tender is the Night particularizes in the most dramatic way, with all his powers of invention and romantic eloquence, what Fitzgerald had written in 1926 in his story 'The Rich Boy':

> Let me tell you about the very rich. They are different from you and me. They possess and enjoy early, and it does something to them, makes them soft where we are hard, and cynical where we are trustful, in a way that, unless you were born rich, it is very difficult to understand. They think, deep in their hearts, that they are better than we are because we had to discover the compensations and refuges of life for ourselves.

Fitzgerald died before he could finish *The Last Tycoon*. Even in the form we have it, incomplete—there are about 60,000 words of it—unrevised, with much in that would undoubtedly have been rewritten, it is plainly the work of a man at the height of his powers, who has suffered bitterly and come through to the other side unembittered and with an immeasurably deeper knowledge of the human lot. And fragment though it is, it is by far the best novel that has been written about Hollywood.

Fitzgerald's strength lies in the creation of his central character, the great film-producer Monroe Stahr. Fitzgerald based his conception of Stahr on Irving Thalberg, but in the character as we have it in the novel, he created, as we realize from Mizener's biography and Budd Schulberg's novel about Fitzgerald's last days in Hollywood, *The Disenchanted*, a figure who was a completely adequate equivalent to himself at the time of writing. Stahr, too, is a desperately sick man, disenchanted with life, but striving still to work, to make something out of chaos, a lonely artist fighting economic circumstances of a kind he cannot possibly control. He is a genuinely tragic figure. In the realization of Stahr's character are evident all the self-knowledge and objectivity we find in the essays, notebooks and letters of *The Crack Up*.

[6]

IT WAS NOT Fitzgerald, however, who created the characteristic idiom of the time, but Hemingway. He was often misunderstood, for the public Hemingway, the 'Papa Hemingway' of legend, was a crude and even brutal parody of the values and life style expressed in his writings. It was a life style unable to adapt itself to industrial civilization, and he had to go further and further afield to find situations that would embody his vision. His best work remains his early work, the three volumes of stories, *In Our Time* (1924), *Men without Women* (1927), *Winner Take Nothing* (1933), the novels *The Sun Also Rises* (1926), called *Fiesta* in England, and *A Farewell to Arms* (1929), together with one or two later stories. His later fiction tends either to degenerate into imitation of his earlier, the Hemingway hero merging as it were into the 'Papa Hemingway' figure, as in *Across the River and into the Trees*, or into what Arnold called *simplesse*, the false simplicity of *The Old Man and the Sea* as compared with the genuine simplicity of the much earlier story on a comparable theme, 'The Undefeated'. A good deal of *For Whom the Bell Tolls* (1940) strikes one now as *simplesse*.

As much as Conrad and Malraux, Hemingway is the dramatist of the extreme situation. His overriding theme is honour, personal honour: by what shall a man live, by what shall a man die, in a world the essential condition of whose being is violence, one in which, moreover, for the Hemingway hero all external sanctions of religion and traditional values have disappeared? The problems are posed rather than answered in his first book, *In Our Time*, a collection of short stories in which almost all Hemingway's later work is contained by implication. It consists of fifteen short stories most of which relate the boyhood experiences of Nick Adams among the woods and lakes of Michigan, initiations as it were into life in the company of his father, a doctor, and of the Indians and guides his father works among. The first story of the sequence, 'Indian Camp', is typical and sets the note of the whole. Nick's father takes him to an Indian camp where a woman is in childbirth. Dr Adams has to perform a Caesarean operation with improvised instruments and without anaesthetic. The operation is successful, and then it is discovered that the Indian husband has killed himself in his fear by cutting his throat. Later, Nick, who has seen it happen, asks his father:

'Do ladies always have such a bad time having babies?' Nick asked.
'No, that was very, very exceptional.'
'Why did he kill himself, Daddy?'
'I don't know, Nick. He couldn't stand things, I guess.'
'Do many men kill themselves, Daddy?'
'Not very many, Nick.'
'Do many women?'
'Hardly any.'
'Is dying hard, Daddy?'
'No, I think it's pretty easy, Nick. It all depends.'

Set in italics between the stories are brief vignettes of violent action and death in the battlefields of Europe—the world war and the war between the Greeks and Turks that followed it—and in the bull-ring. This device is far from being a gimmick; nor is its purpose ironical. The vignettes look forward to the future:

Nick sat against the wall of the church where they had dragged him to be clear of machine-gun fire in the street. Both legs stuck out awkwardly. He had been hit in the spine. His face was sweaty and dirty. The sun shone on his face. The day was very hot. Rinaldi, big backed, his equipment sprawling, lay face downward against the wall. Nick looked straight ahead brilliantly. The pink wall of the house opposite had fallen out from the roof, and an iron bedstead hung twisted toward the street. Two Austrian dead lay in the rubble in the shade of the house. Up the street were other dead. Things were getting forward in the town. It was going well. Stretcher bearers would be along any time now. Nick turned his head carefully and looked at Rinaldi. 'Senta Rinaldi. Senta. You and me we've made a separate peace.' Rinaldi lay still in the sun breathing with difficulty. 'Not patriots.' Nick turned his head carefully away smiling sweatily. Rinaldi was a disappointing audience.

This, both in content and in implication ('We have made a separate peace'), obviously anticipates much of *A Farewell to Arms*; but more immediately it looks forward to the story in *In Our Time*, 'Big Two-Hearted River', which on the surface is merely an account of a trout-fishing trip but which, in its context and in the light of our knowledge of Nick's war experiences, is as it were an account of his return after the war to the healing springs of his early life. There is no discontinuity between the stories and the vignettes. Violence, Hemingway is saying, whether that of hunting and fishing, of sex and childbirth, or of war, is the condition in which a man must learn to live. And, as a technical device, the vignettes have the function of linking the stories, setting them in a context and perspective, in an extra dimension, so that *In Our Time* has a unity far beyond that of a collection of short stories. It is almost a new form of fiction.

In a sense, Hemingway did nothing better than *In Our Time*. Everything is there, the fascination with death and the miraculous rendering of the life of the senses, in the prose that has never been better described than by Ford Madox Ford: 'Hemingway's words strike you, each one, as if they were pebbles fetched fresh from a brook. They live and shine, each in its place. So one of his pages has the effect of a brook-bottom into which you look through the flowing water. The words form a tessellation, each in order beside the other.'

Nevertheless, the main theme has not emerged in *In Our Time*. In his first novel, *The Sun Also Rises*, it is stated in the most intransigent way. Set among American and British expatriates living in France, who do no work that is noticeable, drink too much and are promiscuous, its theme is, how, when all external values have gone, shall a man live? The narrator-hero, Jake Barnes, an American newspaperman, has been castrated by a war wound: alienation, severance from the body of traditional human society, could not be expressed more radically. Barnes is in love with, and is loved by, Lady Brett Ashley, who also suffers from an unhealed trauma of the war: her fiancé had been killed; she has become, seen objectively, a drunk and a nymphomaniac. But in terms of the novel such words are both pejorative and question-begging; in no sense do they contain her, for the important thing is what she does, how she copes with an inescapable situation.

At the heart of the novel is Brett's encounter with the young bull-fighter, Pedro Romero, with whom she falls in love and who falls in love with her. She voluntarily renounces him because she sees that she would ruin him; and she says to Jake:

> 'You know it makes one feel rather good deciding not to be a bitch.'
> 'Yes.'
> 'It's sort of what we have instead of God.'
> 'Some people have God', I said. 'Quite a lot.'
> 'He never worked very well with me.'
> 'Should we have another Martini?'

Wrenched out of context, the passage, and Barnes's pay-off line, may seem almost repellently hard-boiled. It is not in the novel, for one's mind goes back to an earlier passage:

> This was Brett, that I had felt like crying about. Then I thought of her walking up the street and stepping into the car, as I had last seen her, and of course in a little while I felt like hell again. It is awfully easy to be hard-boiled about everything in the day-time, but at night it is another thing.

In context, the burden is plain: one accepts, one makes no fuss, one does the best one can, and one does that by being honest to one's feelings. One must not kid oneself.

This comes out quite categorically in the character that is the foil to Brett: the novelist Robert Cohn. He is, as it were, the victim of literature, so confused by words and the fine sentiments that inhere in words as to be incurably dishonest and therefore dangerous. He cannot distinguish between literature and life. Having had a one-night affair with Brett, he believes that he is in love with her and she with him. He pursues her and her friends to Pamplona, where they have gone for the bull-fighting, and, an ex-middleweight boxing champion of Princeton, beats up Romero on the eve of his appearance in the bull-ring. By contrast with Brett, he does not know himself well enough even to be able to decide not to be the masculine equivalent of a bitch. One might say he has no self-discipline; he is ruled by words.

This comes close to the core of Hemingway. Despite his wide reading, no writer of comparable stature has had a greater distrust for 'literature'. He cut out and dismissed as fiction all the great abstract words. As Frederic Henry says in *A Farewell to Arms*:

> I was always embarrassed by the words sacred, glorious, and sacrifice and the expression in vain. We had heard them, sometimes standing in the rain almost out of earshot, so that only the shouted words came through, and had read them, on proclamations that were slapped up by billposters over other proclamations, now for a long time, and I had seen nothing sacred, and the things that were glorious had no glory and the sacrifices were like the stockyards at Chicago if nothing was done with meat except to bury it. There were many words you could not stand to hear and finally only the names of places had dignity.

Against the great abstractions Hemingway set the small concrete nouns, the names of things one could be sure of, that could be tested by the evidence of the senses. His vocabulary must be the smallest of any major writer, and the restriction was deliberate. He said he wrote *Death in the Afternoon* 'to tell honestly the things I have found true' about bull-fighting. He wrote his novels and stories in order to tell honestly the things he had found true about life; but his criterion of truth was almost what could be assessed in terms of physical impact. It was the one thing he could be sure of. It was both his limitation as a writer and the source of his power. It meant that he was debarred from the expression of whole areas of human experience; it also made him an almost unrivalled interpreter of the life of physical sensation, of the exhilaration of hunting and fishing, of violent exercise, and of the primitive emotions, love and death. For Hemingway honesty to what is felt is all.

Which brings us back to Robert Cohn. In a sense, Cohn is not there at all. He feels at second-hand; he is a puppet controlled by the writers he has read; he has no validity as a man. But there is something else. Hemingway's code could be reduced to that of the stiff upper lip; too easily, because the code is much more positive than this. With the code goes a sense of style, a quality Cohn deplorably lacks; indeed, it might be said that the sense of style is the expression of the code. Style is what Brett Ashley superbly has. In part, it is a disdain of meanness and messiness. In part, of course, it comes from Hemingway's whole rendering of her, when we see her, for example, as 'built with curves like the hull of a racing yacht'.

The code is as much aesthetic as ethical, which no doubt explains Hemingway's devotion to the bull-ring and to big-game hunting, in which the confrontation of violent death is turned into ritual or an elaborate game. Insisting upon nothingness, Hemingway asserts violently man's dignity in the face of nothingness. Man dies: it is intolerable that a man should die less than well, with a sense of style; and as a man dies, so should he live.

In *A Farewell to Arms*, Hemingway's second novel, dealing as it does with events earlier in time than those of *The Sun Also Rises*, the Hemingway code does not quite emerge. As a rendering of battle, *A Farewell to Arms* can stand comparison with *War and Peace* and *Le rouge et le noir*; it is also one of the great pathetic love stories of the world. We have seen how one aspect of the novel is anticipated in the vignette in *In Our Time* in which Nick Adams, fighting with the Italian army and wounded in the spine, tells the dying heedless Rinaldi, 'You and me we've made a separate peace.' In the novel, though Rinaldi remains, Nick has become Lieutenant Frederic Henry. The course of the novel is extremely simple. Henry, wounded on the Italian front, meets in hospital a young English VAD, Catherine Barkley, whose fiancé has been killed in action. They fall in love and, having consummated their love, Henry returns to the front. The time is 1917; there is the disaster of Caporetto in which the Italian army disintegrates in panic retreat. Henry is caught up in this—Hemingway's description of the retreat is probably the finest piece of writing on war in the English language—and makes his separate peace. He and Catherine, who is pregnant, row across the lake by night to Switzerland, where Catherine dies in childbirth. Henry alone is left to tell the story. The end is inevitable. They have opted out of society, which is still society though stinking with death. They have snatched a separate peace, precarious and temporary, which can obviously have no future. They have as it were reduced themselves to a world of two, which the intrusion of a third—their child—must destroy.

One can't, however, make any comment on the story so simple as 'All for love, and the world well lost'. This is not in any normal sense a romantic novel. It is the story of a man and a woman wrought by the intolerable to the pitch of extreme desperation. It is an attempt, at any rate on Henry's part, to get down to some kind of bedrock in a world that has been stripped of all meaning for him. It is Hemingway's triumph that, more than any other novelist, to borrow Empson's line, he learnt a style from a despair.

[7]

To move from Hemingway to Thomas Wolfe is to move from the spare, the laconic, the rigorously selective, to the vast, the exuberantly expansive, the all-embracing; from the distrust of words and emotion to the total subjection to words and emotion. Wolfe was a very big man, six feet five inches tall, and the fact seems more than commonly relevant to his work as a writer, for his energies, appetites and capacities were proportionately large. He wrote always as it were at the top of his voice, and the words poured out of him in full spate, millions of them, and, long as the four novels that we possess are, all were carved out of and assembled from works much longer, assembled, what is more, by other men; left to himself, Wolfe would never have stopped writing, never ended a book.

He was always his own subject; he is the Eugene Gant of *Look Homeward, Angel* (1929) and of *Of Time and the River* (1935); and though in the posthumous novels put together by Edward C. Aswell, *The Web and the Rock* (1939) and *You Can't Go Home Again* (1940), he changed the name of his hero to George Webber and tried desperately to shrink his hero's size, it is impossible to distinguish between Gant and Webber, and Wolfe himself forgets to do so. Both are he.

Throughout his novels—and they are really one novel—we follow the fortunes of Wolfe-Gant-Webber always in full reaction against wherever he may be at any given point in the narrative, fleeing, seeking; fleeing from his family and his only slightly disguised birth-place of Asheville, North Carolina, to the state university, to Harvard, to Paris, to New York, to Brooklyn; constantly fleeing, and seeking—what? Love? An ideal father? An ideal mother? The flight and the search are obviously one and the same thing; the movement is circular. I have no doubt that it is to be explained only in Freudian terms, that Fiedler is correct when he writes: '*Look Homeward Angel, You Can't Go Home Again*: the titles tell the story of the search and the frustration; and beyond them, the books reveal the love of that frustration and the seeking self: the little boy lost, for whom no world is real and satisfactory once mama's breast has been withdrawn, papa has died, and big brother has become a ghost endlessly mourned.'

But Fiedler himself notes that 'of all the avatars of self-pity' in American literature, 'perhaps the only one to approach legendary dimensions is Eugene Gant'. Like his creator, Gant is more than life-size. He has the proportions of a myth-figure. And this is largely because of the style in which the novels are written. Whether one cares for the style is irrelevant. We are presented with words in spate, whole Niagaras of rhetoric. No one word is used if ten are possible. It is grossly repetitive, grossly romantic, grossly inflated, sometimes, it seems, no more than a torrent of sound, so that the only possible comparison seems to be with the later Swinburne. It is much more heavily rhythmical than one expects prose to be; whole paragraphs are suddenly discovered to be in blank verse. Yet, when all this is said, the prose remains a triumph of style, as much, in its totally different way, as Hemingway's is.

The best analysis I know of Wolfe's style is Malcolm Cowley's, who says: 'His writing was a sort of chant, like the declamation of a Homeric bard'; and notes that the patterns or devices so easily to be picked out in Wolfe's prose'—cadence, metre, rhyme, assonance, refrains—are those into which the language naturally falls when one is trying to speak or write it passionately and torrentially'. And this style Wolfe was using as a bard or even as an epic poet: to enlarge and elevate his subject-matter and to maintain the heroic tone. It is this sustained tone that gives Wolfe's work its unity. Its power and head-long impetuous rush are such as to enable it to bear on its surface any amount of absurdity or improbability. One chooses almost at random:

Around him lay the village; beyond, the ugly rolling land, sparse with cheap farmhouses; beyond all this, America—more land, more wooden houses, more towns, hard and raw and ugly. He was reading Euripides, and all around him a world of black and white was eating fried food. He was reading of ancient sorceries and old ghosts, but did an old ghost ever come to haunt this land? The ghost of Hamlet's Father, in Connecticut,

> ... I am thy father's spirit,
> Doomed for a certain term to walk the night
> Between Bloomington and Portland, Maine.

He felt suddenly the devastating impermanence of the nation. Only the earth endured—the gigantic American earth, bearing upon its awful breast a world of flimsy rickets. Only the earth endured—this broad terrific earth that had no ghosts to haunt it. Stogged in the desert, half-broken and overthrown, among the columns of lost temples strewn, there was no ruined image of Menkaura, there was no alabaster head of Akhnaton. Nothing had been done in stone. Only this earth endured, upon whose lovely breast he read Euripides. Within its hills he had been held a prisoner; upon its plain he walked, alone, a stranger.

O God! O God! We have been an exile in another land and a stranger in our own. The mountains were our masters: they went home to our eyes and our heart before we came to five. Whatever we can do or say must be forever hillbound. Our senses have been fed by our terrific land; our blood has learned to run to the imperial pulse of America which, leaving, we can never lose and never forget. We walked along a road in Cumberland, and stooped, because the sky hung down so low; and when we ran away from London, we went by little rivers in a land just big enough. And nowhere that we went was far: the earth and the sky were close and near. And the old hunger returned—the terrible and obscure hunger that haunts and hurts Americans, and that makes us exiles at home and strangers wherever we go.

That is from *Look Homeward, Angel*. Wolfe, one feels, could have kept it up for ever. No doubt it is very adolescent, alike in its content and the manner of its rendering. But if this is so it is adolescence raised to genius, and the adolescence is a specifically American adolescence. Eugene passes without warning from 'he' to 'we'; the individual experience becomes as it were the American experience. Eugene becomes a figure of American myth. He contains the whole novel, and in a sense he contains within himself universal references.

Such passages probably need to be read in adolescence if they are truly to intoxicate. Re-reading Wolfe in later life, one will almost inevitably tend to skip them. But one also discovers qualities in him perhaps missed before, qualities to which considerations of adolescence are quite irrelevant and which place him, at any rate intermittently, among the great novelists. These are most evident in episodes in which Eugene is only one actor among many or is peripheral to the action. Then Wolfe is seen as a wonderful observer and a wonderful re-creator of what he has observed. One remembers the two death scenes in *Look Homeward, Angel*, those of Eugene's father and of his brother Ben. They have a naked intensity of pity and horror in which nothing is burked and which takes in and as it were recapitulates the long squalid history of rancour, hatred and mutual persecution that is the lot of the Gant family. The miracle is that all this is expressed—and also the grief. In these confrontations of death Wolfe does attain objectivity; it is as though he really is seeing his characters *sub specie aeternitatis*. As Pamela Hansford Johnson says in her critical study of Wolfe: '*Dixieland* is the sad house of King Admetus, and those that stand within it have the dignity of immortals.'

Or, in an entirely different mode, there is the whole long Paris episode in *Of Time and the River* recounting Eugene's mystified friendship with the doomed brilliant homosexual Starwick—but the point, of course, is that it takes him a very long time to realize that Starwick is homosexual—and with the two Boston women, Elinor and Ann, whom he sponges on and who, emotionally, sponge on him. These are brilliantly rendered studies in corruption, the more effective because by their side Eugene appears and feels himself to be the lumbering, blundering provincial innocent. The doomed homosexual who has seen through and passed beyond everything is one of the most familiar figures in modern fiction and, one feels, a sentimental conception. What is striking here is that Wolfe succeeds in projecting him as genuinely tragic; while, without overwriting, without moral comment, without, it almost seems, being aware that he is doing so, he reveals Elinor as a monster of rapacity and revenge possessed of almost infinite capacity for cruelty. What comes beautifully through is the horror of the situation; it has a chill, nightmare quality, which makes absolutely right Eugene's reaction:

What was wrong with life? What got into people such as these to taint their essential quality, to twist and mutilate their genuine and higher purposes? What were these perverse and evil demons of cruelty and destructiveness, or anguish, error, and confusion that got into them, that seemed to goad them on, with a wicked and ruinous obstinacy, deliberately to do the things they did not want to do—the things that were so shamefully unworthy of their true character and their real desire?

It is 'inexplicable', and in a way it is Gant's—or Wolfe's—recognition of this that gives the whole long episode its tragic dignity.

It is here that Wolfe's real greatness lies; not in his 'bigness', the obvious Whitmanesque nature of his genius, the endless fury of his search for something impossible of definition, the rhetoric piled on rhetoric, the more than lifesize gestures of repudiation, but in his ability to face the horror and the evil of life and to render it without flinching, stoically to accept it even though it is 'inexplicable'.

[8]

WOLFE HAD a great contempt for what he called the 'European and fancy', such as, more than once in his career, the fiction of Thornton Wilder has appeared to many of his critics. It was indeed the charge, expressed rather more precisely, made against him by the Communist critic and short story writer Michael Gold in 'Wilder: Prophet of the Genteel Christ', which appeared in *The New Republic* in October, 1930. A survey of Wilder's work to that date, the three novels *The Cabala* (1926), *The Bridge of San Luis Rey* (1927) and *The Woman of Andros* (1930), and the collection of plays *The Angel that Troubled the Waters*, it is, on the face of it, a devastating attack, in which Wilder is presented as 'the poet of the genteel bourgeoisie', the prophet of 'that newly fashionable religion that centres around Jesus Christ, the First British Gentleman'. There is much in it with which one has to agree. Neither the novel that made Wilder's reputation, *The Bridge of San Luis Rey*, set in Peru in 1714, nor *The Woman of Andros*, set in the Greek island of Andros some years before the birth of Christ, is very rewarding now. In them, with their weary elegance of style, which suggests the tail-end of the nineties, Gold's contemptuous dismissal of Wilder as 'this Emily Post of culture' seems justified.

But this is not the whole truth about Wilder, as may be seen if we go back to his first novel, *The Cabala*. It relates the encounters experienced by an American postgraduate student with the members of the old aristocracy of Rome called the Cabala, 'a group of people', as another American describes them, 'losing sleep over a host of notions that the rest of the world has outgrown several centuries ago: one duchess's right to enter a door before another; the word order in a dogma of the Church; the divine right of kings, especially of Bourbons'. Wilder's hero, Samuele as the members of the Cabala nickname him, is fascinated by them; he views them, as Gold says, 'with tender irony'. But Gold completely fails to take the point of the novel. Wilder himself has called the setting of his novel 'the purely fantastic twentieth-century Rome', and I suspect he is using the word 'fantastic' in its strict sense. *The Cabala* is a fable, in terms of fantasy, about the necessity, as James saw it, of the Americans' 'fighting against a superstitious valuation of Europe'. The fable is none the less serious for being played out throughout in terms of fantasy. Wilder's Rome is not simply the Rome of today; it is Rome, as it were, in time, one might say the educated American's—or Englishman's—idea of Rome. In the first chapter Samuele is taken to meet a young English poet dying in poverty: the poet is the almost unknown Keats of 1821, though the time is a century later. So it comes as no jarring shock to discover at the end of the book, though they are rendered with exactitude as figures of the present, that the members of the Cabala are the pagan gods of Rome shrunken and grown ineffective through twenty centuries of Christianity.

But this is not the end. Sailing out of Naples for the United States, Samuele cannot sleep for wondering why he is not more reluctant to leave Europe. He invokes Virgil, who appears to him and tells him: 'Romes existed before Rome, and when Rome will be a waste there will be Romes after her. Seek out some city that is young. The secret is to make a city, not to rest in it.' And, for good measure, Virgil goes on to tell him what he has heard of New York, that its 'towers have cast a shadow across the sandals of the angels'.

> The shimmering ghost faded before the stars, and the engines beneath me pounded eagerly towards the new world and the last and greatest of all cities.

That is the novel's concluding paragraph. Despite its wit and charm, the limpidity and grace of its style, the meaning of *The Cabala* could not be more plain. In the most elegant way, Europe is rejected; New York is the modern Rome, the heir of the ages.

The Cabala seems to me to be a completely successful instance of the novel as fable, and it is successful because the fantasy is handled with such tact that it never breaks the surface realism, it is indeed incorporated in it, carried by it. It is, admittedly, very literary; Wilder's whole career, as novelist and dramatist alike, shows that he approaches life from literature; but this does not necessarily invalidate his judgments on life. Admittedly, too, it took Wilder some time to come round to a treatment of the United States in fiction. 'Let Mr Wilder', runs the last paragraph of Gold's denunciation, 'write a book about modern America. We predict it will reveal all his fundamental silliness and superficiality, now hidden under a Greek chlamys.' *Heaven's My Destination* appeared in 1934 and what it revealed was not Wilder's silliness and superficiality but Gold's.

Heaven's My Destination is a strictly contemporary novel set in the South West and Middle West of the depression years, and the first thing that must strike one about it is that here Wilder is competing, more than successfully, with such a novelist as Sinclair Lewis on his home ground. The excellence of the writing might, perhaps, be taken for granted, but not the ease and skill with which Wilder has caught the small towns and small hotels and 'travelling men' of rural America or the comedy with which he displays them. At the same time, he is doing something much beyond Lewis: he is attempting the portrait of a good man, a 'holy fool'. George Brush is a traveller in school textbooks, a Fundamentalist Christian under the influence of Gandhi, who is determined at all costs to lead the Christian life, a course of action that leads him into trouble wherever he goes. When we first meet him he is offending hotel-keepers by his practice of scribbling texts on the virgin blotting paper on public writing desks. He is constantly being arrested, for riding in a Jim Crow car, on one occasion for withdrawing his savings from a bank on the verge of bankruptcy and refusing to take the interest, which he regards as immoral. He is insulted, beaten up, for the logic of his goodness scandalizes all who come in contact with him; the same logic of his goodness makes him impervious to argument or to appeals to common sense:

'Buddy', said Blodgett, 'why did you say that it made you nervous to get raises?'

'Because hardly anybody else's getting raises these days. I think everybody ought to be hit by the depression equally. You see?'

Mrs McCoy said drily: 'Sure, I see. Your ideas aren't the same as other people's, are they?'

'No', said Brush, 'I should think not. I didn't put myself through college for four years and go through a difficult religious conversion in order to have ideas like other people's.'

In the end, Brush does change; or rather, his ideas change. He loses his religious faith and confidence in himself; all his efforts, it seems, lead only to people hating him. But faith in himself is restored, though not his Fundamentalism, by an heirloom from a man he has never met, a Roman Catholic priest named Father Paszieski, who, we are to understand, has been as dedicated to goodness as Brush and who has recognized Brush's vocation. We leave him once again embarked on the pursuit of the good life, with all the misunderstandings and scandalizing of the community it entails.

Brush is portrayed with humour and affection; he is a comic figure; but he is all the same the touchstone by which American society and mores are judged. One of his not-remote ancestors, of course, is Fielding's Parson Adams, and the novel is probably the most successful attempt at the picaresque in the eighteenth-century sense our time has seen. The invention is unflagging and the satire, which is never bitter, always hits its mark. In characters and scenes alike, one feels that the whole of rural America has been encompassed. It was a sad thing for American fiction when Wilder deserted it for the drama.

Another sad defection from the writing of fiction has been Glenway Wescott's, whose main theme has been what might be called the Mid-Western version of the American's complex fate. For the greater part of the thirties Wescott was an expatriate, living in France, but, on the evidence of his fiction, still unable to escape from Wisconsin, his native state, which seems at times almost as much a state of mind as a place. The title of his collection of short stories, *Goodbye, Wisconsin* (1928), is ironical, or at best the expression of a wistful dream. The image of Wisconsin that appears in these stories is in many respects a literary equivalent of the Iowa painter Grant Wood's 'American Gothic'; Mid-Westerners, or those sufficiently emancipated to have got away from the Mid-West, are seen by Wescott as 'a sort of vagrant chosen people like the Jews'. The dream of the narrator of the title story is that one day he may escape from the Middle West into a style of 'rapid grace for the eye rather than sonority for the ear, in accordance with the ebb and flow of sensation rather than with intellectual habits, and out of which myself, with my origins and my prejudices and my Wisconsin, will seem to have disappeared'.

In his first novel, *The Apple of the Eye* (1924), Wescott had as it were defined Wisconsin, with the grim conformity of its repressive puritanism. It is part of Wescott's talent that he sees the beauty of puritanism: 'To live in the spirit instead of the flesh . . . Puritanism appeals to the imagination, but it makes people sick.' *The Apple of the Eye* is a study of puritanism and its consequences.

Wescott's strength as a novelist lies in his very ambivalence towards his subject, and in his finest novel, *The Grandmothers* (1927), it appears in depth and at length and with a nostalgia that is always controlled. The action flows between the present and the past; the novel is a discovery of the past, a coming to terms with it. It is in essence a young intellectual's imaginative reconstruction of the lives of his grandparents and their families and relations, pioneers in the opening up of Wisconsin in the middle years of last century. In a way, it is history become myth, for very early on in the novel we meet Alwyn Tower, the young man who re-creates the past, sitting on a balcony above a French Mediterranean harbour with drunken sailors from an American warship quarrelling below, re-reading an essay he had written as a boy of nineteen on what he has found out about his family, 'as it were, a short biography of America'. He is, in other words, considering what it means to be an American.

> Staring into the dusky Mediterranean, he thought of the Tower stories, the lives of his mother's parents, Ira and Ursula Duff, of pitiful, red-headed Flora, his uncles, the minister and the deserter, his great-aunt Mary, the adventuress, and all the others . . .
> . . . the best way to explain what they meant would be, quite simply, to tell the stories themselves . . . Stories like a series of question marks; questions which did not require an answer, questions at peace. He was content with their ambiguities, so he knew that they were the end of understanding, or at any rate, the end of trying to understand.

Trying to understand, for his own sake, shadowy men, women, and children . . . And as he thought of their lives, he was surprised by regret (their regret) which weakened and then strengthened his will; regret that the time for laughter and ease, even for him, never seemed to come, while work never came to an end.

So the novel spreads out in the stories of Alwyn's forbears to become a remarkably solid evocation of pioneering life in Wisconsin, a summation of a period and a place. In this novel, which is one of the neglected masterpieces of American twenties fiction, Wescott achieves his dream of a style of 'rapid grace for the eye . . . in accordance with the ebb and flow of sensation rather than with intellectual habits', out of which he himself has disappeared.

THE SOUTHERN NOVEL
BETWEEN THE WARS

[1]

> No author can conceive of the difficulty of writing a romance about a country where there is no shadow, no antiquity, no mystery, no picturesque and gloomy wrong, nor anything but a commonplace prosperity, as is happily the case with my dear native land.

THE MODERN reader may well feel that Hawthorne was worrying in undue haste. He died while the Civil War was in progress: for the South, the War and the Reconstruction were to provide quite as much shadow, mystery, picturesque and gloomy wrong as any man of letters could reasonably demand.

But there was to be more to it even than this. According to the South's image of its own past, the result of the War was the destruction, wrought with unparalleled suddenness and vindictiveness, of a civilization different from and superior to that of the North, a civilization consciously aristocratic that opposed to the bourgeois commercial values of the North the notions of honour and the gentleman. The image is seen in all its fullblown magnolia-flower splendour in a sequence of best-selling novels and the films based on them, of which Stark Young's *So Red the Rose* and Margaret Mitchell's *Gone with the Wind* are obvious instances. Significantly, both these novels belong to the thirties, for the image is a recent one. Its historical accuracy is another matter, as W. J. Cash shows in his *The Mind of the South*. Generally the civilization of the Old South was little to boast about: it was complacent, stagnant, uncreative, intensely snobbish. But the fantastic courage of its soldiers during the War and the misery and humiliation that followed, these were real. And in any event, a country's image of itself, no matter how far it departs from objective truth, is a fact of prime importance about the country.

The image is very much a literary one. It was created largely by the 'Fugitives' group of poets and critics at Vanderbilt University, Nashville, Tennessee, the best known of whom are John Crowe Ransom, Allen Tate and Robert Penn Warren. It has been defined by Tate as the 'image of the past in the present: the pervasive Southern subject of our time'.

It was the subject a novelist rather older than the 'Fugitives' had already made her own: Ellen Glasgow, who was born in Richmond, Virginia, in 1874 and died in that city in 1945, the descendant on her mother's side of a Southern aristocratic family that had settled in the Tidewater in the early sixteen-hundreds and, on her father's, of Scottish-Irish pioneers of Covenanter stock who had settled between the Blue Ridge and the Alleghanies. Her first novel, *The Descendant*, was published as early as 1897 and with it began her life's work, conducted through a score of novels, of critical evaluation of the society in which she had her roots and lived all her life.

Ellen Glasgow saw her novels as falling into three groups, 'Novels of the Commonwealth', 'Novels of the Country' and 'Novels of the City'. In the first, in such novels as *The Battle-Ground* (1902), *Virginia* (1913) and *Life and Gabriella* (1916), she deals with the social history of Virginia in the years before the Civil War and during the War itself, and in novels like *The Voice of the People* (1900) and *The Romance of a Plain Man* (1909), with the reconstruction that followed. The theme of the 'Novels of the Country'—*The Miller of Old Church* (1911), *Barren Ground* (1925) and *Vein of Iron* (1935)—is life among the Scottish-Irish families of the country, 'good people', not 'good families', to use her own distinction. The latter, as they existed in the years immediately before and after the first world war, form the material of her 'Novels of the City', the three comedies of manners, *The Romantic Comedians* (1926), *They Stooped to Folly* (1929) and *The Sheltered Life* (1932), all set in Richmond, called Queenborough in the books.

But however Ellen Glasgow's novels are classified, certain constant preoccupations run through them all. She is concerned all the time with the consequences for the South of its fixation upon its past and of its chivalric code, especially as it affects the Southern Lady. In retrospect, certain words and phrases seem to occur repeatedly in her work almost as key-words to it—'fortitude' and the 'streak' or 'vein of iron'—and indicate not only her prescription for the South's curing of its own ills but her attitude towards life's ill generally. Sceptical, pessimistic, stoical, she sees life and frustration almost as synonymous. Her sense of the human condition seems to be summed up by a recurring situation in her fiction, that of true love experienced and then lost early in life and followed by the conscious acceptance of the second best. In this emphasis on frustration as a law of life she is in part at one with her literary generation, which was that of Dreiser and Bennett. She shared the same influences of Darwin and Huxley, reinforced for her by the Calvinism in which she was brought up, though intellectually she repudiated it. But the emphasis on frustration, especially as exemplified in the recurring situation of early love that never fulfils its promises, went beyond the purely literary, and to explain it one is forced back on some such phrase as that Richard Chase applies to her—'feminine narcissism'.

She is at her most brilliant in the 'Novels of the City', particularly in *The Romantic Comedians*. Her powers of wit, epigram and irony, her intellectual insight into self-deception and her sense of the comedy implicit in it make it not absurd to see her as belonging to the same school as Jane Austen, Meredith and Forster, even though she is not quite of their order. The quality and tone of *The Romantic Comedians* are indicated in its first paragraphs:

> For thirty-six years Judge Gamaliel Bland Honeywell had endured the double-edged bliss of a perfect marriage; but it seemed to him on this sparkling Easter Sunday, that he had lived those years with a stranger. After twelve months of loneliness, one impulse of vital magic had obliterated the past. As he arranged his tribute of lilies over Cordelia's grave, he tried with all the strength of his decorous will to remember her features and mourn her as sincerely as she deserved.
>
> 'I am a bird with a broken wing', he sighed to himself, as he had sighed so often in other ears since the day of his bereavement. And while this classic metaphor was still on his lips, he felt an odd palpitation within the suave Virginian depths of his being, where his broken wing was helplessly trying to flutter.

In his capacity for self-deception, Judge Honeywell, 'who could recite the Apostles' Creed so long as he was not required to practise the Sermon on the Mount, and could countenance Evolution until it threatened the image of its Maker', is a considerable comic creation. The novel unfolds the Judge's infatuation with and marriage to a poor but beautiful young woman much less than half his age, a marriage that ends in his being cuckolded and abandoned. It uses, in other words, the traditional material of artificial comedy, but the treatment of it is not quite what might be expected. The Judge's dreams of romantic love are given a genuine lyrical quality that is not destroyed by the irony with which they are presented. His dreams of what might be called the fairy-child are not dissimilar in kind from those of Lewis's Babbitt, but they are much better done, so that, absurd as he may be, the Judge still at the end has a pathos and a dignity.

He is, as it were, an innocent hypocrite, or hypocritical innocent, his hypocrisy that of the society with which he identifies himself and its sexual code, which has ossified into conventions that distort and indeed cripple the personalities of those who accept it. It is in her rendering of the women in this novel that Ellen Glasgow most effectively criticizes the consequences of the code. She does so not only through her portrait of Cordelia, whom we see solely through the Judge's memories of her, and through the presentation of the beautiful, stately spinster Amanda, whom the judge has once loved and still regards as a goddess and who has remained unmarried because of her love for him, but also through the foils to these, his second wife Annabel, his emancipated twin sister Edmona, and above all through Annabel's widowed mother, Mrs Upchurch, a delightful comic creation and, because of her poverty and the necessity to keep respectability alive at all costs, the touchstone by which the pretensions of the code are tested in harsh actuality.

Good as these 'Novels of the City' are, Ellen Glasgow's major achievement and her most sustained criticism of the South lie in the 'Novels of the Country', *Barren Ground* and the first half of *Vein of Iron*, the first half because of the remarkable character of Grandmother Fincastle, who dominates it and who sums up in herself and in her memories of her ancestors the history of the Scottish-Irish dissenters who won and settled the mountains of Virginia. Through her, *Vein of Iron* spans the history of the Commonwealth from its beginnings until the economic depression of the thirties.

It is the portrait of Grandmother Fincastle that gives the novel its real distinction; when she dies much of its interest departs. The quality of indomitability that is hers and that also goes to her making is triumphant throughout *Barren Ground*, which is in essence the story of Dorinda Oakley, a farmer's daughter, in her lifelong struggle to conquer her environment. The pervading symbol in the novel is the broomsedge that is everywhere spreading over what was once good farmland but is falling out of cultivation because of the aftermath of the Civil War and the Reconstruction, the breakdown of the traditional social system, the poverty and ignorance of the people, and also—a criticism Ellen Glasgow makes again and again—what she considers the engrained Southern habit of 'slighting' work.

Dorinda, the daughter of a poverty-stricken farming family whose only assets are a dumb patience and the capacity to endure, is abandoned, pregnant, on the eve of her marriage by her lover Jason Greylock, a young doctor whose will has been broken by his sadistic father and who is forced into a shot-gun wedding with another girl. Dorinda's reaction to her plight is characteristic:

> Yes, whatever happened, she resolved passionately, no man was going to spoil her life! She could live without Jason; she could live without any man. The shadows of her great-aunts, Dorinda and Abigail, demented victims of love, stretched, black and sinister, across the generations. In her recoil from the hereditary frailty, she revolted, with characteristic energy, to the opposite extreme of frigid disdain.

Dorinda runs away to New York, loses her baby, and with luck that is rather too good to be wholly convincing, falls into a situation which allows her opportunity to study scientific farming and, with money borrowed from her benefactors, returns to Virginia to take over the family farm. With single-minded energy and intelligence she prevails, pushing back the broomsedge, bringing back lost land to fertility again, selling her milk and butter in Washington; and we leave her not only with the shattered Jason, dying from drink, taken almost contemptuously into her care, but with his ancestral land hers also, to be rescued in their turn from the wilderness into which they had lapsed.

Barren Ground is a most powerful evocation of stoical courage and determination—and also of a country sunk into decay. It exists in its own right as a major novel, but, along with *Vein of Iron*, it has also an adventitious value for readers outside the South, in that it makes explicit much that is implicit and often mysterious in the work of other Southern novelists, Faulkner in particular. I am thinking especially of the picture of degeneracy it gives, of imbecility as a result of generations of inbreeding. Ellen Glasgow gives us the knowledge of the South, its history and people that Faulkner assumes in us.

In fiction for the past thirty years the South has meant primarily William Faulkner, because it is in his novels and stories that the sense of the past in the present has been most comprehensively embodied, and this despite faults that would have sunk a lesser writer without trace. No novelist ever had less mercy on his readers. He can be obscure to the point of opacity. Sentences four pages long, containing parentheses within parentheses, are not rare. Words pile up like a river in flood and bear with them, like a river in flood, a mass of debris. Yet his genius is such as to surmount these faults.

What is Faulkner's achievement? Not simply, great though it is, the creation of his world, his imaginary Yocnapatawpha County, Mississippi, though it is true that the novels and stories set outside it are generally failures. But to concentrate on Yocnapatawpha County, to take the novels and stories as the source-books of its history, sociology and folklore, is to see Faulkner wrong. Faulkner was not a Southern Balzac, and Yocnapatawpha County is very evidently not Barsetshire. It is what he did with Yocnapatawpha County that matters; and what this is may be shown, perhaps, by contrast with another Southern novel, Caroline Gordon's *None Shall Look Back* (1937).

None Shall Look Back is perhaps the most austere and uncompromising novel about the Civil War that we possess. Its mood is summed up in the words of one of the characters, Cally, when she says: 'There's just two kinds of people in the world, those that'll fight for what they think right and those that don't think anything is worth fighting for.' The only survivors in *None Shall Look Back* are the commercially minded. This is a heroic novel in the strict sense. It contains no consideration of the causes of the War, no criticism of the warring parties, no analysis of the motives of those engaged in the action. It is haunted by images and premonitions of death; its theme is duty and the heroic attitude in the face of death and defeat. Nothing is burked: the battle-scenes are brilliantly done, at the level almost of those in *The Red Badge of Courage*; and the horrors, the devastation and famine the war brings in its wake, are chillingly rendered.

To the outsider, *None Shall Look Back* may appear even fanatical in its author's complete acceptance of the image of the South in its antebellum period. And the image is established right away, in the first chapters, with the description of the gathering of the Allard family at Pleasant Grove for Fontaine Allard's birthday; the image of a patriarchal, feudal society, not sophisticated, but with a simple elegance and a sense of *noblesse oblige* in which duties balance rights. Throughout the novel an aristocratic life-style is beautifully conveyed. Yet the outsider, it seems to me, must have his reservations. Despite the complete absence of high-falutin', of heroics as distinct from heroism, one cannot help wondering whether life has ever been lived at the constantly heroic pitch described in this novel. And beyond this question lies another. Isn't the whole conception of life as described in *None Shall Look Back* a literary abstraction? In retrospect, the characters in this novel seem static, fixed in formal gestures, like the figures on a vase.

Then, in a curious way, the slaves, the Negroes, are hardly present in the book at all. Apart from the faithful old Negro butler, Uncle Winston, the slaves are there to be looked after and done good to. But they are mindless, almost, as animals, shiftless and ungrateful. When the Federal troops occupy Clarkesville they depart from Pleasant Grove 'in great haste'. 'It seemed to her', Lucy Allard thinks, 'that the negroes, furtive and for ever alien race, had got wind of some disaster which as yet was only approaching. "Yes", she thought, "we are sinking, sinking; and they know it and have deserted us."' The Allards are 'good' to their slaves; they are believed to spoil them. They are deserted just the same. So much for the image of the South in its feudal aspect.

Here, I suspect unwittingly, Caroline Gordon exposes the moral corruption that was fundamental to Southern society, the negation of human rights on which it was based. But no character in the novel is even aware of this, and certainly Caroline Gordon never considers through her characters why the Negroes should be 'furtive and for ever alien' or why, indeed, loyalty should be expected of them. Admirable human beings as Caroline Gordon's characters on the whole are, they are wholly creatures of convention, capable of the heroic but not of the tragic. They are doomed. Much of the strength of *None Shall Look Back* comes from the sense of this. It makes the novel a heroic story—but nothing more.

Faulkner's treatment of the South is infinitely more complex. His fiction, one feels, is rooted almost in the folk-memory, not the product of a literary abstraction. It makes him the heir not only of the heroic image of the South but also of something one looks for in vain in the novels that concentrate solely on the heroic: the humour of the South, at its simplest the tall story. Though as a novelist he is in debt to the great Europeans, for much of his content and his characteristic use of it he is in the direct line of descent from Longstreet and Twain. He is a master of the vernacular and a superb comic writer, undilutedly so in *The Hamlet*. It is a side of Faulkner's genius too often neglected. It is intermittent, sometimes inhibited altogether, but never far away. It is the obverse of his preoccupation with the doomed, the bizarre and what Malcolm Cowley has called the tradition of psychological horror in American writing. It is, in the end, the index of Faulkner's humanity.

Faulkner's greatest achievement came relatively early in his career: a handful of short stories and the novels *The Sound and the Fury* (1929), *As I Lay Dying* (1930), *Light in August* (1932) and *Absalom, Absalom!* (1936), with *The Hamlet* (1940) representing a more relaxed Faulkner. It is in these that Quentin Compson's answer to his Canadian roommate's question reverberates most intensely: '"Why do you hate the South?" "I don't hate it", Quentin said quickly, at once, immediately; "I don't hate it", he said. *I don't hate it,* he thought, panting in the cold air, the iron New England dark; *I don't. I don't. I don't! I don't hate it! I don't hate it!'* Quentin Compson is not Faulkner, yet it is difficult not to make the reference to Faulkner himself, so intense, so passionate, is Quentin's reaction to Shreve's question. He doesn't hate the South, for hate, in Shreve's terms, is too simple a word. But hate, as we know, is the other face of love; and in Quentin's—and Faulkner's—attitude to the South both love and hate—love-hate—are involved. The relation of Quentin to the South is that of microcosm to macrocosm; if he could solve the riddle of the South he could solve the riddle of himself. It is in these novels that Faulkner most heroically grapples with the fate and the fatality of being a Southerner.

In the later novels the tension has slackened because, in one sense at least, the riddle has been solved; and the greater degree of explicitness means a descent from the tragic level. Yet just because of this, a late novel like *Intruder in the Dust* (1948) offers a convenient way into Faulkner's world, not only because of the direct statement it contains of his values ('Some things you must always be unable to bear. Some things you must never stop refusing to bear. Injustice and outrage and dishonour and shame.') but also because it expresses his conception of history and of time:

It's all now you see. Yesterday won't be over until tomorrow and tomorrow began ten thousand years ago. For every Southern boy fourteen years old, not once but whenever he wants it, there is the instant when it's still not two o'clock on that July afternoon in 1863, the brigades are in position behind the rail fence, the guns are laid and ready in the woods and the furled flags are already loosened to break and Pickett himself with his long oiled ringlets and his hat in one hand probably and his sword in the other looking up at the hills waiting for Longstreet to give the word and it's all in the balance, it hasn't happened yet, it hasn't even begun yet but it not only hasn't begun yet but there is still time for it not to begin against that position . . .

The prose, incidentally, is characteristic, and what is being said explains the manner in which it is said—the headlong, under-punctuated sentences, the repetitions, the apparently uncouth piling up of synonymous expressions. Faulkner's aim is to show, in the very texture of his writing, the simultaneity of past and present.

He is attempting something akin to what Joyce was doing in *Ulysses* and indeed his first major novel, *The Sound and the Fury*, would not have been possible except for Joyce; which is not to say that it is anything like a pastiche of Joyce. Its theme is the degeneration of a Southern family, the Compsons, who have been prominent in Jefferson, Mississippi, since before the days of the Civil War. But it is scarcely possible to speak of theme as divorced from the form of the novel. *The Sound and the Fury* is best approached in the simplest and most literal way, by a look at the title. It is, of course, from Macbeth's 'She should have died hereafter' speech: life

is a tale
Told by an idiot, full of sound and fury,
Signifying nothing.

The Sound and the Fury is presented quite literally, in its beginnings at any rate, as a tale told by an idiot, Benjy Compson; while the character for whom life may be said to seem nothing more than sound and fury, his brother Quentin, kills himself in order to escape from time, the time that is figured earlier in Macbeth's speech in the words 'Tomorrow, and tomorrow, and tomorrow'.

The novel is composed of four parts, each of which narrates the happenings of a single day; the sequence is April 7, 1928, June 2, 1910, April 6, 1928, April 8, 1928. In the first part we are within the mind of the idiot Benjy, a congenital imbecile of thirty-three, deaf and dumb, whose development has not gone beyond babyhood. Benjy, as the stream of his sensations shows, exists outside time; he lives in a continuous present, in which what happens at the moment and what has happened in the past exist simultaneously, bound each to each by simple association. Thus, when the novel opens he is running along the fence that bounds the golf course which was formerly the Compsons' pasture: 'Through the fence, between the curling flower spaces, I could see them hitting.' The first words of the second paragraph make it plain that it is a golf course he is haunting and later we realize why: Caddie was the childish name of his beloved sister Candace. Benjy's mind works by association; and here Faulkner has helped us by italicizing the associative words and sentences that switch Benjy's mind into the past. Benjy, for all his idiocy, indeed because of it, emerges as a terrifyingly human figure. The isolation that is every human being's is intensified for Benjy by his inarticulateness, but it is still a *human* isolation:

> 'They came on. I opened the gate and they stopped, turning. I was trying to say, and I caught her, trying to say, and she screamed and I was trying to say and trying and the bright shapes began to stop and I tried to get out. I tried to get it off my face, but the bright shapes were going away. They were going up the hill to where it fell away and I tried to cry. But when I breathed in, I couldn't breathe out again to cry, and I tried to keep from falling off the hill into the bright, whirling shapes.'

'I was trying to say, and I caught her, trying to say, and she screamed and I was trying to say': here, in an extreme form, is the general human situation, the attempt to communicate and the failure to do so.

The matter of Benjy's drivellings is illuminated by the second part, which takes us back eighteen years to Quentin Compson's last day as a Harvard undergraduate and his last day on earth. It is in Quentin that the doom of the Compsons comes to consciousness. Through his soliloquies we learn of the family circumstances; of the drunken self-pity of his father, a lawyer who does not practise, a defeated Hamlet who consoles himself with the bottle, the Latin poets and much self-justifying Southern rhetoric; of his mother, who has retreated into illness and family pride; of his sister Candace who, pregnant, has been married off to a man who is not the father of her child. We learn how the Compson pasture has been sold in order that Quentin may go to Harvard; above all, we learn of his furious love for Candace, his shame

at her disgrace, and his furious attempts to convince himself and his
father that he has committed incest with her.

Quentin is the least successfully realized character in the novel.
What reality he has in *The Sound and the Fury* (and one has to put it
like this because he is also the centre of consciousness of *Absalom,
Absalom!*) he takes from the characters about him and the vividness of
the scenes in which he takes part, whether in memory or experienced
on June 2, 1910, the day of his suicide.

Jason Compson, who exposes himself in all his meanness and
vulgarity in the third part of the novel, is a superb comic creation. As
much as Benjy, whom he is planning to have put away in the state
mental hospital, he represents the final degeneration of the Compsons,
the end of all their illusions of grandeur. Objectively, there is much
right on his side. He has recognized the Compson illusions for what
they are. He knows that if the Compsons are to survive it will be by his
efforts alone. He is a realist; but he is also, as his every utterance shows
both in content and expression, graceless, mean-spirited, money-
grubbing, irredeemably vulgar. The whole Jason section is a triumph
of vernacular writing, and as we follow Jason in his daily round of
meannesses the story of the Compsons further unfolds.

In the fourth section, which is straight narration, the novel's area of
reference expands. Until now, the novel has been deliberately claustrophobic: we have been imprisoned within the consciousness first of the
idiot Benjy, then of Quentin, then of Jason. In this last section we break
out, as it were, into the open; and now the Negroes of the Compson
household come into their own. It is in Dilsey, the old cook and the
mainstay of the Compson family, and her children that the human
values of the novel reside. Besides acting as a chorus to the action,
Dilsey by her very presence in the novel distances it and sets the tragic
degeneration of the Compsons in perspective.

Jason Compson, one might say, is an honorary Snopes, as we meet
them in *The Hamlet*: that is one aspect of Compson degeneracy. The
Snopeses, in Faulkner's world, stand for all that is most alien and opposed to the aristocratic values of the Old South. Faulkner's contempt
for them is undisguised; and since they are poor-whites it is sometimes
assumed that Faulkner holds all poor-whites in contempt. This is not
so at all, and if proof were needed *As I Lay Dying* would be enough.
The 'I' of the title is Addie Bundren, the wife of Anse Bundren, a
hill-farmer of Yocnapatawpha County. The novel, on one level at any

rate—its most successful—describes a journey: the journey the Bundren family make, over almost impassable roads and across flooded rivers, to take Addie Bundren's corpse—for she is dead before the immediate action of the novel begins—for burial in Jefferson. It is, admittedly, macabre comedy, shirking nothing of the horrors, for example, of putrescence: its humour is that of men and women very close to the earth. The journey is made because Anse has promised Addie that he will bury her in Jefferson. True, the fulfilment of the promise is not everything. The daughter, Dewey Dell, is pregnant, and getting to Jefferson means for her the possibility of securing an abortion. For Anse, too, Jefferson offers the prospect of acquiring a new set of false teeth—and also, as it turns out, a new wife. But the promise is the main thing; the other reasons for going to Jefferson are entirely subsidiary and represent rather the peasant wish to take every advantage of a journey that has to be made anyway. And in its rendering of the fulfilment, against all odds, of an obligation *As I Lay Dying* is a celebration of piety both familial and natural.

There is an obvious contrast with the comedy of another Southern writer, Erskine Caldwell, a writer all too easy to dismiss because his later work consists largely of self-parody. But an early novel like *God's Little Acre* (1933) deserves to be taken seriously. Like Faulkner's, the characters are poor whites, farmers existing on the subsistence level. But Caldwell is a social critic in a more obvious and cruder sense than Faulkner: his characters are victims of a social system that has dehumanized them to such an extent that they are scarcely human beings at all. 'There was a mean trick played on us somewhere. God put us in the bodies of animals and tried to make us act like people.' The words are Ty Ty's, and the comment is at least partly true: Caldwell's characters are animals in their complete subjugation to sex, and in this are like the very poor everywhere. Sex is what the poor still have when they have nothing else. Sex apart, the characters of *God's Little Acre* are not even animals: they are mindless automata, acting each in his specific way because he cannot do otherwise. They are the puppets of abstract lusts, characters of imbecile simplicity. So Ty Ty obsessionally digs for gold and, as has been pointed out, if he found it he would not know what to do with it. Similarly, Pluto collects his votes; and the end is really of no consequence, action—the one limited, specific, obsessive action—is purposeless.

The comedy arises, I suppose, from the fact that, all the same, the characters are human. Caldwell's is the comedy of degradation, and it is probably the most squalid comedy that has ever been written. Caldwell creates a world in which human dignity does not exist, in which there are neither human rights nor human obligations; and, in *God's Little Acre*, it is horribly funny. And limited though Caldwell is as a writer, he is not as limited as all that. 'If, in *God's Little Acre*, a man should walk on the scene and offer to buy dead souls of negroes, would the reader be surprised?' The question is Robert Hazel's, in *Southern Renascence: The Literature of The Modern South*, and it is surely right. Caldwell is the poor white's Gogol.

The contrast between the two novelists needs no further stressing, but it does help to define the nature of Faulkner's art and genius. And again, so far as the character with whom the novel opens is concerned, it is a natural transition from Caldwell to *Light in August*. For Lena, too, is a poor-white girl; heavily pregnant, carrying her shoes in her hand, she is making a journey, mainly on foot but sometimes by passing wagon, to find her lover, Lucas Burch, who all the people she meets and she confides in know, as we the readers know, has run out on her and will never marry her. She is a figure at once comic, pathetic and—because of her faith and innocence—of great human dignity. This first chapter of *Light in August* is a splendid example of how simply and directly Faulkner can write when he wants to. And though the novel is only partly Lena's story, since she is there at the beginning and the end she enfolds and distances the more sombre main story, sets it in perspective, fulfilling a function similar to Dilsey's in *The Sound and the Fury*. She is a symbol of what endures, of common humanity, of life that goes on, a symbol not only in herself but also as the bearer of new life.

Her arrival in Jefferson coincides with the pursuit of a murderer, a bootlegger named Joe Christmas. Faulkner introduces us to Christmas by a process of indirection, with all the other principal characters on stage before he appears. His history is narrated in flashback against the background of Lena and also against that of Hightower, whose story is the third panel of what has been seen as a triptych. Christmas is that typical figure of American fiction the isolated man, doomed to isolation and doomed to destruction because of his isolation. His life is the quest for an identity he can never find. He is, to all appearances, white, but his father may have been a mulatto. He does not know, nor, indeed, does the reader. Whichever choice he makes he repudiates violently as soon as made; among Negroes he asserts his whiteness; among whites he insists upon his negritude. And fundamental to this is a desire for recognition as a human being who can have meaningful relations with other human beings. Faulkner isolates the determining incident, the traumatic situation, that governs his life. He is a very small boy in an orphanage. He is in the dietician's room eating the woman's toothpaste; she returns and he hides behind a curtain, from behind which he witnesses her copulation with a doctor. But that is not what interests him: shut off from the world, he is consumed with a lust for the toothpaste, eats too much and is violently sick. The woman is terrified that he will tell what he has seen. He expects to be punished for his wrongdoing, which is eating her toothpaste. He wants to be punished.

> He was waiting to get whipped and then be released. Her voice went on, urgent, tense, fast: 'A whole dollar. See? How much you could buy. Some to eat every day for a week. And next month maybe I'll give you another one.'
> He did not move or speak. He might have been carven, as a large toy: small, still, round headed and round eyed, in overalls. He was still with astonishment, shock, outrage.

So the pattern of his life is set, the repudiation of human contact, the retreat into violence.

As much as Dreiser's Clyde Griffiths in *An American Tragedy*, Christmas is entirely the victim of his environment. He is not a tragic hero, and it is perhaps the reluctant recognition of this that leads Faulkner to attempt to build him up as a symbolic figure. He is of course one in his own right as the embodiment of the fatal rift in a culture in which a man must be either a white man or a black man and not simply a man. But the attempts to suggest a Christ-figure in him are a different matter. It may be that Faulkner means us to take him as no more than a scapegoat, but even so the result is a sentimentalization.

For all that its centre of consciousness is Quentin Compson, *Absalom, Absalom!* is much more closely related to *Light in August* than to *The Sound and the Fury*. It takes up, develops and penetrates to a new depth the twin themes of miscegenation and a man's demand to be recognized as a man. On a first reading the most daunting of Faulkner's novels, the most bewildering, the most tortuous, it is also the grandest in conception and execution, the novel in which Faulkner

most profoundly and completely says what he has to say about the
South and about the human condition.

It recounts the rise and fall of Thomas Sutpen. In a sense, *Absalom,
Absalom!* is a detective story with Quentin Compson as the obsessed
detective, and, in its final version, Sutpen's rise and fall and their
consequences are as it were the creation of Quentin and his Canadian
friend Shreve, his room-mate at Harvard. Quentin learns the main
facts of Colonel Sutpen's life from two sources, an old spinster, Rosa
Coldfield, Sutpen's sister-in-law, and from his father, whose own
father was Sutpen's friend. It is through Rosa Coldfield's version of the
Sutpen story that we first meet Sutpen:

> Out of quiet thunderclap he would abrupt (man-horse-demon)
> upon a scene peaceful and decorous as a schoolprize water color,
> faint sulphur-reek still in hair clothes and beard, with grouped
> behind him his band of wild niggers like beasts half-tamed to
> walk upright like men, in attitudes wild and reposed, and
> manacled among them the French architect with his air grim,
> haggard, and tatter-ran. Immobile, bearded and hand palm-
> lifted the horseman sat; behind him the wild blacks and the
> captive architect huddled quietly, carrying in bloodless paradox
> the shovels and picks and axes of peaceful conquest. Then in the
> long unamaze Quentin seemed to watch them overrun suddenly
> the hundred square miles of tranquil and astonished earth and
> drag house and formal gardens violently out of the soundless
> Nothing and clap them down like cards beneath the up-palm
> immobile and pontific, creating the Sutpen's Hundred, the *Be
> Sutpen's Hundred* like the oldtime *Be Light.*

Miss Coldfield's Sutpen is a figure of myth, the product of an outraged and neurotic imagination. The facts themselves are clear.
Sutpen had arrived in Yocnapatawpha County as it were out of nowhere in June 1833 at the head of a band of Negro slaves of a wildness
and ferocity not known in Mississippi before. He had bought one
hundred square miles of virgin country from the Indians and on it
established the plantation of Sutpen's Hundred. In 1838 he had
married Rosa's sister, Ellen, by whom he had a son, Henry, and a
daughter, Judith. In 1861, as Colonel Sutpen, he had raised his own
troop and gone to fight in the War between the States. He had returned
from the War to find his plantation in ruins, and Henry, whom he
had disowned, disappeared. A doomed titan (as Rosa Coldfield sees

him), he set out to re-establish his estate and fortune and beget more sons to inherit it. His wife dead, he proposed to Rosa, but alienated her when he suggested that, before marrying, they should see whether she was capable of bearing a son. Rebuffed by her, he turned to the daughter of 'Wash' Jones, the poor white who worshipped him; but the girl bore him a daughter, whom he repudiated together with her mother with such brutality that Jones killed him.

Rosa Coldfield's version of Sutpen is presented in the first chapter of the novel; General Compson's and his son's follow in the next four. We begin to understand the roots of Sutpen's behaviour. Born among the poorest of poor whites in West Virginia, he had been taken as a boy to Virginia proper and, sent by his father on an errand to the mansion of the plantation on which they were working, had been turned away from the door by the Negro butler. This is the traumatic situation. From then on, he is an obsessed man, and his doom is implicit in his obsession. As he says years later to General Compson: 'You see, I had a design in my mind.' It was to be a landowner like the Virginia planter whose coloured butler had turned him away; the seeds of his tragic fall lay in the fact that his conception of human relations was exactly that of the coloured butler.

In fact, by the time he reached Yocnapatawpha County a first attempt to execute his design had already failed. From Virginia he had shipped to one of the Caribbean islands, where he had saved the life, family and property of a Spanish planter during a slave insurrection, and been rewarded with the hand of the planter's daughter. She had borne him a son, and then only did he realize that she was partly coloured. Thereupon, he had put her aside, disowned both marriage and offspring, and set out for Mississippi with the band of wild Negroes shipped from the West Indies.

It is this disowned, unadmitted son who is the immediate cause of Sutpen's fall. Brought up in New Orleans as Charles Le Bon, he meets his younger half-brother, Henry, as a student at the University of Mississippi, and in the vacation Henry takes him back to Sutpen's Hundred. Charles, who to all appearances is white, knows his relationship to the Sutpens, and Sutpen knows it too, though the rest of the family do not. To the delight of Henry and his mother, Charles seeks to become engaged to Judith, his half-sister. Sutpen will neither consent nor explain his attitude. What Charles seeks is clear: his recognition by Sutpen. Given this, he will give up Judith. But Sutpen never will acknowledge him; and in the end, when the war is almost over and the two young men ride back from the Confederate Army to Sutpen's Hundred, it is Henry who shoots Charles to prevent his marrying Judith, shoots him not in order to prevent incest, for he already knows Charles is his half-brother, but because he has just discovered he has Negro blood in him.

Like Joe Christmas, all that Charles Le Bon asks for is the moment of recognition, as a son, as a human being. It is refused him; and herein lies Faulkner's diagnosis and criticism of the South. Sutpen is a symbolic figure. In a sense, he *is* the South; that he has built his great house and established himself in a very short time is merely the dramatic telescoping of a process that in Virginia and North Carolina had taken generations. Sutpen symbolizes the profound impiety on which the South was based, the impiety which sees human beings not as ends in themselves but as means, as property, as things. It was an impiety that degraded both owned and owners. It is as though the institution of slavery was bearable, even to the slave-owners, only when the slaves were not men like themselves, but black men; yet since white owners never scrupled to sleep with slave women and beget more slaves, the institution itself perpetuated with an increasing intensity a perversion of human relations. In terms of human beings, the South was based on rape.

Sutpen, like the South, is self-doomed to destruction, doomed by his own impiety towards other men and women. And the fall of the house of Sutpen is terrifying in its thoroughness. At the end all that remains of the Sutpens is the idiot Jim Bond, Le Bon's grandson, howling and gibbering in the overgrown plantation.

[2]

FAULKNER is nothing if not a romantic writer, with all that that implies of criticism and of praise. In this respect, the perfect foil to him is Allen Tate, whose one novel, *The Fathers*, appeared in 1938. Tate, primarily a poet and critic both of literature and in the realm of ideas where literature, morals and politics exist side by side, was one of the theorists of the Fugitives Group, and *The Fathers* could be taken as a dramatization in fiction of his ideas of society and tradition. It is that, but it is much more. It is a beautifully articulated novel whose author, one feels, knows throughout exactly what he is doing and saying. Tate is in complete control. He intended, he has said, 'to make the whole structure symbolic in terms of realistic detail, so that you could subtract the symbolism, or remain unaware of it, without losing the literal level of meaning . . . but if you subtract the literal or realistic detail, the symbolic structure disappears.' Apart from perhaps one instance where a single literal or realistic detail is allowed to obtrude too much in order that the symbolic point may be made, he achieves his intention almost perfectly, and the result is a peculiarly satisfying novel, satisfying in the classical sense that its beauties spring from the conscious observation of conscious limits.

Tate's South is not Faulkner's; it is, rather, the old South that the Sutpens and the Compsons set out to imitate, the South of Virginia, the Old Dominion. The novel is narrated by an old man, Lacy Buchan, looking back on the events of his boyhood more than half a century earlier, events that have obsessed him throughout that time. He writes:

> Is it not something to tell, when a score of people I knew and loved, people beyond whose lives I could imagine no other life, either out of violence in themselves or the times, or out of some misery or shame, scattered into the new life of the modern age where they cannot even find themselves? Why cannot life change without tangling the lives of innocent persons? Why do innocent persons cease their innocence and become violent and evil in themselves that such great changes may take place?

This device of the narrator who participated, without understanding them, in the events described allows Tate to move backwards and forwards in time and to comment, through Lacy, on the events themselves. Lacy is at once narrator and chorus, and his reflections on the events are as important as the descriptions of them.

The action covers the period 1860–1, the months immediately before and after the outbreak of the Civil War. But *The Fathers* is not a war novel as Caroline Gordon's *None Shall Look Back* is. The theme is rather the break-up of a culture, a way of life. The war is a symbol of that break-up, but the immediate symbol, in the novel itself, is Lacy's brother-in-law George Posey, whom he hero-worships. Significantly, Posey's first, and binding, gift to the boy is a gun, which, on his first attempt to fire it, knocks him down and winds him. The order into which Posey erupts is personified in Lacy's father, Major Buchan. Major Buchan is a feudal landowner—Buchan of Pleasant Hill —who refers to his neighbours by the names of their plantations, Carter of Ravensworth, Carey of Vaucluse. His life is ruled by ceremony; manners, one feels, have made the man. As Lacy says: 'Our lives were eternally balanced upon a pedestal below which was an abyss that I could not name. Within that invisible tension my father knew the moves of an intricate game that he expected everybody else to play.' Elsewhere Lacy returns to the image of the abyss: 'Is not civilization the agreement, slowly arrived at, to let the abyss alone?'

Lacy recalls 'the only time I had ever seen my father blush; someone had tried to tell him his private affairs, beginning, "If you will allow me to be personal", and father had blushed because he could never allow anybody to be personal'. Yet, ruled by forms though he is, Major Buchan is not merely a formal man; or, if he is, then the forms themselves have bred in him a generosity of spirit and conduct which makes it appropriate to call him a great gentleman. Thus, at his wife's funeral, it is her old Negro maid, Lucy, whom he takes by the hand to head the procession following the coffin. His closest friend is his old Negro valet, Coriolanus, who shares his study. His values are almost alarmingly uncommercial; his attitudes are entirely feudal, his life governed by obligations in which money has no part. In fact, he is heavily in debt, but would never think of selling his Negroes: they are part of the family. He believes, indeed, that he has freed them: ironically, they are sold after his death. An anti-secessionist, he disinherits his elder son for following the Confederate cause. When the Federal troops arrive and a Northern officer gives him half an hour to leave his house before it is burnt, 'There is *nothing* that you can give to me, Sir', he retorts—and goes away and hangs himself.

Major Buchan's very fineness of breeding makes him defenceless against a world increasingly contemptuous of the values he lives by; and it is a very considerable achievement of Tate's to render the Major in such a way that we never think of him as comic. He is touchingly unarmed against life; though he knows the moves of the intricate game that he expects everybody else to play, he is utterly lost when other people do not know them. George Posey does not know them. He too is a Southerner, but an uprooted one. Once landowners in Maryland, the Poseys now live in Georgetown. They no longer have any function in society and, George apart, have degenerated into eccentricity. And George himself, a man of violent energy, is defenceless because he has no code which can mediate between him and life; he 'receives the shock of the world at the end of his nerves'; the boy Lacy always sees him as 'a horseman riding over a precipice'.

He does not know how to behave; his conduct is a constant affront to Major Buchan, whose daughter he marries. Posey, it is plain, is a representation of modern man, who errs because his responses to life are no longer dictated by tradition. His attitude towards the Buchans and their values is expressed in his behaviour at Mrs Buchan's funeral, when he mounts his horse and rides away:

> 'I can't even remember their names. I meet them but I don't know who they are. And by God they'll starve to death, that's what they'll do. They do nothing but die and marry and think about the honour of Virginia.' He rammed his hands into his pockets and shouted: 'I want to be thrown to the hogs. I tell you I want to be thrown to the hogs.'

And perhaps his lack of any kind of piety is most clearly shown when, in order to buy the bay mare whose excellence enables him to win the tournament at which he proclaims Susan Buchan Queen of Love and Beauty, he sells a Negro for fifteen hundred dollars, saying, 'You're liquid capital, I've got to have the money.' 'He rode away on the back of a bay Negro', is the comment of one of the Buchans; and their horror at his behaviour is due not simply to the fact that he has sold one of his slaves but that the slave in question is his own half-brother. Nothing could be further removed from the mores of Major Buchan.

George Posey is the emblem and agent of destruction. Not, of course, the only agent of Major Buchan's destruction; the war itself would have looked after that. But, unbridled as he is, recognizing no limits, Posey is as it were the immediate domestic emblem and agent of destruction; the violence within him mirrors the greater violence of the war; and if it is the war that destroys Major Buchan it is Posey who destroys the Major's family.

The action described in Tate's novel is as violent as anything in Faulkner, but the texture of the writing is anything but violent. *The Fathers* is a work of great formal beauty, the product of a most distinguished mind; implicit in it is a profoundly conservative moral and political philosophy; and, as with the best of Faulkner, we realize, having read it, that it transcends its region and the time of its setting. The South and its troubles have become a metaphor for the human situation generally.

I do not think this can be said of the novels of Robert Penn Warren, the youngest of the 'Fugitives' group. Distinguished as poet and critic, he is a highly conscious novelist, perhaps too much so. Reading his work, one feels it is no accident that he is also the co-author, with Cleanth Brooks, of *Understanding Fiction*, a textbook very influential in American universities. Warren's novels are elaborate and formidably well planned, organized, it has been said, like 'metaphysical poems, as well as like the later Elizabethan dramas—as that drama has been interpreted, at least, by modern "expanded metaphor" analysis'. But this does not necessarily make them the better as novels, and though Warren is not to be blamed for the enthusiasm of his critics, there are times when one rebels. According to John M. Bradbury in his *The Fugitives: a Critical Account*:

> *All the King's Men* is a novel of redemption and the only one of Warren's, therefore, which permits the protagonist, who is again a personification of modern man in quest of self-identification, to emerge from his ordeal in the hope of a new and orientated life. The symbolic fable of this book embodies the world of fact in Willie Stark ('stark' fact) and the world of idea or abstraction in Adam (innocence of the world of fact) Stanton, while the Eves of the piece, Anne Stanton and Sadie Burke, are the agents by which knowledge of evil is transmitted to Jack Burden (who must finally bear the full burden of knowledge, as he is regenerated).

If this is a correct interpretation, then it diminishes rather than enhances; for it imposes an absurdly heavy weight on one of the oldest devices of the novelist, seen in such character-names as Veneering in Dickens and Quiverful in Trollope, and beyond that, tempts one to translate into allegory a novel which in the last analysis should be finally untranslatable into other terms.

For all the illustrative imagery, it is very doubtful whether anyone has ever read *All the King's Men* (1946) as primarily a novel of redemption and rebirth. Primarily, it is a novel about the nature of politics, rooted in a traditional and pessimistic view of man. All action, Warren suggests, is flawed because of the natural corruption of man. Politics is the art of the possible; and in a state not unlike Louisiana

Warren shows us politics, the struggle for and control of power in a state, as it might have existed in any Italian principality throughout the middle ages until a century and a half ago.

The view of politics expressed is not so remote from Machiavelli's. At the centre of the book, dominating it, giving it its *raison d'être*, is the Governor, Willie Stark, a not-unsympathetic representation of a politician suggestive of Huey Long. Willie, the champion of the poor and dispossessed, is a genuinely tragic figure—and this is the index of the novel's achievement. He is the disillusioned idealist who, discovering the political naïvety of his pristine idealism, must fight his political enemies with their own dirty weapons. Corruption, in the circumstances of his time and place, is the element in which he must exist; he has no alternative; corruption belongs to the realm of what is given. Stark is brilliantly created in all his ambiguities, his idealism, his class-consciousness, his lust for revenge, his sensuality; and as brilliantly described is the whole complex of events, the clash of loyalties, the intrigues, the personalities, that bring him first to power and then lead him to his downfall, the assassination by another idealist's bullet. All this is the guts of the novel, and Warren renders it with great authority. Here, one feels, are the facts of government in a community politically backward to the point of barbarism.

Unfortunately, it is not the whole of the novel. We see the action through the eyes of Jack Burden, a newspaperman who has helped to make Stark and has become one of his henchmen. Burden is a renegade from his class; by birth and upbringing he belongs to the families of the founding fathers of the state, men as ruthless as Stark and more selfish, even though their ruthlessness and selfishness were masked by a parade of the gentlemanly virtues. Burden is both narrator and chorus; he is telling and analysing a tragic history, the tragic history not only of Stark but of himself and of his family. In the end he is relating the story of his own redemption.

But—and this is the fatal flaw in a most ambitious novel—what most strikes one is the inadequacy of Warren's rendering of Burden. He is presented as very much the typical American newspaperman of the thirties as we know him from such films as *The Front Page*: unillusioned, cynical, sardonic, consciously tough, his speech a continuous explosion of wisecracks. He is intolerably prolix, and the manner in which he is prolix is so vulgar in expression and so coarse in feeling that it is impossible for the reader to accept him either as a fitting chorus to the tragedy or as a fitting exponent of Warren's values. Which is why, remembering *All the King's Men*, Burden's redemption and rebirth are the last things that come to the reader's mind. He is, in terms of the novel's total effect, the least significant part of it; yet, since the whole action is as it were framed in his consciousness, he imparts to the novel a tone of almost unbearable pretentiousness.

The reader recognizes pretentiousness when he senses, as the author himself apparently has not done, the gap between the end the author has set himself and the means which he has used to reach it. Pretentiousness is essentially a failure in self-criticism, in self-knowledge. It has been, it seems to me, Warren's besetting sin. It seriously mars *All the King's Men*; it ruins *World Enough and Time*. Warren is a native of Kentucky, 'the dark and bloody ground' of the Indians, and embedded in *World Enough and Time* is what could obviously have been a fine novel of Kentucky's dark and bloody past. But 'embedded' is the word. The novel is based on a famous and well-documented murder trial held in Frankfort, Kentucky, in 1826, an unusual murder in that the murderer—called Jeremiah Beaumont in the novel—killed his patron Colonel Cassius Fort out of sheer romantic idealism, to avenge a girl whom Fort had seduced and abandoned. It is the pursuit of an ideal that leads Beaumont to disaster; and here again Warren is concerned with the place of idealism in a world which is pledged to and lives by violence. The violence of the time and place is extraordinarily well caught. Beaumont's career is made the basis of what might be called a philosophical melodrama; both Beaumont in his diaries and the anonymous, present-day narrator of his story examine his actions and motives from every angle. The result should be impressive and is not. It is neither the melodrama nor the philosophy one objects to, but the appalling prolixity which has the effect of inflating the subject beyond what it can bear. One sees what Warren is after: the equivalent in horror and violence of Jacobean tragedy. But, in *World Enough and Time* to a degree even beyond *All the King's Men*, he appears as the principal inheritor in our time of the most dubious element in the tradition of the South, Southern rhetoric, that love of words, even to the extent of being possessed by them, not primarily for their meaning or aptness but for their grandiloquence, their ability to intoxicate. The tradition is not, of course, by any means wholly bad. Much of the textural richness of contemporary Southern writing, as compared both with the narrow range of Hemingway's style and vocabulary, for instance, and with the pedestrian flatness of Farrell, can be attributed to it. All Southern writers share in it, Faulkner conspicuously, and there are times when it runs away with him, just as there are times when, like Tate in *The Feathers*, he sees the funny side of it and burlesques it. Thomas Wolfe was almost entirely its victim; but, since he was his own hero and the central character of his novels, the consequences were less fatal for him than for Warren. Warren, after all, purports to tell us things philosophically important.

Which is why Warren's best novel is still his first, *Night Rider* (1939), simply because it is so much more compact than his later fiction: the moral is not elaborated but is there, plain enough, for the reader to deduce himself. Again, the scene is Kentucky, at the beginning of the present century; again we have the tragedy of idealism and of lack of self-knowledge or lack of awareness of personal identity, which for Warren seems to go hand in hand with the precipitate actions of idealism.

In the interests of what seems to him social justice, the hero, Percy Munn, a young lawyer, finds himself a leader of the Night Riders, a Ku-Klux-Klan-like organization that comes into being to fight the tobacco-buyers' ring which threatens to ruin the small tobacco-growers of Kentucky. Inevitably it becomes an instrument of violence, breeding counter-violence, riots and murder. And as its nature changes so does Munn's; the outer world of destruction in which he is involved is mirrored within himself; indeed, inner and outer are hardly to be separated. The action takes place very largely at night, in darkness; Munn has given himself to the night side of life. His wife leaves him; destruction and violence become increasingly more necessary to him. In the end, he is an outlaw, wanted for a murder he has not committed, exposed as essentially a hollow man, identityless, as hollow as Senator Tolliver, his erstwhile patron whom he has come to hate and who is in some sense his *alter ego*. It is, perhaps, significant that throughout the novel Munn is referred to as Mr Munn, for his identity is wholly public and formal.

Night Rider is an impressive tragic novel, rich in sharp characterization of Munn's associates, men driven by power or destructive idealism, and abounding in extremely dramatic scenes of riot and crowd violence. These latter indicate probably the true nature of Warren's talent. He has a vision of human life as condemned to violence almost by definition, and the violence springs impartially as it were from noble motives and from evil. Its resemblance to the view of life of a late-Renaissance writer like Webster is plain enough; but the success of *Night Rider* suggests that Warren does better when he plans his fiction not in terms of Jacobean drama but in terms of the visual imagery of cinema.

[3]

FAULKNER apart, the most remarkable novelist the South has produced seems to me Carson McCullers. At the time of writing, Katherine Anne Porter has published nothing of novel-length, and Eudora Welty is much more distinguished as a short-story writer than as a novelist. Carson McCullers's genius is at least as strange as Faulkner's, but expressed with lucidity and precision, a classical simplicity. However tortured her vision may seem, there is nothing tortured or odd in the texture of her prose; and the raw material of her art is the world as commonly observed.

Except in *Reflections in a Golden Eye*, her scene is the industrial South of small mill towns. Her first novel, *The Heart is a Lonely Hunter* (1940), remains the ideal introduction to her work. The title is an exact description of theme and point of view. It opens: 'In the town there were t vo mutes, and they were always together'; and the book is built round one of them, John Singer, who, when the action begins, is living with the other, a Greek, Spiros Antonapoulos. One can think of it as a marriage, though there is no suggestion at all of a homosexual relation, between opposites. Singer is tall and thin, neat, intelligent; Antonapoulos lazy, stupid, obese. In this relationship, Singer is, as it were, the adorer, the giver, Antonapoulos the careless, ungrateful recipient of his love. Antonapoulos has a permanent 'gentle, flaccid smile' which for Singer contains something very subtle and wise: the Greek is in fact a mental defective and before the first chapter ends has been taken away to the state mental hospital. Singer is now doubly alone, isolated by his physical condition and also by the loss of love. He rents a room in a boarding-house and eats his meals at the New York Café, which is owned by Biff Brannon.

Restlessly Biff turned his attention to Singer. The mute sat with his hands in his pockets and the half-finished glass of beer before him had become warm and stagnant. He would offer to treat Singer to a glass of whiskey before he left. What he had said to Alice was true—he did like freaks. He had a special friendly feeling for sick people and cripples. Whenever somebody with a harelip or T.B. came into the place he would set him up with beer. Or if the customer were a hunchback or a bad cripple, then it would be whiskey on the house. . . .

Singer, too, is a freak, and through the special nature of his freakdom becomes a magnet for a number of characters who may also be called freaks. To them all Singer appears in sort as their saviour; he is a kind of catalyst: without knowing it, certainly without being changed by it, he helps them to realize their dreams and themselves.

But if the girl Mick, the drunken socialist Jake and the Negro Dr Copeland are freaks, so, Carson McCullers seems to suggest, is the rest of the world, for their attitude towards Singer is everyone else's taken to extremes:

Now it came about that various rumours started in the town concerning the mute.

The Jews said that he was a Jew. The merchants along the main street claimed that he had received a large legacy and was a very rich man. It was whispered in one browbeaten textile union that the mute was an organizer for the C.I.O. A lone Turk who had roamed into the town years ago and who languished with his family behind the little store where they sold linens claimed passionately to his wife that the mute was Turkish . . .

As for the mute, he lives only for the visits he can make to Antonapoulos in the mental hospital and the gifts he can take him, gifts carelessly received as of right; and when the Greek dies he kills himself.

The Heart Is a Lonely Hunter is a parable of the human condition, of human isolation, of the craving to communicate and of the impossibility of communication; and also, perhaps, of the inescapable delusions attendant upon the inescapable human need to love. There is a double irony in the novel. Mick, Jake Blount, Biff and Dr Copeland all re-create Singer in the image of their own desires. For Mick he is almost God: 'Everybody in the past few years knew there wasn't any real God. When she thought of what she used to imagine was God she could only see Mister Singer with a long, white sheet around him.'

But he, too, re-creates according to his own desires and mutely adores a god beyond him—and the god of his worship, love which gives meaning to his life, is a mental defective.

Yet the impression made by *The Heart Is a Lonely Hunter* is not terrifying. It is, rather, that of a grave, sad beauty, a diffused poetic pity. For two reasons. The first is the nature of Carson McCullers's prose, which is not in any obvious sense poetic or heightened and which looks plainer than in fact it is. It is actually a very cunning style, ever so slightly removed from the contemporary. Then, the town and its life are rendered in concrete detail. The town is not, we feel, conceived in any arbitrary manner in order to point a moral or impose a reading of life. And though the characters may be freaks they are not merely dotty, like the characters of T. F. Powys. If they differ from other human beings they do so only in degree; the laws that govern their being are universal laws. And all the time, almost as the soil from which they spring, the common business of human existence is going on, the common joys, anxieties and endurances.

In *The Heart Is a Lonely Hunter*, Carson McCullers creates a fictitious world that can stand for the real world in its depth and variety. In *Reflections in a Golden Eye* (1941), her second novel, she does nothing like this, and because of it it is much the lesser book. A ground-bass of common humanity is lacking in *Reflections in a Golden Eye*; we are in a world inhabited entirely by freaks, freaks different, certainly, from those of the earlier novel, but all the same freaks. The novel is of a grotesque violence. We see the characters act, but why they act as they do we must deduce from the actions themselves, which are reflections, if we are to take seriously the passage in the novel from which the title comes, in the golden eye of a peacock: 'A peacock of a sort of ghastly green. With one immense golden eye. And in it these reflections of something tiny and—grotesque.' The eye reflects but does not interpret; and anyway, the peacock itself is merely a figment of fancy, something glimpsed momentarily in the embers of a fire. It is as though Carson McCullers has surrendered in despair to a conviction of the utter meaninglessness of life.

The Member of the Wedding, published five years later, is much warmer and more human. It is a novel of growing up and initiation, initiation, perhaps, into the acceptance of human limits. 'It happened', the novel begins, 'that green and crazy summer when Frankie was twelve years old. This was the summer when for a long time she had not been a member. She belonged to no club and was a member of nothing in the world. Frankie had become an unjoined person who hung around in doorways, and she was afraid.' In the beginning, Frankie, motherless, alone except for the Negro cook Berenice and the small boy John Henry West, seeks simply to escape from her solitary condition—she dreams of leaving her father's house, of going to the war as a Marine, of becoming a film star—by becoming a member.

She is, one might say, tired of being a freak. She has seen and been haunted by the freaks at the annual fair, The Giant, The Fat Lady, The Midget, The Wild Nigger, The Pin Head, The Alligator Boy, The Half-Man Half-Woman. 'She was afraid of all the Freaks, for it seemed to her that they had looked at her in a secret way and tried to connect their eyes with hers, as though to say: we know you.' But there comes a day in that green and crazy summer when she can say: 'I doubt if they ever get married or go to a wedding. Those Freaks.' For what she has suddenly decided she can become a member of is her soldier-brother's wedding. Her brother and his bride, she says, are 'the we of me'. She identifies herself with them absolutely, and dreams of being with them always. She has no realization at all of the sexual side of marriage. Only in the most oblique sense is her initiation an initiation into sex.

Of course she is disillusioned: she cannot become a member of the wedding. On her return home, she sets out to run away—and is picked up by a policeman almost immediately. 'The plans for the movies or the Marines were only child plans that would never work, and she was careful when she answered.' She never speaks about the wedding again; she becomes thirteen and Frances and acquires a girl friend named Mary Littlejohn with whom she reads Tennyson. They go to the fair together but do not see the Freaks, for Mrs Littlejohn said it was morbid to gaze at Freaks.

Frances has become a member. The freakishness at the heart of things is still there: John Henry dies of meningitis: 'He died the Tuesday after the Fair was gone, a golden morning of the most butterflies, the clearest sky.' But the freakish has become peripheral: 'He came to her once or twice in nightmare dreams . . . But the dreams came only once or twice, and the daytime now was filled with radar, school, and Mary Littlejohn.'

In *The Member of the Wedding*, Berenice, the Negro cook, is the emblem of acceptance and endurance as Etta is in *The Heart Is a*

Lonely Hunter. She stands, as it were, for the ground-bass of human experience. In the short novel *The Ballad of the Sad Café*, this is represented by the singing of the chain-gang, which ends the work like a coda:

> The voices are dark in the golden glare, the music intricately blended, both sombre and joyful. The music will swell until at last it seems that the sound does not come from the twelve men on the gang, but from the earth itself, or the wide sky. It is music that causes the heart to broaden and the listener to grow cold with ecstasy and fright. Then slowly the music will sink down until at last there remains one lonely voice, then a great hoarse breath, the sun, the sound of the picks in the silence.
>
> And what kind of gang is this that can make such music? Just twelve mortal men, seven of them black and five of them white boys from this county. Just twelve mortal men who are together.

The Ballad of the Sad Café is the strangest, the most haunting of Carson McCullers's work. It has the timelessness and remoteness of a ballad. There is the lonely, dreary Georgia mill town, in which 'there is nothing whatsoever to do', and at its very centre the largest building in the town, entirely boarded up except for one window in the second floor, out of which sometimes in the late afternoon a face looks down on the town, that of Miss Amelia Evans, who once ran the house as a café. The story describes a sort of ritual dance in which the loved one always turns from the lover to love another who also turns away. It is told with a beautiful economy and precision in a prose of singular purity that transmits both the ambience of the town and its inhabitants and the timeless quality which broods over the action.

Mrs McCullers's most recent novel, *Clock without Hands* (1961), comes much more close to the novel as we ordinarily know it than anything she has written before. By the same token, it is her most obviously 'Southern' novel, since it deals with the threat of desegregation in a small town in Georgia in 1953. Owing to the greater degree of surface realism, the characters can scarcely be regarded as freaks in the old sense; they are more broadly humorous.

The novel is an investigation of Southern guilt, the guilt being represented in all its ambiguity by the octogenarian politician Judge Fox Clane. The Judge is a very considerable comic figure, but pathetic also, caught in a web of evasion and rationalization in which goodwill to the Negro is one strand. Without that, there could be no guilt; and the symbol of his guilt is the blue-eyed Negro Sherman whom he makes his secretary and whom he is bound to, also, through the Negro's associations with his dead son. The *dénouement* of the novel is the death of Sherman at the hands of a mob of poor-whites whom the Judge himself has egged on to resist Negro encroachment on their privileges. As he says to the dying druggist J. T. Malone:

> 'Another thing, you and I have our property and our positions and our self-respect. But what does Sammy Lank have except those slews of children of his? Sammy Lank and poor whites like that have nothing but the colour of their skin. Having no property, no means, nobody to look down on—that is the clue to the whole thing. It is a sad commentary on human nature but every man has to have somebody to look down on. So the Sammy Lanks of this world only have the Nigra to look down on. You see, J. T., it is a matter of pride. . . .'

One says the *dénouement*. It is not quite that; for the immediate action of the novel is played out against a larger background. At the beginning of the book we learn that the druggist has just discovered that he is suffering from leukaemia and has not more than fifteen months to live. It is within this period of Malone's slow dying and increasing loneliness in the knowledge that he is dying that the action takes place. Malone is the clock without hands. He is utterly alone. Because of Malone, the novel exists in a dimension additional to those that condition realistic fiction generally. And for all the brilliance of the portrayal of the Judge and, even more so, of Sherman, with his fantasy-world of self-aggrandizement, it is to Malone and his fate—the ultimate human fate—that the mind first returns when remembering the novel.

THE THIRTIES: AMERICAN

[I]

THE TWENTIES, as Scott Fitzgerald observed, ended in October, 1929; and not only in the United States but throughout the Western world, for the Wall Street crash set off a chain-reaction of disasters everywhere, culminating in the outbreak of the second world war in 1939. The thirties was a decade of fear, misery and panic, of mass unemployment, the continuing defeat of democracy at the hands of Fascism and Nazism, and of the threat of universal war. The twenties had been many things, among them an age of liberal hope: for many people in the thirties, appalled by the paralysis that appeared to have stricken the liberal democracies, whatever hope remained was remote, desperate and radical. For some it centred in the fact that the Soviet Union still existed and that within its territories men seemed to control their destinies; for others, it lay in the violent assertion of the principles of order and discipline that were the public face of Fascism. It was a time when even the most retiring of private citizens was compelled, by the spectacle of the poverty on all sides of him and by the obvious and ever-increasing danger of war, to consider the nature of economic power, to commit himself to political action and, in the end, to take sides.

In such an age, it would have been remarkable if the main theme in literature, among the younger writers particularly, had not been the social and economic malaise of the time. 'What do you think about England, the country of ours where nobody is well?' Auden's famous question, with America substituted for England where necessary, re-echoes through the imaginative writing of the decade. Not that either the diagnosis or the prognosis of the disease was invariably expressed in political terms. Those English and American writers who joined the Communist Party were rarely anything but very amateur Communists, with the shakiest grasp of Marxist theory and practice, and few of them remained in the Party for long. Both in Britain and the United

States there was much talk of the proletarian novel and the left-wing novel, and some examples of the former, with 'proletarian' interpreted according to Marx, can be isolated. More often, what lay behind the characteristic fiction of the age was not any view of it that could be intellectually formulated but rather a general sense of its malaise. What emerged was a literature of protest at the spectacle of human misery that seemed intolerable in the light of the technological progress the century had made. Many of the novels of the day read now as simple cries of pain and indignation.

It seems generally true, at any rate so far as England is concerned, that the thirties novels which are most alive today are precisely those least directly concerned with the social questions of the time. Yet even so, it is not quite so simple as it seems. We don't in these days think of Graham Greene as a social novelist, but his novels of the thirties had an immediate topical reference; they could scarcely have been more 'contemporary'. And even with a novelist like Evelyn Waugh, whose political views were quite unlike those we normally think of as characteristic of English novelists in the thirties, the ending of *Vile Bodies*, 'the biggest battlefield in the history of the world', chimes perfectly with the feeling of the time.

Moreover, the social and political preoccupations that dominated the English and American novel during the thirties made these fictions part of an international movement in writing. The problems, of unemployment, poverty and waste, were universal, and the enemy, as fascist movements sprang up in country after country, was everywhere. But both had been experienced more intensely and earlier outside Britain and America, and it was in European novelists that English and American writers found their greatest exemplars, in André Malraux and Ignazio Silone especially. Their novels became the standards by which the socially and politically committed novels of Britain and America had to be judged. Malraux and Silone could both say, with Whitman, 'I am the man, I suffer'd, I was there'. What they had suffered seemed to be what men throughout the Western world might very soon have to suffer; and their literary ability was such as to give their experiences memorable expression.

It was the sense of this international movement in writing, of the solidarity of writers of many countries, that was behind such magazines in England as John Lehmann's extremely influential *New Writing*. The first number, which appeared in spring, 1936, announced that 'though it does not intend to open its pages to writers of reactionary or Fascist sentiments, it is independent of any political party'. That was vague enough. It was also good enough: everybody knew what it meant. The novels of social protest in England and America in the thirties cannot be pegged down to any one political party. Politically, the decade ended, after all, with the concept of the Popular Front; and what still seem its characteristic novels were the product of a common climate of opinion, the outcome of common experience whether suffered in the English Midlands, in Chicago or in California.

Only in this very wide sense, indeed, can one speak of a thirties movement; and looking back on it now, one sees how part of its origins lay in a somewhat earlier but similarly vague and widely diffused movement. This was the sudden appearance, round about 1928, simultaneously in several of the combatant countries, of novels and memoirs of the world war. There had, of course, been war books before this. Barbusse's extremely influential *Le Feu* had appeared as early as 1916. In the United States John Dos Passos's *Three Soldiers* was published in 1921 and E. E. Cummings's *The Enormous Room* a year later; only dubiously a novel, so close is it to the author's own experiences in a French prison, it remains a notable and highly individual piece of experimental prose. In England, there was Ford Madox Ford's Tietjens series, and the unjustly neglected *The Spanish Farm* trilogy by R. H. Mottram, which appeared from 1924 to 1926. In England, however, it was the poets, Owen, Sassoon, Rosenberg, who most adequately recorded the initial impact of the war on the serving soldier and his reaction against it.

Yet despite the existence of these books, it still seems as though in the years immediately after the end of the war there was a general conspiracy of silence between writers, publishers and readers; as though by common consent, memories of the war were to be repressed. They broke to the surface round about 1928; it was as though, throughout the world, it had taken the writers who had been fighting soldiers ten years to come to terms with their experience. The Austrian novelist Arnold Zweig's *The Case of Sergeant Grischa*, one of the best of the war novels, appeared in 1927. It was followed in 1928 by the most successful and, one suspects, the most influential of them all, the German writer Erich Maria Remarque's *All Quiet on the Western Front*; and to that year also belong the two best English memoirs of the war, Edmund Blunden's *Undertones of War* and Robert Graves's

Goodbye to All That, autobiographies and not novels, and both the work of poets. Richard Aldington's *Death of a Hero*, a formless novel, incoherent and hysterical, reading as though written in the white heat of battle itself, followed in 1929, as did Hemingway's *A Farewell to Arms*. Sassoon's *Memoirs of an Infantry Officer* appeared a year later.

These and others—Ludwig Renn's *War*, Ernst Jünger's *Storm of Steel* and William March's *Company K* among them—are the books inspired by the first world war that we remember. Their interest to us here, though, is in the mood they reflect. With the exception of Jünger's book, they are, if not pacifist, at any rate absolute in their revulsion against modern war. They were written, many of them, as warnings to the future from the past; but they were also written, one can't help feeling, as though what was written about could not possibly occur again. In this, they were idealistic and liberal in spirit—and they appeared on the very eve of the great depression and the leap of Fascism it unleashed.

The social novelists of the thirties were mostly too young to have fought in the war, but they had grown up in it. It had been the great formative experience in their lives; and they had read the war books at the very outset of their literary careers. They had come of age in what later looked like an artificial paradise, only to find almost immediately after that the world lay in ruins all about them. Contemplating this world in ruins, attempting to render it in fiction, they took over the mood of the war books, a mood of anger and contempt for those who seemed responsible, the politicians and the industrialists, and of pity for their helpless victims.

This was common to social novelists on both sides of the Atlantic; but when we set the American and English social novels of the thirties side by side we see differences between them. The American novels, as a whole, are much the more violent and radical. The twenties boom had soared to far greater heights in the United States than in England; the slump was therefore the greater, and so was the sense of shock, outrage and betrayal. The violence of the novels reflected, too, a tradition of violence in American industrial relations that had no parallel in English life; one may contrast the extraordinarily vicious terrorization of the striking miners of Harlan County, Kentucky, in 1931, with the almost Sunday School atmosphere in which the British General Strike of 1926 ran its course.

Then, miserable as was the lot of the unemployed in Britain, it was probably never as wretched materially as that of the workless in America. There had, after all, been some measure of social security in Britain for nearly twenty years; there were unemployment insurance benefits. They were inadequate and early on in the decade they were in a great many cases cut by the abominated and abominable means test; but the unemployed man in Britain was to some small extent cushioned against complete poverty, as the American was not until later. Significantly, in the novels written by British unemployed workers the emphasis is on the humiliation of being workless, of having to queue for the 'dole' at labour exchanges, of having to submit to the indignity of the means test. Again in contradiction to the English novel of the time, the American has, besides its violence and radical anger, a resolution to grapple with the political and economic situation and to change it, a resolution that pointed beyond the violence and the anger to a native and fundamental optimism in the writers. In the realm of government this resolution found expression in the mass of legislation and projects that made up the New Deal. No British government during the thirties showed energy or imagination at all comparable to that of the Roosevelt administration, and these facts are reflected in the mood and tone of the novels of the two literatures.

Finally, in the absence of a novelist great enough to transcend it, the British class system itself was enough to prevent the appearance of an English novelist large enough to take in the experience of the time. Good social novels were written, but they were small, dealing with isolated pockets of personal experience. Some of the novels by working-class authors remain moving, but their authors lacked the necessary literary skill and education to make them more than pathetic documentaries. Novelists with the necessary skill lacked the equally necessary experience of working-class life. There were almost no novelists with anything like the range of first-hand knowledge of the way in which ordinary people of more than one social class live that American writers like Cantwell, Farrell and Steinbeck had. The closest to them was Henry Green, whose *Living* remains among the best English novels of working-class life, but, having written it, Green moved away to other scenes and material.

The Americans had the advantage, too, almost as soon as the decade opened, of having a powerful exemplar in a novelist of considerable skill and enterprise, John Dos Passos, whose trilogy, *U.S.A.*, consisting of *The 42nd Parallel* (1930), *1919* (1932) and *The Big Money*

(1936), is the most ambitious work of fiction attempted by any writer in English during the thirties. If the work fails, it does so in the most honourable and heroic way.

Dos Passos's second novel, *Three Soldiers*, was one of the earliest of the war novels. It now reads somewhat oddly; but its oddity is characteristic of Dos Passos. Therein lies its interest today. It traces the fortunes of three young American private soldiers during the war: Dan Fuselli, whose ambition is to be a regular guy and get promotion; Chrisfield, a farm boy from Indiana who loathes the regimentation of army existence and pines for home; and John Andrews, a sensitive, educated youth who wants to be a musician. He and Chrisfield desert. Andrews hides with a French girl and begins to compose a symphony, only to face the firing squad with the work unfinished. Fuselli and Chrisfield are destroyed by the war no less than Andrews, yet there is considerable point in the criticism that Dos Passos seems to be implying that the loss of Andrews's symphony is the major tragedy of the war. One gets the impression of a tiresome aestheticism, a moral unseriousness, compared, say, with the attitude towards the war of a poet like Wilfred Owen. But then, it strikes one, the real target of Dos Passos's hatred is not the war at all: it is the United States Army, and the Army precisely because the inevitable circumstances of Army life impose an intolerable restriction on the rights of the individual human being. To the European, this seems a very American attitude.

This repudiation of regimentation, whether by the army or by society itself, is the constant factor in Dos Passos's fiction. He is the great nonconformist, if you like the original Jeffersonian democrat. For part of the thirties he was probably the most illustrious American writer the Communist Party secured as a fellow-traveller, but he was never a Communist, and what he saw in Spain during the Civil War led to his disillusionment with the Left. In his most recent novels the target of his hatred is trade unionism. But this is not to say he has become a reactionary. He is continuing to attack, in the name of individual freedom, power that he believes has become monolithic. He remains essentially an anarchist.

The writer he is closest to is Whitman; but he is, as it were, a Whitman who has fallen from the state of innocence. Whitman could preach the brotherhood of man and see it actually materializing in mid-nineteenth-century America: for Dos Passos the facts of life in twentieth-century America frustrate the brotherhood of man. One sees this in his third novel, *Manhattan Transfer*, published in 1925. In a sense, the central character of the novel is the whole teeming city of New York, which is rendered impressionistically, almost in terms of Imagist poetry:

> Three gulls wheel above the broken boxes, orangerinds, spoiled cabbage heads that heave between the splintered plank walls, the green waves spume under the round bow as the ferry, skidding on the tide, crashes, gulps the broken water, slides, settles slowly into the slip.

Here, Dos Passos is in the tradition of nineteenth-century Naturalism: like Zola and the Impressionist painters, he is attempting to create a kind of beauty out of raw materials normally conceived as ugly. Within the city itself, he follows a dozen or more contrasted lives: all are defeated, defeated by the materialistic, anti-human values of the great city.

Like everything else Dos Passos wrote before it, *Manhattan Transfer* prepares the way for the trilogy *U.S.A.*, just as everything else he has written after it seems anticlimax. *U.S.A.* has been extremely influential technically, not only on the American novelists who have followed him but also on European novelists, Sartre in particular. The scope is vast; the work is an attempt at an American epic of the twentieth century. It embraces the whole of the United States and its history from the beginning of the century with the Spanish-American War to the execution of Sacco and Vanzetti in 1927. It follows the lives during this span of time of some nine principal characters and takes in industry, the arts, labour politics, the new profession of public relations, the war, the peace, industrial unrest.

The characters are set in a context of a number of technical devices the aim of which is to give dimension to their separate existences, to implicate them in the whole history of their times. There is, first of all, what Dos Passos calls Newsreel, a montage of newspaper headlines, extracts from newspaper reports, snatches of popular songs. It is as it were the panorama of events large and small, significant and trivial, against which the characters move. Then, appearing rather less frequently, there are the biographies, written in a typographically patterned prose which may be considered a form of free verse, of representative Americans of the quarter-century—among them Debs, Luther Burbank, Big Bill Haywood, Bryan, Carnegie, Edison, La Follette, John Reed, Theodore Roosevelt, Wilson, Veblen, the

Wright brothers, the Morgans, Henry Ford, Frank Lloyd Wright, Insull. The last biography of all ends the book: the biography of an anonymous young vagrant trying to bum a lift.

The third device Dos Passos calls 'The Camera Eye'. Written in impressionistic prose in stream-of-consciousness, approximating often typographically to free verse, it exists in counterpoint to the narratives of the characters proper. It is essentially subjective; we are, as it were, at one with the interior life. But whose? The author's, probably; certainly Dos Passos's own experiences of war are part of it; but even more, I think, of a figure comparable to the 'I, Walt Whitman' of 'Leaves of Grass', a figure who is not quite the author but the author generalized, universalized, the Whitmanesque 'I am the man, I suffer'd, I was there'.

These devices constitute the framework in which what one is tempted to call the novel proper, the adventures of Mac, J. Ward Moorehouse, Eleanor Stoddard, Joe Williams, Richard Ellsworth Savage, Charley Anderson, Mary French and the rest, is set. After a quarter of a century, *U.S.A.* remains an impressive book but increasingly a less impressive novel. The force of the ambition is still there and also something of the achievement. But as a novel, while it is complicated, it is not at all complex. The novel seems to me to survive as a notable but too orderly ruin. Dos Passos makes his point time and time again and brings it to brilliant summation in the final pages, with the biographical section, 'Vag', describing the young hitch-hiker looking for a lift across the North American continent:

> Eyes black with want seek out the eyes of the drivers, a hitch, a hundred miles down the road.
>
> Overhead in the blue a plane drones. Eyes follow the silver Douglas that flashes on in the sun and bores its smooth way out of sight into the blue.
>
> (The transatlantic passengers sit pretty, big men with bank accounts, highly paid jobs, who are saluted by doormen; telephone girls say goodmorning to them. Last night, after a fine dinner, drinks with friends, they left Newark. Roar of climbing motors slanting up into the inky haze. Lights drop away. An hour staring along a silvery wing at a big lonesome moon hurrying west through curdling scum. Beacons flash in a line across Ohio. . . .
>
> Chi. A glimpse of the dipper. Another spiral swoop from cool into hot air thick with dust and the reek of burnt prairies. . . .

Omaha. . . .

The transcontinental passenger thinks contracts, profits, vacationtrips, mighty continent between Atlantic and Pacific, power, wires humming dollars, cities jammed, hills empty, the indian trail leading into the wagon-road, the macadamed pike, the concrete skyway; trains, planes; history the billiondollar speedup,

and in the bumpy air over the desert towards Las Vegas,

sickens and vomits into the carton container the steak and mushrooms he ate in New York. No matter, silver in the pocket, greenbacks in the wallet, drafts, certified checks, plenty restaurants in L.A.)

The young man waits on the side of the road; the plane has gone; thumb moves in a small circle when a car tears hissing past. Eyes seek the driver's eyes. A hundred miles down the road. Head swims, belly tightens, wants crawl over his skin like ants:

went to school, books said opportunity, ads promised speed, own your home, shine bigger than your neighbours, the radio-crooner whispered girls, ghosts of phantom girls coaxed from the screen, millions in winnings were chalked up on the boards in the offices, paychecks were for hands willing to work, the cleared desk of an executive with three telephones on it;

waits with swimming head, needs knot the belly, idle hands numb, beside the speeding traffic.

A hundred miles down the road.

The point is truly made. Here is the United States in mid-continent in all its contrasts, which are mutually exclusive: progress in the air, on the roads—and the hungry man still walks, mocked by the promise of opportunity, mocked by the American promises. It is the negation of brotherhood. Whenever Dos Passos is celebrating injustice, the palpable and obvious lack of love of man for man, his prose still has the power of a clenched fist.

As a novel, though, *U.S.A.* has become curiously flat. This is due partly to the flat style in which the characters are rendered. One cannot complain of any lack of documentation on their behalf; their dossiers are complete. But they seem now entirely dossiers and, for all their great differences, not always easily distinguishable one from another as we read them.

The trip to Mexico and the private car the Mexican government put at the disposal of J. Ward Moorehouse to go back north in was lovely but a little tiresome, and it was so dusty going through the desert. Janey bought some very pretty things so cheap, some turquoise jewelry and pink onyx to take home to Alice and her mother and sisters as presents. Going up in the private car J. Ward kept her busy dictating and there was a big bunch of men always drinking and smoking cigars and laughing at smutty stories in the smoking-room or on the observation platform. One of them was that man Barrow she'd done some work for in Washington. He always stopped to talk to her now and she didn't like the way his eyes were when he stood over her table talking to her, still he was an interesting man and quite different from what she'd imagined a laborleader would be . . .

That is Janey Williams, Moorehouse's secretary, who later becomes the corrupt Labour leader Barrow's mistress. Twenty pages on we find this:

She and J. W. went out a great deal together, to all the French operas and first nights. There was a little French restaurant where they ate hors d'oeuvres way east in Fiftysixth Street. They went to see the French paintings in the galleries in Madison Avenue. J.W. began to get interested in art, and Eleanor loved going round with him because he had such a romantic manner about everything and he used to tell her she was his inspiration and that he always got good ideas when he'd been talking to her. They often talked about how silly people were who said that a man and a woman couldn't have a platonic friendship.

That is Eleanor Stoddard, an interior decorator of a different upbringing and social class from Janey; but the flatness of Dos Passos's irony, rendered in terms almost of baby talk after Gertrude Stein, reduces them to nearly identical characters.

Part of Dos Passos's trouble, of course, comes from the old difficulty that always faces the naturalistic novelist: how, if character is wholly determined by social and economic factors, are you to produce a character who appears to the reader and to himself something more than a mere emanation of his environment, who possesses at any rate the illusion of free choice? Obviously, Dos Passos is most successful with those characters who are consciously at odds with and in revolt against society, Mac McCreary, the former 'Wobbley' turned Mexican revolutionary, Joe Williams, the merchant seaman, and Mary French. But the real failure of *U.S.A.* is apparent as soon as it is compared with the one contemporary novel with which it is comparable, *Ulysses*. Dublin is as much the all-pervading, circumambient element in that work as the United States is in Dos Passos's; but the relationship to Dublin of Bloom and Stephen Dedalus is much closer, more organic: the city and what happens in it on Bloomsday echo what happens to the characters, exist in a symbolic relation to them. One cannot, indeed, draw a hard and fast line between the characters and Dublin. *Ulysses* is a highly integrated formal structure; and though the means that Joyce uses to build up his extraordinarily complex composition can be isolated, named and analysed, they are not detachable; they are structural parts of a magnificently composed whole; and they never serve merely one single purpose. But you can take away, and keep on taking away, section after section of *U.S.A.* without structural loss: whole passages from the news reels, for example, even the biographies. One could extract the Camera Eye sequences—do they ever, in practice, at the time of reading, appear as the unifying element of the novel?

All this is to say that *U.S.A.* lacks form, is not an organic whole, is without any centre apart from Dos Passos's own indignation. One sees the point of the devices, but they remain devices, and the form has not crystallized out. We have instead an orderly procession of fragments, of which some—the biographies conspicuously—are now of much greater value than others.

[2]

Dos Passos attempted to use the techniques of symbolism in the service of naturalism; but James T. Farrell, for all his indebtedness to Joyce, began as a naturalist and has remained one, unrepentant and defiant. He is the true heir of Dreiser. If he lacks Dreiser's tragic sense, he has an icily relentless passion that transforms his best work into a formidable indictment of society. His best work seems to me quite certainly the trilogy with which he made his reputation, *Studs Lonigan* (*Young Lonigan*, 1932, *The Young Manhood of Studs Lonigan*, 1934, and *Judgment Day*, 1935). It is among the most depressing novels ever written, and one of the most honest and disturbing. In the character of

Studs, the lower middle-class Irish boy living on the South Side of Chicago, a youth with nothing in his environment worthy of the response of his imagination, so that his mind becomes sodden with dreams of the seedy violence of the films and the pulps, one aspect of American civilization is caught and fixed, arraigned with a cold power, a controlled disgust, unlikely to be surpassed. To *Studs Lonigan* Farrell prefixed a quotation from Plato which seems to sum up his point of view exactly: 'Except in the case of some rarely gifted nature there never will be a good man who has not from his childhood been used to play amid things of beauty and make of them a joy and a study.' Young Studs is not a rarely gifted nature. Farrell is the novelist of Megalopolis as Mumford has defined it, the great barren urban agglomerations from which the things of beauty that should surround the child are so strikingly absent.

In précis, as summarized for example in the *Oxford Companion to American Literature*, *Studs Lonigan* cannot help appearing as a *reductio ad absurdum* of naturalistic fiction. But this is not how it seems either as one reads it or as one remembers it, for a précis necessarily ignores the richness and concreteness, the finely particularized nature, of the detail with which the book is built up, and also the superbly sustained scenes in which Studs appears as a character. And then, of course, précis disengages Studs from his milieu. In the novel, Studs is merely the figure in the foreground of what is the whole teeming world of the South Side of Chicago, and it is that teeming world that makes him what he is. In terms of the novel itself, it is utterly fitting that Studs, unemployed, unhappily married, the father of an unwanted child, should die of a weak heart at the age of twenty-nine.

Nor, as has often been attempted, in order to persuade us that it need not be taken seriously as art, can the novel be dismissed as 'sociology'. Farrell's naturalism, his apparent objectivity, his Marxism, should not blind us to the fact that here we have an authentic lyric cry of horror at the human condition, expressed in considered art. Farrell's theme is one universal in our time: the effect of the desert of modern city life upon human beings who live in it. His novel has affinities with those of Céline and Döblin and Graham Greene, even at points with Eliot's *The Waste Land*. It is a waste land Farrell is describing.

> Studs Lonigan, on the verge of fifteen, and wearing his first suit of long trousers, stood in the bathroom with a Sweet Caporal pasted in his mug. His hands were jammed in his

trouser pockets, and he sneered. He puffed, drew the fag out of
his mouth, inhaled and said to himself:

Well, I'm kissin' the old dump goodbye tonight.

Studs was a small, broad-shouldered lad. His face was wide
and planed; his hair was a light brown. His long nose was too
large for his other features; almost a sheeny's nose. His lips were
thick and wide, and they did not seem at home in his otherwise
frank and boyish face. He was always twisting them into his
familiar tough-guy sneers. He had blue eyes; his mother rightly
called them baby-blue eyes.

He took another drag and repeated to himself:

Well, I'm kissin' the old dump goodbye . . .

The old dump Studs is kissing goodbye is St Patrick's Grammar
School, 'a jailhouse which might just as well have had barred windows'.

The novel opens, then, with Studs's liberation from school; but not
from the Church, and this is so even though his catholicism amounts to
nothing more than a sullen captivity to superstition. On Farrell's
showing, the Church in Chicago can offer him nothing better, and the
novel is as much an indictment of the Catholic Church in America as of
the nature of American society. The Church is represented as bleakly
puritanical and illiberal, the forcing-house of anti-semitism, racialism,
anti-communism, one hundred per cent Americanism. As a Catholic
critic of Farrell, Professor Frank O'Malley, has observed, it seems to
come naturally for Farrell's Catholic citizen to say:

> 'Mother, you can never trust a nigger or a Jew. The Jews
> killed Christ, and the nigger is a Jew made black till the Day of
> Judgment as a punishment from God. The niggers are descended
> from Cain. Cain slew his brother Abel and God turned on Cain
> for killing his brother, and said that all the descendants of Cain
> would be black, and they would have to live in Africa where it is
> uncivilized. And to this day they are an outcast people, and their
> skins are black like monkeys. You can never trust them.'

The Church as depicted by Farrell is wholly repressive; it rules by
fear, by the threat of damnation. It is as it were the hated policeman
who cannot be evaded, the super-ego in its crudest and most monstrous
form; but it can offer Studs neither ideals nor moral values. At the
beginning of the book, the dominating image of the desirable life for
Studs is the street-corner pool-room, entrance to which is almost an
initiation into manhood. Later, the dominating image becomes the

brothel. Not that Studs hasn't his moments of higher aspiration. They are represented by his ambition to become a professional baseball player and by his half-hearted love for his childhood sweetheart Lucy Scanlon, who, in *The Young Manhood of Studs Lonigan*, finally rejects him after he has picked up venereal disease from a tart but whose memory haunts him on and off for the rest of his life.

His aspirations are abortive, for he is controlled entirely by circumstances and environment, so much so that he is almost personalityless. He accepts uncritically the code of the herd in which he lives, and the central item of that code is to be a tough guy. He passes his life in a continuous fantasy of himself as tough guy, the fantasies being based closely on films seen, as when he dreams of cornering the Kaiser in personal combat in Flanders, which seems now a reminiscence of an early Chaplin film, and on the folk-lore of the pool-rooms and saloons. Any action he commits is the attempt to translate fantasy into reality, on the baseball diamond, in saloons and brothels and the violence of the streets at night. He is terrifyingly immature but also utterly convincing, so minutely is his fantasy-life particularized. Dreiser's tragic pity has no place here. Studs is shown simply as the product and the victim of a corrupt and vicious social order which must be destroyed. As the novel ends with Studs dying in the early days of the economic depression, his father's drunken grief is set against a Communist demonstration marching to the words and music of the Internationale.

Studs Lonigan is still a powerful feat of imaginative writing, impressive and disturbing in its truth. Its power is not invalidated by the fact that its truth is a limited one. It is one man's story, not a universal one, as Farrell obviously realized since he followed *Studs Lonigan* with the sequence of novels—*A World I Never Made, No Star Is Lost, Father and Son* and *My Days of Anger*—depicting the life of Danny O'Neill, a marginal character in the *Lonigan* books, with whom Studs had been at school and who breaks through from the prison of Irish-Catholic Chicago and its values to become a student at Chicago University and in the course of time a writer. O'Neill, it seems fair to assume, is a version of Farrell himself. Ideally, one feels, if Farrell was intent on producing a novel representative of the human condition, a novel that could be accepted as universal, he should have fused his two sequences into one. As it is, their existence side by side brings us up against the limitations of naturalism, what may be called the Calvinism that seems to be implicit in it. The circumstances in which Studs and O'Neill grow up are much the same: one is damned by them, the other triumphs over them and escapes; but why one and not the other? Somewhere in the dark background there seems to lurk a doctrine of Election.

As it happens, with these novels the problem is academic, for the O'Neill sequence, however close it may be to the facts of autobiography, is not nearly so convincing as *Studs Lonigan*, which remains Farrell's master work, though a much more recent one shows qualities of tenderness and sympathy of which one scarcely thought him capable. This is *The Face of Time*, published in 1954. In it—it is not quite easy to see how—he manages to produce an effect of beauty. *The Face of Time* describes the life of the O'Flaherty family in working-class Chicago during the early years of the century. O'Flaherty, an immigrant, has retired from his work in the Chicago transport system and, unknown to himself, is dying of cancer. It comes as no surprise to learn that his youngest daughter is tubercular and another the mistress of a married man; and the scene is no more agreeable than that of *Studs Lonigan*. Yet, in the characters of old O'Flaherty and his wife, Farrell achieves something like a pastoral quality.

For the reason, we must go back to the quotation from Plato prefixed to *Studs Lonigan*. As compared to Studs, the native-born American, the O'Flahertys are, as it were, so much nearer grace. They are immigrants, and for both of them the reality is still the Ireland of their childhood, and America something not understood, essentially mysterious and, the much greater degree of material prosperity around them notwithstanding, consisting of broken promises. They have in their time, unlike Studs, played among things of beauty, and innocence has been kept; so that the O'Flahertys emerge as images of simple goodness. The tact with which Farrell created his images is nowhere better shown than in his rendering of the O'Flahertys' Catholicism. Bitter critic of Catholicism as Farrell is, he is an honest novelist and in *The Face of Time* he shows us the Church as it exists in the minds of his immigrant hero and heroine.

[3]

I realized with amazement how rapidly the human psyche can strip itself of its awareness and its emotional contacts, and reduce itself to a sub-brutal condition of simple gross persistence. It is not animality—far from it. These boys are much less than animals. They are cold wills functioning with a minimum of consciousness. The amount that they are *not* aware of is perhaps the most amazing aspect of their character. They are brutally and deliberately unaware. They have no hopes, no desires even. They have even no will-to-exist, for existence even is too high a term. They have a strange, stony will-to-persist, that is all.

THESE WORDS of Lawrence's could apply to the characters of *Studs Lonigan*; in fact, they appear in his introduction to Edward Dahlberg's *Bottom Dogs*, which appeared in 1930, two years earlier than Farrell's novel. It covers the first twenty or so years of Lorry Lewis's life as a child in Kansas City, a boy in a German orphanage in Cleveland, Ohio, a worker in the Kansas City stockyards, a hobo in California, a bum in Los Angeles. It ends with his vaguely fearing, in a curious way even hoping, that he may have contracted venereal disease from a dance-hall pick-up. It is quite a short novel; unlike Farrell, Dahlberg does not employ the saturation technique of the Naturalists, the relentless accumulation of tiny detail, but is much more impressionistic. For whole stretches of the novel Lorry seems hardly there at all—until one realizes, as in the orphanage chapters and the very fine bitterly funny Y.M.C.A. chapter at the end of the book, that he is there in the sense that a mirror could be said to be there. His mind seems so empty that the only thing it can do is reflect what is outside it, characters and scenes of meaningless violence.

The novel conveys a sense of utter hopelessness far beyond Farrell's. Studs, at any rate, has his fantasies, crude as they are: Lorry lacks even fantasy; and in the Lonigan trilogy there is always its author's passionate indignation, which manifests itself in the continuous irony that pervades Studs's existence. This means that Studs is seen all the time in perspective: he is distanced; he stands, by plain implication at least, in relation to alternative ways of life, to values that, if never stated, can easily be inferred. But there is, as it were, nothing that mediates between Lorry and the reader; we are as much within his consciousness, such as it is, as we are, say, within that of Virginia Woolf's Mrs Dalloway; and his consciousness is expressed in the language in which the novel is written.

Dahlberg's vernacular is the language of city streets. It is in itself debased, so that it can express only the debased. As Lawrence noted: 'The boy Lorry "always has his nose in a book"—and he must have got things out of the books.' There is no evidence in the novel that he did, and it comes as a shock to learn that Lorry has at any rate tried to read Thackeray. Yet against this failure in totally communicating Lorry must be set Dahlberg's total success in creating Lorry's feckless, bewildered, over-working mother the 'lady barber'; and the medium is perfect for the expression of the raw and the violent unqualified by any interpretation of them. It still transmits to the reader shocks of crude sensation, the sensation, for instance, of jumping a freight train, of sleeping for the first time in a flop-house, or of not having eaten for two days. And above all it communicates hopelessness, the hopelessness of the last sentences of the novel:

> Anyway, if he got the clap he would go to Los Angeles City Hospital; maybe, those enamelled iron beds, the white sheets, the medical immaculateness of it all, might do something to him. Something had to happen; and he knew nothing would. . . .

The lives of the bottom dogs, men and women who can sink no lower in the social and economic system, have provided Nelson Algren with his chosen material. His first novel, *Somebody in Boots*, published in 1935, follows the early life of Cass McKay, who, brought up in a slum home in Texas, becomes a hobo, goes to prison for vagrancy, reaches Chicago, lives with Norah Egan, who works in a sweatshop, associates with Negroes and Communists and is beaten up for doing so. At the end of the novel, girlless and jobless, he is again a hobo. *Somebody in Boots* contains as section-headings quotations from *The Communist Manifesto*, which gave it the right tone at the time; but over the years Algren's Marxism has fallen away from him. He has remained faithful to his bottom dogs, though he now tends to see them in rather more sensational conditions than those resulting from mass unemployment: his bottom dogs are now drug-addicts as in *The Man with the Golden Arm* or haunters of New Orleans brothels as in *A Walk on the Wild Side*.

There can be no question of the immediate reality of his characters. Horrible though they are in their subhumanity, his small-time hoods and punch-drunk pugs and brothel-keepers convince from the word go. Richard Wright has described Algren's imagination as 'innocent, bold, vivid, and poetic', and this seems just. He writes in an altogether more vicious and crude vernacular than ever Dahlberg did and achieves considerable poetic intensity in doing so. Farrell's characters were members of Irish immigrants in Chicago: Algren's in *Never Come Morning* (1942) come from Polish immigrant families in the same city. But whereas Studs Lonigan's fall is essentially from lower middle-class respectability, one is never made aware of any fall at all in Algren's characters. In part, this is because, being from the beginning at the bottom of things, there is nowhere they can fall; but in part, also, it is the index of Algren's innocence. Algren's Bruno Bicek has his affinities with Lonigan. His life is governed by crude fantasies of grandeur, specifically, to be heavyweight champion of the world. When the novel ends, he is being indicted, at the age of 18, for murder. What is interesting is Algren's attitude to his characters. Algren is Whitmanesque: 'I feel I am one of them—I belong to these convicts and prostitutes myself.' This identification makes for warmth, immediacy and sympathy, but it scarcely mitigates the hideous monotony of his novels. It reveals his fundamental sentimentality. A slackening of the poetic power, and his Chicago with its racketeers, gangsters, tarts, junkies, hoodlums, could be almost interchangeable with Steinbeck's Monterey.

It is not accidental that the characters in these bottom-dog novels all belong to ethnic groups peripheral, because of their recent arrival in the United States, to the mainstream of American life. But there is one ethnic group in the United States that has been in the country for as long as all but a relatively small minority of Americans and is still largely peripheral: the Negroes. One of their traditional functions in society is stated brutally by Judge Clane in Carson McCullers's *Clock without Hands*: 'Sammy Lank and poor-whites like that have nothing but the colour of their skin. . . . It is a sad commentary on human nature but every man has to have somebody to look down on. So the Sammy Lanks of this world only have the Nigra to look down on.'

The Negro, in other words, is the bottomest dog of all; and after Dahlberg, Farrell, Algren appeared the Negro bottom-dog novel, Richard Wright's *Native Son*, in 1940. Not that Wright was the first

American Negro novelist, but he was essentially of his time; he had experienced in his own life the twentieth-century transformation of American Negro life generally, the transformation from the country labourer to the urban proletarian. Born in 1908 in Mississippi, he had gone to Memphis, Tennessee, at the age of fifteen and worked at a variety of unskilled jobs; and then, during the depression years of the thirties, had drifted north to Chicago, there to join the Communist Party in 1936. One sees how great a liberation this must have been for him. It changed the whole problem of being a Negro in the United States; it taught him that Negroes were not doomed to live in perpetual semi-servitude because of the colour of their skin but belonged to a great mass of the exploited, irrespective of colour, throughout the world. It gave the Negro at once new dignity and new hope. All this is in *Native Son*, Wright's first novel but second work of fiction. In it he brought to violent consciousness the Negro's assertion of himself, his refusal any longer to be what the white man had cast him to be; and *Native Son* remains a most powerful novel both of Negro assertion and of radical protest. For Wright—and much of the book's power comes from this—they were different sides of the one coin.

Part of the novel's strength comes, too, from the reader's realization that Wright's protagonist, the Negro youth Bigger Thomas, is not at all a persona for the author himself. Bigger is no sensitive adolescent with literary aspirations. He is already, when we first meet him, a young tough with a criminal record and in violent repudiation of the religious values of his hard-working mother with whom, along with a younger brother and sister, he lives in a rat-infested single room on the Chicago South Side. Violence is indeed the key to his character. As the novel opens, he has the chance of a job with a wealthy white family, which his mother implores him to take. He half-promises to do so but at the same time he is planning a drug-store hold-up with his friends. The druggist is a white man, and Bigger has always carefully avoided white people in his criminal activities. He eggs his friends on to undertake the stick-up but he is terribly afraid. In order, therefore, to make the stick-up impossible, he accuses one of his friends of the cowardice he himself feels and terrorizes him with his knife.

He is in fact compact of hatred and the sense of a radical deprivation. Hence the fearful attraction of holding up Blum's drug store.

> They had the feeling that the robbing of Blum's would be a violation of ultimate taboo; it would be a trespassing into

territory where the full wrath of an alien white world would be turned loose upon them; in short, it would be a symbolic challenge of the white world's rule over them; a challenge which they yearned to make, but were afraid to. Yes; if they could rob Blum's, it would be a real hold-up, in more senses than one. In comparison, all their other jobs had been play.

The challenge when made goes far beyond the robbing of a white drug store, but is the result of no act of will on Bigger's part: rather, it is purely accidental, the consequence of blind panic in circumstances over which he has no control. He gets his job as chauffeur to the Daltons, millionaire real-estate agents known for their philanthropy towards Negroes, is caught up bewilderingly and resentfully in the world of their daughter, Mary, a university student, and her Communist friends, and within a matter of hours has quite unwittingly killed her and, in order to destroy the body, pushed it into the kitchen furnace.

He kills, then, by completely unforeseeable accident; but the effect on him is of liberation, of a sudden sense of power; and thinking to turn the killing to his own account, he sends the Daltons a note saying the girl has been kidnapped and demanding ransom money, clumsily implying that the kidnapping is the work of Communists, people of whose existence he has until a few hours back been in entire ignorance. Again within a matter of hours, the murder has been discovered, and Bigger flees. He is cornered by police and vigilantes, attempts to shoot it out with them on the roof of a tenement house, but is finally brought down by jets of water from fire hoses.

Thus the first two parts of the novel. They are executed with tremendous power. Bigger is not a hero; he is not even very intelligent; but he is not sentimentalized or falsified. And he is presented all the time in close-up, as it were. He is conceived and rendered with such passion that, willy-nilly, the reader becomes implicated in *his* panic, *his* flight, *his* struggle against overwhelming odds, for by the end of this second part it is this one Negro boy against the whole of white Chicago, city government, police, press and an enraged and frightened public.

The third part is much less good. Bigger is defended by a Communist lawyer and is reduced from the heroic stature which is his in the earlier parts to that of a counter in an argument. What Max, the lawyer, says of him is excellent and largely true; but it is all much too explicit.

And Bigger's feelings on the eve of the electric chair, his dawning awareness of human solidarity, strikes one as altogether too *voulu*, the party moral at the end.

Wright never fulfilled his remarkable promise. He became the leading American Negro intellectual of his day but lived not in the United States but in France. His only other novel, *The Outsider* (1953), must be judged a failure. The nature of its subject is such that, had it succeeded, one would have had to invoke Dostoevsky as the obvious measure of judgment. As it is, *The Outsider*, one feels, falls short of Sartre. In a sense, it reverses the thesis of *Native Son*. It has great power, but in the end it has to be taken rather as an intellectual thriller than the something more it should have been; one's final interest is in the ideas propounded, not in the characters that should embody them. Cross Damon, the Negro hero, is the Existentialist for whom God is dead, who is conscious of 'the full flood of a senseless existence' and who must learn how to live in accord with his knowledge. On his deathbed, he realizes that in his conduct he has fallen into the pattern of behaviour of the Communists themselves and that his efforts to be free were futile. 'Alone a man is nothing.'

Wright's thesis overrides his characters: one isn't conscious of them as human beings so much as exponents of ideas. This intensifies the sense of melodrama, which in turn perverts Wright's true aim, which was not, one assumes, primarily to write an anti-Communist novel.

[4]

WRIGHT's experience of Communism was one shared by the great majority of those American and British novelists of the thirties who saw themselves at the time as 'proletarian', 'political', 'Marxist'. The common pattern was of sudden conversion to Communism followed by disillusionment. It is easy to see now that most of the novelists who thought themselves political were in fact politically innocent. For some writers, however sincere they may have believed themselves, it is plain now that Communism—and not all the novelists by any means who used Marxist jargon or exploited class-war situations in their fiction were paid-up members of the Party—was simply the latest literary fashion. That this was realized at the time can be seen from Albert Halper's novel of 1933, *Union Square*, a novel now of historical interest only. 'What the hell', the already disillusioned Communist poet Jason Wheeler asks a meeting of left-wing writers, 'do workers care about art? And why should they be made conscious of your so-called "proletarian" twaddle about the masses rising up to greet a new workers' culture?'

Yet the emotional appeal of Communism to the generous-minded young at this time cannot be over-estimated. It was simple and direct. It was put with a brilliance and power beyond anything British and American novelists were capable of by André Malraux in his *La Condition Humaine*, the seminal left-wing novel of the age. The function of Marxism in Malraux's novel is to give validity to the concept of dignity; it is its function, too, in the American left-wing fiction of the time. Admittedly, little of this fiction remains readable today, and it is doubtful whether any but literary historians will again pick up the novels of Halper, Grace Lumpkin, Jack Conroy, Thomas Bell or Josephine Herbst. But one of these novels still seems to me to exist in its own right: Robert Cantwell's *The Land of Plenty*, published in 1934.

The title is, of course, ironical. The theme of the novel is the education of the workers, and of one young worker in particular, through a spontaneous strike caused by the inefficiencies of capitalism in a wood-veneer factory in a city on the north-west coast. The strength of the novel, apart from its considerable ambition and its considerable literary expertise, derives largely, it seems to me, from the quality of personal experience that permeates it. Before becoming a journalist in New York, Cantwell himself worked as a plywood factory veneer clipper operator, so that the novel is saturated with the sense of the actual.

The novel is divided into two parts, 'Power and Light', and 'The Education of a Worker'. The symbolism of the first part, indicated in its title, is clear and unstrained. It is the eve of the Fourth of July, the employees of the factory are working overtime, there have been wage-cuts, there are rumours that hands will be laid off. As the book opens, the lights in the factory have just failed. The workers switch off their machines almost by instinct and through long experience of the plant are at home in the dark; whereas the new efficiency expert, Belcher, is lost in the darkness, in a state of near-panic. The moral is obvious. It is

Hagen, who oils the motors, who investigates the stoppage and advises Belcher. In the confusion caused by the failure of the lights there has been an accident; a hoist-man has been injured by a swinging log. The manager of the factory, MacMahon, is summoned from his home to look into the trouble. He and Belcher lose themselves on the mudflats beneath the factory, are caught up in the bushes by the shore and, frightened of the incoming tide, are marooned there until there is light enough for them to see their way back. By the time they return the workers have released the hoist-man from the log that pinned him down; but when the lights finally go on Belcher fires Hagen and another man. The workers compel MacMahon to countermand Belcher's order.

The action of this part of the novel covers scarcely more than an hour. Cantwell focuses his attention on the leading characters in turn; the first chapter is called 'Carl', the second 'Hagen', and so on. But the almost anonymous minor characters are not much less important than those in the foreground, for while the main actions are being conducted Cantwell uses the situation—the power failure, the bosses' loss of control, the accident to the hoist-man, the injustice done to Hagen— to crystallize the workers' fears, discontent and, finally, their sense of solidarity, so that by the end of this first part its title has taken on a new meaning: the power is the workers', and they have seen the light.

The second part of the novel, 'The Education of a Worker', concentrates on the education of one specific worker, young Johnny Hagen, Hagen's son, who has had to give up his ambitions of going to college in order to help support his family. When they return to work after the Fourth of July holiday the workers find that twenty men have been laid off the night-shift, and both shifts strike. Cantwell does not, of course, neglect to use the Fourth of July celebrations to point the contrast between the promises of the American dream and the nature of the American reality; and the contrast is heightened by the events of the days that follow as experienced by Johnny. The strike and what it involves—picketing, the hazards of police brutality, the hostility of middle-class opinion—are tantamount to an initiation into manhood for the boy, an initiation paralleled by his first experience of sex, on a night when the workers drive out the scabs and the police and take over the factory.

What strikes one now about *The Land of Plenty* is its quality as a heroic novel. Cantwell has said that he was moved to write it precisely for the reason that Malraux's Kyo became a Communist: 'in order to give working people a sense of their own dignity'. And though it would be absurd to attempt to set *The Land of Plenty* beside Malraux's masterpiece, it does at least partake of its spirit, its heroic and defiant temper; and it is the only left-wing novel of the thirties in America or Britain that does.

[5]

JOHN STEINBECK'S strike novel, *In Dubious Battle*—it was his fourth novel—appeared in 1936. The central characters of the book are professional Communists, Mac, a veteran in the field, and Jim Nolan, a younger man who comes to the Party because his 'whole family has been ruined by this system', and the novel still has considerable interest as an account of the organization of the itinerant fruit-pickers in California. On the face of it, it is a story of Radical heroism, of the illiterate and oppressed restored to their dignity as men by their own efforts and by those of dedicated revolutionaries, of Nolan's increasing stature as a clear-eyed and ruthless organizer, and of his murder by vigilantes; it ends on a note of fervent rhetoric, with Mac addressing the strikers at night, Nolan's corpse illuminated by a lantern beside him:

> Mac shivered. He moved his jaws to speak, and seemed to break the frozen jaws loose. His voice was high and monotonous. 'This guy didn't want nothing for himself——' he began. His knuckles were white, where he gripped the rail. 'Comrades! He didn't want nothing for himself——'

As one reads the novel now, however, one realizes not only its occasional naïvety—Mac and Nolan are two-dimensional figures of proletarian heroism endowed with an almost boy-scout simplicity of motive and action—but also its essential ambiguity. It emerges quite plainly in the dialogue of Dr Burton, the fellow-traveller whom Mac brings in as medical officer of the striking fruit-pickers' camp. As a character, Burton scarcely exists but he is, as it were, the reflective centre of the novel, and it can scarcely be doubted that his values are

Steinbeck's. It is Burton who says to Nolan: '. . . you've got something in your eyes, Jim, something religious. I've seen it in you boys before', and to Mac: 'You're the craziest mess of cruelty and *Hausfrau* sentimentality, of clear vision and rose-coloured glasses I ever saw.' Burton, in other words, sees through the Communists, and though he may admire and even perhaps envy their single-mindedness, which to him is almost simple-mindedness, he has no illusions about the final issue of their struggle.

Why, then, is Burton risking his life and his reputation working with Communists at all? Challenged by Mac, he replies: 'I don't believe in the cause, but I believe in men . . . I guess I just believe they're men, and not animals. Maybe if I went into a kennel and the dogs were hungry and sick and dirty, and maybe if I could help those dogs, I would. Wouldn't be their fault they were that way.' Yet Burton's attitude is not quite as simple as this may suggest. His attitude is much more that of a kind of scientist, perhaps an anthropologist working in the field. He is a man with theories about life, about group-man as a new species, of which strikes are a manifestation. As he says to Mac:

'It might be like this, Mac: when group-man wants to move, he makes a standard. "God wills that we recapture the Holy Land"; or he says: "We fight to make the world safe for democracy"; or he says: "We will wipe out social injustice with communism." But the group doesn't care about the Holy Land, or democracy, or communism. Maybe the group simply wants to move, to fight and uses these words simply to reassure the brains of individual men . . . You might be an effect as well as a cause, Mac. You might be an expression of group-man, a cell endowed with a special function, like an eye cell, drawing your force from group-man, and at the same time directing him, like an eye. Your eye both takes orders from and gives orders to your brain.'

This is the most explicit statement of the biological unanimism that seems to lie behind all Steinbeck's work and that goes far towards explaining its nature and where it succeeds and where it fails. This biological unanimism has obvious affinities with Whitman's notion of 'the en-masse' and, as stated by the preacher Casy in *The Grapes of Wrath*, comes, according to R. W. B. Lewis, straight out of Emerson, is indeed his notion of the over-soul.

One might say that Steinbeck's theme is life and the processes of life at a certain place at a certain time. But the processes of life that interest him are those common to the spirochaete, the tiger and man. They are evolutionary processes, relatively undifferentiated; and this plainly presents him with difficult problems as a novelist, who is normally concerned with something diametrically opposed to Steinbeck's view, namely individuation. Values, except the values that make for the animal survival of the species, are absent from Steinbeck's work —or almost so; he has a generous indignation at the spectacle of human suffering. But apart from this, he is the celebrant of life, any kind of life, just because it is life; and against his passionate sympathy with the Joads of this world must be set his woozy sentimentality over the bums and whores-with-hearts-of-gold he celebrates in *Tortilla Flat* and *Cannery Row*.

In effect, this means that Steinbeck is at his best as a novelist when he is dealing with human beings living at something approaching the animal level. These are made acceptable and indeed moving because of the genuine sweetness one feels in Steinbeck's nature and because he sees these human beings as being at least as dignified as animals. He doesn't, in other words, reduce them; his view of life would prevent his doing that. One sees this in the short novel *Of Mice and Men*, which only fails to be a small masterpiece because of the unconvincing nature of Lennie's hallucinations in the final chapter. In one sense, of course, in its picture of the relationship between the two ranch hands, George the little guy and Lennie the feeble-minded giant whom he protects, *Of Mice and Men* is another example of what might be called the eternal American 'buddy novel' with its inescapable suggestion of latent homosexuality; but part of Steinbeck's strength generally is his very Americanness; he is essentially a *native* writer. And he handles the buddy theme with great tact. At first glance, the success is the more remarkable because what happens, what is bound to happen, cannot come as a surprise: we know that Lennie, who loves soft small things and kills mice and puppies by accident, not knowing his own strength, will certainly kill a girl in the same way before the book ends. At second glance, we see how the success comes about. From the beginning, from the page in which Lennie comes into the action, he is associated, we see him, with some small soft helpless animal; and in the end these small soft helpless animals symbolize Lennie himself. He may be a giant in physique but, all the same, in essence, he too is a small soft helpless animal doomed to be killed like one. Mice and men, if not identical in Steinbeck's view, are at least interchangeable.

Of Mice and Men is a pathetic story of human beings at what is almost the lowest level of articulateness, to be distinguished from animals mainly, perhaps, by their capacity to dream, though what they dream can never be fulfilled in reality. The dream is the same as that which motivates the 'Okies' in *The Grapes of Wrath*, the dispossessed sharecroppers of Oklahoma who pour in their broken-down old cars across the mountains and the desert into the rich valleys of California, the promised land where there's a little white house standing in its own few acres at the end of the trail. Their progress is in a sense a repetition of that which brought their ancestors across the Atlantic from Europe to the Eastern seaboard; and the promised land of California is to be proved no less delusive than America itself.

The Grapes of Wrath, of course, exists on a much vaster scale than *Of Mice and Men*. It includes within itself a considerable part, however dramatically or melodramatically heightened, of the experience of a considerable number of Americans during the thirties; and though it can be faulted in many ways—it is at times pretentious, at times sentimental, and the characters never quite become three-dimensional—it is still a novel that deserves respect and even admiration. It is, for one thing, superb simply as narrative; and many of the incidental things in it, the inter-chapters which enhance the significance of the migration by setting it in a larger context of history, are brilliant. There is, admittedly, a tendency to inflate in these chapters, but Dos Passos himself in *U.S.A.* did nothing better than, for instance, Chapter Seven, the impressionistic rendering of the used-car lots where the migrants plead to be allowed to buy their wretched vehicles and spares.

And, once again, the theme is given dignity by being seen *sub specie aeternitatis*, at any rate biologically. For what one is observing in *The Grapes of Wrath*, one can't help feeling, is a whole species on the move. The Joads and those they represent really are behaving as 'the en-masse', an en-masse of lemmings, perhaps.

> The cars of the migrant people crawled out of the side roads on to the great cross-country highway, and they took the migrant way to the West. In the daylight they scuttled like bugs to the westward; and as the dark caught them, they clustered like bugs near to shelter and to water. And because they were lonely and perplexed, because they had all come from a place of sadness and

worry and defeat, and because they were all going to a new mysterious place, they huddled together; they talked together; they shared their lives, their food, and the things they hoped for in the new country. Thus it might be that one family camped near a spring and another camped for the spring and for the company, and a third because two families had pioneered the place and found it good. And when the sun went down, perhaps twenty families and twenty cars were there.

They are group-man, a species in which the individual counts for as much and as little as an individual cell in the human body. And this impression of group-man is further strengthened by being felt to exist within the whole order of nature; group-man is, as it were, one species among a host of species. There is, for example, the very fine third chapter, which describes the progress of a turtle climbing a wall and crossing a road. The turtle exists in an obvious symbolic relation to Tom Joad, just out of jail, returning to his family and about to set out with them on the long trek to California. But, having said that turtle and Tom exist in a symbolic relation to each other, one has to discriminate. Each exists in his own right and dignity, so that, even if one were to equate Tom with the turtle, one couldn't say he was diminished in consequence. The turtle, for all he appears only for a page or two, is as fully realized as any human character in the novel, and rendered with no less empathy and love.

On the plane of what I have called biological unanimism *The Grapes of Wrath* is a remarkable *tour de force*. The trouble is, it cannot always remain on that plane. We are, after all, tracing the fortunes of a limited number of human beings, the Joad family and the friends and acquaintances they make on the way. Steinbeck's representations of them are adequate enough for what may be considered propaganda purposes— on its publication *The Grapes of Wrath* was commonly compared with *Uncle Tom's Cabin* and perhaps had a similar influence in spotlighting social injustice. Beyond that, they seem adequate no longer. Ma Joad is an easily-understood paradigm of courage and endurance, but with her, as with the other characters, we are in the presence of the flat character. What the personages do and say is monotonously predictable from page to page. They are all too simply conceived, much too close to the popular stereotypes of poor-whites and hill-billies to be found in comic strips and cartoons. As human beings, they cannot carry the significance Steinbeck would have us read into them, and this is especially so of the two characters who are in some sense Steinbeck's spokesmen, Tom Joad and Casy, the ex-preacher. When Tom Joad, after the murder of Casy, decides to take up the preacher's job of labour organizer, and says to his mother:

'Well, maybe like Casy says, a fella ain't got a soul of his own, but on'y a piece of a big one—and then—'
'Then what, Tom?'
'Then it don' matter. Then I'll be aroun' in the dark. I'll be ever'-where—wherever you look. Wherever they's a fight so hungry people can eat, I'll be there. Wherever they's a cop beatin' up a guy, I'll be there. If Casy knowed, why, I'll be in the way guys yell when they're mad an'—I'll be in the way kids laugh when they're hungry an' they know supper's ready. An' when our folks eat the stuff they raise an' live in the houses they build—why, I'll be there. See God, I'm talkin' like Casy. Comes of thinkin' about him so much. Seems like I can see him some-times.'

one can only think that, if this rhetoric worked once, it does so no longer; just as now Casy's prayer over Grampa Joad's body—

'This ol' man jus' lived a life an' jus' died out of it. I don't know whether he was good or bad, but that don't matter much. He was alive, an' that's what matters. An' now he's dead, an' that don't matter. Heard a fella tell a poem one time, an' he says: "All that lives is holy." Got to thinkin', and purty soon it means more than the words say'—

strikes one as intolerably phoney.

[6]

WHAT IS lacking in Steinbeck and indeed in most of the novelists of the political thirties is found in the work of three writers who achieved little fame in their own time, were re-discovered years after and are still little known in England—Nathanael West, Henry Roth and Daniel Fuchs. Perhaps all that these three novelists have in common is that they are Jews, but to their treatment of the American scene their Jewishness adds a dimension of significance comparable to that which Silone's Christianity, however unorthodox, gives to his picture of Italy under Fascism. We are lifted right above the purely economic, mechanical interpretation of life and are confronted with the human condition in its naked terror.

Nathanael West lived in Paris in the middle-twenties and came under the influence of the Surrealists. His first novel, *The Dream Life of Balso Snell*, which appeared in 1931 to be almost entirely ignored, is a surrealist fantasy about the eponymous hero's wanderings within the Trojan Horse where, among other things, he meets a naked man in a bowler hat who is writing the life of Saint Puce, a flea who lived in Christ's armpit. Fiedler has suggested that West's apprenticeship to Surrealism enabled him to restore the Gothic to the American novel. Certainly it is true, as Fiedler says, that: 'Putting down a book by West, a reader is not sure whether he has been presented with a nightmare endowed with the conviction of actuality or with actuality distorted into the semblance of a nightmare; but in either case, he has the sense that he has been presented with a view of a world in which, incredibly, he lives!'

West's theme is the horror and anguish of the human condition. He expresses it in comedy that is shocking and grotesque, bitter and savage. His two major works are *Miss Lonelyhearts* (1933) and *The Day of the Locust* (1939). Besides these novels and *Balso Snell*, he also wrote *A Cool Million* (1934), a brilliantly funny satire on the Horatio Alger myth of the rise to success of the virtuous poor boy. It is, as it were, a twentieth-century American version of *Candide*. It has been overshadowed by West's other novels, for by writing it in a heavily mock-heroic style, West had necessarily to sacrifice his extraordinarily economic and nervous prose; and he was probably the most economical novelist who ever wrote. Much of his power comes from this, from an extreme and desperate concentration, the sense we have that the books have been wrung out of the guts of the man in all his agony.

West's major work springs out of his confrontation with America— by which one obviously means the entire western world—at its most meaningless and absurd. But the meaningless and the absurd are as it were the essential conditions of life: they are what man and woman are reduced to. The hero of *Miss Lonelyhearts* is—Miss Lonelyhearts. We never know his real name. He is the sob-sister of the New York *Post-Dispatch* ('Are-you-in-trouble? — Do-you-need-advice? — Write-to-Miss-Lonelyhearts-and-she-will-help-you'). The trouble is, the people who pour out their souls to Miss Lonelyhearts really do need help. He is appalled and obsessed by their sufferings. He visits a girl who is sometimes his mistress:

> Betty reached for his brow. 'What's the matter?' she asked. 'Are you sick?'
> He began to shout at her, accompanying his shouts with gestures that were too appropriate, like those of an old-fashioned actor.
> 'What a kind bitch you are. As soon as any one acts viciously, you say he's sick. Wife-torturers, rapers of small children, according to you they're all sick. No morality, only medicine. Well, I'm not sick. I don't need any of your damned aspirin. I've got a Christ complex. Humanity. . . . I'm a humanity lover. All the broken bastards . . .' He finished with a short laugh that was like a bark.

West describes Miss Lonelyhearts's colleagues telling dirty stories in a bar:

> Miss Lonelyhearts stopped listening. His friends would go on telling these stories until they were too drunk to talk. They were aware of their childishness, but did not know how else to revenge themselves. At college, and perhaps for a year afterwards, they had believed in literature, had believed in Beauty and in personal expression as an absolute end. When they lost this belief, they lost everything. Money and fame meant nothing to them. They were not worldly men.

Miss Lonelyhearts's case differs from theirs only in one respect. They might all be he; except that, as he explains to his girl friend:

> 'A man is hired to give advice to the readers of a newspaper. This job is a circulation stunt and the whole staff considers it a joke. He welcomes the job, for it might lead to a gossip column, and anyway he's tired of being a leg man. He too considers the job a joke, but after several months at it, the joke begins to escape him. He sees that the majority of the letters are profoundly humble pleas for moral and spiritual advice, that they are inarticulate expressions of genuine suffering. He also discovers that his correspondents take him seriously. For the first time in his life,

he is forced to examine the values by which he lives. This examination shows him that he is the victim of the joke and not its perpetrator.'

In his agonized helplessness in the face of the wretchedness that crowds itself upon him, he becomes momentarily the persecutor of the suffering. 'He was twisting the arm of all the sick and miserable, broken and betrayed, inarticulate and impotent. He was twisting the arm of Desperate, Broken-hearted, Sick-of-it-all, Disillusioned-with tubercular-husband.' He is really twisting his own arm because, as he realizes himself, he is 'capable of dreaming the Christ dream'. He is indeed a Christ figure, even if an impotent one; and this is emphasized in the novel by the part played by his editor, Shrike, a man of vast cynicism who appears a sort of Satan offering him the kingdoms of the earth and exposing to him the hollowness of his illusions.

The novel ends on a note of farcical irony. Miss Lonelyhearts has a religious experience in which he becomes at one with God. His doorbell rings, and he sees coming up the stairs the crippled husband of a woman who has written to him for advice, whom he has met and who has seduced him. Miss Lonelyhearts rushes down the stairs to embrace the cripple, persuaded that when he embraced him 'the cripple had been made whole . . . He did not understand the cripple's shout and heard it as a cry for help from Desperate, Harold S., Catholic-mother, Broken-hearted, Broad-shouldered, Sick-of-it-all, Disillusioned-with-tubercular-husband. He was running to succour them with love'. As the cripple struggles to escape from his embrace, the cripple's gun goes off and kills him.

The human condition, for West, is outrageous and intolerable; it can be borne, one feels, only when translated into the comic, when the cosmic absurdity is as it were clowned into further absurdity. West's anguish drives *Miss Lonelyhearts* along like the propeller of a steamer. Its pulsations are never absent for a moment. Though more mature, more ambitious than *Miss Lonelyhearts*, *The Day of the Locust* lacks its intense drive. The pulsations of anguish are more intermittent. This is partly for technical reasons. In the earlier novel, we feel and see everything through the tortured hero himself; it is his world we inhabit. In *The Day of the Locust*, West's values are enshrined much less dramatically in the figure of Tod Hackett, a painter working at a film studio, who, though involved in the action, pities rather than suffers. Miss Lonelyhearts does both simultaneously. Tod is much more of an observer, and that this is so is shown by the fact that he has come to work in Hollywood partly in order to paint an apocalyptic painting called 'The Burning of Los Angeles'. The people whom he meets and whom he is concerned for are, so to speak, characters in his canvas. He expresses, in other words, a normality that is not found in *Miss Lonelyhearts* and this undoubtedly diminishes the nightmare intensity, the surrealistic quality, which makes the earlier novel so powerful and disturbing.

And apart from this, there are passages where it seems that West has forgotten that Tod is his central character; and his place is taken by Homer Simpson, the clerk who has come to California from Iowa for his health. Homer is much more like the lame-duck figures of *Miss Lonelyhearts* but is still a described figure, a character rendered from the outside; he does not encompass within himself the whole of the action as Miss Lonelyhearts does.

All this is to say that *The Day of the Locust* approximates much more closely to the novel as normally understood. For all that, it is still an extraordinary work that rises to an apocalyptic climax which is the counterpart in words of Tod's painting, 'The Burning of Los Angeles'. Just as in *Miss Lonelyhearts* West had seized upon the newspaper-sob-sister's column as a symbol of hopeless sufferings, so in *The Day of the Locust* he seizes on Hollywood as a symbol of the unreality in which western man largely lives. The novel is not concerned with the film industry—except in so far as the film industry, on the fringes of which most of the characters live, represents the pursuit of unreality as an end in itself.

The novel opens with a brilliant brief impression of a film set. Tod looks out of his office window at the studio to see an eighteenth-century battle in progress; the armies disappear behind 'half a Mississippi steamboat'. But as we walk with Tod immediately after through Los Angeles we realize that what is depicted in the studio is no more unreal than what lies outside:

> ... not even the soft wash of dusk could help the houses. Only dynamite would be of any use against the Mexican ranch houses, Samoan huts, Mediterranean villas, Egyptian and Japanese temples, Swiss chalets, Tudor cottages, and every possible combination of these styles that lined the slopes of the canyon ...
> On the corner of La Huerta Road was a miniature Rhine castle with tarpaper turrets pierced for archers. Next to it was a little

highly coloured shack with domes and minarets out of the *Arabian Nights*. Again he was charitable. Both houses were comic, but he didn't laugh. Their desire to startle was so eager and guileless.

It is hard to laugh at the need for beauty and romance, no matter how tasteless, how horrible, the results of that need are. But it is easy to sigh. Few things are sadder than the truly monstrous.

In West's Los Angeles we are in the realm of the truly monstrous. Nothing is what it is. Its inhabitants? There are the hangers-on of the studios, cowboys who have never roped a steer, and in particular Faye Greener, whom Tod and Homer both love, the blonde who wants to be a star, who is caught completely in a world of illusions and at the same time is as hard as iron, without scruples or morals:

> She was supposed to look drunk and she did, but not with alcohol. She lay stretched out on the divan with her arms and legs spread, as though welcoming a lover, and her lips were parted in a heavy, sullen smile. She was supposed to look inviting, but the invitation wasn't to pleasure.
>
> Tod lit a cigarette and inhaled with a nervous gasp. He started to fool with his tie again, but had to go back to the photograph.
>
> Her invitation wasn't to pleasure, but to struggle hard and sharp, closer to murder than to love. If you threw yourself on her, it would be like throwing yourself from the parapet of a skyscraper. You would do it with a scream. You couldn't expect to rise again. Your teeth would be driven into your skull like nails into a pine board and your back would be broken. You wouldn't even have time to sweat or close your eyes . . .

And behind Faye and her father, a broken-down music-hall actor, the studio cowboys, and 'Honest Abe Kusich', a dwarf in a perpetual fury, there is the nameless mob, the locusts that have borne down on California. It is impossible now to read *The Day of the Locust* without thinking at the same time of *The Grapes of Wrath* and Steinbeck's Okies flooding west like lemmings. But they were in search of the good earth, whereas West's locusts are the middle-class retired middle-aged who have crawled from Iowa to die in an exacerbated boredom in a Never-Never Land that has deceived them. So the novel rises to its magnificent conclusion, with the vacant, hopeless hordes of displaced Mid-Westerners pouring into Hollywood to watch the goings-on at a première at Kahn's Persian Palace Theatre. As the mob goes berserk and Tod is crushed almost to death, he sees almost as in a vision his completed canvas of 'The Burning of Los Angeles'. It is on this apocalyptic note that *The Day of the Locust* ends. It is as though one has witnessed the final ironical presentation of the American Dream.

Henry Roth's only novel, *Call It Sleep* (1934), the *New Masses* dismissed snottily on publication with the comment: 'It is a pity that so many young writers drawn from the proletariat can make no better use of their working-class experience than as material for introspective and febrile novels.' Today, it reveals by contrast the inadequacies of most of the proletarian fiction of the time.

The reviewers, seeking comparisons, invoked Farrell's *Studs Lonigan*, but they also invoked *Portrait of the Artist*. The comparisons do indeed tell us something about the nature of the novel, but Fiedler comes closer to indicating it when he applies to it C. M. Doughty's epigram Nathanael West quotes in *The Dream Life of Balso Snell*: 'The Semites are like to a man sitting in a cloaca to the eyes, and whose brow touches heaven.' This very well suggests both the social environment in which Roth's characters exist and the state of aspiration amounting to ecstasy in which the central character has his being. *Call It Sleep* is profoundly Jewish in much the same way as *Portrait of the Artist* is sometimes described as profoundly Catholic, but it is no more a 'Jewish' novel than Joyce's is a 'Catholic' novel.

Call It Sleep, after a brief prologue, tells the story of David Schearl's life in the slums of New York between the ages of six and eight. The prologue is important. It describes the meeting on Ellis Island in 1907 between Albert Schearl, a Jewish immigrant already working as a printer in New York, and the wife and infant son who have just landed from Europe to join him in what the epigraph ironically calls the Golden Land. In the prologue Roth establishes right away the relationship between the husband and wife, which we see for the greater part of the book through the boy David's eyes and through its effects on him. The father, proud, bitter, inordinately suspicious, is permanently and radically estranged from everything in the world about him. His paranoiac self-regard causes him to lose job after job, just as it makes all personal relations impossible: his encounters with his wife's immigrant sister who comes to lodge with them before she finds a widower to marry are very funny indeed. And more and more he turns against his son who in the end he believes is not his child at all but a bastard conceived by his wife after he had left the old country for the Golden Land. His wife Genya is warm-hearted and sensual, but virtually imprisoned in an utterly strange environment whose language she cannot speak. More and more, forced in upon herself by her husband's harshness and coldness towards her, she turns to the child, who finds in her lap his only sure refuge from the nightmare jungle of the New York slums. And even so, the refuge cannot last for ever.

In its Oedipal quality the family situation is purely Freudian, and it increases in intensity throughout the two years covered by the action of the novel. Lost, bewildered, friendless, the small boy David scurries through the streets of the Lower East Side like a frightened little animal lost in a jungle inhabited by the larger carnivores, trying desperately to dodge the bigger boys waiting to bait him because he is a Jew. Viewed from this aspect, *Call It Sleep* must be the most powerful evocation of the terrors of childhood ever written. We are spared nothing of the rawness of cosmopolitan slum life. There is, for instance, the horrified boy's initiation into sex by a crippled girl. The braces on her legs creak as she embraces him: 'Between the legs. Who puts id in de poppa. De poppa's got de petzel. You de Poppa.' And all the terrors the boy experiences in the streets of New York are brought together, recapitulated, in his apprehension of the tenement houses in which he lives, the dark, rat-infested cellars with their overwhelming suggestion of mindless and brutal animality, the dark stairways to be fearfully climbed to the apartment at the top of the house which means security and warmth because his mother is there, and the roof above, the escape to which means freedom. Obviously, the structure of these tenement houses could stand for the structure of the psyche in Freudian terms.

Roth plunges us into a child's mind more directly and more intransigently than any other novelist has done. We share the child's instantaneous apprehension of his world. Compared with Roth's rendering of this, the chapters on the early childhood of Stephen in *Portrait of the Artist* are easily translatable, almost conventionalized shorthand notations of the working of a child's mind. And the child David is a most unusual child. Timid, sensitive, intelligent, above everything else he is imaginative. He re-creates, transmutes, the world he lives in not into any simple fantasy of make-believe—we're a long way here either from Tom Sawyer or the young Studs Lonigan—but with the desperate, compulsive imagination of a poet. He is, indeed, for all the grotesque difference in milieu, much closer to the boy Wordsworth of *The Prelude*.

Racked by a guilt he cannot understand and obsessed by notions of a God who is incomprehensible, he still has intimations of transfiguration. He glimpses their meaning when the teacher at the *Chedar*, the Hebrew school, Reb Yidel Pankower, translates a passage of scripture in which an angel touches the lips of the prophet Isaiah with a fiery coal so that he may speak in the presence of God. As Rideout says in *The Radical Novel in the United States*, the passage 'becomes a shaping concept which ultimately brings together the disunified elements of David's experience—the cellar, the street, the tenement apartment, and the roof'. It bursts into living reality for the boy when he is forced by three young Gentile toughs to drop a strip of zinc into the slot between the streetcar tracks that carries the live rail. The resulting flash terrifies him, but from then on he associates God's coal with what he thinks of as the cellar beneath the track, with all its associations for him of the cellar beneath the tenement house. And when later, fleeing his father's rage both at his possession of a rosary and what seems his precocious sexual depravity, he runs distraught through the streets, it is to the streetcar tracks that he stumbles, to push the ladle of a milk can into the slot between them. Knocked out by the electric shock, as he comes round he has a vision that unifies his fragmented world and reconciles him to his experience of that world.

This climactic flight through the streets is brilliantly done, counter-pointed against a chorus of voices representative of the varied life of the city. One of them is the voice of a street-corner left-wing orator. This is the only political note in the novel and, even so, it is taken up by other voices, echoed, changed, distorted, given a sexual gloss, a scriptural connotation, so that it remains essentially ambiguous.

Roth's artistry is seen at its clearest in his handling of speech. He renders with horrible fidelity the degraded mutilations of English as spoken by the children of European immigrants: 'My ticher calls id Xmas, but de kids call id Chrizmas. Id's a goyish holiday anyways. Wunst I hanged op a stockin' in Brooklyn. Bod mine fodder pud in a eggshells wid terlit paper an' a piece f'om a ol' kendle. So he leffed w'en he seen me. Id ain' no Sendy Klaws, didja know?'

But when the characters are speaking in Yiddish, Roth puts into their mouths a remarkably pure English. It is as though a kaleidoscope has suddenly been shaken, and we see the characters in quite a new light, with, as it were, a double vision. We are made sharply aware, as in no other novel I know except possibly Willa Cather's *My Antonia*, of the degradation, the diminution in human dignity, that was the immigrant's lot as he transplanted himself from a society with a traditional culture to one with no culture at all. In the novel this is seen at its most striking in the representation of the Hebrew teacher Reb Yidel Pankower. At first sight a dirty, irascible, petty sadist, a Dickensian character conducting an almost Dickensian parody of religious education, it is he who realizes the calibre of his pupil David and makes the final comment on the Golden Land to which his parents have brought him: 'A curse on them! He glared about him at the children and half-grown boys and girls who crowded the stoops and overflowed in the sidewalks and gutter. The devil take them! What was going to become of Yiddish youth? What could become of this new breed? These Americans? This sidewalk-and-gutter generation?' With Reb Yidel Pankower we are back once more with Doughty's 'The Semites are like to a man sitting in a cloaca to the eyes, and whose brow touches heaven'.

There is no such spanning of the gulf between heaven and hell in Daniel Fuchs's fiction. *Call It Sleep* is among the great achievements in American writing this century. One wouldn't claim this for *Summer in Williamsburg* (1934), *Homage to Blenholt* (1936), or *Low Company* (1937). But Fuchs is a most entertaining writer and something more than that. His novels are 'Jewish' novels in the limited sense, warm-hearted, funny, ironical, self-mocking. They have a lot in common with such a novel of Saul Bellow's as *Seize the Day*; reading them, one feels inclined to parody Yeats's famous remark on Housman's poetry in his introduction to *The Oxford Book of Modern Verse*: 'A mile further and all had been *schmaltz*.' But Fuchs's novels are not *schmaltz*; the warm-heartedness is controlled and never inhibits the irony; the pathos never deliquesces into sentimentality. It is typical of Fuchs that *Summer in Williamsburg* should end with Mr Papravel, who somehow makes gangsterism as respectable as any other form of business, announcing to his hoodlums:

'America', he repeated with conviction through the smoke, 'I don't care what anybody says, America is a wonderful country. Seriously, seriously, I mean it. Look at me, look how I worked myself up in four short years. In America everyone has an equal chance. I don't know how things are in Russia now, even God

Himself doesn't know what's going on there these days, but even so, where, I want to know, where in the world could a Jew make such a man of himself as right here in America?'

The terrain of Fuchs's novels is Brooklyn, the time the depression of the thirties. His characters, however, are less crippled by poverty than Roth's of twenty years earlier; they are much more adjusted to American life; and the young people, first-generation Americans, have been through high school and some have been to college. They have become part of the overwhelmingly Jewish city of New York. Fuchs's great theme is frustration, its comedy and pathos, frustration as an inescapable fact of life, not simply as a consequence of economic depression. Thus the central character of *Homage to Blenholt* is a young man, Max Balkan, the despair of his family, friends and the girl who wants to marry him because he refuses to find a job, being intent on producing an invention that will make his fortune, for instance, 'individual wrappers around toilet seats in public places'. Yet he is much more than the innocent Horatio Alger hero in an unpropitious world; he is a dumb poet drunk on visions of glory, on Marlowe's *Tamburlaine the Great* in particular. It is this that leads him to make his homage to Blenholt; as he says to his girl friend: 'Don't you see, Ruth? . . . Blenholt is Tamburlaine. He is what I want to be, Tamburlaine in New York, now, and I want to pay him homage if it's only for the sentiment.' And so he drags Ruth, who wants only to see Joan Crawford in the film at the neighbourhood cinema, with him to attend Blenholt's funeral. And who is Blenholt? A petty party boss, Commissioner of Sewers. The account of Blenholt's funeral and of the memorial service to him is a splendid piece of comic writing.

Balkan is a Quixote in Brooklyn; and not the only Quixote-figure in the novel either; there is also his friend Mendel Munves, the dedicated philologist ('I know men', he assures the girl who hopes to marry him, 'who have given up their lives for the ideals of the National Spelling Reform Society'), for whom a job would get in the way of his researches into Anglo-Saxon place-names. But Quixotes in the end must yield to reality, and both Max and Mendel have finally to surrender to marriage, domesticity and the search for the 9-till-5 job. The last word is Max's father's, the old Yiddish tragedian from Yudensky's People's Theatre on the Bowery, whose King Lear knocked them cold in London, Paris, Amsterdam, Copenhagen, Budapest, Chicago and Melbourne and who now tramps the streets dressed as a clown and carrying sandwich boards advertising 'Madame Clara, Scientific Beauty Treatments by Skilled Experts':

> In his wife's earthy guffaws he recognized the clamorous demands of the world, its insistent calls for resignation and surrender, and he knew now that Max would never be the same again. His son would grow old and ageing, die, but actually Max was already dead for now he would live by bread alone. That was the rule and few men were strong enough to disobey it. It had happened to Mr Balkan himself, he knew, and now it happened to his son. And regretting the way of the world, Mr Balkan realized that he had witnessed the exact point at which his son had changed from youth to resigned age. Walking out of the house and shifting the shoulder straps to get the signs comfortably settled, it seemed to the old man that this death of youth was among the greatest tragedies in experience and that all the tears in America were not enough to bewail it.

Fuchs's third novel, *Low Company*, is his surest and most accomplished. In it, the violence beneath American city life of the thirties is brought to the surface, is no longer simply a matter for humour but is shown as a conditioning factor in the lives of the characters. In this novel, too, there is a great advance in dramatic intensity. The individual episodes are rendered with a vividly sharp economy. And the range of characters is wider and more varied. Best of them all is Shubunka, the owner of a chain of brothels, a man grotesquely fat and ugly and of a monumental sadness, who is driven out of his small empire of vice by vice-czars more ruthless and unscrupulous than himself.

> For eight years he had built up his organization, and now they would take everything away from him. There would be no more money, no fine suits, no respect no matter how unwillingly wrung. Without the prestige of his money, he had nothing and he might as well be dead. He could not run away and it made no difference whether they shot him and killed him.
>
> And it comes to me, the fat man said calmly, staring at the patches travelling on the ceiling. It is only what I deserve. He told himself he had no right to be spared for he, too, had been faithless and had spoken cruelly, had robbed and done evil, and lied and exploited and persecuted and crippled. He had committed all the sins, not heeding their significance, arrogant and presumptuous within himself. When Karty, the poor gambler,

came to him for money, it had pleased his fancy to turn him
aside, and now the fat man regretted bitterly that he could
not find him, give him the money, make him happy. Evil was
rewarded by evil and his punishment was just.

Shubunka's soliloquy echoes the Jewish prayer to be said on the eve
of the Day of Atonement which Fuchs uses as epigraph to the novel.
It establishes the values in terms of which the novel is written. But all
the time the humour is there, lighting up the characters, placing them
in perspective. It is an attribute of Fuchs's charity.

[7]

THE CODA to the politically orientated fiction—in however vague a
sense—of the thirties in America is a novel published when it was
all past, Lionel Trilling's *The Middle of the Journey* (1947). This, as
one would expect from the author's distinction as a critic of the novel,
is a most intelligent work. Indeed, there are times when it seems even
a little too good, as though Trilling was demonstrating, from his vast
knowledge of the theory of the novel, just how a novel should be
written. It is all—the symbolism, the moments of revelation, the
unexpected unfolding of character—perhaps a little too pat. Yet it
sums up the American intellectuals' long love-affair with Communism
as no other novel has done.

It does so by exploring the reactions of a number of middle-class
fellow-travellers, who may be taken as representative figures, to the
defection from the Communist Party of Gifford Maxim, a man in some
sense the mentor of them all since he is a professional revolutionary,
the committed man. The centre of consciousness of the novel is John
Laskell, a sociologist, who, as the book opens, has just as it were risen
from the dead—reluctantly; he has been very ill and has cherished his
illness. As we meet him in the first chapter, he is in the train bound for
Connecticut, where he is to recuperate with his young friends, Arthur
and Nancy Croom; and with him for part of the journey, almost as
though under his protection, is Maxim, whose defection from the Party
and his sudden espousal of Christianity seem to the well-intentioned,
socially conscious, progressive Crooms acts of treachery too disgusting

to be contemplated. They are, as the course of the novel makes plain, political innocents living in a world of illusions, and dangerous because of their very innocence and good intentions. They have no real knowledge of Communism as a political creed as distinguished from a philosophy; the world of melodrama in which Maxim has lived as a professional revolutionary, which has involved his killing a man and may involve his being killed in turn, is so meaningless to them as to be unbelievable. They live as it were in a world of fictions, and it is part of Laskell's re-initiation into life to discover this.

There is, for example, Nancy Croom's refusal to admit the existence of death; there is, too, the self-deception implicit in their apotheosis of the shiftless, irresponsible, brutal Duck Caldwell as the noble worker uncontaminated by bourgeois values; there is their failure to see in his wife Emily anything more than a tiresome figure of dated Greenwich Village artiness. Duck kills his daughter in a drunken accident, and it is this event that becomes the focal point of the final confrontation of Maxim with the Crooms:

> Duck can be forgiven. I can personally forgive him because I believe that God can forgive him. You see, I think his will is a bad one, but not much worse, not different in kind, from other wills. And so you and I stand opposed. For you—no responsibility for the individual, but no forgiveness. For me—ultimate, absolute responsibility for the individual—but mercy. Absolute responsibility: it is the only way that men can keep their value, can be thought of as other than mere *things*. Those matters that Arthur speaks of—social causes, environment, education—do you think they really make a difference between one human soul and another? In the eyes of God are such differences of any meaning at all? Can you suppose that *they* condition His mercy? Does He hold a Doctor of Philosophy more responsible than a Master of Arts, or a high-school graduate more responsible than a man who has not finished the eighth grade? Or is His mercy less to one than another?
>
> None of them had ever heard language like this, although they may have read it, and they did not know how to respond.

As a dramatization of ideas and of the clash between the ideologies of our time, *The Middle of the Road*, for all it lacks their obvious dynamic, is a novel that must be placed beside *The Power and the Glory* and *The Revenge for Love*.

[8]

I HAVE BEEN writing as though the social scene, the lives of men and women in a time of cataclysmal economic and political upheaval, were the concern of American thirties fiction, except in the South, which had its other additional preoccupations, to the exclusion of everything else. Of course this was not so. Not all the expatriates left Paris at the end of 1929 to return to and rediscover the United States; and to some writers, reading their copies of *transition* and *This Quarter*, Paris still seemed the literary capital of the Anglo-Saxon world. Djuna Barnes's novel, *Nightwood*, appeared as late as 1936, a vision of life among sexual perverts in Paris, written in a highly poetic prose, though poetic in what at the time was a very modern way, part of the movement of which Cummings's *The Enormous Room* is also an example. T. S. Eliot said when the book appeared that it has 'a quality of horror and doom very nearly related to that of Elizabethan tragedy'. It is not easy to see it in such terms now; it strikes one much more as American Gothic engrafted on French decadence *à la* Huysmans.

Then there was Kay Boyle, whose novel *Plagued by the Nightingale* appeared in 1931. It remains, in its subdued lyricism, an interesting study of French family life as seen by an American girl who has married into it, and it still touches the nerve of horror.

The most famous expatriate writer of the thirties, however, is probably Henry Miller, with *Tropic of Cancer* (1934), *Black Spring* (1936) and *Tropic of Capricorn* (1939). Miller is only marginally a novelist. Indeed, he is perhaps best seen as an anti-novelist, as the epigraph to *Tropic of Cancer* from Emerson suggests: 'These novels will give way, by and by, to diaries or autobiographies—captivating books, if only a man knew how to choose among what he calls his experiences that which is really his experience, and how to record truth truly.' This means for Miller in *Tropic of Cancer* 'the recording of all that which is omitted in books'. Miller is his own hero: *Tropic of Cancer* is a fragment of autobiography dealing with his life in Paris in the early thirties. He is writing a book and is very poor, at times almost at the starvation level. He sponges on rich American expatriates for meals and is not above picking up a few francs by pimping. For a time he has a job as a proof-reader on the Paris edition of an American newspaper and he is also for a time in intolerable exile from Paris as an English teacher in a *lycée* in Dijon.

But the structure of events scarcely matters. What is much more important is the tone of the book and Miller's attitude towards life, which is anarchic in a way that has now become familiar. Civilization, he cries, is doomed; the only realities are sex and art. But if here he links up with a French contemporary like the Céline of *Un voyage au bout de la nuit*, he has his roots deep in nineteenth-century America. It is not by chance that he quotes Emerson, and when he philosophizes on art and civilization he writes like a sub-Whitman, windy and half-baked. When he deals with sex he seems to me to achieve a crudity unsurpassed except by the *graffiti* on the walls of public urinals, and the crudity is the more striking—and sometimes the more comic—because of the high-falutin to which it is juxtaposed. In my view, *Tropic of Cancer* is obscene in the simplest sense; but it is anything but pornographic: a book less aphrodisiac it is scarcely possible to imagine.

Yet though autobiography, it is for the qualities it shares with fiction that one reads *Tropic of Cancer*. It has been much overrated by its admirers and has, one suspects, been kept alive artificially by the inaccessibility caused by its having been banned for nearly thirty years in the United States and Britain. But it is still not negligible. It exposes one aspect of what might be called American Paris at the rock-bottom of the morally and physically squalid and does so with a curious kind of innocence. In the descriptions of the Paris scene there are, too, passages of real poetic beauty. And there is something else. Edmund Wilson wrote of it in 1938: 'If you can stand it, it is sometimes quite funny.' Parts of it I find very funny indeed, in an old-fashioned way, that of the picaresque, especially in the comedy in which Miller's friend, Fillmore, marries a French girl, becomes the victim of her family and is finally smuggled off to the States by the author. By making his characters concerned almost exclusively with sex, Miller reduces them to the condition of automata, and men behaving like machines are always comic.

Whether Miller intended this is another matter. He seems to me essentially a naïve writer of considerable raw power but little art, and his influence as the spiritual father of the Beats has been strong on younger writers as naïve artistically as himself.

Nevertheless, it is true that American fiction in the thirties was concerned overwhelmingly with the social scene, and how unavoidable the preoccupation was is suggested by the publication in 1935 of Wilder's *Heaven's My Destination* and in 1937 of Hemingway's *To Have and Have Not*, novels that still seem like radical departures from their authors' normal interests. And for novelists who came of age as writers during the thirties the condition of society as a major theme was all but inescapable. It was not necessary for them to be Communists or even vaguely Left Wing. The great strength of John O'Hara, for example, has always lain in his precise, exhaustively detailed descriptions of provincial society. John McCormick has described *Appointment in Samarra* (1935) as 'almost *The Great Gatsby* of the 1930's'. Certainly it seemed so to many young English writers who read it when it first came out. That it does so no longer is because it contains no character remotely comparable in stature and significance to Gatsby. Indeed, the novel now seems curiously hollow at the centre, for the behaviour of the principal character remains unmotivated and unexplained.

Appointment in Samarra relates the downfall and suicide of Julian English, a member of one of the best families of the town of Gibbsville, Pennsylvania, over the three days of Christmas, 1930. The downfall and suicide are precipitated by English's sudden impulsive throwing of a highball into the face of Harry Reilly, a rich parvenu to whom he owes money, at a Christmas Eve party at the country club. Why English behaves as he does is never made sufficiently clear, and though one can make guesses they remain guesses; we do not have evidence adequate enough to support them. There are suggestions of a faulty heredity; or it may be that English is reacting against his father's appalling rectitude. We are obviously in the presence of a profound death-wish that finds expression in an *acte gratuit*. But that gets us little further; English's behaviour is as much a mystery to himself and to his wife and friends as it is to the reader.

So there is not much scope for interest in English; he is a snob and a drunk, and there is little else to be said about him. The treatment of English's environment, Gibbsville, a centre of the anthracite-mining industry, is another matter; and English's *acte gratuit* and the further aberrations of behaviour it leads him into serve to expose the life of a community with astonishing particularity. *Appointment in Samarra* gives us a complete anatomy of Gibbsville. O'Hara's knowledge of the mores of the country club, the subtle gradations of the locker-room, is inexhaustible; his awareness of snobbery as a factor in conduct, of the all-pervasiveness of social emulation in the behaviour of, for example, men at dances, is as keen as Thackeray's; and he knows just as precisely how antagonisms in religion and the herd-like conflicts between religious or racial groups operate. *Appointment in Samarra* may not be a profound novel or even in the last analysis a successful one, but it remains fascinating.

In an interesting note on David Riesman, Lionel Trilling says that 'the novelist, in his ideal character, is the artist who is consumed by the desire to know how things really are, who has entered into an elaborate romance with actuality'. He then suggests that in the fiction of our time this sensitivity and curiosity have become less and less manifest and that they seem to have taken refuge in sociology and cultural anthropology. Significantly, Trilling exempts O'Hara from his generalization about contemporary fiction; and in fact one reads O'Hara with a similar fascination to the way in which one reads sociologists like Riesman and William H. Whyte and the cultural anthropologists reporting as it were direct from the field. And for all it is fiction, *Appointment in Samarra* is probably the best and most illuminating account we have of the class system of a white American town. It also—and here there is a real parallel with *The Great Gatsby*—catches exactly the feel and quality of life at a specific time in a specific place. On the evidence of *Appointment in Samarra* O'Hara ought, one feels, to have developed into a great novelist. There, he is half a great novelist. But *Appointment in Samarra* remains his best novel. His work, *10 North Frederick* (1955), for example, which again is set in Gibbsville, still has a strong sociological or anthropological fascination, and he knows as well as ever he did men and women in terms of their ratings according to Dun and Bradstreet and to Kinsey alike; but his insight into human nature, into the way men and women behave as they do, and why, is as rudimentary as it was thirty years ago.

One cannot say John P. Marquand's insight into human nature was rudimentary; but it was scarcely piercing. He was a novelist of great technical facility whose achievement never quite matched his skill. Marquand is at once the satirist and the celebrant of Boston in its traditional aspects of plain living, high thinking, great wealth, conscious rectitude and the snobbery that goes with all these—the Boston to which the word 'Brahmin', with its indication of caste-exclusiveness, is automatically added. But the satirist and the celebrant in Marquand tend to cancel each other out. Or rather, the celebrant takes over from the satirist. One might compare him to Howells, but one would have to go on to add that the kind of criticism of Boston and its traditional values implicit in Howells's *The Rise of Silas* is something Marquand is incapable of. The complacency of his characters, gently made fun of though it is, seems at bottom to be the complacency of their creator. Marquand has it, as it were, both ways:

> 'I don't know why it is you make me laugh', Bill said, 'because, frankly, you've always been a straight.'
> 'What's a straight?' I asked.
> 'A straight', Bill said. 'Don't you know what a straight is? A straight's someone in a skit who has all the jokes thrown at him. I start to tell you a joke. I say, "I was walking down the street the other day", and you say, "Yes, you were walking down the street? Go on". And I say, "I met a dame", and you say, "Oh, you met a dame, did you?" That's what a straight is.'
> Bill always had something to say that was new and interesting.
> 'I see', I said. 'I guess I've always been a straight.'
> I thought Bill would laugh, but instead he finished his drink and poured out another one.
> 'Maybe, but maybe it's better than being a smart man. He's mighty lonely and there're lots and lots of straights.'

That is from *H. M. Pulham, Esquire* (1942), the record of Henry Pulham's life as relived by himself when he sets out to write his life story for the twenty-fifth anniversary reunion of the Class of 1915 at Harvard. There should, one feels, be a contrast between the inner truth of Pulham's life and the facts of his career, which look, as he says himself, like something on a tombstone; but though Pulham rediscovers the compromises, evasions and cautions that have shaped his life, there is very little contrast and contradiction between the private truth and the official, no revelation, no exposure, because there is nothing either to reveal or to expose, only the renewed realization that, like Eliot's Prufrock, at the most his role in life is to be 'an attendant lord, one that will do To swell a progress, start a scene or two'. What one expects, and never gets, is something akin to Strether's outburst to little Bilham in *The Ambassadors*: 'Live all you can; it's a mistake not to.' One doesn't get it because it seems that Marquand no more than Pulham has any real notion of an alternative way of living to that of Boston as expressed here.

Marquand's craftsmanship, his humour and his wit, which are

delightful, are all of the surface. One reads him from page to page, from chapter to chapter, with admiring attention, but in the end Katherine Mansfield's comment on E. M. Forster seems infinitely more true of him: 'Feel this teapot. Is it not beautifully warm? Yes, but there ain't going to be no tea.' And this is just as true of what seems to me Marquand's best novel, *Wickford Point*, a lovingly satirical re-creation of a New England family in its decadence. The subject itself invokes comparisons, which the novel cannot possibly sustain, with Hawthorne and with Faulkner. Marquand's charm, which is real, is that of superior soap-opera, of the action as it unfolds, not of any cumulative effect, for there is no cumulative effect.

James Gould Cozzens's is a much more solid achievement than either Marquand's or O'Hara's, and it was unfortunate that after years of writing fiction that had won him little except critical esteem he should have burst into fantastic success with *By Love Possessed*, not by any means his best novel and one marred by a fascinated loathing of sex and by an absence of any feeling that could normally be recognized as love. Until Cozzens wrote *By Love Possessed*, one had not associated his novels with either love or sex. He is pre-eminently the novelist of man in society, of man as a member of an organization, of man, indeed, seen under the aspect of his vocation or profession. He is concerned with what is possible for a man to do in a given context of place and time. He is not only anti-sentimental, he is anti-romantic. His characteristic spokesmen are middle-aged men who have seen much of the world and have learnt from experience that frustration is the inevitable lot and that man cannot do what he wants but only what circumstances—the nature of society, the constitution of human institutions and the clash of interests all about him—allow him to do. There is a possible comparison with C. P. Snow. Both are students of human ecology; but Snow is much more sanguine than Cozzens and much more interested in the vagaries and contradictions in the behaviour of individual human beings. Cozzens has a much more deterministic view of human nature; in his consideration of man in society the main emphasis is on society itself, as the factor constraining the individual man.

His most beautiful treatment of what is possible to a man in a given society is *The Just and the Unjust* (1942). This novel poses, in an account of a murder trial in a small New England town, the whole problem of justice and its execution in a democratic community. We see the action mainly through the eyes of the prosecuting counsel, young Abner Coates, the assistant district attorney; and the last lines of the novel, a dialogue between Abner and his father, a retired judge, express what seems Cozzens's abiding view—stoical, unillusioned—of man's life in society:

'. . . Yes, there'll be more war; and soon I don't doubt. There always has been. There'll be deaths and disappointments and failures. When they come, you meet them. Nobody promises you a good time or an easy time. I don't know who it was who said when we think of the past we regret and when we think of the future we fear. And with reason. But no bets are off. There is always the present to think of, and as long as you live there always will be. In the present, every day is a miracle. The world gets up in the morning and is fed and goes to work, and in the evening it comes home and is fed again and perhaps has a little amusement and goes to sleep. To make that possible, so much has to be done by so many people that, on the face of it, it is impossible. Well, every day we do it; and every day, come hell, come high water, we're going to have to go on doing it as well as we can.'

'So it seems,' said Abner.

'Yes, so it seems,' said Judge Coates, 'and so it is, and so it will be! And that's where you come in. That's all we want of you.'

Abner said, 'What do you want of me?'

'We just want you to do the impossible,' Judge Coates said.

The exploration of what is possible for a man is scarcely less interesting in *Men and Brethren* (1936). This recounts a day in the life of Ernest Cudlipp, the Episcopalian vicar of a parish in New York City. Cudlipp is not a saint: he is merely a very busy clergyman who must solve, as best he may, the problems as they arise of those about him, who may not be Christians at all. There are things he cannot do. He would like, for example, to shelter an old friend, a priest who has abandoned his orders after involvement in a sexual scandal. Christianity itself seems to dictate that he should do so; but his duty to the Church as an institution forbids it. Without the Church as an institution he is nothing, and the edicts of ecclesiastical policy have to be accepted even when they seem to be opposed to those of Christianity, if he is to function as a priest at all.

In a sense, the sense in which politics has been defined as the art of the possible, Cozzens is a political novelist. In *Guard of Honour* (1948), his most massive work to date and one of the most notable feats of organization in contemporary fiction, he investigates the nature of military discipline in the army of a democratic state in total war. The scene is a United States Air Force training field in Florida in 1943; Cozzens re-creates the life of the camp, which is almost a city in itself, in enormous and minute detail. The action, which covers only three days, deals with the crises of administration, the tensions arising from politics at every level, racial conflicts and personal antagonisms, confronting 'Bus' Beal, the commanding officer, the youngest two-star general in the Army, and a man who, by his very training and experience, is ill-prepared for the administration of an organization that is the state in miniature. The roll of characters is almost Tolstoyan in its amplitude, and all are drawn together into a highly complex action that hinges upon the practical difficulties, in a Southern state, of fulfilling the requirements of the United States Army ordinance demanding complete integration of white and coloured soldiers.

Cozzens, outside of *By Love Possessed*, is the least sensational of novelists. He builds up his picture of society by a patient accumulation of detail and conceives his characters solidly, without apparent subtlety; but they are there in three dimensions and can, as it were, be walked round. He is excellent with professional men, with men who, by the very nature of their work, are conscious of obligations to a code of professional behaviour. It is almost entirely a man's world that he creates. His deficiencies are obvious; they can be summed up in the complete absence in his work of anything that can be called poetry. His view of life, it must be admitted, is daunting: his awareness of the limits imposed on man's freedom to act, both by the nature of society and by human nature as Cozzens sees it, leads him to a deep conservatism. But he has expressed his view in three or four novels whose scope goes far beyond that of practically all his contemporaries in English and American fiction, novels rooted as deeply as O'Hara's in the close and dispassionate scrutiny of the actual.

THE THIRTIES: BRITISH

▲▼▲▼▲▼▲▼▲▼▲▼▲▼▲▼▲▼▲▼▲▼▲▼▲▼▲▼▲▼▲▼▲▼▲▼▲▼▲

[I]

AMONG THE English novelists who began to publish in the twenties, although their reputations belong to a later time, are I. Compton-Burnett, Elizabeth Bowen, Graham Greene, William Plomer, Henry Green and Evelyn Waugh. Miss Compton-Burnett's first novel, *Dolores*, had indeed appeared as early as 1911, but her second, *Pastors and Masters*, the novel which initiates the method she has made her own, did not follow until 1925. She remains, after sixteen novels, completely *sui generis*. Her world is hers alone, and so is her way of rendering it, the product of a high degree of abstraction. The period of her novels is roughly that of the last decade of the nineteenth century, though 'period' is certainly not a quality she is concerned with. At the centre of her novels there is always a middle-class family existing generally in three generations, living as a rule on unearned income in the country and exclusively concerned with its own intense family life. There are also servants and friends and hangers-on; but the world that results is a closed one and very small.

Miss Compton-Burnett has said: 'Real life seems to have no plots. And as I think a plot desirable and almost necessary I have this extra grudge against life. But I do think there are signs that strange things happen, though they do not emerge. I believe it would go ill with many of us, if we were faced by a strong temptation, and I suspect that with some of us it does go ill.' In her novels, the strange things emerge— from the tyranny of family life, and they would be very strange indeed if Miss Compton-Burnett were a realistic novelist, which she is not. She writes of what is possible rather than of what normally is; her characters commit the crimes that people more often dream of than commit. One could almost say that in her novels unconscious desires become conscious and are acted upon. So that in her novels the factor of violence is extremely high: wills are forged or suppressed, incest is not uncommon, murder takes its course, power exercises itself, emotional blackmail is constant; all this despite the surface decorum of her work.

Two very brief synopses of plots may well stand for all Miss Compton-Burnett's work. In *Men and Wives* (1931), the tyrant is Lady Haslam, a hypochondriacal, obsessive mother who, after an attempt at suicide, which is an exercise in blackmail rather than an act of genuine despair, goes for a time into a mental home. In her absence, her husband and children discover a new freedom to grow and be themselves; so that when she comes home her son Matthew murders her to prevent the old regime being re-established and in order that he may marry Camilla. Camilla refuses him when she learns what he has done; and when he confesses his crime to the family no one will believe him. And the family settles itself, as it were, into a new pattern of tyranny and obsession.

In *More Women than Men* (1933), Josephine Napier, the head-mistress of a girls' school, kills the wife of her nephew Gabriel by exposing her to a draught while she is suffering from pneumonia, kills her because she has an obsessive passion for Gabriel herself.

The manner of Miss Compton-Burnett's novels exists in the strongest possible contrast to the matter. Miss Compton-Burnett conducts her novels, to a degree beyond any other novelist with the exception of Firbank, through dialogue, though there is rather more description than is sometimes recognized. The descriptive passages point to the one novelist who may be considered her literary ancestor. When one reads a passage like this, in *Men and Wives*—

> Her second son, Jermyn, was a serious young man of twenty-four, who combined in his looks the best points of both his parents, and whose Christian name had been given him because it was his mother's surname, a reason seemingly valid only for a younger son, since it had not been applied to his elder brother. Her daughter, Griselda, was a handsome, unstable-looking girl a year or two younger, whose wide grey eyes continually sought her mother's, and never seemed at rest. The youngest son, Gregory, was an overgrown, featureless youth of twenty, with prominent, colourless eyes and at first sight no expression. The eldest son observed a custom of being late . . .

—Jane Austen comes to mind.

But it is on her dialogue that she relies. There was a time when critics, attempting to describe it, invoked Congreve; and the comparison at least indicates its formal structure and stylization, its extreme artificiality. But there is something not in Congreve. This is the impression we have that the characters are saying not only the things that are said in normal conversation but also those things that are consciously suppressed.

It is not easy to quote effectively from Miss Compton-Burnett's dialogue; it is so tightly knit and builds up to its climaxes by subtle gradations and exchanges; but here is an excerpt from the first chapter of *Men and Wives*, the family meeting at breakfast after morning prayers:

'Well, now, breakfast!' said Godfrey, receiving his world on secular terms. 'Now a good breakfast to make up for the bad night, Harriet. Don't stand about loafing, you two boys. Good morning, all of you. How is Father's girl today?'

'Quite well,' said Griselda, giving him a startled smile, and leaning towards her mother.

'Mother, how did you sleep?'

'Not at all, my sweet one. Never mind, as long as you slept well.'

Griselda held her eyes down, and Jermyn strolled to the table.

'Well, bad news of the night?' he said with a deliberate ease.

'There is no news, dear, but not in the sense that no news is good news. It must certainly be no news to you now, and you speak as if you were reconciled to it.'

'Oh, now, Harriet, now you are making a mistake,' said her husband in a manner of making a last effort before yielding to fate. 'We keep all our sympathy for you, but, as you say, it is not news to us now. Nor is it to you, my poor girl. Gregory, don't stand there, kicking your feet like a child.'

Gregory took his place by his mother, and looked into her face with simple affection.

'Well, how did you employ the night watches, since you had them at your disposal?'

'In pacing up and down the corridors, my son,' said his mother in a soothed and gentle voice, and with almost a light of humour in her eye over words ominous to any other ear. 'I knew I shouldn't wake any of you. You all sleep so soundly.' Even this was not a reproach to Gregory. 'I don't feel so wrought up as I generally do after a night without sleep.'

'Oh, come, come, that is a good word, Harriet. Come, this is a brave speech,' cried Godfrey. 'Now we shall have a better day. You will have a better day. You will be able to amuse yourself a little.'

'Amuse myself? Shall I, Godfrey? It has taken all my effort for years to get through the day, and to face the night, the night!' Harriet dropped her voice and bent her head as much in suffering as in the acting of exasperation, and Jermyn rose to the demand.

'What an offensive thing to say, Father! What worse insult than to be accused of amusing oneself? Amusing oneself, when life is but toil and duty?'

From that one can see how and why Miss Compton-Burnett is able to rely almost on dialogue alone. Then, two of the characters at any rate, Sir Godfrey and Lady Haslam, have already exposed themselves; and one theme at least, Lady Haslam's tyranny over her family through hypochondria, is already evident. What remains remarkable, of course, is that she is able to handle her themes at their greatest and darkest moment of revelation, when, as Pamela Hansford Johnson has said, they 'would bear some relation to the themes of Greek tragedy, if we could conceive Greek tragedy with the Furies impotent or non-existent', through dialogue alone. But Miss Compton-Burnett's dialogue is extraordinarily flexible and subtle. It is often said that all her characters talk alike, irrespective of age, sex or class; but the comparison is not so much with prose dialogue as we normally think of it, as with blank verse or the heroic couplet in Elizabethan and seventeenth-century drama. It has a similar function. Abstracted from life as they are, Miss Compton-Burnett's characters are further abstracted by the dialogue. Through it, they expose themselves; their self-regard is stripped of its mask of high sentiments. But they are, every one of them, vehicles of style, and they have in turn a tremendous sense of style. They are a little larger than life, like characters in heroic drama. The dialogue from its very nature elevates both action and personages; and this is why, though her view of life is implacable and intransigent and she offers no comfort, nothing beyond a stoical acceptance of things as they are, she delights even as she scarifies. And she achieves a perfection in her work beyond anything reached by her contemporaries; and she does so because, like Jane Austen, she knows her limits and never transgresses them.

Jane Austen, though more remotely, is an ancestor of Elizabeth

Bowen also, whose first book, *Encounters*, a collection of stories, appeared in 1923 and whose first novel, *The Hotel*, followed four years later. In her earlier work, the scene is commonly Ireland, in her later, more often London, though the characters she deals with have remained largely the same, members of the cultivated, liberal upper middle-class. Her first reputation was as a witty observer of manners, a delicate satirist of social absurdities; but from *To the North* (1932), social comedy, though always there, if sometimes uneasily, has been secondary to a conception of human relations verging upon the tragic. It is as though Henry James has been superimposed upon Jane Austen. The overriding theme of what are probably her three best novels, *To the North*, *The House in Paris* (1935) and *The Death of the Heart* (1938), is the confrontation of experience by innocence. The affinity with James here needs no stressing.

It emerges most powerfully and explicitly in *The Death of the Heart*, the initial situation of which is the introduction into the family circle of the Quaynes, a well-to-do, cultured, childless couple living in one of the more agreeable areas of central London, of the husband's almost unknown sixteen-year-old half-sister Portia. The novel opens with Anna Quayne's telling a friend of the discovery of the diary which Portia is keeping and of the disturbing effect it is having upon her. 'As I read', she says, 'I thought, either this girl or I are mad.'

The clue to the book lies in its title. But whose heart is dead, or killed? Not necessarily Portia's, despite the succession of disillusions and betrayals she suffers, culminating in the realization that her diary is being read even as she writes it. No, the dead hearts are those of the Quaynes and their circle, and the full final effect of Portia upon them is to force them to realize it. They are neither evil nor cruel; they are as kind as they know how to be; in accepting the care of Portia they have assumed a duty—dutifully. But they have forgotten or grown cold to what Keats called 'the holiness of the heart's affections', and their coldness and sterility—the result, it is implied, of their own experience of life, their acquiescence in the second-best—are exposed by the candour of Portia's innocence and the integrity of her natural, unassuming demand for love. As they realize at the end of the novel, the artlessness of the girl's diary is the mirror in which their true natures are reflected: hence the horror felt by Anna Quayne when she first reads it.

Elizabeth Bowen is a highly conscious artist who has evolved over the years a prose style that has the elaboration, the richness of texture, the allusiveness of poetry, a prose as carefully wrought, as subtle in its implications, as that of Henry James in his last phase. She has, too, an intense awareness of, and sensitivity to, place and weather, to the living character of houses, for example, and the indefinable yet readily palpable relation set up between them and the people who dwell in them. Her characters are always people living in particular places during particular seasons and in particular climatic conditions; and she uses her settings in place and time symbolically, to further our responses to the characters that move in them. One recalls the brilliant opening scene of *The Death of the Heart*, of Anna Quayne and her friend the novelist St Quentin walking in Regent's Park. It is more than a description, however vivid, of a winter scene in London. The frozen lake in Regent's Park connotes the frozen heart of Anna Quayne.

Elizabeth Bowen remarks of one of the characters in her late novel, *The Heat of the Day* (1949): 'One of his eyes either was or behaved as being just perceptibly higher than the other. This lag or inequality in his vision gave her the feeling of being looked at twice.' There are times when Miss Bowen's own vision as a novelist has seemed not unlike this character's, for her vision as a symbolic novelist and her vision as a writer of social comedy do not always match; and though *The Death of the Heart* seems to me Miss Bowen's profoundest novel, yet there is an inequality of vision, almost a squint, in it that in my view seriously flaws it. This is the delineation of the wretched Heccombs, with whom Portia is sent to stay. They are extroverts as raw and unsubtle as the winds that sweep across Romney Marsh to their house, 'Waikiki', at Seal-on-Sea. The interlude at 'Waikiki' is a most malicious and entertaining piece of social comedy, executed with real gusto:

> 'And another thing you had much better not begin to do is putting stuff on your nails. That sort of thing makes the majority of men sick. One cannot see why girls do it.'
> 'Perhaps they don't know.'
> 'Well, I always tell a girl. If one is to know a girl, it is much better to tell her what one thinks. Another thing I don't like is messed-up mouths. When I give a girl tea, I always look at the cup. Then, if she leaves any red muck on the rim, I say, "Hallo, I didn't know that cup had a pink pattern." Then the girl seems quite taken aback.'

It is deadly, but so different in character from the rest of the book as quite to spoil its unity. More than this, it operates against one's sense of Miss Bowen's fairness. On any objective valuation, the Heccombs are as morally worthy as the Quaynes: they are less sensitive, and lower in the social scale; that is all. Yet the spectacle of them appears to inhibit the poetic insight with which their creator views the Quaynes, and they become figures of fun.

For all that, *The Death of the Heart* seems to me one of the best English novels of the century. *The Heat of the Day*, which followed it, is less successful, and though in parts extremely brilliant, its strengths are closely related to its weaknesses. The distinctive quality of this novel is what, in Henry James, Stephen Spender has called 'described poetry'. The following is an instance of this—the heroine, Stella, is dining with her lover:

> But they were not alone, nor had they been from the start, from the start of love. Their time sat in the third place at their table. They were the creatures of history, whose coming together was of a nature possible in no other day—the day was inherent in the nature. Which must have always been true of lovers, if it had taken till now to be seen. The relation of people to one another is subject to the relation of each to time, to what is happening. If this has not been always felt—and as to that who is to know?— it has begun to be felt, irrevocably. On from now, every moment, with more and more of what has been 'now' behind it, would be going on adding itself to the larger story. Could these two have loved each other better at a better time? At no other would they have been themselves: what had carried their world to its hour was in their blood-streams. The more imperative the love, the deeper its draft on beings, till it has taken up all that ever went to their making, and according to what it draws on its nature is. In dwelling upon the constant for our reassurance, we forget that the loves in history have been agonizingly modern loves in their day. War at present worked as a thinning of the membrane between the this and the that, it was becoming apparent—but then what else is love?

This passage is surely a lyric in reverse, as it were. With extreme brilliance, by analysis and amplification and the matching of ambigui- ties, it teases out the meaning of what is essentially a poetic idea. It is a method which demands great powers of intuition into subtleties of feeling and the utmost precision in the use of language; and since its material is such as cannot ordinarily be expressed in prose, it demands, too, an expression which is bound to use many of the devices of poetry. Almost inevitably, it leads Miss Bowen from time to time into a distortion of normal sentence-structure and word-order suggestive of a prose Hopkins. Indeed, if the process were carried much further the result would be a disintegration of language, as seems to me to occur in her next novel *A World of Love* (1955).

But the passage is important not simply as an example of Elizabeth Bowen's method; it also states the real subject-matter of the novel. 'Their time sat in the third place at their table', and the time is 1940 to 1944, as London, 'the intimate and loose little society of the garrison', experienced it. The surroundings of the characters in *The Heat of the Day*, then, are the war-years in London, and with the atmosphere of the place and the time Miss Bowen is in almost mediumistic *rapport*. The novel is the most completely detailed evocation of it that we have in fiction; it does for the period 1940–44 what Henry Green's *Caught* does for 1939–40. We are immersed in wartime London as in a palpable, tangible medium like an element. Unerringly, exquisitely, Miss Bowen has caught the very feel of the time. The characters, too, live in the period like an element.

This is at once the novel's strength and the source of its weakness. The war has uprooted, dislocated them all. They are caught in the war as in the glare of a searchlight; but in the lives they have lived before, in the darkness outside the circle of light, Miss Bowen is scarcely interested. And this is fatal to her plot, the theme of which is treason. Robert Kelway, a self-confessed traitor in the end, never convinces as a traitor, though he does as a lover.

Rosamond Lehmann's fiction has incidental resemblances to Elizabeth Bowen's rather than any real affinity, resemblances springing from a shared influence, that of James, and from a roughly similar background of upper-class life. Her first novel, *Dusty Answer* (1927), demonstrated what was to be her abiding subject in fiction, the anguish of women in love. It reaches its fullest expression in *The Echoing Grove* (1953). The novel is most elaborately composed. At its centre is the triangular relationship between Madeleine, her husband Rickie, and her sister Dinah, who becomes Rickie's mistress. The culmination revealing the psychological significance of the whole comes eight pages before the end when the two sisters, long estranged, talk in the small hours. Madeleine, whose lover has just rejected her, says:

'... We were so happy—not always, but most of the time, as he agrees. Do I understand *nothing*? He says I don't. Does it always wear out? Are men bound to get sick of making love to the same woman, even if it's—if it seems to her—very successful? Is that all there is to it?'

Glancing at the childishly quivering face, Dinah said with pity and kindness:

'It's not all there is to it by any means; but it does seem almost insoluble. I can't help thinking it's particularly difficult to be a woman just at present. One feels so transitional and fluctuating ... So I suppose do men. I believe we *are* all in a flux—that the difference between our grandmothers and us is far deeper than we realize—much more fundamental than the obvious social economic one. Our so-called emancipation may be a symptom, not a cause. Sometimes I think it's more than the development of a new attitude towards sex: that a new gender may be evolving— physically new—a sort of hybrid. Or else it's just beginning to be uncovered how much woman there is in man and *vice versa*.' She pondered. 'Perhaps when we understand more, unearth more of what goes on in the unconscious, we shall manage to behave better to one another. It's ourselves we're trying to destroy when we're destructive: at least I think that explains the people who never can sustain a human relationship. It's not good and evil struggling in them: it's the suppressed unaccepted unacceptable man or woman in them they have to cast out ... come to terms with.'

The situation is exhaustively examined in all its aspects and rendered with a quite extraordinary intensity through a series of complex flashbacks from the first meeting of the two sisters, both widowed now, after their long alienation from each other. Technically, *The Echoing Grove* is most impressive, yet the end of the technique, it seems to me, is, rather than anything else, to produce a suffocatingly claustrophobic work in which never for a moment are we allowed the least relief from the masochistic self-torture suffered by the principal characters. They never transcend their misery. One feels of them the full force of Lawrence's complaint against Poe: 'These terribly conscious birds, like Poe and his Ligeia, deny the very life that is them; they want to turn it all into talk, into knowing.' Whether Miss Lehmann intended it or not, she shows us here personal relations become obsessive, indulged in, as it were, as an end in themselves. And with

Rickie she seems to me to fail completely, by destroying him for the reader before she begins the task of creating him; for much the most powerful scene in the novel is the very early one in which the two sisters make common cause for the first time in many years in the drowning of a rat that Dinah's dog has savaged. It is a quite terrifying scene, and whether intended or not, it can only be interpreted as symbolic of the two women's ganging up against Rickie, as the killing of the male.

[2]

WILLIAM PLOMER'S first novel, *Turbott Wolfe*, was published in 1926, when he was a very young man. A distinguished poet and autobiographer, he has, one feels, obstinately refused to be a professional novelist. In fiction his best work has lain in the short story, and there his achievement, especially in volumes like *I Speak of Africa* and *A Child of Queen Victoria*, has been remarkable. All the same, his novels cannot be ignored and, taken with the short stories, their influence has been seminal. If today there is such a thing as a characteristically South African fiction—one thinks of the work of such diverse talents as Nadine Gordimer, Daphne Rooke, Doris Lessing, Dan Jacobson, Alan Paton, Jack Cope, David Lytton—then Plomer was its ancestor. As Laurens Van der Post has said, Plomer's 'was the first imagination to allow the black man of Africa to enter into it in his own human right ... He was the first to accept him without qualification or reservation as a human being'.

Plomer was born in the Transvaal, educated in England, returned to South Africa at the age of sixteen, and was first a farmer and then kept a native store in Zululand before coming to England to live for good. Through all his fiction runs one single preoccupation. In the preface to a collection of his stories, *Four Countries*, he writes: '... luck apart, it does seem to me that my transplantations have not been uncharacteristic of this age of dislocation, disorientation and exile, this age of the Displaced Person. In their way I think most of my stories reflect the age by isolating some crisis caused by a change of environment or by the sudden and sometimes startling confrontation of different races and classes'. His theme has always been that of the Displaced Person in the larger and literal sense of the phrase.

Turbott Wolfe is an account of a Young Africa movement, the main principles of which are that South Africa is not and never can be a white man's country and that the only way Africa may be secured for the African is through miscegenation. Written in the form of a continued conversation, a monologue, the narrative has at once the charm and the disadvantage of conversation. Conversation is hardly a subtle enough medium for the presentation of character, so that such an important character as Friston, for instance, remains always shadowy. But the creation of Turbott Wolfe himself is a brilliant and successful persona for Plomer himself and makes possible the expression of a dominant mood that could scarcely have been expressed in any other way. And the inconsequence of conversation is admirably adapted both to the contemptuous descriptions of white settlers and the idyllic passages on native life, such as the portrayal of the girl Nhliziyombi, with whom Wolfe falls in love.

Turbott Wolfe remains an extremely interesting novel. Plomer's second novel, *Sado*, about Japan, also remains interesting, but less so as a novel. As an artist in the rendering of scenes, Plomer is a virtuoso; but with this goes an inability, it seems, to make up his mind whether he wishes to write travel sketches, paint landscapes or tell a story. This is very evident in *Sado*. Sado, the young Japanese, with his inferiority feelings, his apathy, his thoughts of suicide, is Japanese certainly but not an uncommon figure anywhere. A sentimental friendship develops between him and the young Englishman Lucas. They drift apart through a trivial misunderstanding:

> A conscientious egoist, he had not been quite conscientious enough, and had surrendered to the feminine, introverted, Asiatic part of his nature, instead of relying on the masculine, European frankness in Lucas. And what, after all, was this fearful crime of which Lucas had been guilty? Why, simply that he had failed to introduce Sado to Elsa Nicolai!

It is plain that, strictly, the question of race and colour is irrelevant here: given the inferiority feeling, a similar drifting apart could have occurred had Sado been not a Japanese student but an English working-class youth. But the weakness of the novel lies in Lucas. We are told many things about him, we know his attributes; but he remains a lay figure, a cultured young Englishman in Japan, our guide round the Islands. He is dim, vague, admirably analysed, capable of charming and witty generalizations on life and art, but never alive. He is the first of a number of such characters in Plomer's fiction.

Sado was followed by *The Case Is Altered*. In form, this novel follows one of the favourite patterns of thirties fiction in England, what might be called, after Vicki Baum's sensational best-seller, the *Grand Hotel* formula, in which a number of very different and contrasted characters are brought together through the purely adventitious unity of place. For Plomer, the place is a boarding-house in London. But the characters are not merely inhabitants of a boarding-house; they are also to be seen as dwellers in an interregnum, lost, conscious of the death of the old world and waiting for a new one to be born. They are to be taken as typical figures of the England of the day. Unfortunately, the characters dissolve, as it were, in description and analysis; it is as though we had been given the blueprints for characters but not the characters themselves.

The same criticism must be made of *The Invaders*. The subject is the unemployed who, during the thirties, flocked into London from the provinces, pathetic, hopeless, lost; and beyond them, the middle-class drifters, all sufferers from a maladjustment to society, from that feeling of being unwanted by society that runs through Plomer's work at this time. All the characters are aimless, adrift, wandering round and round their little universes like goldfish in a globe. Units of a crowd, they are symbolic of men in society today, like the crowds that wander forever round Marble Arch, which Plomer describes so brilliantly in his first chapter. But they are described from their externals, faintly at that. One gets the impression that working-class characters are far more remote from Plomer, less real to him, than the Negroes of Zululand ever were. And writing about Negroes, Plomer had a target for his anger. Nothing, it appeared, sharpened his vision so much as indignation, as hate; in England, one felt, he had found much to baffle and depress him, little to hate.

Plomer's next and most recent novel, *Museum Pieces*, appeared in 1952, eighteen years after *The Invaders*. It seems to me by far his best, and it springs out of affection, not indignation or hatred. The satirist of the early books has become a humorist. The subjects are again displaced persons, museum pieces whom time has passed by. The principal character, Toby d'Arfey, is the last of an old family, a man who, by his very upbringing and traditions, is unfitted for the modern world. He is a man, as Plomer demonstrates in the flesh, of exuberant wit and genuine talent. It is not so much that he lives in the past as that he can find no place for himself in the present. At first sight, he seems an obvious butt for the satirist. The narrator of the novel, a woman who knew him well, describes him as follows:

> As a speculator, he had been in a fur coat to Riga. In search of love, pleasure, art, new sensations, heaven knows what, he had been half-way round the world. He had been half-way, or further, towards becoming an opera singer, and a painter, and had lately set out to be a high-flying milliner, and a maker of animated cartoons. He had been ready to present himself to me as a lover, and to Seddon as a gambler. He had always been something of a playboy, but seriousness was always breaking in. And now he was writing a play.

So we see him, with his adoring mother as foil to him, moving through the twenties and thirties, always out of step with the times, becoming poorer, trying in vain to adapt himself to the age; until, a sick man in the early days of the war, which if he had been in health might have given him real scope for his abilities, he commits suicide.

Plomer expresses his final attitude to D'Arfey in the last sentence of the novel, in which the narrator says: 'As I looked back, that one precarious life seemed to me even then in its frivolity to have a certain grandeur, like a joke made on the scaffold by a man about to be put to death not for what he has done or not done, but for what he is.' And, through Plomer's art, he does emerge as a heroic figure, larger than the life that has defeated him.

The displaced person, of course, was a familiar figure in fiction long before we knew the term, generally in the shape of the uprooted man adrift in urban society, Megalopolis, and he has been the chief theme of another novelist who, though one feels a certain discrepancy between his talents and his actual achievement, still never has had quite the recognition he deserves—Patrick Hamilton. His three related novels, *The Midnight Bell*, *The Siege of Pleasure* and *The Plains of Cement*, were collected into one volume, with the title of *Twenty Thousand Streets under the Sky*, in 1935. Centred largely on a small, very ordinary public house, The Midnight Bell, near Euston Station, they convey admirably the sense of the vastness and impersonality of London, the quality suggested by the titles both of the last novel in the sequence and of the trilogy as a whole. The first novel recounts a young barman's obsessive love for a prostitute; the second, the steps by which the girl Jenny became a prostitute; the third, a barmaid's embarrassed courtship by an older man whose very being baffles her. They strike one as being completely authentic; there is neither melodrama nor sensationalism in them; and the characters are presented with a controlled sympathy.

If these novels are not the minor masterpieces of naturalism one feels they might have been it is because of a defect of style. Hamilton is dealing with the inarticulate, and with his principal characters he succeeds: he knows that lack of education and a poverty-stricken vocabulary do not preclude either intelligence or goodness. It is with the minor characters, the frequenters of the saloon bar, Jenny's prostitute friends and so on, that he fails, or relatively fails, by presenting them humorously, in terms of an elaborate irony, so that they become sub-Dickensian types. He is, as J. B. Priestley observes in his perceptive introduction to the sequence, 'too determinedly facetious, too lavish with what we might refer to as his Komic Kapitals'.

All the same, in these novels Hamilton catches superbly one aspect of London life in the twenties; and in his later novels, *Hangover Square*, *The West Pier* and *Mr Simpson and Mr Gorse*, without departing widely from his chosen scene, he has very largely purged himself of his facetiousness, his tendency towards a ponderous irony. In his last two novels, *The West Pier* and *Mr Simpson and Mr Gorse*, Patrick Hamilton is relating the life of the criminal psychopath Ernest Ralph Gorse, who seems pretty closely modelled on one of the most notorious murderers of recent times, Neville Heath. Hamilton gives us an almost clinical description of Heathmanship in action; and this defines both the fascination of these novels and their limitations. The fascination is that of the seven hundred volumes of the *British Trials* series: there is the same impressive density of documentation, the same impressive omniscience after the event.

In these novels, Hamilton shows himself as the poker-faced connoisseur of the seedily third-rate; he clumps through the spiritual slums of urban man like a plain-clothes police sergeant, and he has them all taped, the semi-detached villas, the cocktail lounges, the saloon bars and their denizens; so that when Ernest Ralph Gorse meets the colonel's widow, Mrs Joan Plumleigh-Bruce, among the chromium and faked oak of The Friar in Reading, everything is set for a complete demonstration of the exploitation of the worthless by the vicious. The weakness is that it is so completely a demonstration. Hamilton's characters are as dingy a set of people as it is possible to imagine, distinguished only by small-time sordidness, mediocre snobberies and unambitious lusts, interesting only because of what is going to happen to them, which in turn is interesting only because we know that one day Ralph Ernest Gorse will hang. They are not explored in depth; had they been, they might have achieved some sort of dignity, jumped out of their two-dimensional police-photograph flatness.

They are, as it were, accretions of generalizations about broad categories—real or otherwise—of human beings, given the illusion of life by their author's air of knowingness about their habits and haunts; so much so that at times they appear almost as the secretions of their circumstances. Challenge the generalizations and the conviction departs. But this said, the fact remains that these novels compose a chillingly impressive exposure of spiritual death.

[3]

THE FIGURE of the displaced person can, of course, be taken as a symbol of man's essential situation on this earth. In our time, the leading English novelist of the displaced person in this fundamental sense is Graham Greene. A masterly story-teller, he has learnt much of his narrative art from Stevenson and Conrad but not less from the film. And though he sees his characters in what he believes to be the fundamental human situation they are always given a strictly contemporary setting. He is in almost mediumistic *rapport* with the temper of the times. Thus, though his preoccupations were very different from those of the poets who are generally thought characteristic of the thirties in England, Auden in particular, when one turns to the novels Greene wrote in the thirties one sees immediately that they could have been written at no other time. He shares with Auden a common symbolism of frontiers, spies and betrayal; and his prose, at any rate in individual phrases and images, is the nearest equivalent we have to Auden's verse.

Again, his thirties novels, superficially at least, rehearse the great thirties themes: strikes and political murder in *It's a Battlefield*, the irresponsible power of international finance in *England Made Me*, the machinations of armament manufacturers in *A Gun for Sale*, the Spanish civil war in *The Confidential Agent*, culminating in *The Power and the Glory* with the confrontation of Marxism and religion. In the later novels, the stories are played out, sometimes with what seems an uncanny prescience, with the world's most disturbed areas as their background. The scene of *The Quiet American* is Vietnam during the war against the French, that of *Our Man in Havana* Cuba on the eve of the Castro revolution, that of *A Burnt-out Case* the Congo just before the Belgian withdrawal.

Yet Greene is not by any means the special correspondent as novelist. Rather, the outer violence mirrors, as it were, the violence within the characters, gives a universal situation a local habitation. These representations of contemporary history as the element in which his characters live come as naturally to Greene as the use of the thriller in its simplest and most classical form, that of the hunted man, to express what seems to him the truth about man's fate.

From the beginning he has been obsessed with the plight of fallen man, with the split in man's mind, the insidious attraction of evil, the insidious attraction of good; and he has always been obsessed by the meaninglessness, the seediness (perhaps, in its adjectival form, his favourite word), the vulgarity of a society living without a sense of God. The world he describes is very largely the world of rootless, beliefless urban man, and he describes it with compelling vividness and in terms of a fascinated loathing in which there is always an element of love entwined with the hate. He contemplates it and renders it with horror and with pity. As a Christian, he sees his characters, even in the less serious novels he calls entertainments, under the aspect of eternity, so that in his work, as he has said of Trollope's, 'we are aware of another world against which the actions of the characters are thrown in relief'.

The obsessions were there from the beginning, but the art, of course, needed time to mature. Greene's first novel, *The Man Within*, was published in 1929. It is a very accomplished first novel set among smugglers in Sussex at the beginning of the nineteenth century. Its theme of betrayal was to occupy Greene for the next few years. *Stamboul Train, It's a Battlefield, England Made Me* and *A Gun for Sale* were published between 1932 and 1936. In them, the fractured surface of the strictly contemporary scene, whether in eastern Europe, London, Stockholm or Nottingham, is rendered extraordinarily vividly, cinematically. Their merits are unequal. The most successful is the least ambitious, *A Gun for Sale*, which was presented simply as an entertainment, the story of a political assassin and his pursuit by the police in a world on the verge of war.

Greene became a Catholic in 1926, but his first explicitly Catholic novel, *Brighton Rock*, did not appear until 1938. It is his first major work. In form, the novel is a thriller, a story of betrayal, murder and revenge set in the underworld of a great, glittering seaside resort. But this is to take it simply at the surface level. It is also, and much more importantly, a dramatization of the clash between two opposed attitudes to life and man's total experience, that represented by the good-hearted, sentimental, life-loving and good-time-loving, promiscuous Ida Arnold, who, as she says herself, knows 'the difference between Right and Wrong' ('God doesn't mind a bit of human nature'), and that represented by Pinkie, the stunted, seventeen-year-old gangster-leader, who as a Catholic thinks in terms not of right and wrong but of good and evil and in his demoniac ambition and ruthlessness—towards himself as towards others—deliberately opts for evil and damnation.

These two views of life, the secular and the religious, are at eternal enmity one with the other, and it is in Ida that Pinkie recognizes his enemy. She is indeed almost the pursuing fury with her passion for justice, for fair play, for seeing Right done and Wrong punished. Ida, with her frank enjoyment of sexuality—

She was cheery, she was healthy, she could get a bit lit with the best of them. She liked a good time, her big breasts bore their carnality frankly down the Old Steyne, but you had only to look at her to know you could rely on her. She wouldn't tell tales to your wife, she wouldn't remind you next morning of what you wanted to forget, she was honest, she was kindly, she belonged to the great middle law-abiding class, her amusements were their amusements, her superstitions their superstitions (the planchette scratching the French polish on the occasional table, and the salt over the shoulder), she had no more love for anyone than they had . . .

—stands for everything that is loathsome to Pinkie, the ex-choirboy who has dreamed of being a priest and in whom as a child horror of sex has been awakened by the spectacle of the Saturday-night copulations of his parents. The battle between them and the principles they embody is fought out to the bitter end, to Pinkie's death.

Brighton Rock is an extremely powerful delineation of the 'terror of life'. It is executed throughout in images of squalor, dirt and disgust; there is no saying yea to life here. Whatever illusions the characters have are denied; and the novel ends on a note of almost unbearable irony with the pathetic child-widow Rose about to hear for the first time the terrible words of the gramophone recording Pinkie had made for her, 'God damn you, you little bitch, why can't you go back home for ever and let me be?'

Pinkie, with his 'starved intensity, a kind of hideous and unnatural pride', his ruthless suppression in himself of any stirring of pity, his conscious dedication to evil, is extraordinarily vividly realized. We see a whole world through his eyes; and because we also see him through the eyes of others, witness his inadequacies and incomprehensions, he carries with him an awful pathos. All the same, he remains inherently implausible; to convince us, Greene would have had to make him a figure comparable to Rimbaud in life or to Raskolnikov in literature. Indeed, he and the other main characters in the novel strike one as figures in a morality rather than as characters in their own right.

And there is another difficulty, more fundamental. There is the Jansenistic contempt for everything, virtues included, that does not spring from grace, a lack of charity that one doesn't find, for example, in the Catholic novels of François Mauriac. In many ways, as his first fully mature work, *Brighton Rock* may be taken as the archetypal Greene novel in which the sinner seems nearer to God, more likely to receive the visitations of grace, than the innocent humanitarian. There is, as Morton Dauwen Zabel has noted in his essay on Greene in *Craft and Character in Modern Fiction*, a long-established tradition of the 'sanctified sinner' in modern literature from Baudelaire onwards. In Greene's case, it was vigorously attacked by George Orwell, reviewing *The Heart of the Matter* in *The New Yorker*, who claimed that 'by trying to clothe theological speculations in flesh and blood, it produces psychological absurdities'. It had led Greene to assume, of Pinkie, 'that the most brutally stupid person can, merely by having been brought up a Catholic, be capable of great intellectual subtlety', a charge that seems to me very near the mark, as indeed I find his comment on Scobie, in *The Heart of the Matter*: 'if he were capable of getting into the kind of mess that is described, he would have got into it earlier. If he really felt that adultery is mortal sin, he would stop committing it; if he persisted in it, his sense of sin would weaken. If he believed in Hell, he would not risk going there merely to spare the feelings of a couple of neurotic women'. But then I find *The Heart of the Matter* the least satisfactory of Greene's major novels, and Scobie himself conceived in sentimentality. Moreover, Greene here has surely become the victim of his own style, so that more than once he is on the point of writing self-parody. The brilliantly sharp images, perfectly focused to present types of men and women and to evoke an atmosphere of seediness or despair, become almost stereotyped here, predictable and monotonous.

One cannot say this about the novel that followed, *The End of the Affair*. There is no suspicion of self-parody. Yet it raises problems even more acute than those started by *Brighton Rock* and *The Heart of the Matter*. As a study of obsessive love, obsessive jealousy, it is masterly. The story is told by the jealous lover himself, Maurice Bendrix, a novelist and an unbeliever; not an attractive or likeable man but one who at least tries to be honest about himself. He has begun an affair with Sarah Miles, the wife of a senior civil servant, merely to get copy about the lives of senior civil servants for a novel he is writing, and then finds himself in love with her. But the affair ends suddenly and inexplicably after the house in which they are making love is blasted by a V.1. Tortured by jealousy, Bendrix sets a private inquiry agent—a most deftly contrived and appealing character—on Sarah's trail. The agent manages to purloin her diary and so Bendrix discovers the identity of the rival who has supplanted him. The rival is God. When one reads Sarah Miles's diary one realizes that the real theme of Greene's novel is not sexual jealousy at all but the working of divine grace.

For obvious reasons, few novelists have taken the working of divine grace as their subject. Greene succeeds up to a point and then fails by attempting too much. Bendrix argues that what appear to be the miracles of which Sarah is the agent are in fact coincidences. Coincidence in fiction is the less convincing the more often it is invoked, and this must be even more true of miracles. Greene errs similarly, and even more gravely, when we learn after her death that Sarah, entirely unknown to herself, had been surreptitiously baptized into the Roman Church as a small child. There comes a point, in other words, when the novel is overlaid by the parable; an element that is outside literature, in that it cannot be judged in literary terms, takes over.

This is not true of *The Power and the Glory* (1940), which, though conforming to the archetype laid down in *Brighton Rock*, rises triumphantly clear of the parable. One has only to read the first paragraph to realize one is in the presence of the Greene whose skill, to quote Zabel, 'puts him in the descent of the modern masters—James, Conrad, Joyce—in whom judgment and imagination achieved their richest combination'. No doubt the immediate object of our attention is his conception of the priest, the one priest left in this remote Mexican state in which the Church is banned and its clergy outlawed, a priest who on any ordinary view, including his own, must be considered a bad priest, a coward who keeps himself going only with the help of brandy, a priest, moreover, who has fathered a child, but who, partly because he is a priest, a man in a special relation to God, is yet capable of the ultimate heroism, of something like martyrdom. It is the index of Greene's success here that we do, without any sort of strain, accept him at the end as possibly among the fellowship of the saints.

But the imaginative achievement would not have been possible had the novel not also been an achievement of judgment; indeed, the two are inseparable, though it is the rightness and strength of the judgment that distinguish this novel from Greene's other works. For the first and almost the only time the representative of the secular interpretation of life, the non-religious, humanist view, is treated with a dignity and seriousness comparable to that accorded to the representative of the religious. The police lieutenant is conceived in imaginative understanding and is shown as equally dedicated as the priest. If there are secular saints this man is one. This means that the argument—or rather, the dramatization of the argument—is lifted on to a plane that transcends anything in Greene's other fiction. It gives the novel a genuinely tragic quality. Both the priest and the police lieutenant are men who love and who are moved by love; and in the end they come together, however momentarily, in something that can be called human companionship. 'You're a good man', the priest says; and the police lieutenant: 'You aren't a bad fellow.' So the novel exists in a charity we find nowhere else in Greene.

[4]

THERE IS a constant element in at any rate a majority of the novels Evelyn Waugh has written from *Decline and Fall* (1928) to *Unconditional Surrender* (1961): the hero is an innocent caught up in and done down by the machinations of a wicked world. But the nature of the world changes.

In *Decline and Fall* we are in a world as remote from moral considerations as a fairy story or a Marx Brothers film, a world refracted partly through Firbank, partly, perhaps, through P. G. Wodehouse. The novel opens with the annual dinner of the Bollinger Club at Scone College, Oxford, which precipitates Paul Pennyfeather, who is reading for the Church, into a sequence of adventures the more fantastic and bizarre for being narrated deadpan. Debagged by the youth of the English county families, Paul is sent down for indecent behaviour, becomes a schoolmaster at Llanabba Castle in North Wales, enters high society as the fiancé of Mrs Margot Beste-Chetwynde, later Viscountess Metroland, finds himself in Egdon Heath Prison, having taken the rap for Margot, who, unknown to him, owns Latin-American Entertainment Co., Ltd, a chain of brothels in South America, and then, almost by magic, is back at Oxford under a different name reading for the Church once again. He moves, an innocent, in a world of immortals, Margot Metroland, Dr Fagan, Captain Grimes, Solomon Philbrick, Mr Prendergast, beings as indestructible as the forces of nature that, in comic terms, they represent.

One calls *Decline and Fall* satire for lack of a more accurate word. But very largely, we are outside satire because we are outside moral considerations, as much as we are in Lewis Carroll. The clue to Waugh's controlling attitude may be found in Paul's reflections in prison on his behaviour in shielding Margot from the consequences of her crimes as a white-slaver:

> As he studied Margot's photograph, dubiously transmitted as it was, he was strengthened in his belief that there was, in fact, and should be one law for her and another for himself, and that the raw little exertions of nineteenth-century Radicals were essentially base and trivial and misdirected. It was not simply that Margot was very rich or that he had been in love with her. It was just

that he saw the *impossibility* of Margot in prison; the bare connection of vocables associating the ideas was obscene.

The point is made again when Paul, back at Oxford, talks to Margot's son, Peter Pastmaster, now an undergraduate prominent in the Bollinger:

> '. . . You know, Paul, I think it was a mistake you ever got mixed up with us; don't you? We're different somehow. Don't quite know how. Don't think that's rude, do you, Paul?'
> 'No, I know exactly what you mean. You're dynamic, and I'm static.'

To the dynamic, all is forgiven; the concept of forgiveness is irrelevant: they triumphantly *are*.

With *Vile Bodies* (1930), we are out of fairyland and into Mayfair. *Vile Bodies* is one of those rare novels, like *The Great Gatsby*, that seem to define and sum up a period. It can stand for one aspect of life in the England of the twenties. Its theme is stated in a parenthesis:

> 'Oh, Nina, *what a lot of parties*.'
> (. . . Masked parties, Savage parties, Victorian parties, Greek parties, Wild West parties, Russian parties, Circus parties, parties where one had to dress as somebody else, almost naked parties in St John's Wood, parties in flats and studios and houses and ships and hotels and night clubs, in windmills and swimming baths, tea parties at school where one ate muffins and meringues and tinned crab, parties at Oxford where one drank brown sherry and smoked Turkish cigarettes, dull dances in London and comic dances in Scotland and disgusting dances in Paris—all that succession and repetition of massed humanity . . . Those vile bodies . . .)

The plot is of the slightest: the attempts, continually thwarted through lack of money and loss of jobs, of Adam Fenwick-Symes and Nina Blount to get married. *Vile Bodies*, like *Decline and Fall*, is a fantasy, but a fantasy based on the observable reality of the times. So there is much more satire, of the kind one might find in a very brilliant theatrical revue; its targets are essentially the world as reflected in the popular press, which means the press itself, the Bright Young People it helped to bring into being, evangelists like Aimée Semple MacPherson, the world of motor racing, the book-banning activities of Sir William

Joynson-Hicks, and so on. The truly remarkable thing is that it has survived its topicality; it is a triumph of style and the comic spirit.

Waugh is as detached as he was in *Decline and Fall*; yet there is a difference in his attitude. When Paul Pennyfeather sees the *impossibility* of Margot Metroland in prison, one feels that Waugh is seeing it too; he is seeing her and Grimes and Fagan and Philbrick as Immortals immune to the laws that govern human beings. In *Vile Bodies*, there is, instead, a recognition of the futility of the characters, of a lost generation. It is not stated; the comment is implied in the way the book is written and composed, implied very occasionally as well by the kind of juxtaposition of the noble past with the bathetic present that T. S. Eliot uses in his Sweeney poems; as in the account of the gossip-writer Lord Balcairn's suicide:

> So the last Earl of Balcairn went, as they say, to his fathers (who had fallen in many lands and for many causes, as the eccentricities of British Foreign Policy and their own wandering natures had directed them; at Acre and Agincourt and Killiecrankie, in Egypt and America. One had been picked white by fishes as the tides rolled him among the tree-tops of a submarine forest; some had grown black and unfit for consideration under tropical suns; while many of them lay in marble tombs of extravagant design).

In a way, *Vile Bodies* is a monitory book. A rendering in comic terms of futility, it expresses the end of an era and what must follow after. But to leave it simply at that would be to ignore the complex tone of the novel, which is the consequence of Waugh's double vision of his characters. He sees their silliness and futility quite dispassionately; but his response to them is one not of contempt but of affection; the love affair between Adam and Nina, for instance, is made curiously touching. He sees them, one feels, and the characters of *Vile Bodies* generally, as children, as innocents dancing on the edge of nothingness. Alas! regardless of their doom, the little victims play.

Fantasy disappears altogether in *A Handful of Dust* (1934). Here we are in the real world, and innocence is well and truly done down. At once comic and grim, *A Handful of Dust* is one of the best novels of our time. Contempt for the social scene depicted and for those who inhabit it has entered in, and so has bitterness. It is a story of the destruction of Tony Last by his wife Brenda, a destruction motivated not by malignance, indeed scarcely motivated at all, but the outcome of boredom and irresponsible selfishness.

The title of the novel is, of course, from *The Waste Land*, and poem and novel meet at many points, though in the novel there is no promise of the fructifying waters. As ever, much of the strength of the novel comes from the author's detachment. Last in his way is a good man; but he is also absurd. He gets not perhaps what he deserves but certainly what he must expect. He is betrayed as much by the nature of his illusions as by his wife. And this is made plain in the novel. He is pathetic but no more; no more is claimed for him. He is not sentimentalized in any way.

Between *Vile Bodies* and *A Handful of Dust* Waugh published *Black Mischief*, a rogue-novel, as it may be called, set in an African kingdom closely resembling Abyssinia. The rogue-hero is Basil Seal, of whom there is nothing good except that in his ceaselessly resourceful villainy he is a splendid comic character. He turns up again, very much in his element, in Waugh's novel of the first months of the war, *Put Out More Flags*. In these novels, satire in any real sense, or moral indignation, is in abeyance; but they are superbly funny. Once again, perhaps, they signalize Waugh's admiration for the dynamic.

Brideshead Revisited (1945), subtitled *The Sacred and Profane Memories of Captain Charles Ryder*, is, according to the author, 'an attempt to trace the workings of the divine purpose in a pagan world'. Ryder, who narrates the story, finds himself stationed during the war near Brideshead Castle, the seat of the Marchmains, a great Catholic family. We switch back to 1923, to Oxford and Ryder's meeting with Sebastian Flyte, Marchmain's younger son, who becomes his closest friend. This Oxford section is Waugh at his best. Here the romantic note is right. But then we pass on to Ryder's discovery of the Flytes, this great, traditionally Roman Catholic family, and his lifelong love-affair with them. The characters whom Waugh dislikes are still etched in comic savagery; but with the Flytes we move further and further into unreality, almost, indeed, into the territory of Disraeli and Ouida. The apotheosis of unreality is reached in the deathbed scene of Lord Marchmain, who, when he left his wife, had also repudiated his faith. Marchmain makes the sign of the cross; and as he dies soliloquizes about his ancestors:

'They dug the foundations to carry the stone for the new house; the house that was a century old when Aunt Julia was born. Those were our roots in the waste hollows of Castle Hill, in the briar and nettle; among the tombs in the old church and the chantry where no clerk sings.

'Aunt Julia knew the tombs, cross-legged knight and doubleted earl, marquis like a Roman senator, limestone, alabaster and Italian marble; tapped the escutcheons with her ebony cane, made the casque ring over old Sir Roger. We were knights then, baronets since Agincourt, the larger honours came with the Georges . . .'

If one says the passage shows remarkable breath control for a dying man, one isn't being flippant so much as pointing out that Waugh has soared into rhetoric and forgotten about his character altogether.

The trilogy, *Men at Arms*, *Officers and Gentlemen* and *Unconditional Surrender*, presents something of a problem. When *Officers and Gentlemen* appeared in 1955 Waugh said: 'I thought at first that the story would run into three volumes. I find that two will do the trick.' Nevertheless, *Unconditional Surrender* was published in 1961. It is perhaps difficult not to see a split between the first two volumes and the third. In the first two books Catholicism asserts itself as the core of a nostalgic dream of an ideal past by which the present is judged and found wanting. These novels record Guy Crouchback's infatuation and subsequent disillusionment with the Army in the first years of the war.

The Crouchback of these two novels is not unlike Ford's Tietjens: he is a man who has no place in the modern world: his ideals, his own conception of himself as a man of honour, serve only to hinder him and trip him up in his traffic with the world as it is. Yet, compared with Tietjens, Crouchback seems the expression of a wistful dream of the author's rather than a solid creation; and the two novels taken together seem a series of brilliant fragments rather than a composed whole or even part of a whole. There is splendid incidental comedy, of course, centred on Apthorpe in *Men at Arms* and Corporal-Major Ludovic in *Officers and Gentlemen*. At the same time, an extremely unpleasant vein of snobbery runs through both books.

Yet one's impression of these two earlier novels of the trilogy has been substantially altered by *Unconditional Surrender*. What happens in *Unconditional Surrender* is that Crouchback comes alive as a sympathetic character, even as the positively good man. By the end of *Officers and Gentlemen* all his illusions have been ruthlessly destroyed, and perhaps the title may stand for, among other things, his final acceptance of the truth about man in the temporal world. One instance of this is Waugh's delineation of Crouchback's ex-wife Virginia. She is a wanton, a twenties girl, as Waugh makes plain. Pregnant by another man, she sets out deliberately to make Crouchback re-marry her. Waugh presents her without condemnation or satire, with full understanding of her frailties and also of her gallantry, and has Crouchback re-marry her knowing exactly what he is doing. He is performing a private act of charity, the only kind of action that in the temporal world is incorruptible.

Crouchback is no more in control of circumstances in this novel than in the earlier ones. He volunteers for service with military government in Italy, undergoes training and finds himself in Jugoslavia as a liaison officer with the Partisans. The account of this corner of the war is as brilliant as the description of the evacuation from Crete in *Officers and Gentlemen*. Crouchback is still the victim of events but again he asserts himself in a purely private act of charity, the rescue of a collection of displaced persons, Jewish refugees. Their leader says to him:

'Is there any place that is free from evil? It is too simple to say that only the Nazis wanted war. These Communists wanted it too. It was the only way in which they could come to power. Many of my people wanted it, to be revenged on the Germans, to hasten the creation of the national state. It seems to me there was a will to war, a death wish, everywhere. Even good men thought their private honour would be satisfied by war. They could assert their manhood by killing and being killed. They would accept hardships in recompense for having been selfish and lazy. Danger justified privilege. I knew Italians—not very many perhaps—who felt this. Were there none in England?'

'God forgive me', said Guy. 'I was one of them.'

This is surely one of the most affecting passages in contemporary fiction, and it represents Crouchback's final attainment of self-knowledge.

At the moment of writing, it seems that *Unconditional Surrender* may very well mark a turning-point in Evelyn Waugh's development as a novelist. Yet, as one looks back over the three novels and compares them with *Decline and Fall* and *Vile Bodies*, one is struck not so much by the differences as by the underlying similarity. Paul Pennyfeather and Adam Fenwick-Symes are the victims of what seems inconsequent action in a world that is certainly not naturalistic but is more than fantasy. But Guy Crouchback is the victim of action just as inconsequent in a real world no less fantastic, the world of war as many thousands have experienced it. Perhaps the earlier novels are more true to life than we had believed.

[5]

HENRY GREEN has been the least predictable of contemporary English novelists and, Ivy Compton-Burnett excepted, probably the most original. His first novel, *Blindness* (published 1926), was written while he was still a schoolboy; his second, *Living* (1929), written when he was twenty-four, remains after more than thirty years the best English novel of factory life, though to put it in such terms is almost inevitably to see it wrong, as it was for years. Green was born in 1905, the son of an industrialist, and educated at Eton and Oxford, from which he proceeded to the family factory in Birmingham. There for a while he worked as a foundryman, writing *Living* in his spare time. It predated Auden's first volume of poems by a year, and its subject-matter and style gave its author honorary membership, as it were, of a literary movement to which he never really belonged; but in the thirties it was the subject-matter, life among factory workers in Birmingham, that gave it its immediate attraction.

The theme is a familiar one: the displacement of labour by reorganization and the infatuation of a girl who wants marriage and children before anything else with a young man who finally, and comically, deserts her. The novel is composed as a sequence of mainly very short episodes rather in the manner of a film, the author cutting from character to character, from scene to contrasted scene, taking in workers, members of the management, the managing director and his family. At the centre of the book is Mr Craigan, the old moulder, and Lily Gates, who is virtually his daughter, for though Craigan is unmarried he owns his own house in which he lives as a patriarch with his mate Joe Gates and his family. It is Mr Craigan's intention that Lily should marry the young man of his choice, Jim Dale, but his plans are frustrated by the girl's elopement with Bert Jones. She returns home unmarried, with Mr Craigan, suddenly old, more dependent on her than ever and fearful that one day she will marry and leave him.

The weakness of most novels of working-class life has stemmed from an over-emphatic naturalism. Characters have been shown as the passive victims of an overwhelmingly hostile and capricious environment, will-less automata helpless in the grip of circumstance. The consequence is that most working-class novels are bleak and grey. *Living* is not. The very title of the novel is defiant, as though Green had discovered life for the first time. The author's delighted sense of novelty is carried over to the reader; and what Green captures, as it has scarcely been done before or since, is what can only be called the poetry of working-class life.

Sometimes it is a poetry of incident:

> Then, one morning in iron foundry, Arthur Jones began singing. He did not often sing. When he began the men looked up from work and at each other and stayed quiet. In machine shop, which was next iron foundry, they said it was Arthur singing and stayed quiet also. He sang all morning.
>
> He was Welsh and sang in Welsh. His voice had a great soft yell in it. It rose and rose and fell then rose again and, when the crane was quiet for a moment, then his voice came out from behind noise of the crane in passionate singing. Soon each one in this factory heard that Arthur had begun and, if he had 2 moments, came by iron foundry shop to listen. So all through that morning, as he went on, was a little group of men standing by door in the machine shop, always different men. His singing made them all sad. Everything in iron foundries is black with the burnt sand, and here was his silver voice yelling like bells. The black grimed men bent over their black boxes.
>
> When he came to the end of a song or something in his work kept him from singing, men would call out to him with names of English songs but he would not sing these. So his morning was going on. And Mr Craigan was glad, work seemed light to him this morning who had only 3 months before he got his old age pension, he ought to work at his voice he said of him in his mind and kept Joe Gates from humming tune of Arthur's songs . . .
>
> Still Arthur sang and it might be months before he sang again. And no one else sang that day, but all listened to his singing. That night son had been born to him.

More often, it is a poetry of observation, which becomes symbolism. The background of drab streets and public parks, with the factory at their centre, is dominated by the flights of homing pigeons. They recur again and again throughout the novel, sometimes in simple description, sometimes as images of the shifting impulses of the characters. They are symbolic at once of escape, of the life beyond the labyrinth of brick, and of the attachment to home and the familiar scene. They give *Living* a unity beyond its formal structure, and it is on the juxtaposition of homing pigeons with a small baby 'which laughed and crowed and grabbed at it', that the novel ends.

The style accurately matches the novelty of the scene as Green saw it. Bare, repetitive, harsh, angular, sometimes deliberately clumsy, it is an admirable expression for the blackness and din of the foundry, at the same time as it is attuned to the vernacular speech of the characters.

In content, Green's third novel, *Party Going* (1939), is as different from *Living* as it could be. We are in the world of Evelyn Waugh—with a difference. A party of upper-class young people are going to France as the guests of an absurdly rich young man; they meet at the station, fog holds up the train, and they are marooned in the upper rooms of the station hotel while the hordes of workers, waiting for trains below, singing community songs, thicken until they threaten to swamp the hotel itself. The situation is as simple as that; but while in a sense the subject lessens in importance, the style becomes more rotund and involved, the symbolism deepens. There is, for example, the incident—its repercussions sound throughout the novel—of the spinster aunt at whose feet a dead pigeon falls at the station entrance. She picks it up, takes it to the ladies' lavatory, washes it and makes it up into a brown-paper parcel. The discovery disturbs the party, as it disturbs the reader; the incident is funny, but it is more than that, and its meaning cannot be paraphrased. *Party Going* is a comic novel, which may be read simply as such; as it may be read as a satire on people with wealth but without responsibility. It is both these things, and something more; obstinately itself and irreducible to a single moral. It is, to use the phrase Green has applied to his own prose, 'a gathering web of insinuations', and it showed, when it appeared, Green to be one of the very few successful symbolists among English novelists.

This is equally apparent in his wartime novel, *Caught* (1943).

Judged merely as documentary, *Caught* is the best novel we have of London during the phoney war and the early days of the blitz. But it is much more than a documentary novel. For what exactly is *Caught* about? Life in the Fire Service. The lives of men and women held in unwelcome proximity for too long and with too little to do, gossip-ridden and corroded by suspicion. The mutual distrust of the working-class man and the middle-class man. The overwhelmingly disastrous effect of sudden authority and hero-worship combined on a man totally unprepared for them. In part, an account of the first night raids on London; in part, of a father's puzzled devotion for his son and a brother's puzzled devotion to his sister. All these go to make up *Caught*, but all as it were simultaneously, fused together, so that no one single strand can be isolated and drawn out without the whole fabric perishing. From one point of view, *Caught* is a tragi-comedy of mis-understanding; everyone talks at length, but there is no communica-tion. There is no communication between the middle-class auxiliary fireman Roe and his five-year-old son, as there is none between Roe and his officer Pye, whose lunatic sister abducted Roe's son. The novel is summarized in its title; it is the incomprehension and incommunica-bility of Kafka played out in an exactly defined historical context; and the tangle of thwarted understanding and frustrated urge to communi-cate can be resolved only by Pye's suicide and the liberation of the firemen by enemy aeroplanes from the emotional Black Hole of Calcutta into which they are cast.

Green, as a maker of titles, is as literal-minded as Fielding and Jane Austen. Thus *Loving* (1945) is summed up by the title; it is about loving—not love, but the condition expressed by the verbal noun. Practically every character in *Loving* is in a state of loving. Again, the characters are set in a confined space, marooned as it were on a desert island too small for them, cut off from the great world to which they really belong. The desert island of *Loving* is a castle in Ireland staffed mainly by English servants. The period is that of the blitz, 1941–2; they are well out of it, glad of it, and guilty about it. The castle, like the hotel rooms of *Party Going* and the fire station of *Caught*, is a web of gossip, intrigue, scandal and misunderstanding. As in *Caught*, the whole book revolves round one nuclear incident: 'Mrs Jack', the daughter of the owner of the castle, is surprised one morning, by a housemaid, in bed with her lover. It is the beginning of the end; every-thing follows from it. From then on it is inevitable that Raunce, the butler, and Edith, the housemaid, should run away together to England.

Though perhaps on a smaller scale than *Caught*, *Loving* is much more closely knit and the symbolism much more pervasive. There is the ring which is lost, found, lost again and recovered by Edith. This is part of the essential structure of the novel, a precipitant of action. Then there are the peacocks and the doves whose presence and display irradiate the whole book, 'complex symbols', as Edward Stokes has said in his fine critical study, *The Novels of Henry Green*, 'of pride, vanity, beauty, sex and greed'. And continually there are scenes which illuminate magically, the scene, for example, of the two young house-maids waltzing in the deserted ballroom among the dustcloth-shrouded furniture:

> They were wheeling wheeling in each other's arms heedless at the far end where they had drawn up one of the white blinds. Above from a rather low ceiling five great chandeliers swept one after the other almost to the waxed parquet floor reflecting in their hundred thousand drops the single sparkle of distant day, again and again red velvet panelled walls, and two girls, minute in purple, dancing multiplied to eternity in these trembling pears of glass.

Green conducts the novel almost entirely in terms of dialogue and external description. There is no attempt to enter the characters' minds. Yet, rendered wholly from the outside as he is, the central character, the butler Raunce, is a triumph. Green continually surprises us with new facets of his being. At first he seems to be no more than a petty fiddler, then a hypocrite, then a lecher; but as facet after facet is exposed we realize that he is more complicated than our preconceived notions had allowed for, that he is a character completely in the round, surprising us disconcertingly, as people do in life.

After *Loving*, there seems to me a fragmentation of Green's talent. In *Back* (1946) and *Concluding* (1948) poetry, one might say, takes over almost to the exclusion of everything else. What one takes away from *Concluding*, which is at once a novel about old age and about the future, is something similar to the effect of a late Impressionist paint-ing: action, plot, character, scene are dissolved in the play of light and colour. The effect is obtained consciously and carefully; but it is obtained at the cost of the work as a novel.

In Green's two most recent novels, *Nothing* (1950) and *Doting* (1952), the poetry has been jettisoned. They are brilliantly entertaining renderings of upper-class life in London in the decade after the war; but in them Green relies on one strand only of his talent, his ear for speech, and uncannily accurate though it is, it is not nearly strong enough to bear the weight of a whole novel. *Living*, *Party Going*, *Caught* and *Loving* are a different matter altogether. They succeed as novels in the most mundane sense. All have passages of haunting visual beauty, passages which are immediately poetic in their effect. But they do not take the reader away from the scene Green is rendering; indeed, they serve to render it more intensely and more particularly, bring it into sharper focus. Their function is to heighten, but they are still subordinate to the prose narration.

[6]

BETWEEN 1931 and 1939 Anthony Powell published five novels, *Afternoon Men*, *Venusberg*, *From a View to a Death*, *Agents and Patients* and *What's Become of Waring?* Almost as a matter of course, they were compared with Evelyn Waugh's novels of the same period. When he published his next novel, in 1951, it was plain that he had embarked upon a distinctly different type of fiction. *A Question of Upbringing* was the first of a long series of novels to be called *The Music of Time*, of which *A Buyer's Market*, *The Acceptance World*, *At Lady Molly's*, *Casanova's Chinese Restaurant* and *The Kindly Ones* have appeared. What resemblances there are between Powell's early novels and Waugh's are technical. Waugh's early novels are more than half fantasies; by comparison, Powell's is the world as commonly observed. *Afternoon Men* may be taken as representative of Powell's early novels. Contrast the names of Powell's characters with those of Waugh's: Margot Metroland, Miles Malpractice, Agatha Runcible. None of Powell's characters is called anything so extravagant. In other contexts, his names would probably not appear as even slightly eccentric, though in their context they have the unquestioned rightness of *le mot juste*: the name Naomi Race, for an old Bohemian lady who knew Rossetti—what could be better?

Again, though the world of *Afternoon Men* is as small as Waugh's, it is not Mayfair but Bohemia, the near-slums of art; its inhabitants the seedy denizens of Chelsea and Bloomsbury whose focal points are the pubs and clubs of Soho. It is an altogether more slovenly world, and, as Powell describes it, one of the minor circles of hell, though rarely has hell been depicted with such wit or with such elegant contempt:

> Slowly but very deliberately the brooding edifice of seduction, creaking and incongruous, came into being, a vast Heath Robinson mechanism, dually controlled by them and lumbering down vistas of triteness. With a sort of heavy-fisted dexterity the mutually adapted emotions of each of them became synchronized, until the unavoidable anti-climax was at hand. Later they dined at a restaurant quite near the flat.

In this description there is more than a suggestion of Wyndham Lewis, and reading these novels one recalls Lewis's 'Dogmatically I am for the Great Without, for the method of external approach—of the eye rather than that of the ear.' In *Afternoon Men*, Powell too is for the Great Without, though he combines the wisdom of the eye with that of the ear in a sense not intended by Lewis. His visual descriptions are sketched in a minimum of words. But a good half of his effect Powell gets through his extraordinarily precise ear for speech. On the first page of the novel we find this—the scene is a night club: 'If you pay for this round and give me three-and-ninepence we shall all be square.' That is Pringle; it establishes him completely.

In *Afternoon Men* Powell's victims do not have a chance; they are isolated in all their portentous silliness by the gestures and utterances in which he surprises them. There is no direct comment. Built up in a succession of brief shots like a film, the novel from beginning to end describes a full circle. As the form indicates, there is no reason at all why the action described, the round of drinks, parties, seductions, should ever stop. It is as confined, as stuffy, as restless, as endlessly repetitious as the world of goldfish in a bowl. It has the same kind of pointless busy-ness, which is brilliantly conveyed by the use of characters who may be strictly supernumerary to the plot but move constantly backwards and forwards across it. There is, however, this difference between the world of *Afternoon Men* and a goldfish bowl:

goldfish are dumb. Their world is silent: that of *Afternoon Men* echoes and re-echoes with gossip and scandal, with the latest news of everybody's private lives.

To the extreme messiness of these lives, the promiscuity and the drunkenness, the sprawling confusion of the parties, the inefficiency and the dirt ('We none of us wash much here'), Powell opposes not moral indignation or outraged denunciation but what might be called an aesthetic disdain expressed in the austerity, the formal order, of the novel itself.

The Music of Time is obviously an immensely more ambitious work than *Afternoon Men*. The world Powell describes remains one in which Society and Bohemia meet and at times merge, as Mayfair and Soho do in simple topographical fact. The sense of formal order is as strong as ever: Powell sees life aesthetically, as it were. On the first page of *A Question of Upbringing*, what seems to be the whole aesthetic of the work is laid bare. Powell looks down from a window and sees in the street below workmen round a brazier in the falling snow. He writes:

> For some reason, the sight of snow descending on fire always makes me think of the ancient world—legionaries in sheepskin warming themselves at a brazier: mountain altars where offerings glow between wintry pillars: centaurs with torches cantering beside a frozen sea—scattered, unco-ordinated shapes from a fabulous past, infinitely removed from life; and yet bringing with them memories of things real and imagined. These classical projections, and something in the physical attitudes of the men themselves as they turned from the fire, suggested suddenly Poussin's scene in which the Seasons, hand in hand and facing outward, tread in rhythm to the notes of the lyre that the winged and naked greybeard plays. The image of Time brought thoughts of mortality: of human beings, facing outward like the Seasons, moving hand in hand in intricate measure: stepping slowly, methodically, sometimes a trifle awkwardly, in evolutions that take recognizable shape: or breaking into seemingly meaningless gyrations, while partners disappear only to reappear again, once more giving pattern to the spectacle: unable to control the melody, unable, perhaps, to control the steps of the dance. Classical associations made me think, too, of days at school, where so many forces, hitherto unfamiliar, had become in due course uncompromisingly clear.

Immediately, Powell's narrator, Nicholas Jenkins, is back at Eton.

The spectacle of the workmen round the winter brazier is the equivalent for Powell of Proust's *madeleine*, and the work moves forward in ever-expanding circles, beginning with Eton and Oxford, continually returning to the characters met there but taking in more and more as Jenkins's acquaintance with life widens, so that in the end a relatively large area of metropolitan society has been netted. The passage quoted is a good example of the way Powell enhances his narrative, gives dignity to characters and events, by making Jenkins see them, usually at the moment of initial encounter, in pictorial terms, always, I suspect, with reference to specific paintings. This means that momentarily at any rate the character takes on a quality of myth, a timeless quality. But even more important is the image of human beings as participants in a dance, a dance over which they have no control since its movements and their steps in it are governed by the music of time, to which Powell returns repeatedly. As they dance, his characters are 'facing outward', as in Poussin's painting. Facing outward to whom? Not to the reader directly, but to Jenkins. And here, all questions of difference of scale and scope apart, we have the great difference between *Afternoon Men* and *The Music of Time*. The only comment permitted in *Afternoon Men* is what we may deduce from the complete absence of comment. In *The Music of Time* Jenkins mediates between us and the action; he interprets it for us.

While Jenkins is plainly a persona for the author himself, he is a solid creation: we take his word for what happens in the work. He has, after all, the authority of a prose style at once witty and subtle. But there is a whole side of him, as there used to be with the moon, that exists only by inference. In *At Lady Molly's*, for instance, he meets Lady Isabel Tolland and by the end of it is engaged to be married to her. In *Casanova's Chinese Restaurant*, we learn that he is now married to her. But all this, his courtship, his emotional life, is conducted off-stage, as it were. In *Casanova's Chinese Restaurant*, his wife has a mis-carriage; but in terms of the novel this incident exists only to enable Jenkins to meet Widmerpool in the unfamiliar surroundings of an expensive nursing home. It is the index of Powell's control over us that we never begin to wonder about Jenkins's feelings about his wife at this time. Jenkins's function is to be an extremely subtle recording instrument, and he comes alive by virtue of what, out of the whole range of phenomena about him, he chooses to record.

He is very intelligent, but he is intensely selective in what he chooses to record. He is a connoisseur of paintings and of people. His curiosity about people is insatiable, and he has acquired an uncommon talent for placing people, placing them, that is to say, in the social hierarchy. His interest is in the analysis of human behaviour and in the motives behind it. The main motive appears to be the will to power, seen at its most grotesque and also at its most formidable in Widmerpool. But it is no less apparent in careerists like Quiggin and Mark Members and in intriguers like Sillery. The converse of the will to power is the envy of failure: against Widmerpool must be set Uncle Giles; and one sometimes feels that it is his early experience of these two contrasted types that has provided Jenkins with the standards of reference by which he judges the men he meets in later life.

But though his curiosity is insatiable it is also limited. One could make a longer list of the things Jenkins is not interested in than of those he is. To take an obvious example: he seems to have met no one who is religious even in the most conventional way, much less anyone who has undergone conversion. He has his being in a world of self-regard, which he takes at its own valuation. That amiable old silly, Mr Deacon, painter, antique dealer and homosexual, leaves his copy of *War Never Pays* under a chair at Mrs Andriadis's party. But how and why did Mr Deacon get mixed up in the pacifist movement? We are not told. Jenkins sees a procession marching in protest against the Means Test: it is led by the Oxford don Sillery and includes the eminent novelist St John Clarke, pushed in his wheel chair by the critic Quiggin. Are they to be taken to represent intellectual left-wing politics in the thirties? One does not know, and one cannot be sure that Jenkins knows either. Against this must be set the seemingly ceaseless proliferation of characters, so that, at one level, the fascination *The Music of Time* exercises on us seems as much akin to a work like Creevey's diary as to fiction.

We shall not know how good *The Music of Time* is until we have the whole of it. Powell himself practically forces us to make a comparison between the work and *A la recherche du temps perdu*, not only because of the title but also because of his style, which in *A Buyer's Market* is Proustian to the point almost of pastiche. But Proust's is not only a picture of a society in decay: it is also the embodiment of a philosophy of time; and so far any such unifying philosophy has been lacking in Powell's sequence. What we await now is the great generalization, the equivalent of *Le temps retrouvé*.

[7]

THE NOVEL and the short story are very different forms and out-standing talent in the one is no more a guarantee of outstanding talent in the other than success in either is a guarantee of success in prose drama, for example. Some of the best English short-story writers of the twenties and thirties, Katherine Mansfield, A. E. Coppard, H. A. Manhood, Malachi Whitaker, did not attempt novels at all, and those of H. E. Bates, for all their careful craftsmanship, have for me nothing like the vitality and poetic quality of his short stories. V. S. Pritchett is a somewhat different case, for though it is on his short stories that his reputation mainly rests, he has written novels of a quality of interest that more than compensates for their frequent failure of structure.

The character he has made particularly his own he has described in his essay on Gosse's *Father and Son*:

> Extreme puritanism gives purpose, drama and intensity to private life ... Outwardly, the extreme puritan appears narrow, crabbed, fanatical, gloomy and dull; but from the inside—what a series of dramatic climaxes his life is, what a fascinating casuistry beguiles him, how he is bemused by the comedies of duplicity, sharpened by the ingenious puzzles of the conscience, and carried away by the eloquence of hypocrisy.

There is an interesting anticipation of this view of puritanism in *Nothing Like Leather* (1935), a novel which, as its title indicates, has the leather trade as its background. Matthew Burkle, for whom sex is evil, is courting Dorothy Sparkes. They have reached the point of discussing ideal love:

> Burkle was sensitive and glad, telling no one. He was seeing holiness, he who had once been sunk into the pit of shame. There were hot, shameful moments when in imagination he lay with Daisy and called her Dorothy in a whisper which made his heart scamper lest his conscience should hear: but he emerged again into holiness, laving the senses in that pure cold water! And was there not some pleasurable duplicity in his impurity? Ah aha, to be a man with a conscience! To have a fascinating labyrinth in which one could wander!

But Burkle is still the puritan seen from the outside, the hater of sex, whose energies are canalized into the making of money. The puritan has not yet caught Pritchett's imaginative sympathy.

Nor has he in *Dead Man Leading* (1937). Harry Johnson is an explorer who deserts the expedition he is with in Brazil in order to look for his father, who has disappeared. A celibate and a masochist, Johnson, while preparing for the expedition with which the novel deals, has been seduced by the step-daughter of its leader. Irrationally, he is convinced the girl is pregnant. Pritchett comments: 'The conscience of the puritan has need of its melodrama and mythology and he went up the river towards Wright, in the final stage, with the speechless fear of a son guiltily approaching his father.'

Johnson himself is something of a myth figure, Pritchett's variation of a type that haunts English writing in the thirties, the type whose exemplar in history is T. E. Lawrence. Like Burkle, he strikes one as a construction from intellectual premises rather than a creation of the imagination. Every so often in *Dead Man Leading*, however, Pritchett allows the comic writer in him to take over, and then one has, in contrast to the surrounding constriction, a sense of liberation, of ease, of delight, expressed in characters like the cockney-gone-native Calcott indulging in table-rapping with clever Mr Silva.

Such passages point the way to the stories of *You Make Your Own Life* and the novel, *Mr Beluncle* (1951), in which the comedy of extreme puritanism is really explored. Mr Beluncle is a small furniture manufacturer who has been, among other things, a Congregationalist, a Methodist, a Plymouth Brother, a Baptist, a Unitarian, a Theosophist, a Christian Scientist. All these changes in belief have some connection with his economic circumstances at the moment of change. As we meet him in the novel, he is a disciple of Mrs Parkinson, a member of an American sect called the Church of the Last Purification, Toronto, which denies the objective existence of evil.

The first thing that strikes one is Pritchett's depth of imaginative sympathy. He places himself at the centre of Mr Beluncle, as it were; he accepts him completely; and there are no reservations in his sympathy, moral or aesthetic. He reveals Beluncle as a man who can scarcely be judged by ordinary standards of behaviour because he is living out, one might almost say is lived by, a dream. His conduct, which is frequently disastrous to his wife and children, has scarcely reference to the external world at all. He is the self-isolated man, with a hard black line drawn round him. Self-deceiver, liar, cheat, hypocrite, domestic tyrant—he is all these, and yet all these are beside the point. He is the victim of a compulsive fantasy that rules his life and turns everything and everybody he meets into its accomplices. His beliefs give him all the sanction he needs. If they did not he would change them and join another sect whose beliefs did.

Mr Beluncle is a comic character in the Dickens tradition. The novel however, remains curiously static. Beluncle's situation can obviously never change. The dream we watch him enact is always the same dream; which means that the few months of his life that Pritchett deals with are no more significant than any other period of his life before or after. Nevertheless, the comedy is the vehicle of a profound imaginative insight, seen in the treatment not only of Beluncle himself but of his family. It is an uneasy family, and not a happy one, but knit together by a sort of pride in the sense of being different from other families, for life with Beluncle is conducted at a higher pitch than the normal. It is nothing if not dramatic.

Pritchett's lower middle-class milieus and material link him to a number of other novelists of the time, who had an original distinction and idiosyncrasy that make them still significant. One of these was John Hampson, whose best novels, *Saturday Night at the Greyhound*, *O Providence* and *Family Curse*, appeared between 1931 and 1936. The scenes of these novels differ: Saturday night at a pub in a remote Derbyshire mining village during which the conflicts within the inn-keeper's family come to a head; the childhood of a sensitive small boy, the youngest of a large family that has suddenly fallen into penury; the members of a middle-class Birmingham family waiting for the wealthy grandmother to die. But all bear Hampson's thumbprint. The style appears at first harsh, even crude; it is in fact the natural expression of an abhorrence of anything like fine writing or verbal decoration or the obviously charming. Its angularity reflects the angularity of a mind intransigently honest, not cynical but unillusioned and sardonic, stoic. In almost all Hampson's novels there appears the figure of the young man, often a youngest son—Tom in *Saturday Night at the Greyhound*, Johnny in *Family Curse*—who is, or sees himself to be, in permanent estrangement from society because he is homosexual. He is wiser, more clear-sighted, more disinterested, than the other characters; he sees through them and foresees the consequences of their behaviour, even though he may be powerless to prevent them; though he participates

in the action, he is also its chorus. There is obviously room for sentimentality here, yet sentimentality is the last quality one finds in these
novels. They have a remarkable objectivity. Both in texture and in
attitude they seem to me very Anglo-Saxon. They have a bedrock
quality, and though Hampson was in fact learned in the modern
novel, and a craftsman of a high order, they seem to owe nothing to
anything that has gone before.

A similar bedrock quality is found in the fiction of James Hanley, a
much less careful craftsman than Hampson but possessed of remarkable
imaginative power. Indeed, one can apply to Hanley Sean O'Faolain's
comment on Faulkner: 'It is always provoking when a writer has more
genius than talent'. Genius is a large word, but it is not inappropriate
in Hanley's case, however intermittent it may be. His faults are so
obvious as to be glaring. Hanley has no humour and therefore little
perspective; he lacks a sense of selection; and in what sets out to be
realistic fiction he can on occasion indulge in a reckless disregard of
probability. Nor is his prose normally more than pedestrian. This
means that his novels rarely stand up by themselves. Yet at the same
time there is intermittently a quite extraordinary intensity of vision
which, while it lasts, lifts his work on to a plane altogether other than
that at which at first sight it seems to exist.

This was apparent in the novel that first made his name, *Boy*, which
was prosecuted and suppressed under the iniquitous British obscenity
law of the time. It is the story of the persecutions, miseries and indig-
nities suffered by a boy on his first voyage on a merchant steamer.
Looked at coldly, the events narrated may strike one as being altogether
too bad to be true; but at the moment of reading, it seems impossible
to look at them coldly, so intense is the passion that informs their
narration.

There are few of Hanley's novels in which there are not at least
moments of similar intensity which, once read, are not forgotten, so
that in memory they seem to be the book itself. One remembers the
episode in *The Ocean* (1941), a novel of the war at sea as experienced
by merchant seamen, in which torpedoed sailors drifting in a ship's
life-boat suddenly see, though they do not immediately recognize it,
the spouting of a whale; a passage of mysterious and hallucinatory
clarity that takes us suddenly in the realm of poetry. If Hanley could
sustain these moments he would be among the great novelists; as it is,
they more than justify his work.

His chief subject has been the sea and the lives of those who work on it or near it, sailors and dockers, and his principal monument to it the four novels that constitute the *Furys Chronicle*, *The Furys*, *The Secret Journey*, *Our Time Is Gone* and *Winter Song*, novels devoted to the fortunes of the Furys, Liverpool-Irish, the father Dennis, a seaman who for a spell is a docker, his wife Fanny, and their children, one of whom goes to prison, while another becomes a trade union leader and a third a sailor. It is a chronicle of life lived for much of the time at the subsistence level, of struggle between husband and wife, to whose ambition to make one of the sons, Peter, a priest, the whole family is in a sense sacrificed. The work as a whole is often raw and claustrophobic and never quite reaches the tragic level one feels it should. Yet its end, in *Winter Song*, is of real beauty, with the reconciliation in old age of Fanny and Dennis, broken by his experiences as a naval stoker whose ship has been torpedoed, and their return to Ireland. The opening of this novel, describing the old sailor's return, as human derelict, to the Catholic seamen's mission in Liverpool, is particularly fine; and there is a memorable picture of simple unsentimentalized goodness in the character of Kilkey, the Furys' son-in-law. This whole last novel of the sequence is conceived and executed with what can only be called a moral grandeur based on the author's sense of the dignity of human endurance and his compassion for it.

Frank Tilsley was the author of a number of highly successful popular novels characterized by sound feelings and a somewhat old-fashioned technique of broad realism reminiscent of Arnold Bennett. His second novel, *I'd Do It Again*, was, however, something more, and a landmark in what may be loosely called the English novel of revolt during the thirties. It is told in the first person by a young clerk who steals in order to buy his wife a fur coat and is not found out. The point of view is clearly stated in the title; the narrative has a vernacular rasp; and alike in its boldness of method and in its defiance of poverty and sordid living conditions, a revolt with no political basis whatever, it has more in common with American fiction of the time than with English.

[8]

DESPITE THE YEARS of mass-unemployment, of hunger marches, of the means test, the English novels of social protest of the time seem in retrospect altogether more tepid, more genteel affairs than their American counterparts. There were plenty of novels exposing the misery of unemployment, the most effective, as it was almost the most violent, being the first of them, Walter Greenwood's *Love on the Dole*: today it does not seem much more than a crude morality, though its raw power is still there. Much more typical of these novels, though, were such books as Walter Brierley's *Means Test Man*, a careful description of a week in an unemployed miner's life. One couldn't call it revolutionary or even in any sense political in its implications; it is essentially the cry of outrage of a serious-minded working man who has suddenly found himself deprived of function and status. Its prevalent tone strikes one now as middle class; it is certainly very far removed from that of Dahlberg, Cantwell or Algren. Both in the United States and in Britain there was much talk of what was called the proletarian novel. Generally it was used as a loose synonym for the working-class novel. In the only sense in which it has meaning, in the Marxist sense, there were very few examples indeed of it in Britain, the only one that still has interest as a positive literary achievement being the trilogy *A Scots Quair*—*Sunset Song* (1932), *Cloud Howe* (1933), *Grey Granite* (1934)—by Lewis Grassic Gibbon, who died at the age of thirty-four in 1935.

'I am a revolutionary writer', he said; and to an English reader he will still probably seem revolutionary in more ways than one. He was by far the best novelist produced by the Scottish Literary Renaissance. This means that Gibbon writes in Scots, and though his prose is by no means inaccessible to English readers, it still presents difficulties, not of literal understanding—one rarely feels the need for a glossary—but of evaluation; the non-Scot can have little sense of the associations which the words carry. It is not so much that the words are unfamiliar as that they show the Scottish characters as suddenly unfamiliar. Whether this means that Gibbon has, as it were, broken through to the real Scots, to Scottishness, an English critic can scarcely know. My own feeling is that Gibbon's use of Scots gives his work a folk quality, the sense of a whole people speaking through the author, almost impossible for a novelist to achieve in British English.

The novel relates the life from girlhood to middle age of Chris Guthrie, a crofter's daughter in the Mearns country of Kincardineshire. In *Sunset Song* we see her at home as a girl and then as the wife of a young crofter, Tavendale. The Mearns country and the life there, her God-fearing, brutal father, 'bedding his wife like a breeding sow' until she will have no more of it and kills herself, are most vividly described. But Chris is at the centre, the clever girl whom her father sees as a teacher; yet when she has the chance to go to Aberdeen University she refuses, unable to leave her country:

> Two Chrises there were that fought for her heart and tormented her. You hated the land and the coarse speak of the folk and learning was brave and fine one day; and the next you'd awaken with the peewits crying across the hills, deep and deep, crying in the heart of you and the smell of the earth in your face, almost you'd cry for that, the beauty of it and the sweetness of the Scottish land and skies.

In *Cloud Howe* we find her widowed—Tavendale has been killed in France—left with a small son, Ewan, and married again, to Robert Colquohoun, minister of Seggett, a small mill-town. Colquohoun is an idealist, liberal in theology and politics, who after an excursion into 'practical' christianity, lapses into a watery mysticism. In *Grey Granite* Chris is again a widow, partner in a boarding-house in the seaport town of Duncairn. But in this volume the main interest shifts from her to her son Ewan, an engineering apprentice who becomes converted to socialism by a pretty English school teacher boarding at Chris's, moves on to Communism, becomes a strike-leader, is viciously beaten up by the police and, as we leave him, has become a professional Communist agitator about to lead a delegation of hunger-marchers to England. The novel ends with Chris, having made a third, unsuccessful marriage, returning to the Mearns to become a farmer.

Chris is at the centre of the trilogy, but not quite at the centre of events. She becomes more passive as the work proceeds, and in terms of it as a whole she is often only one of the centres of its consciousness. In *Grey Granite* Ewan increasingly takes over, so that we interpret the action partly through him; but throughout the work much of what happens is reported to us through the speech of the people themselves, the corporate voice, so to speak, of the bourgeoisie of Seggett, for example, girding, jeering, flyting at the Rev. Robert Colquhoun and what seem to them the snobbish pretensions of Chris, and of the 'keelies', the unemployed workers, of Duncairn. We are here, one realizes, very much in the tradition of Scottish backbiting and sardonic satire; but, much more important, it enables Gibbon, without sacrificing the unity of the whole, to show us the whole action from a multiplicity of points of view.

The more closely one examines *A Scots Quair* the more elaborate a work one realizes it is. And this elaborateness, this sense of the work as existing simultaneously in many dimensions, goes far towards cancelling out its many defects. The lyricism of the writing is at times so uncontrolled as to fall into a breathless, ecstatic emotionalism. Many of the minor characters, especially in *Grey Granite*, have the crudity of figures in political cartoons in Communist newspapers; and of the major characters, Ewan certainly raises question-marks in the mind. Austere, disciplined as it were by nature, by temperament a scientist, contemptuous of his fellows, singleminded to the point of ruthlessness, Ewan seems to be modelled on no observed human being but rather on an ideal notion of the professional Communist leader in an age of transition. Yet, though the character is never quite believable, the conception of it is impressive and testimony of Gibbon's own revolutionary integrity. He makes no attempt to soften Ewan's character, to make him sympathetic. When the English school teacher, Ellen, who has led him to socialism in the first place and who has become his mistress, leaves the Communist Party, sickened by it and by the apparent hopelessness of the fight, he repels her with the words, 'I can get a prostitute anywhere'. He is, one must assume, the Just Man made Perfect, or History, in the Marxist sense, incarnate; in other words, a heroic concept. He has put off temporal weakness, as much a man apart as in other religions priests are, as comes out in his talk to Big Jim Trease, the Party agitator, towards the end of the novel:

> Ewan nodded and said that he saw that, there wasn't much time for the usual family business when you were a revolutionist. And Big Jim twinkled his eyes and said No, for that you'd to go in for Socialism and Reform, like Baillie Brown, and be awful indignant about the conditions of those gentlemanly coves, the suffering workers. And Ewan grinned at him, and he at Ewan, neither had a single illusion about the workers: they weren't

heroes or gods oppressed, or likely to be generous and reasonable when their great black wave came flooding at last, up and up, swamping the high places with mud and blood. Most likely such leaders of the workers as themselves would be flung aside or trampled under, it didn't matter, nothing to them, THEY THEM-SELVES WERE THE WORKERS and they'd no more protest than a man's fingers would complain of a foolish muscle.

'They themselves were the workers'—in capital letters: that indeed is the point. We are in the presence of the real stuff, the Marxist theory of the dictatorship of the proletariat.

All this is a long way from the merely local and temporary issue of working-class life and struggle as we find them recorded and inter-preted in the novels of Walter Greenwood and Walter Brierley or even Hanley. Whether we like it or not, it is a grand conception; we are in the world of ideas and of faith that is debated, admittedly at much greater length, in Arthur Koestler's *Darkness at Noon*.

Each of the three novels deals with a different stage in the develop-ment of production; we move from peasant cultivation by way of the small industrial unit to modern capitalist organization in the engineer-ing works of Duncairn. And there is a much larger movement of history as well. Indeed, in the druidical remains of the Mearn and in the flints the boy Ewan picks up in the foothills of the ruined Kaimes, there is as it were a recapitulation of pre-history; while throughout we are conscious of the background of Scottish national history. All the time the emphasis is on the process of history and of life. And here we come back to Chris, who may be taken in at least two, perhaps three, ways. She is, first of all of course, a woman, a striking representation of an individual woman at that. But she is also, increasingly as the volumes move forward, the personification of life, whose child history is. She encompasses the whole, and it is the sense we have of this that makes the Communist element in the work, presented as history in its latest phase, imaginatively acceptable.

Ralph Bates was also a revolutionary writer and for some years a professional revolutionary. After serving in the British Army during the first world war, he lived and worked in Spain, as a Communist agent helped to organize the dockers of Barcelona, and was active both in the Spanish Revolution of 1931, which led to the abdication of King Alfonso XIII, and in the Civil War. He joined in himself a profound knowledge of Spain with a passion for music—he is the author of a life of Schubert; and the central character of his first novel, *Lean Men* (1934), Francis Charing, an English Communist expert on Spain and an amateur of Elizabethan music, must, one feels, derive closely from Bates himself. Charing returns to Barcelona as a Communist agent to organize the dockers. In this he is largely successful, but in the chaos following the 1931 Revolution the workers are defeated, and the novel ends with Charing in hiding: 'When next would he be able to serve the Revolution? He could not hazard a guess. "I believe and I will serve", he murmured.'

Lean Men is much too long, and though much happens the story-telling is very confused. The Spanish characters tend to suffer from a poster-like idealization, and the two women in England who love Charing are very shadowy indeed. What remains of interest is the self-portrait, as one assumes it is, of the Communist agent and the revela-tion of the agonies of conscience attendant upon the idealist as Com-munist. This, expressed in the tug between Charing's desire to live for music and his stronger desire to work for the revolution, remains moving.

The Olive Field (1936) is a much better novel, though the story-telling is still defective. Set in a small town in Andalusia, from which the action shifts to Asturias, it describes, first the sufferings of the olive workers, and then the Asturian miners' rising of October 1934. Here there is no English revolutionary to mediate between us and the Spanish scene; the character-drawing is stronger and more rounded. There are, indeed, some finely rendered characters, especially among the reactionaries—the aristocratic landowner, his majordomo, and the parish priest. And there is a number of excellent scenes of violence and civil war. There is no question of which side the novel is on, but it is not partisan in any petty spirit. Throughout, there is a deep feeling for the Spanish people and countryside. Yet, scarcely less than *Lean Men*, its interest now seems mainly historical. It does not transcend the events it describes; and all the time one is reminded, by its general theme and also by specific incidents, of Silone's *Fontamara*, and it cannot live up to the comparison one is bound to make.

As one reads English fiction of the thirties, one cannot help but be struck by the price exacted by the English class and educational system. Novels that take in the whole of English society, or express it in any acceptable way, are not there; there is no equivalent to *The Olive Field* in this respect, and one can only conclude that this is so because of the English novelist's ignorance of life outside his own class, ignorance that no amount of political sympathy for other classes could compensate for. One thinks of Christopher Isherwood, who had to go to Germany to find the working class he could write about.

[9]

IN ONE RESPECT, Isherwood is the greatest disappointment in the history of contemporary fiction. It seems clear, after his most recent novels, *The World in the Evening* and *Down There on a Visit*, that his best work is essentially of the thirties. It is certainly one of the most considerable achievements of that time, and not only because of the Berlin books, which have tended to overshadow the two brilliant novels that preceded them, *All the Conspirators* (1928) and *The Memorial* (1932). They are still technically interesting; and in their matter and the attitude informing them they remind us of Isherwood's close association with W. H. Auden. They may be considered, indeed, as equivalents in fiction of Auden's early verse, their characters particular examples of what Auden was attacking generally, embodiments almost of the codified lists of symptons in *Poems* and *The Orators*.

The conspirators of the title of his first novel are conspirators in an Audenesque sense—conspirators against life, those who avoid life's issues by taking refuge in neurotic illness or obtain the desired object by substituting a rationalization for the recognition of the impulse itself. The situation in the novel is the relationship between a spoiled son and his mother, a widow, who seeks to keep him always as a child, dependent upon her. Love on both sides is perverted. Philip Lindsay, the central character, thinks of himself as an artist and poet and is forced to work in an office. He wants independence and in the end gets it by the simple process of developing rheumatic fever. Rheumatic fever had prevented Philip from going to a public school, saved him from something feared and kept him in the comfort of his mother's home. Rheumatic fever represents a means of having the best of both worlds: of being independent and having every whim gratified by his adoring mother.

While the characters are presented in themselves, with no going behind or telling about them, to borrow James's phrase from his preface to *The Awkward Age*, they are always presented ironically, through their self-exposure in dialogue or through very brief flashbacks. For example, Philip's neurotic state, his compensatory notion of himself as artist-poet, is rooted in the past. Yet the past is never described in detail: his unhappy prep-school days are conveyed in two paragraphs:

> 'But it is really too absurd of Allen to say that I like Page because he flatters me,' Philip thought. 'Imagine feeling flattered at his ridiculous sporting terms. One might think, to hear him talk, that one was useful in the slips.'
>
> Into the boot-room they crowded, clumsy as puppies, wet-haired, muddy in their shorts and sweaters. Kicking sparks from the stone floor with their boot-studs. Jostling to wash their knees at the tap. What was it like on Lower? Oh, we had a juicy victory, didn't we, Flea? I scored all six. You liar. Well, Lindsay booted one of them in by mistake. Lindsay. Where's Linseed? Where's the Linseed Poultice? Pig said you booted one into your own goal. Did you? Did you? Oh, good effort. Jolly smart. Highly cute. Don't you think you were cute? Look, he's blubbing. Linseed's blubbing. The Poultice is damp. Does didums want nana? Never mind. Hard luck, Linseed. Cheer up, Linseed. Anyway Linseed threw in jolly well this afternoon. Yes, he did. He threw in right over Flea's head. Good old Linseed. Three cheers for Poultice. Thumping his back, they clustered round a moment, grotesquely soothed him. Look out, here's Major Frith. You're all right, aren't you, Poultice? May I ask how much longer you Juniors propose to hang round the lavatories? Out before I count ten. We're coming, sir. Sorry, sir. Oh, *sir*. All clattered away.

The technique is cinematic, an arrangement of scenes, episodes, images, flashbacks, in which the linking is done simply by the juxtapositions. *All the Conspirators* is a montage-novel, and though conceived and rendered in irony, it is through the montage that the irony comes out.

The economy of means, the lightness of touch, the wit are no less evident in *The Memorial*, though it is a more ambitious novel. The memorial is a war memorial, and it is symbolic of the characters, who have all been conditioned by the war, the arc of their development twisted by it. Futility hangs over them; they live as it were in a vacuum, in a period of unreality, an interregnum. There is no comment; what is implied is Auden's 'What do you think about England, this country of ours where nobody is well?' That is the essence of the novel, which has the clinical detachment of a collection of X-ray photographs: nobody is well. Given significance, Edward Blake, the war-shattered homosexual airman, would be a tragic figure; deliberately, he is not given significance and is merely pathetic, a case; as is Mary, a woman of the same generation, with her plucky fight against the circumstances in which she has placed herself, a fight that takes the form of running a gallery-cum-restaurant and acting Queen Victoria at arty parties. The actions that express her are admirably chosen; they seem to expose the pointlessness of a whole generation and class. Maurice's undergraduate escapades at Cambridge, Lily Vernon's retreat into the memory of her dead husband, her living in the past and her dabblings in archaeology, and old Mr Vernon, paralysed, a huge baby revelling in his second childhood, somehow take on a significance that transcends the characters themselves and makes them representatives of whole groups of people.

This impression is intensified by the structure of the novel. It is in four parts, the first of which introduces us to the characters as they are in 1928. In the second we see them as they were in 1920; in the third we go forward to 1925; in the last further forward to 1929. In a sense, the first part, 1928, is the climax of the novel. Thence, we trace the characters backwards; and in the last section, we are shown what progress they have made since 1928. They have made none; their drifting continues. In the first part, in a notably economical piece of writing, Edward Blake attempts suicide in Berlin and bungles it; in the last part he is again in Berlin, living with a German boy scarcely old enough to remember the war. It is he who provides the ironical last sentence of the book: 'That war . . . it ought never to have happened.' Even the gesture of suicide has been arrested; and it seems significant that the gesture should be made at the beginning of the novel.

In a quite short novel we meet nearly a dozen characters and learn all that is necessary to know about them through a series of flashbacks introduced only by a row of asterisks. Isherwood's method is that of the miniaturist; he seems to see his characters as through the wrong end of a pair of field-glasses; they are caught in an exquisite clarity of detail yet, as it were, in isolation, somehow abstracted from the booming, buzzing hurly-burly of life. It is from this, I think, that their power to stand as symbols proceeds. According to Isherwood himself, his technique derives from E. M. Forster:

> The whole of Forster's technique is based upon the tea-table: instead of trying to screw all his scenes to the highest possible pitch, he tones them down until they sound like mothers' meeting gossip ... In fact, there's actually *less* emphasis laid on the big scenes than on the unimportant ones. That's what's utterly terrific. It's the completely new kind of accentuation—like a person talking a different language.

The full effect of this 'tea-tabling' manner, as Isherwood calls it, is apparent in the Berlin books, *Mr Norris Changes Trains* and *Goodbye to Berlin*, which, though written as a series of short stories, have something very close to the unity of a novel owing to the continued presence of 'Herr Issyvoo', the narrator. He defines himself in the second paragraph of *Goodbye to Berlin*: 'I am a camera with its shutter open, quite passive, recording, not thinking. Recording the man shaving at the window opposite and the woman in the kimono washing her hair. Some day, all this will have to be developed, carefully printed, fixed.'

But he is also the man who controls the camera, who chooses the angle from which the camera is to be used, who will develop, print and fix the films and will decide which are worth mounting. He is a trick-photographer of enormous skill, whose art consists in posing his bizarre characters at unexpected angles, in shocking juxtaposition to the terrifying, tragic background of historical events. Mr Norris, the homosexual masochist, is a minor crook who might almost have stepped out of the novels of Ronald Firbank. Isherwood makes no moral judgment on him, accepts him for his own sake as a comic character, a source of joy to the beholder. But—

> Berlin was in a state of civil war. Hate exploded suddenly, without warning, out of nowhere; at street-corners, in restaurants, cinemas, dance-halls, swimming baths; at night, after breakfast, in the middle of the afternoon. Knives were whipped out, blows were dealt with spiked rings, beer-mugs, chair-legs or leaded clubs; bullets slashed the advertisements on the poster-columns, rebounded from the iron roofs of latrines. In the middle of a crowded street a young man would be attacked, stripped, thrashed and left bleeding on the pavement; in fifteen seconds it was all over and the assailants had disappeared ...

This is the scene through which Mr Norris zig-zags like a butterfly; and it is the juxtaposition that gives him his significance.

Isherwood's originality is to show us the collapse of German civilization obliquely, through characters eccentric or bizarre, characters who for one reason or another—sexual, racial, economic—are lost. These books are tragedy approached almost as farce, or, one might say, pocket epic, epic in miniature. They capture the disintegration of Germany, the years of crisis and chaos, of mass unemployment, internecine warfare between Nazis and Communists, the whole horror of a nation's degeneracy, as no other work of fiction has done.

George Orwell's influence on the younger English writers of the past fifteen years has been greater probably than that of any author of the immediate past except Lawrence, but it is not his fiction that has influenced them. It has been much more the idea of Orwell himself and what he stood for, his blunt, suspicious, no-nonsense, anti-romantic attitude, his resolute and ruthless honesty, towards himself and the world about him. He was a novelist largely by the accident of his times. His last novel, *Nineteen Eighty-four*, achieved worldwide fame as an awful warning of a possible totalitarian future. Its power is unquestionable, but its permanent interest will almost certainly lie in its incidentals, its investigation of political truth and the idea of 'Newspeak', subjects Orwell had touched on in essays that preceded the novel. And of all his fiction the finest is his fable *Animal Farm*.

The novelist of the past he seems most to have admired was George Gissing, with whom one feels he had a temperamental affinity. His own novels are like Gissing's in that they are the expression of a powerful, sombre and intransigently honest mind that is yet deficient in human sympathy.

His best novel is his first, *Burmese Days* (1934). Like his other fiction, it stems out of his own experience, but its hero, Florey, though he may have much of Orwell in him, is certainly not Orwell. It is written with a hard, angry brilliance; it is indeed a prolonged outburst of contemptuous disgust at a situation that makes personal freedom, with its corollaries of loyalty to friends that need be conditioned by no considerations of snobbery or race prejudice, impossible for the white rulers. As an exposure of one consequence of Anglo-Saxon colonialism it could hardly be bettered, yet ultimately the deficiency in human sympathies one feels in it works against it. It is not that, with the doubtful exception of Florey, the English characters are shown as nasty, and that their victims the Burmese as little better—the only admirable human being in the book is the Indian doctor Veraswami, who is the victim of both the English and the Burmese; it is rather the total impression of misanthropy that finally chills. Florey and Veraswami excepted, all the characters are caricatures executed in anger and rancour; so that the novel strikes one now as having been written by a man with one skin too few protesting not so much about the condition of Burma in the early thirties as about the human condition.

His novels after *Burmese Days* are really monologues in which he himself is the hero and speaker. They are, one might say, expressions of highly personal prejudice. Witness *Coming up for Air* (1939), which seems to me the best of the other novels. It is the work of a man who quite simply hates most of the things we regard as characteristic of the modern world, whether we locate the modern world in America or in Russia. This comes out by implication in the beautiful passages—the nearest he ever got to lyricism—in which his hero, playing truant from his job, returns to the scenes of his Edwardian childhood in a country town, and openly in the rest of the novel, in the passage, for example, describing the eating of a sausage in a milk-bar: 'It gave me the feeling that I'd bitten into the modern world and discovered what it was really made of.' *Coming up for Air* still has the power to move one, but it does so because it is about Orwell himself: Orwell contemplating England under the shadow of the coming war.

[10]

DURING THE thirties fantasy suddenly appeared as a medium of social criticism. In one way, it was a specifically English—and politically conscious—adaptation of European influences, surrealism, the novels of Kafka, the plays of the German Expressionists; and somewhere near the centre of the forces making for their adaptation we find, as so often during these years, the twin figures of Auden and Isherwood, whose *The Dog beneath the Skin* is a prime example of thirties fantasy in the theatre. Even so, when one has invoked the surrealists, Kafka and the rest, one may still think the fantasy would have developed without their influence. They gave the method a validity and, up to a point, offered models; but one remembers Isherwood's description in his autobiography, *Lions and Shadows*, of how he and Edward Upward, as undergraduates at Cambridge, devised a private surrealistic world called 'Mortmere' which, they realized, was the counterpart in fantasy of the actual world in which they were living, and a criticism of it.

In Isherwood's fiction 'Mortmere' makes no appearance. Upward, however, developed it, among Marxist lines, in a few short stories and in *Journey to the Border* (1938). The hero of the novel is a middle-class young man working as a tutor in the country house of a rich man, constantly struggling against the position but unable to resolve it. Against his will, he is persuaded to accompany his employer to a race meeting. On the way, and while he is there, he undergoes a series of hallucinations, mounting in intensity, based on what is going on all about him. These hallucinations are, as it were, the counterpart of the debate that is going on in his mind, a debate which proceeds dialectically until it is borne in upon him that the only solution to his problem, the only way to reality, is to identify himself with the struggle of the working class.

The dream-like quality of the novel is admirably sustained, as is the sequence of hallucinations. This is, one feels, the genuine Kafka country. And then the imaginative excitement gutters out in overexplicitness. What had promised to be a symbolic novel proves to be a simple allegory.

This is the criticism to be made also of the much better known novels of Rex Warner. Comparisons with Kafka, which were almost *de rigueur* when the novels first appeared, now seem entirely beside the point, and intelligent and admirably written though it is, Warner's fiction increasingly appears very much—perhaps too much—of its time and movement. His first novel, *The Wild Goose Chase* (1938), recounts the adventures of three brothers who set out to find the wild goose, which stands perhaps for freedom or political justice. They cross the frontier—the frontier is a constantly recurring symbol in the fiction and poetry of the thirties—into a mysterious country dominated by a Fascist group. There is no attempt at a plausible surface realism; everything depends upon the invention of continually surprising episodes of allegorical satire directed at Fascism or imperialism. These vary greatly in effectiveness, the best probably being the burlesque rugger match, the result of which has been decided beforehand.

The Professor (1939) is an allegory of the dilemma of the liberal politician in a state threatened by Fascism. It has points of similarity with Stephen Spender's verse play *Trial of a Judge* (1938), and of both it can be said that, while the statement of the problem and the moral drawn are impeccable, the sense of reality that comes through is faint indeed compared with the actuality of history. The process of allegory itself leads to a thinness and abstraction. This is true, it seems to me, of Warner's best novel, *The Aerodrome* (1941), which describes the taking over of a village by a mysterious Air Force, an authoritarian movement dedicated to efficiency and the proposition 'that the world may be clean'. When it was published, no doubt because of the times, it was taken as an allegorical satire on Fascism or Nazism, but the Air Force now appears much more like an allegorical representation of Communism. In a foreword to *The Aerodrome* Warner says, 'I do not even aim at realism', yet by disregarding realism he could do no more than produce a parable that, for all its neatness—partly because of its neatness—has very little relevance to the dilemma and the historical situation it is supposed to represent and illuminate.

They are indeed simplified almost out of existence. The village, dominated as it is by squire and parson, cannot stand in any adequate way for the world of traditional, democratic values because it bears almost no relation to the actual world in which those values have to exist. And this remoteness from observable reality is emphasized both by the style in which the novel is written and the mechanism of the plot. Both derive from eighteenth-century models. The prose, good as it is, has a formal quality that removes it from the contemporary scene; while the mechanism of the plot, with its confusion of births and parentage, strikes a note of irrelevant archaic ingenuity.

The remoteness, of course, is intentional; its aim is to distance the conflict of values, and by doing so to present it in its essence. But essences are not the material of fiction, and though we may admire the ingenuity of the author in having given us the essence of the conflict it is precisely the ingenuity that impresses us, not the presentation of the conflict itself. This is plain, it seems to me, as soon as we contrast Warner's novel with other novels dealing with the same theme but rooted in existence, with Greene's *The Power and the Glory* or with Arthur Koestler's *Darkness at Noon*. But Koestler's novel was written in German, and the novels he was to write later in English cannot match it in power and profundity.

WAR AND POST WAR:
BRITISH

▲▲▲▲▲▲▲▲▲▲▲▲▲▲▲▲▲▲▲▲▲▲▲▲▲▲▲▲▲▲

[I]

JOYCE CARY came to the novel comparatively late in life—his first novel was not published until he was forty-four in 1932—after a career unlike that of most novelists, a career in the Nigerian Political Service spent among primitive peoples and largely concerned with government and administration. In approach, matter and tone his fiction differs significantly from all other written in England during his lifetime, which no doubt explains why, though his work was highly praised from the beginning, it was almost fifteen years before his real stature was perceived.

His output was uneven. There are times when he seems the victim of his own exuberance, his capacity for invention; and this is particularly noticeable in his later work, in his novel of the General Strike, *Not Honour More*, where his picture of the Strike seems to have little relation to recorded history. He is often, one feels, impatient of the detailed observation essential to the novel of social history. His range of characters is also narrower than at first sight appears, and very narrow indeed where women are concerned. Yet, more than any writer of our time, English or American, he is the novelist of the creative imagination, for the creative imagination is the quality he most values in human beings. And the creative action of the imagination is unceasing and continuous, each man trying, in Cary's words, 'to create a universe which suits his feelings'. Since each man is unique and his shaping fantasy unique, it clashes inevitably with those of his fellows and, often, with the established order of society. For the individual the consequences may be tragic; equally, from the point of view of society, they may be comic: in Cary's novels the comic and the tragic are different sides of the same coin. In the end, the creative imagination becomes equated with the spirit of life itself.

Artistic development in the usual sense is absent from Cary's novels. Yet a general movement may be traced through his work from the treatment of the relatively simple theme to that of the much more complex; and in retrospect his novels seem to fall into four main groups; the African novels, *Aissa Saved* (1932), *An American Visitor* (1933), *The African Witch* (1936) and *Mister Johnson* (1939); the novels of childhood, *Charley is my Darling* (1940) and *A House of Children* (1941); the Sara Monday-Wilcher-Gulley Jimson sequence *Herself Surprised* (1941), *To Be a Pilgrim* (1942) and *The Horse's Mouth* (1944); and the Chester Nimmo trilogy *Prisoner of Grace* (1952), *Except the Lord* (1953) and *Not Honour More* (1955). The classification omits *Castle Corner* (1938), which was published during Cary's African period and which, despite the extraordinary vividness, through a huge gallery of characters, of its description of Anglo-Irish life and the rise of colonial imperialism in the eighteen-nineties, must be accounted a failure, as Cary realized himself; *The Moonlight* (1946); *A Fearful Joy* (1949); and the posthumous *The Captive and the Free*, which was assembled, as it were, by other hands after his death.

In the African novels, Cary dramatizes his overriding theme of the creative imagination of the individual in conflict with those of others or with authority as the conflict between races and colours, between modes of being alien to each and therefore more or less incomprehensible to each other. In these novels we see primitive peoples faced with a new and largely unintelligible civilization, taking what they want from the white man's religion and way of life and making of it a new thing satisfying to them but baffling to the white administrators and missionaries.

The African world described, then, is one in which everybody is at cross-purposes with everyone else. Inevitably, the tragic and the comic are inextricably mixed. As renderings and interpretations of primitive psychology, these novels are among the best we have in English, and one mark of Cary's success is the fact that the white characters are revealed as no less essentially strange than the black. Rudbeck, the resident magistrate in *Mister Johnson*, is just as much caught by compulsive fantasy, the fantasy of himself as a maker of roads, as is the infinitely comic, infinitely pathetic Johnson himself, the clerk from the mission school who identifies himself with the white man's way of life and, full of lordly exuberance and expansiveness, combines the ingenuousness of a child with the myth-making mind of a poet, to his ultimate and ironic catastrophe, death at the hands of the white man's justice.

Of these African novels, the best is certainly *Mister Johnson*, partly because of its very simplicity. Form was not Cary's strong point and could scarcely have been in view of his method of 'assembling' his novels; but in *Mister Johnson* everything is subordinated to the rendering of the enchanting tragi-comic hero, whose gaiety and resilience Cary seems to capture in the texture of the prose itself and whose situation and innocent vainglory he dramatizes in the most delightful invention.

It was a natural step for Cary to pass from the representation of relatively primitive peoples to that of children, and typical of him to write in rapid succession two novels depicting children placed in almost grotesquely dissimilar circumstances. *Charley is my Darling*, published in April 1940, stemmed out of the revelations of urban working-class poverty and dirt forced upon the British people by the mass-evacuation of children to the country that took place when war broke out in 1939. The novel must have been written at high speed and perhaps it suffers from this. Certainly it suffers from inaccuracies in the rendering of the social scene. A great pity, for Charley Brown, the young hero of the novel, is a striking embodiment of 'that hunger of the imagination', to use Dr Johnson's phrase, 'which preys incessantly on life', and the novel moves through comedy that, though often tender and affecting, becomes progressively wilder almost to the point of farce, to end in near-tragedy.

The second of this pair of novels, *A House of Children*, autobiographical in origin, describes life among the children of a large upper middle class in Northern Ireland during the eighteen-nineties. It might in its way be considered Cary's tribute to Proust. There is no attempt to recreate childhood in itself; what happens exists in memory; and what are admirably caught are the changes, the growth, the discontinuities, even the regressions of childhood when looked back upon from adult life, and, above all, the sudden sense of glory which, however intermittently, illuminates every childhood at some time.

A House of Children was followed by the sequence *Herself Surprised, To Be a Pilgrim* and *The Horse's Mouth*. In these Cary is writing not in his own person or out of a convenient persona, but in turn as Sara Monday, Mr Wilcher and Gulley Jimson, a performance, so complete is the impersonation in each case, of remarkable virtuosity. These novels compose not so much a trilogy as a triptych, the link between each being the character of Sara Monday, the narrator of *Herself Surprised*, which is the story of Sara's associations with Wilcher and Jimson. Sara recalls, in the warmth and simplicity of her feelings and in the innocence of her sensuality, Renoir's nudes. She is writing her novel in prison, in a state of repentance; like Moll Flanders, in Defoe's novel which *Herself Surprised* sometimes reminds us of, she thinks of her life as a moral object-lesson. She is woman in her twin roles of mother and mistress; despite her good intentions and her early religious education, she is incapable of resisting the demands that man, the male child, makes on her. If she cannot square her behaviour with her sincerely held religious beliefs it is because they cannot in the nature of things be squared. In her own eyes she is a sinner; but to the reader her life is a hymn of praise to creation and to the Creator.

Along with *Mister Johnson* and *A House of Children*, *Herself Surprised* is the most perfect of Cary's novels, but compared with the two other novels in the triptych, it is on a small scale; and *To Be a Pilgrim* and *The Horse's Mouth* remain Cary's richest novels and the most authoritative as expressions of his attitude to life. The authority in each comes from the strength and freshness, the three-dimensional solidity, of the main character, the narrator.

On the face of it, the creation of Gully Jimson, in *The Horse's Mouth*, is the more striking triumph, for here Cary achieves a convincing representation of artistic genius. As we know him in the novel, Jimson is an old and battered man just out of prison; a man for whom the visible world exists in an almost overpowering intensity, which he transmits to us in a completely idiosyncratic idiom, extravagant, rhetorical, slangy, as though he were the child at once of James Joyce and William Blake. Blake, indeed, is his great exemplar, the Prophetic Books the nearest thing to his bible. Like Blake, he is a visionary painter whose work is wildly unfashionable; but he lives wholly for his painting, and though stricken with poverty and continually engaged in ingenious and largely criminal schemes for obtaining money, all the time he keeps his integrity as a painter.

We see the world as he sees it. Through him, Cary creates a whole world, eccentric certainly, but still a genuine image of the real one. *The Horse's Mouth* is Cary's most sustained effort in comedy, and one has to go back to *Peregrine Pickle* to match the speed and vigour of the writing and its author's ability to keep it going; as in the masterly climax of the novel, in which Jimson and his young disciples furiously paint the wall of a building that the local authorities are even then busily demolishing as unsafe.

Yet the creation of Wilcher in *To Be a Pilgrim* is the greater feat. Wilcher is a true original: there is no other character like him in the range of our fiction. An old man, aware that he is regarded by the young as a fogey, he has played second fiddle all his life, ministering as a lawyer to his elder brothers and sisters, men and women more vital than himself, men and women of action. He is pedantic and fussy, personally a little ridiculous, and he knows it:

> We were sailing in his cranky little boat, a pursuit which caused me acute misery. For wet, especially in the seat, always gave me rheumatism; the motion of a boat, even on a calm day, made me ill; the necessity of continually getting up and moving to the other side of the boat, and ducking my head under the boom, at the risk of my hat, broke up every conversation and exasperated me extremely; and finally, I could conceive nothing more stupid than to proceed by zigzags, from nowhere to nowhere, for the sake of wasting a fine afternoon. Neither, if I may mention such a point, though it is probably unimportant, have I ever been able to understand why there was no accommodation provided on small yachts, for things like sticks and umbrellas; whereas land conveyances, such as gigs and even governess carts, always have a basket designed for their proper storage and protection.

Moreover, as we see him in his journal—and the novel is really his journal—he is a little cracked, an old man on the verge of senility whose emotional life has been so repressed that it is now breaking out in ungovernable tendencies towards indecent exposure, so that he has to be kept under restraint. At the same time, as is made clear throughout, he is a man of real intellect and real religious faith.

In *To Be a Pilgrim*, Cary handles three stories at once. In his journal Wilcher is concerned with his own immediate problem, how to escape the restraint he is under and join Sara, who feels only pity for the comic, inhibited, fierce old man; concerned, too, first in a spirit of hostile scrutiny, with the lives of his niece, a doctor, and her husband, a nephew, who are struggling to bring the family estate at Tolbrook into cultivation again; and at the same time reliving his past, exploring his relations with his parents, brothers and sisters in order to discover the sources of their strength and of his failure. It is here the novel becomes a magnificent evocation of English history from 1890 to 1939 from the standpoints of political liberalism and religious nonconformity. His brothers and sisters were people of force and power; Wilcher himself is not, but he is a man of imagination, and as he relives his past he brings his family to life again in all its strength and sense of obligation.

The three stories of *To Be a Pilgrim* are told in such a way that each is set off against and given significance by the others; and all are bound together, fused into one, by the darting generalizations, the constant reinterpretations of experience, of Wilcher. By the end of the novel, we have realized that Tolbrook, with Ann, Wilcher's doctor-niece, writing her father's biography in what was his study, and Robert her husband using the threshing machine in the great saloon, among the Adam panelling, under the Angelica Kaufmann ceiling, is a symbol of England herself; a more successful one, in my view, than Forster's similar identification of a house with England in *Howards End*.

This brings us to what is fundamental both to *To Be a Pilgrim* and to *The Horse's Mouth*. The Nonconformist tradition has been one of the most potent and formative in English life, in politics no less than in religion. Cary's beliefs are central to that tradition, and in his fiction, in *To Be a Pilgrim* and *The Horse's Mouth* above all, he has re-stated it for our time.

After *To Be a Pilgrim* there was a decline in Cary's powers as a novelist. Up till then, part of the excitement he generated came from his restless experimentation, what seemed his endless fertility of scene and situation. But, with the *Herself Surprised–To Be a Pilgrim–The Horse's Mouth* sequence, he seemed to have found a formula; so that, after the intervening novels *The Moonlight* and *A Fearful Joy*, he wrote another trilogy, the Chester Nimmo series, which, brilliant though it is, is too near the earlier sequence in manner to be as interesting as it ought to be. At the same time, his mind darkened; the comic exuberance grew less; and, one feels, he became more and more preoccupied with his philosophy, more and more impatient with fiction. Certainly, his grasp of the external world slackened; or it ceased largely to interest him. In a sense, his philosophy became his religion and ran away with him; but until that happened he had done more than any other novelist of our time, Lawrence in his very different way alone excepted, to reinterpret in fiction one enduring tradition of

English life and feeling, without which England and the English would be very different from what they are.

[2]

IT WOULD be difficult to find a greater contrast to Cary than C. P. Snow; Cary romantic, exuberant, caught up in what at bottom is a religious view of man; Snow unromantic, cautious, worldly in the sense that he is very much of the actual world of the here and now, committed at most to a stoicism proceeding from a view of man that might be called moral agnosticism. Yet Snow has at least this in common with Cary, that he is writing in terms of fiction the history of his own times as interpreted through his own experience, an experience, like Cary's, rather different from that of most English novelists. Lewis Eliot, the narrator of the series still in progress made up of *Strangers and Brothers* (1940), *The Conscience of the Rich* (1958), *Time of Hope* (1950), *The Light and the Dark* (1947), *The Masters* (1951), *The New Men* (1954), *Homecomings* (1956), *The Affair* (1960), is a man who has made his own way from the provincial lower middle class to become first a barrister, then a lecturer in law and fellow of a Cambridge college, and at the end, as a result of the war, a senior civil servant: Snow was a physicist, not a lawyer, but the parallel between author and character is plain enough.

This does not mean that *Strangers and Brothers*, which is the general title of the sequence, is anything like an autobiographical work in the sense that *Sons and Lovers* is. The most one can say is that Eliot, like Jenkins in Powell's *The Music of Time*, is a convenient persona for the author. The stories that make up the sequence are, for the most part, Eliot's only at a remove. His degree of involvement in the action varies from book to book, and his main function is to be the observer of the action and its chorus. 'The inner design' of the work as a whole, Snow has said himself, consists of 'a resonance between what Lewis Eliot sees and what he feels'; the greater his emotional involvement the greater the resonance, and the more satisfying. Otherwise, as in

The Affair, he tends to appear too baldly as the man of goodwill, the man who sees all sides, the 'fixer' of problems.

These novels of Snow's constitute an investigation into human ecology—'the mutual relations between organisms and their environment'—or at any rate certain areas of human ecology. Snow is always concerned with the limits of the possible. It is not, as is sometimes suggested, that his theme is anything so crude as that of power; but the world that concerns him is a very masculine one. He knows men particularly well in what are their traditionally masculine attributes, men as they are in the company of other men and in competition with other men. There is little he does not know, one feels, about ambition and about the conflicts between ambition and conscience or the stresses of the private life.

This knowledge, which pervades the whole series, comes to its finest fruition in *The Masters.* In a Cambridge college the master is dying, and a new master must be elected by the fellows from one of their number. The motives of the contending candidates are mixed; the factions that combine, split and sometimes come together do so from disinterested concern for the college no less than from self-interest, even though the necessity of the characters to align themselves into factions exposes animosities, grudges, ancient rivalries, secret passions and hopes hitherto concealed, just as it breaks up old friendships. The real success of the novel is that, having read it, we realise we have been reading a novel on the nature and practice of politics: the senior common room, on Snow's showing, is a microcosm of one aspect of the world.

A great part of this success comes from Eliot's—or Snow's—moral agnosticism. He observes, reports, analyses, comments, but passes no moral judgment: he knows that motives are always inextricably mixed. The result, for the reader, is an impression of massive fairness, as, for instance, in this analysis of Jago:

> Jago enjoyed the dramatic impact of power, like Chrystal: but he was seeking for other things besides. He was an ambitious man, as neither Brown nor Chrystal were. In any society, he would have longed to be first; and he would have longed for it because of everything that marked him out as different from the rest. He longed for all the trappings, titles, ornaments, and show of power. He would love to hear himself called Master; he would love to begin a formal act at a college meeting 'I, Paul Jago,

Master of the college . . .' For him, in every word that separated the Master from his fellows, in every ornament of the Lodge, in every act of formal duty, there was a gleam of magic.

There was something else. He had just said to Chrystal 'we can make it a great college'. Like most ambitious men, he believed that there were things that only he could do. Money did not move him in the slightest; the joys of office moved him a great deal; but there was a quality pure, almost naïve, in his ambition. He had dreams of what he could do with his power. These dreams left him sometimes, he became crudely avid for the job, but they returned. With all his fervent imagination, he thought of a college peaceful, harmonious, gifted, creative, throbbing with joy and luminous with grace. In his dreams, he did not altogether know how to attain it. He had nothing of the certainty with which, in humility, accepting their limitations, Chrystal and Brown went about their aims, securing a benefaction from Sir Horace, arranging an extra tutorship, making sure that Luke got a grant for his research. He had nothing of their certainty, nor their humility: he was more extravagant than they, and loved display far more; in his ambition he could be cruder and more predatory; but perhaps he had intimations which they could not begin to hear.

Frank Kermode has suggested, in *Puzzles and Epiphanies*, that Snow 'is never much interested in, probably doubts, the existence of', what Lawrence called 'the last naked him'. Certainly the 'last naked him' is not Snow's concern in his fiction; but this does not mean that he is concerned solely with public faces. Indeed, what gives his work its authority is his recognition of the private incommunicable agony behind the public face. When he is analysing the behaviour and feelings of the dons in *The Masters* and *The Affair*, the scientists in *The New Men* or the civil servants in *Homecomings*, Eliot in a sense is guessing; in other words, he is acting as each one of us does in the ordinary commerce of the world. But his guesses are based on a theory of human nature based on a wide experience of men and women—and himself. As he says in *The Light and the Dark*,

I believe that some parts of our endowment are too heavy to shift. The essence of our nature lay within us, untouchable by our own bonds or any other's, by any chance of things or persons, from the cradle to the grave. But what it drove us to in action, the actual events of our lives—those were affected by a million things, by sheer chance, by the interaction of others, by the choice of our own will.

Kermode finds that 'Snow, for all his gifts of pathos, is, like most scientists, a meliorist at least'. This seems to me to be true, so long as we see Snow's meliorism as a working hypothesis about human beings in society which is based all the same on something very close to a tragic view of individual human beings. In Snow's world the race does not necessarily go to the swiftest or the most brilliant. 'Some parts of our endowment are too heavy to shift', and Snow is permanently fascinated by those whose brilliance or whose goodness is frustrated and defeated by an intractability or recalcitrance in the depths of their being; George Passant, in *Strangers and Brothers* and *Homecomings*, and Roy Calvert, in *The Light and the Dark*, come to mind at once. Snow's way is not the way of tragedy, but these are characters all the same brought down by a flaw within.

The clue to Snow's view of human beings is really to be found in the overall title of his sequence. Men are brothers—because they have to be: society and in the last analysis existence itself are impossible without co-operation. But even while they are brothers, men are still strangers one to another, doomed to be strangers by virtue of their being human. Take *Homecomings*, which, more than any other novel in the sequence except *Time of Hope*, is Lewis Eliot's personal story. It relates the breakup of his marriage and the happiness he finds in his second marriage; and rarely have the muteness and incommunicability of adult human suffering, the suffering a man may carry within him behind the façade of a successful public life, been more surely or movingly conveyed.

Throughout these novels there run a humility and a largeness of mind in the face of the extraordinary variety, and of the vagaries, of human nature which much more than compensate for Lewis Eliot's occasional pomposities and pretentiousness. The impulse is always to see and to understand, not to judge. And it is Snow's sense of the reality of individual, private human suffering that makes us accept his picture of men in society.

In many respects, the novels of William Cooper exist as comic counterparts of Snow's. In the first of these, *Scenes from Provincial Life* (1950), the opacities, discontinuities, contradictions of human behaviour are taken for granted and are seen as entertaining in themselves. The novel is told in the first person by Joe Lunn—the

overtones of the name will be immediately audible to English readers
—a young physics master in a provincial secondary school in 1939. Joe,
the hero as anti-hero, tells his story, which relates his successful efforts
to avoid marrying the girl he is sleeping with, in an extremely adroit
approximation to colloquial speech, the colloquial speech, admittedly,
of an educated man. Indeed, in a sense the speaking voice is everything
here; more important than what happens is the manner in which we
are told what happens, a manner which owes something, I suspect, both
to the Italian novelist Italo Svevo and to William Gerhardi. It is light,
mocking, irreverent, anti-culture, anti-literature, anti-art, in the more
portentous senses of these words: 'ah, novels, novels, Art, Art, pounds
sterling!' It conveys, at the same time, in its deliberately casual,
throw-away manner, an exact impression of one aspect of provincial
life among the educated young in the last years of the thirties, almost
to the point of being a comic version of *Strangers and Brothers*. At
times the style becomes too arch, too facetious, and then one is
conscious of the author in the wrong way, as a show-off; and there is
the danger that it may become altogether too relaxed, as I feel it does
in the sequel, *Scenes from Married Life* (1962).

But Cooper has another, more conventional manner. It is evident
notably in *Young People* (1958):

> The first moral compulsion ought to be to understand. I'm not
> saying *tout comprendre, c'est tout pardonner*, far from it. But I am
> saying that passing moral judgments should be open to you only
> when you understand what you're judging, not before.

Thus Swan in the novel. Swan's way is Cooper's. He makes no moral
judgments; he is content to describe his characters and their behaviour
with affection and ironical sympathy; and much of the excellence of
Young People springs from this. The young people of the title are four
young men of working- or lower middle-class origin who are students
in the early thirties at a small provincial university college. They have a
good conceit of themselves and of one another, because, though they
are *gauche* and know it, they also know they are very promising young
men. They have already set out on an expedition of conquest, and their
mentor is the eldest among them, Swan, a research student who is to
win a scholarship to Cambridge, and is already writing a novel.

The progress of the novel is leisurely, and Cooper begins by
establishing firmly his provincial background, not only through the

young men but also through Mr and Mrs Gunning, a delightful couple who are the parents of one of them and prepared to be parents to them all. It is some time before we realize that Cooper's camera is in the end to focus on one in particular of the four, the dashing, romantic Leonard Harris, and even longer before we—or his friends—discover that his romanticism is that of the pathological liar. Harris's career is very subtly unfolded; and it is exactly here that Cooper's refusal to be drawn into moral judgments, whether directly or by implication, stands him in such good stead. Harris is a bad lot; he trails unhappiness and disaster in his wake. And yet—perhaps Swan's is the final word on him: 'If we want to weigh the whole thing up fairly, we have to think what life would have been without it.' The point is, without the deceiving self-deceiver in their midst, the lives of Cooper's characters would have been in some way the poorer. What impresses in *Young People* is the acceptance, as good in itself, of the many-sidedness of life and of its unpredictability.

[3]

BEHIND the fiction of L. P. Hartley one feels the ghostly presences of James and Hawthorne: they indicate both the nature of his art and his moral preoccupations. Before the war, he was known as the author of two volumes of short stories and of a *nouvelle, Simonetta Perkins*, written very much in the manner of James, but the constant theme of his work was established in the *Eustace and Hilda* trilogy— *The Shrimp and the Anemone* (1944), *The Sixth Heaven* (1946) and *Eustace and Hilda* (1947): the relationship of man to his conscience, his sense of right and wrong, and right behaviour. This comes out most explicitly in *My Fellow Devils* (1951), which might be called Hartley's *Mansfield Park*; like Jane Austen's novel, it cannot make for comfort in readers who shun or do not understand a rigid morality. The problem posed is how we should behave in the presence of evil, and his answer is unambiguous: we should have no truck with it.

Hartley's range is narrow. His manner is quiet, and though he has written some of the best comedy of our time it is muted comedy, tinged with sadness. Yet though his world is a small one, and apparently demure, the smallness and the demureness are deceptive, for his world can uncannily reflect the violence and the conflicts from which it is seemingly isolated.

Admirable as *The Go-Between* (1950) is, the peak of Hartley's achievement seems to me still the *Eustace and Hilda* trilogy, a work, it has been said, 'comic in manner but full of terror in its implications'. The essential situation is stated in symbolic terms in the first paragraph of the first novel of the sequence, *The Shrimp and the Anemone*:

> 'Eustace! Eustace!' Hilda's tones were always urgent; it might not be anything very serious. Eustace bent over the pond. His feet sank in its soggy edge, so he drew back, for he must not get them wet. But he could still see the anemone. Its base was fastened to a boulder, just above the water-line. From the middle of the other end, which was below, something stuck out, quivering. It was a shrimp, Eustace decided, and the anemone was eating it, sucking it. A tumult arose in Eustace's breast. His heart bled for the shrimp, he longed to rescue it; but, on the other hand, how could he bear to rob the anemone of its dinner? The anemone was more beautiful than the shrimp, more interesting and much rarer. It was a 'plumose' anemone; he recognized it from the picture in his Natural History, and the lovely feathery epithet stroked the fringes of his mind like a caress. If he took the shrimp away, the anemone might never catch another, and die of hunger. But while he debated the unswallowed part of the shrimp grew perceptibly smaller.

This first paragraph fixes Eustace for us: the gentle, sensitive, over-scrupulous little boy already obsessed with problems of morals and behaviour, fixes, too, his relationship with his sister—for who is Hilda if not the anemone, and who Eustace if not the shrimp?—and his ultimate destiny. Implicit in the paragraph is the whole trilogy; throughout the three novels almost every one of Eustace's actions is done in consciousness of Hilda. To say Hilda is the anemone and Eustace the shrimp is not thereby to make a moral judgment to the effect that Hilda is the villain and Eustace the hero-victim. They are both victims—of each other, fated by the nature of their relationship to destroy each other; and if it is Hilda who is finally responsible for Eustace's death—the quietest, most subtle and therefore most shocking death in contemporary English fiction—it is Eustace who puts himself in the position to be killed by his manœuvring, if the word is permissible for so innocent a scheming, the disastrous engagement between Hilda and his hero Dick Staveley.

In *The Shrimp and the Anemone* Eustace is a little boy, in *The Sixth Heaven* an undergraduate at Oxford, in *Eustace and Hilda* a young man mainly on holiday in Venice. Hartley works out his story with all the concentration on a single issue of classical French tragedy, but all the same, it is comedy that he has written. His theme is essentially that of a morbid relationship, but it is sterilized of morbidity by the treatment. Hartley's detachment, which is that of the affectionate comic writer, not only sets Eustace in perspective but also universalizes him; as we see from the fantasies of ambition and terror, always written with the sharpest economy, in which Hartley allows Eustace to indulge. The following is typical, a flight of fear experienced on a first visit to a great country house:

'Did you ring, sir?'
'Yes, I did. I'm afraid I can't find my white flannel trousers.'
'If you'll excuse my saying so, sir, it's not likely you'll find them under all that mess. That mess will take me at least fifty-five minutes to clear up, and this is my evening out.'
'Oh, I am so sorry.'
'It's no good your apologizing, sir. I was only saying to them in the Hall, that, of all the guests who've ever stayed here in my experience, man and boy, you've given far the most trouble. We wondered where you had been brought up, sir, we did, straight. Not in a gentleman's house, I said, believe me.'

But there is also the perspective in which the whole relationship between Eustace and Hilda is placed. It comes out, I think, in the figures of Eustace's other sister Barbara and her husband Jimmy, who appear as symbols of normality, of health; they represent a world of happy acceptance of living into which neither Eustace nor Hilda can ever enter. The revealing passage occurs in a discussion, ostensibly on Communism, between Hilda and Jimmy:

'Mind you, I don't agree with what they stand for,' Hilda continued, leaning her elbow on the table and shaking her clenched hand at Jimmy, who recoiled slightly. 'They think a thing becomes right if enough people can be persuaded to do it. They have no sense of personal moral responsibility. I hope you're not like that.'

'Oh no,' said Jimmy, recovering himself. 'But I believe in sharing it. Too much responsibility does no one any good.'

Too much responsibility does no one any good. Is it not precisely this, a too overwhelming sense of moral responsibility for each other, that is at the heart of the tragedy of Eustace and Hilda alike?

Eustace seems to me among the most completely successful character-creations in contemporary fiction, and, at first glance, everything might seem to have been against Hartley here. A nervous, diffident, timid, over-scrupulous, as it were professional delicate little boy who grows into a delicate, unsure, charming young man with literary ambitions: one of the stock characters of English fiction since Butler wrote *The Way of All Flesh*, one might think. Yet Eustace is a fresh, unique being both as a small boy and as a young man at Oxford and in Venice. He is so because of the special quality of his mind. This is seen at its clearest in the first part of *Eustace and Hilda*, that wonderfully delicate evocation of the effect of Venice on the young man's awakening mind. One says 'awakening' because it is the especial characteristic of Eustace that throughout the three books his mind is continually unfolding: shy as he is, and naïve, he has all the same a real capacity for certain kinds of experience, the aesthetic and what, for want of a better word, one must call the mystical. Following Eustace's fortunes, we are always at the growing point of his mind, a mind reacting, discovering, discriminating, absorbing.

Above all, perhaps, Eustace is successful because he is not merely the hero of a biographical novel. He is, as it were, abstracted from the flux of time, so that his sensitivity and his capacity for the exercise of conscience are not left to winnow the air in the casual encounters of life but are borne along and given direction by the exigencies of the situation symbolically enacted in the first paragraph of the trilogy. The plot enhances him, elevates him to his full significance. At the same time, by striving to squeeze from the situation the last drop of drama inherent in it, Hartley has been repaid in these three novels, which together make one, by beauty of form, the rarest quality in English fiction. Eustace partakes of that transfiguring quality.

Hartley is one of a number of contemporary novelists who strike one as being very much at the centre of the English tradition of the novel. They are concerned with the behaviour of men and women in society, with the making of choices; and they are also scholarly novelists in the way that some painters and musicians are called scholarly. They approach the writing of fiction with a full knowledge of what has been done in the art before. They are conscious of the great exemplars. They are not the less original for this, but it means that generally they know precisely what it is they are doing, and what they are doing may very well be ambitious indeed. Such a novelist is Robert Liddell, an unprolific writer whose finest novel, *The Last Enchantments*, was published in 1948. This novel is closely related to his critical book, *A Treatise on the Novel*, which appeared a year earlier. Here, Liddell, whose attitude towards fiction almost out-Jameses James's in its austerity and is altogether too limiting for my taste, preaches what he calls the 'pure novel', 'concentrating on human beings and their mutual reactions'. 'So rare is such concentration in the English novel', he goes on, 'that any writer who conscientiously practises it is almost sure to be accused of "imitating Jane Austen" whether their minds are alike or not.' In fact, at that point Liddell is writing upon I. Compton-Burnett, whose mind he finds in many ways like Jane Austen's.

Together, they are Liddell's ideal novelists. Whether his mind is like theirs I cannot say; as I encounter its direct expression in *A Treatise on the Novel* I find it too prissy and governessy to be quite admirable. When I meet it in the narrator of *The Last Enchantments*, however, it is another matter. On the surface, the novel is composed largely of gossip over the teacups of North Oxford. The characters are scholars, minor men of letters, landladies, servants, members of the lunatic fringe of the University. The novel could scarcely have been written, one feels, without Jane Austen and Miss Compton-Burnett. Liddell catches a considerable part of their uncompromising, astringent qualities of wit and verbal precision; and the gradual stripping away of the pretensions of the central character, Mrs Foyle, is very funny indeed. But also, explicit in the novel, is the analogy between Mrs Foyle and Balzac's Goriot. Whether Goriot is a tragic character or not is arguable, but it is Lear he is commonly compared with; and this aspect of Goriot is there in Mrs Foyle. It is the index of Liddell's power and skill that he so successfully and movingly creates a female Goriot in terms of North Oxford tea-parties.

Pamela Hansford Johnson's views on the novel are nothing like Liddell's, yet it seems to me that, on his definition, she too can be considered a pure novelist. She too brings to its contemplation of human beings and their mutual reactions a rare degree of concentration. Like

Liddell, Miss Hansford Johnson is a learned novelist: she is an expert on Dickens, can meet the Proust scholars on their own ground, and has sympathies wide enough to take in Thomas Wolfe and I. Compton-Burnett, on both of whom she has written persuasively. And all this seems relevant to her own fiction. She has been a professional novelist for many years now; *This Bed Thy Centre* (1935), a study of working-class life in south London, written when she was twenty-two, remains one of the most interesting first novels of the thirties. But through the years her talents have steadily deepened and her insights broadened until now she writes with complete authority. By that I mean that, having read her, one feels that the whole truth has been told about the characters and the situations in which they find themselves. One has a sense of her complete knowledge of them, and this sense is the effect, it seems to me, of her technical mastery and of her moral discriminations.

Such novels as *The Last Resort* (1956) and *The Humbler Creation* (1959), render beautifully the complexities, the discontinuities, the contradictions of human behaviour and the necessary recognition of the frustrations attendant upon it. They seem to me to have the sad, honest, lucid acceptance of life we find in George Eliot, and, like George Eliot, Pamela Hansford Johnson is concerned, in her later novels at any rate, with the problem of right doing, of duty. The central character of *The Humbler Creation* is an Anglican parson, vicar of an unfashionable London parish, saddled with a silly neurotic wife and with too many family burdens, a good man tempted into the sin of love outside his marriage. But this is very much to over-simplify, for in these novels complexity of detail is everything, and it is through the complexity that the author's discrimination asserts itself.

So, in *The Last Resort*, it is possible to isolate the moral element that sunders the two lovers in the words of one of them:

'Underneath it is all the undertow of the Ten Commandments. They make dreadful fools of us. They're like our grandmother's sideboard, which we don't use any more, but can't bring ourselves to sell. There it is, all the time, weighing us down from the attic or biding its time in the cellar.'

But beyond this is the whole intricate pattern of character-relations and the events that spring out of them, a pattern that has to be intricate in order acceptably to suggest the complexity of life itself. This is essential to Miss Hansford Johnson's purpose, and she achieves it. In *The Last Resort* particularly she is, one is persuaded, seeing life steadily and, if not whole, seeing sufficient of it to stand for the whole. She persuades us of this by the sobriety of her realism, her ability to render specific places and their inhabitants, by her sure grasp of her characters, who are many and diverse and who are never seen statically but are always capable of surprising us with new facets of their personalities, and, not less important, by her tone. In this novel, Pamela Hansford Johnson uses a narrator, a novelist who is the friend and confidant of the main actors. As an example of the tone:

> It occurred to me, as the train drew out beyond the downs, that she was of the company of those who can make and keep resolutions which must change a whole life; a member of that most incomprehensible of companies, in which are the martyrs and the saints. For most of us can conceive the noble idea, suggest it to ourselves, even go so far as to begin to put it into practice: but the secret planner of the mind knots the invisible safeguards, weaves the safety-net beneath us. We are in no danger of falling too far. We do not quite speak the irrevocable word: we only suggest that we are about to speak it. We envy the saints and martyrs, sometimes with passion: we long to match them. At moments we believe that there is, between them and ourselves, only a filament thin as the spider's, and that if we can make the one supreme effort of will we shall send it torn and floating into the air. But it is in the difference between the desire and the performance that the mystery lies, the mystery we shall never solve. The vast majority of us are expert recanters; we can do it with infinite grace and the minimum of blameworthiness when the time is ripe. During the whole period in which we are planning our gesture of complete self-abnegation, of total change, the daemon inside us keeps up its perpetual murmur, 'Stop! You're not quite committed'; when the time comes, we ourselves say, 'Stop!'—in the human voice.

In *The Last Resort* it became apparent that she was steadily extending the range of her fiction. It is not that the types she describes, or their milieus, are new; but she makes them new: the retired, angry, self-absorbed doctor, his wife neurotically possessive of her daughter, the homosexual architect, and the rest. She sees all round them and catches them in a new light, in a new significance, so that in the end they are somehow bigger, richer as emblems of the human condition, than one might expect them to be. And what is strikingly absent from their delineation is what Norman Douglas called 'the novelist's touch', the falsification of life through failure to realize 'the complexities of the ordinary human mind'.

How much Pamela Hansford Johnson is extending her range may be seen in the novel that followed *The Last Resort*—*The Unspeakable Skipton* (1959). Her subject here is the paranoiac artist. Familiar enough in life, in fiction treatment of him has been mainly marginal. In life the great exemplar is Frederick Rolfe, 'Baron Corvo', and Miss Hansford Johnson has admittedly drawn on him for her portrait of Daniel Skipton, Knight of the Most Noble Order of SS. Cyril and Methodius. But Rolfe is no more than the starting-point: Skipton exists in his own right and in our time, a separate creation.

Skipton is a monster. We see him in his austere garret in Bruges writing blackguarding letters to his long-suffering publisher even while trying to borrow from him; we see him attempting to blackmail the elderly cousin who has never met him and who makes him an allowance out of sheer kindliness. He scours the town for English tourists to pimp for. He is a monster of satanic egoism, and with diabolical glee he translates all who offend him—by their mere existence—into figures of fun, effigies of depravity, that go straight into his interminable, unpublishable novel. A monster—and yet, as Miss Hansford Johnson reveals him, the mind, called to pass judgment, wavers. That ferocious anal-eroticism, that passion for cleanliness, that revulsion from the contacts of the flesh, don't they come very near to a perverted saintliness? And certainly the intransigence of his appalling lunatic self-regard makes him almost one of the saints of art.

Skipton is a splendid comic creation; and yet, without abating the rigour of her sardonic comedy, Pamela Hansford Johnson brings out the full pathos of the poor wretch and his fate, which is in essence that of the dedicated artist who is devoid of talent. She embodies his fate in a plot marked by continuously amusing invention and by a set of characters that are excellent foils to him. And the setting of the novel, Bruges with its bells and its canals, places the comedy in a further dimension of poetry.

A novelist in mid-career whose more recent work has shown considerable expansion not so much of talent as of range is Olivia Manning. Ever since her first novel, *The Wind Changes*, appeared in 1937, she has possessed an exceedingly pure and exact style, together with what one thinks of as a painter's eye for the visible world, that has enabled her to render particularly well the sensual surface of landscape and places, as in *School for Love* (1951), a novel of Jerusalem in wartime as seen through the consciousness of a sixteen-year-old boy stranded there. It is a prose and an eye that seem accurately to take the measure of things. Yet this exactness of rendition, when applied to human beings, has sometimes seemed to have a diminishing effect, as of a lowering of vitality, a sense of Gissing-like hopelessness in the face of life. One felt this in *A Different Face* (1957), in which a man returns to Coldmouth, a town on the south coast of England, only to discover that the money he had invested in a private school there has been lost. The name of the place, vividly and chillingly described as it is, seems altogether too apt.

Olivia Manning's work in progress, however, of which two parts have now been published, *The Great Fortune* (1960) and *The Spoilt City* (1962), is something quite different and promises to be one of the major works of the sixties in English fiction. The first part deals with Bucharest during the first year of the war; the second ends with its occupation by the Germans after the fall of France. The action is necessarily complex and the canvas large. We see the events as they unfold through the eyes of Harriet Pringle, the newly married wife of Guy Pringle, a member of the staff of a British cultural mission in Rumania. As a recreation of history in fiction these novels are entirely admirable; the place and the time, the corruption and the sense of doom, seem caught perfectly; and the characters, British and Rumanian alike, are drawn with delicacy and strength, so that they come alive on the page, often absurd, but even so always as suffering human beings. The result is a poignant comedy of a very rare kind.

On this level alone, as recreation of history, these novels are remarkable. But they exist on another level, too, for central to them is the relationship between Harriet and her husband, a relationship not static because throughout the two novels Harriet is in process of discovering new sides of him. Already the drawing of Guy Pringle is one of the best explorations of character in contemporary fiction, a man of great physical presence, an intellectual from the working class, who seems sometimes a saint, sometimes a fool, and who appears to take his wife so much for granted while he is bent on his errands of mercy:

> Guy's attitude impressed her, though she had no intention of showing it. He had the advantage of an almost supernatural confidence in dealing with people. It seemed never to occur to

him they might not do what he wanted. He had, she noted with surprise, authority.

In the past she had been irritated by the amount of mental and physical vitality he expended on others. As he flung out his charm, like radium dissipating its own brilliance, it had seemed to her indiscriminate giving for giving's sake. Now she saw his vitality functioning to some purpose. Only someone capable of giving much could demand and receive so much. She felt proud of him.

This exploration of the relationship between a wife and husband who are utterly different in temperament is very movingly done, and it lies at the heart of the historical tragi-comedy Olivia Manning is describing.

[4]

THE 'WAR NOVEL' as we knew it in the twenties was not, in England, a product of the second world war. There were of course memorable novels written about the soldier's life in action: Alexander Baron's *From the City, From the Plough* (1948), on the Normandy landings, Walter Baxter's *Look Down in Mercy* (1951), on the fighting in Burma, and earlier books such as Howard Clewes's *Dead Ground* (1945), Alun Lewis's short stories *The Last Inspection* (1943) and J. MacLaren Ross's extremely amusing stories *The Stuff to Give the Troops* (1944). But in these the appeal is not to a special *mystique*, that of the fighting soldier baptized by fire, but to common experience. No rigid distinction between war novels and others is possible, and Evelyn Waugh, Elizabeth Bowen, Henry Green, Graham Greene, H. E. Bates, James Hanley, for instance, are as much novelists of the war as Baron and Baxter. Since war was the inescapable experience of everyone, civilians as much as soldiers, we find the war present throughout the fiction of the forties and the decades that follow, not necessarily shown directly but there as the ineluctable shadow under which characters and events have their being. As P. H. Newby wrote in 1951: 'It is only natural that most novelists content themselves with the traditional materials of love and "a-political" adventure—yet conferring upon them that special quality which springs from an appreciation of the larger issues which confront society.'

This is true even of Malcolm Lowry's *Under the Volcano* (1947). One says 'even' because it belongs to a category of the novel in which normally social and economic factors have little place. It seems to me the finest and profoundest work of fiction written by an Englishman during the decade. Lowry, who died in 1957 at the age of forty-eight, published a first novel, *Ultramarine*, in 1930 while still an under-graduate; very much an experimental novel, it recounted the experiences of a very young middle-class Englishman as a deck-hand on a cargo ship. It was, one assumes, based on immediate experience, experience later to find its way into *Under the Volcano*. Lowry spent most of his life in Mexico, the scene of *Under the Volcano*, the United States and British Columbia, and as a novelist could probably be regarded as no less American than English. Certainly if one were looking for his affinities in contemporary fiction one would find him closest to Faulkner.

This is because of their common heritage: both are the sons of Conrad and of Joyce and learnt, better perhaps than any others, the real lessons to be learnt from Joyce. Apart from the first chapter, which is set a year ahead and has the function almost of a chorus to the action, *Under the Volcano* is concerned with the events of a single day, the Day of the Dead, November 1938, the last day in the life of Geoffrey Firmin, British Consul in the town of Quauhnahuac in Mexico, a town lying beneath the two volcanoes of Popocatepetl and Ixtaccihuatl. The point is made more than once in the novel that the ancients placed Tartarus under Etna: *Under the Volcano* is a novel about hell.

Firmin is a compulsive drunk. Remembering his meeting with his wife in Spain, he thinks:

How many bottles since then? In how many glasses, how many bottles had he hidden himself, since then alone? Suddenly he saw them, the bottles of aguardiente, of anis, of jerez, of Highland Queen, the glasses, a babel of glasses—towering, like the smoke from the train that day—built to the sky, then falling, the glasses toppling, crashing, falling downhill from the Generalife Gardens, the bottles breaking, bottles of Oporto, tinto, blanco, bottles of Pernod, Oxygenée, absinthe, bottles smashing, bottles cast aside, falling with a thud on the ground in parks, under benches, beds, cinema seats, hidden in drawers at Consulates, bottles of

Calvados dropped and broken, or bursting into smithereens, tossed into garbage heaps, flung into the sea, the Mediterranean, the Caspian, the Caribbean, bottles floating in the ocean, dead Scotchmen on the Atlantic highland—and now he saw them, smelt them, all, from the very beginning—bottles, bottles, bottles, and glasses, glasses, glasses, of bitter, of Dubonnet, of Falstaff, Rye, Johnny Walker, Vieux Whisky, blanc Canadian, the apéritifs, the digestifs, the demis, the dobles, the noch ein Herr Obers, the et glas Araks, the tusen taks, the bottles, the bottles, the beautiful bottles of tequila, and the gourds, gourds, gourds, the millions of gourds of beautiful mescal. . . . How indeed could he hope to find himself to begin again when, somewhere, perhaps, in one of those or broken bottles, in one of those glasses, lay for ever, the solitary clue to his identity? How could he go back and look now, scrabble among the broken glass, under the eternal bars, under the oceans?

The Consul is a man who is in the deepest sense alienated, knows himself alienated and, clear-sighted in the imprisonment of his sloth, is yet unable to make the necessary gestures, speak the necessary words, that would heal the breach between himself and the world. The theme of the novel is the necessity of love and the appalling difficulty of love; and during the Consul's last day on earth we watch him in his drunken progress of flight from those who love him and would save him, his wife, an ex-Hollywood film star who has divorced him but returned to him that day, and his half-brother Hugh, an anti-Fascist journalist haunted by the Spanish Civil War; a progress of evasive action from bar to bar, made almost against his will, until it ends with his murder by Fascist thugs who throw his body into the ravine—one of the novel's most powerful symbols—that splits the landscape. One says the flight is almost against his will. He is more in love with damnation than with being saved; he can think the words of love but is unable to say them aloud. In a sense, the climax of the book, in that it represents the point of no return, is the argument he has with Hugh on the value or otherwise of political action. The Consul is a man who in every conceivable way has abdicated. To his wife's pleadings, to all the demands made on him to save himself, he might have said, with Eliot's Gerontion:

> I have lost my passion: why should I need to keep it
> Since what is kept must be adulterated?

It is Lowry's great achievement that he has made the Consul a genuinely tragic figure who never loses our respect and our admiration. There are many echoes of Marlowe in the novel: the Consul's friend Laruelle, a French film director, is planning a Faust film; and we think of the Consul as Marlowe thought of Faustus: 'Cut is the branch that might have grown full straight'. And though the novel is a vision of hell, given the most precise and vivid actuality in terms of the Mexican scene, and certainly, one feels, the most thorough-going rendering of dipsomania that has ever been written, there are still glimpses of heaven, of the possibility of a good life. Heaven, though not for the Consul, is even attainable, and, while the novel abounds in symbols of hell, it also has its symbols of release, of freedom, of which the freeing of birds is the most obvious, and of the possibility of natural happiness, as in the beautiful description of Yvonne's and Hugh's morning ride round the environs of Quauhnahuac, with the foals trotting beside the mares they are riding and, going before them, the dog hunting snakes.

Then there are the wider implications. It is not by chance that, when the book opens with Laruelle's contemplation of his dead friend, the war in Europe has already begun and that during the main action Chamberlain has returned only a few weeks before from Munich and the war in Spain is dragging to its end. The novel is set firmly in the context of its time, and the wider relevance is established even to the point of being rammed home when Hugh, who has been trying to cure his brother's alcoholism, bursts out: 'Good God, if our civilization were to sober up for a couple of days it'd die of remorse on the third—'

Though its indebtedness in a general sense both to *Ulysses* and to *The Waste Land* is obvious, *Under the Volcano* stands uniquely by itself as a great tragic novel, a masterpiece of organization and of elaborate symbolism that is never forced or strained but right, springing largely as it does out of the scenes in which the action takes place. The harmony between the characters and the phenomena of the external universe through which they move is complete; and so are the correspondences between them. In this respect, Joyce in *Ulysses* did no better.

P. H. Newby finds in his own novels 'a curious air of hurry about them, as though time were running out, and I suppose this is one of the qualities I was seeking'. This 'curious air of hurry' seems to me a constant element in Newby's novels from the first, *A Journey to the*

Interior (1945), to the most recent, *The Barbary Light* (1962). All his novels with the possible exceptions of the two related comedies, *The Picnic at Sakkara* (1955) and *A Guest and His Going* (1959), explore a common theme, which might be called the quest and the test. In *A Journey to the Interior* this is executed in almost Conradian form, with the hero, Winter, an employee of an oil company near the Red Sea, recovering from illness and broken by his wife's death, setting out on a journey into the desert to find a mysterious Kurtz-like figure called Ryder, and returning as though a new man, risen from the dead.

Newby is probably best approached through his two related novels *A Step to Silence* (1952) and *The Retreat* (1953). The first of these, set in Worcestershire, indicates one of his literary ancestors: Lawrence. It is difficult to think of any novelist since Lawrence who can so magically illuminate and transfigure the common scene as Newby does. The Worcestershire countryside, the afternoon sun suddenly breaking through the clouds over a town, the interior of a country church being decorated for Christmas on a dark December afternoon, these are seen and described as with entirely fresh eyes, put down in words that seem to match the freshness of the vision, rendered, indeed, with a delicacy and intensity reminiscent of Lawrence in *The Rainbow*.

Like Lawrence, too, Newby catches his characters at the very moment of living, before the intellect has had time to intervene and generalize the moment experienced. In *A Step to Silence* the central character, Oliver Knight, is an adolescent fumbling his way to a knowledge of himself and of life, the victim, often, of his misconceptions about people, institutions and society, and bewildered by them. Since he is at the centre of the novel's consciousness, the reader shares his bewilderment. Oliver is a student at a teachers' training college. The time is 1937, and Oliver leaves the college before his course is ended in order to join the R.A.F.

On one level, the novel deals with the disillusionment which is part of growing up, but the circumstances in which the action is played out lift it on to another plane altogether. The circumstances of the time—1937, with Munich and the war just round the corner—become almost a character in the novel and give it its especial ambience. The state of the world, in particular the part played in it by Fascism, is represented —I think without strain—by the training college with its elaborate student ritual and initiation ceremonies, its demand for conformity for conformity's sake, against which Oliver revolts and which his friend

Hesketh, one of the best grotesques in contemporary fiction, so pathetically wants to satisfy.

The two comedies apart, *A Step to Silence* is probably the most immediately accessible of Newby's novels. Its sequel, *The Retreat*, is less so. It begins in May 1940, with Oliver Knight, now a fighter-pilot, convalescent after illness, making his way to Dunkirk for evacuation, his one thought to see the wife whom he married just before leaving England. The boat he embarks on is bombed. He is blown into the water and, when picked up, stripped of his clothes and all marks of identity, gives the authorities a false name and number. Landed in England, he sets out to find first of all, not his wife, but his friend Hesketh and Hesketh's wife, Jane, who has recently given birth to a dead baby. She is crazed with grief, and Knight runs away with her. So begins a confused chase across England in which his wife, Hesketh, the R.A.F. and the civil police all join in. At an early stage in their flight Knight thinks:

> Jane and I are lost in the wood and we are trying to find our way. We can scarcely see and are afraid of feeling. And, as we press on, the trees are closing behind us and barring our retreat. There is no retreat. We must go on and on.

Towards the end of the novel, when he is returning to his wife, what has happened appears to him as 'a mysterious ritual . . . the movements of a ceremony for the composure of troubled spirits'. This sense of being lost seems to express Newby's view of the human lot; and the wood in which the Newby hero is lost is a wood made up both of personal relationships and of the contemporary situation. For Newby these mirror each other. In this wood, the Newby hero has to guide him only a suspicious common sense and a stubborn independence, a natural habit of nonconformity.

Most novelists—it is what we normally ask of them—give us a rationalization of life. Newby does not: he gives us, instead, the bewilderment of minds in crisis at the moment of crisis itself, renders his characters in what might be called a state of hallucinated vision. For all the obvious differences between them, the novelist he is closest to seems to me Henry Green. In both, the effect aimed at and got is strange and complex, in texture of writing and in ambiguity of meaning alike kin more to poetry than to prose fiction as we normally know it.

A quest of a different kind is the main theme of a very different writer, Denton Welch, whose *Maiden Voyage* (1943), *In Youth Is Pleasure* (1945) and the posthumous *A Voice through a Cloud* (1950)— Welch died at the age of 31 in 1948—exist very much in the border country between autobiography and the novel. The quest of the earlier books is the quest for experience, the quest for self-discovery construed almost entirely in sexual terms. What is remarkable is the innocence—there seems no other word for it—with which the central character, a boy who is plainly Welch himself, explores and translates into action a world of homosexual transvestist fantasy. The scene of *Maiden Voyage* is China; and there is an astonishingly pure response to the sensual surface of things, the experience of sight, smell, touch. In *A Voice through a Cloud* Welch recreates with an equal freshness the life of illness, of the sick man in hospital. In Welch nothing seems to come between the perception and its expression. These novels are sensational in the literal meaning of the word. They have a lack of inhibition, a total frankness, which comes, one can only think, from a total innocence; and while I respond to them as psychological case-books rather than as fiction, they are the case-books of a writer who was touched with genius. They do not plead; they state; and the pity one reads into them oneself, if one wishes to.

Another writer for whom the sensual surface of things seems to offer the greater part of experience is William Sansom, who made a reputation towards the end of the war first with his short stories based upon his experiences as a fireman during the bombing raids on London and then with a number of stories reminiscent of Kafka. His first novel, *The Body* (1949), which recounts the jealousy of Henry Bishop, a middle-aged barber, for a stranger he thinks is in love with his wife, is still perhaps his best. It is, as it were, a comedy of exacerbation in which the distorted vision of the hero-narrator is expressed mainly through a minute rendering of the objects that make up the external world. They are seen in an unnatural clarity, magnified as though through an eye that is not a human eye. One cannot quite speak of these objects—flies, plants, the interiors of saloons, river scenes—as the background of the novel, since the human beings in it are seen in the same way and are transformed into objects also, so that they tend to merge into and become part of the fabric of things. The result suggests the literary equivalent of paintings Rousseau might have made had he been turned loose in London immediately after the war. Sansom's world is essentially decorative and two-dimensional. It seems plain that such fantasticated writing as Sansom's, delightful as it is and even stimulating in that it makes the familiar world unfamiliar by showing it to us from unexpected angles, must exclude him from at least nine-tenths of the usual material of fiction. When he subdues his style and relies on a more nearly normal angle of vision, as in *The Cautious Heart* (1958), he can write sad, muted comedy of middle-aged love set in a notable evocation of London after dark.

[5]

OF SOME English novels of the present time, the fiction for example of Emyr Humphreys and Roy Fuller, which one enjoys and admires for the adult qualities of seriousness, sensibility and lucidity, one feels in the end that not enough has been risked. An essential trace element seems to have been left out, that suggested by Yeats when a character in one of his plays says: 'What if there is always something that lies outside knowledge, outside order?' It is the sense of this, the quality that defies and defeats neatness, that for me enriches J. D. Scott's *The End of an Old Song* (1954). Scott's novel is a criticism of romanticism; it is also a study in national character. These are the two poles of the book, and between them an admirable tension is set up, a tension of ambiguity. The theme is romantic nationalism, Scottish nationalism. Patrick Shaw, the character who tells the story and through whose eyes we see the action, is himself only half-Scots; in many ways he is the outsider from the south and because of this almost by reflex action a romantic. He is conscious, as he crosses the moors as a boy from his Scottish public school to visit Captain Keith at Kingisbyres, of 'the history of a graceful, violent, aristocratic past with which I had no contact at all'.

> And then, sometimes, in association with Kingisbyres I would suddenly have, almost overwhelmingly, the sense of the past, not so much a particular episode or period of history, as of some essence of the past of Scotland, its dark, fated, cruel quality, and the contrasting strain that ran through it of lightness

and grace and gaiety; and even then it seemed to me that this
historic past was like a kind of collective subconscious, something to which the respectable, censored mind does not normally
have access, something powerfully charged with love and hate,
pride and violence, which, in given circumstances, it might
discharge in some tremendous flash of lightning.

Scott's symbols for this highly charged romantic past are the house
Kingisbyres, with its bedroom in which the fire is kept permanently
alight against the arrival of Prince Charles Stuart, and its owner
Captain Keith, who still toasts the King over the Water, no longer
Charles Stuart but Rudolph of Bavaria. Patrick's friend Alastair, the
brilliant village boy and Keith's *protégé* (as it comes out in the end, his
son), is the anti-romantic, the enemy of small nations and their
nationalisms. He is in a sense the modern man: 'There are always some
people', he says, 'who want to get into the biggest competition in
sight, and they'd sooner die than do anything else.' He is also the
traditional ambitious Scot, dreaming as a boy of a career at the English
Bar. But he is more than this, as Patrick sees him:

And all the time the look deepened on Alastair's face, the look of
a victorious commander, giving permission to loot a city, a look
of brutality, pleasure, and recklessness, all masked and stilled by
pride.

He too is an expression of the 'collective subconscious . . . powerfully
charged with love and hate, pride and violence'.

J. D. Scott can make the sudden leap into the unexpected which
renders an invention not merely acceptable but imaginatively convincing. Thus Captain Keith's enthusiasm for the principle of legitimacy ends in his narrowly escaping jail during the war as a Nazi
sympathiser—the link between nationalism and Fascism is made as it
were in passing; and Kingisbyre passes, before it is burnt down, into
the hands of the National Coal Board. But the most daring leap into
the imaginatively convincing occurs in the unfolding of the character
of Alastair, whose repudiation of the past is so total as to involve a
repudiation of England, too. England offers this twentieth-century
Scottish reiver too little in the way of plunder, and by the end of the
book, director of an international economic research organization, he
is about to become an American citizen.

Of Angus Wilson's novels, also, it would be quite false to say that not enough has been risked. Wilson is the most ambitious novelist in British English who has appeared since the war; more than any other, he has attempted to bring back into fiction the amplitude and plenitude of the Victorians, so much so, indeed, that at times he seems in conscious competition with one or another of them. His first novel, *Hemlock and After* (1952), would have caused a sensation in any event because it contains a much more open recognition of homosexuality than was current in English fiction at that time. Its theme is the inadequacy of liberal values in the face of the evil, the representative of liberal values being a famous novelist, Bernard Sands, married and with children, who in late middle age gives way to the hitherto repressed and frightening homosexual tendencies within him and so becomes vulnerable as never before to the machinations of his enemies. His end is tragic, with, it seems, his life's work undone.

As its title, with its ironic reference to the death of Socrates, suggests, *Hemlock and After* is a most ambitious novel, with a large gallery of characters. It has a quality of nightmare intensity, especially in the descriptions of the homosexual underworld, the world of 'camp', which is revealed with a terrifying brilliance that rasps the nerves. But any novel that sets out to criticize society and man's life in it must contain a representation of it that we feel can stand for the actual society being criticized, as for example the worlds depicted in *Our Mutual Friend* and *The Way We Live Now* can. Wilson is unsuccessful here, partly because he falls into the trap that commonly awaits the moralist, the tendency to see human beings either as crude black or as whiter than white. At times *Hemlock and After* becomes moral melodrama; and the writing is at its most powerful when the action is most melodramatic. The principal embodiment of evil in the novel, the procuress Mrs Curry, has a vitality so galvanic that it is difficult to think of any character she can be compared with outside Dickens. But in the end one feels that she is too bad to be true, has been caricatured out of existence; and as soon as one feels this she is no longer plausible as a symbol of evil. At the same time, Sands, who is at the heart of the novel, remains unexplained. If he is to be understood it is by reference to actual human beings—to André Gide, for instance.

Wilson's creative vitality is shown by the fact that in the four very long novels he has so far written he comes nowhere near repeating himself. Yet *Hemlock and After* does in a way establish the pattern underlying his novels. All his novels seem to illustrate the descent or the disintegration of a man or a way of life into chaos, even though at the end there may be, as in *Anglo-Saxon Attitudes* (1956) and *The Middle Age of Mrs Eliot* (1958), an emergence from chaos, a restoration of order. One of Wilson's most serious and important qualities is his awareness of the black nightside of life. But his rendering of it and of its relation to the public world of man's life in society seems not to be quite under his control. It is as though the realistic novel he seems to have set out to write, the novel that can stand as an acceptable paradigm of society, is always disrupted by compulsions from the world of private fantasy below. The clearest instances are to be found in *The Old Men at the Zoo* (1961). Admittedly the novel is set in the future, though a future only ten years hence; but plainly it is a novel about the health and state of England today to a degree at least comparable with Cary's *To Be a Pilgrim*. It abounds in the gratuitously bizarre: a young keeper at the London Zoo killed by a mad giraffe's stepping on his testicles; a young woman savaged to death by the Alsatian with which she has sexual relations; 'Roman games' in which political prisoners are thrown to wild beasts by a demented Fascist dictatorship. It is as though the dominating image of the novel, the Zoo and its inhabitants, has taken over Wilson's imagination entirely, and what seems meant to be a statement about England has been obscured by a riot of bestial imagery.

The Old Men at the Zoo is an extreme example; yet the more I read Wilson's work the more it seems to me that temperamentally he is not a realistic novelist at all. It is true that characters and scenes in his novels could scarcely be more 'actual', more immediately evident to the senses. But this undoubted actuality chimes only intermittently with a sense of observed reality. And the nature of Wilson's actuality is an interesting one. It seems to have the same relation to the 'real' as mimicry does.

Anglo-Saxon Attitudes provides convenient illustrations of this mimicry, which is admittedly superb, in the characters of Mrs Salad, Gerald Middleton's ex-charwoman, and of Inge, his Scandinavian wife. They are both eminently 'there' though they are instances of different kinds of mimicry. Mrs Salad, the cockney char, could only have been created, one thinks on first meeting her, by Dickens. She might be Mrs Gamp's half-sister, and Wilson puts phrases into her mouth that would not have shamed Dickens. But Mrs Gamp is so brilliantly idiosyncratic a creation, so utterly *sui generis*, that a second

Mrs Gamp, or even a half-sister to her, is unthinkable. Mrs Salad emerges as a remarkable piece of pastiche. As soon as this is realized the sense of her reality departs. She comes out of literature, the mimicry of literature, rather than out of observation of life.

Inge Middleton, one feels, is mimicry of life: a monster of silliness, selfishness and self-deception, a gigantic middle-aged little girl—her stature is emphasized continually. Her speech is reproduced with what seems horrible exactitude: she sets one's teeth on edge with every word she utters. In her way she is a triumph, a triumph of a kind Wilson seems able to bring off at will. Yet it is a limited one, for at the end of the novel we know scarcely more about Inge than we did at the beginning: she remains frozen in her postures of malign and self-deluded silliness.

Wilson is fascinated by vulgarity, the gratuitous cruelty of offensively bad manners, and by the raw indecency, strictly the obscenity, which quarrels within a family sometimes display. He can reproduce them—and does from book to book—with a quite startling fidelity. Wilson says of Gerald Middleton in *Anglo-Saxon Attitudes*: 'Perhaps marriage to Inge had taught him that the ludicrous was too often only a thin covering for the serious and the tragic.' As a generalization this is obviously true, but it is not the final impression one gets from the ludicrous in Wilson's fiction. Vulgarity remains vulgarity, and obscenity obscenity, no matter with what *trompe-l'œil* illusionism they are reproduced, and they are no more bearable to read about for long than they are endurable for long in actual life; which is why Wilson is still at his most satisfying within the limits of the short story. And they make up much too large a part of his novels for the world described there to be acceptable as a representation of the real world. His world, indeed, suggests the real world distorted by private nightmare.

Wilson's most considered attempt to render the real world, to show a human being whole and in the round, is *The Middle Age of Mrs Eliot*, an extremely interesting book for several reasons, one of which is that it is a very literary one. The rival—one can scarcely say the model —he sets himself up against here is George Eliot. During the course of the novel it is made explicit that Wilson is attempting a heroine of a distinct kind, one that has engaged the talents of some of our greatest novelists. In her various avatars she has been Jane Austen's Emma, George Eliot's Maggie Tulliver and Dorothea Brooke, Meredith's Clara Middleton and James's Isabel Archer. The very loftiness of her view of herself means that she lives at first in a state of self-delusion, and her progress is the painful one of discovering the real nature of life and of herself. As we first meet her, Wilson's Meg Eliot is the apparently highly successful wife of a successful barrister, beautiful, devoted in the most practical way to good works, lacking only a child to have achieved fulfilment in life. She is perhaps a little too pleased with herself, a trifle smug. It is all shattered when her husband is killed by a stray bullet in a political assassination and she finds herself suddenly a widow and poor, face to face with the test of reality.

The Middle Age of Mrs Eliot strikes one as a prodigious feat of self-discipline on Wilson's part. It has few of the faults of the other novels, but its failure suggests that it is in these very faults that his creative impulse really lies. It is told in massive detail and, as it were, in extremely slow motion; but Mrs Eliot does not emerge from the detail with the significance she is clearly intended to have: she remains, it seems to me, a literary conception. There are excellent things in the book; the snapshots of the contemporary scene are as accurate and brilliant as they always are. But it is as nearly as dull a book as it would seem possible for Wilson to write; and in the final section one has the disconcerting impression that he is taking with deadly seriousness what in a short story he would have turned into heartless satirical comedy.

Cards of Identity (1955) showed its author, Nigel Dennis, to be the most considerable satirist to have appeared in English fiction since Wyndham Lewis. His novel is a brilliant invention, packed with fundamental brain-work and making a radical criticism of one aspect of contemporary man, the situation summed up by the old woman in the nursery rhyme who fell asleep on the King's highway and had her petticoats cut to the knees by a naughty pedlar named Stout. When she woke, 'she began to cry, Lackamercyme, this is none of I!'

Dennis's theme, then, is the problem of identity. He sees contemporary man as lacking in identity or at least easily deprived of his sense of it, uneasily aware that there is no constant factor in his conception of himself: cut off his petticoats, rob him of assumptions he has taken for granted, for example, the inherent superiority of the American way of life or the infallible disinterestedness of Marxism, and he cries, 'This is none of I', knowing no longer who he is, and with relief accepts an identity as it were tailored for him, as after brainwashing. Dennis's novel opens with a grand country house, long empty, being taken over by a fine old English gentleman, his wife and stepson. They are not what they seem: they are the advance guard of the Identity Club. They kidnap a seedy hanger-on of the landed gentry and his sister, erase their identities and even their knowledge of the relationship between them, and turn them into a butler and a widowed housekeeper. A local doctor, harassed to the point of breakdown by the exigencies of the National Health Service, is brainwashed into a gardener and his nurse into his assistant. And so on. But all this is preparation for what, in effect, are the real guts of the book, an account of the annual conference of the Identity Club and the three case-histories read before it.

The point is, they are not histories of actual cases. They are as it were cases awaiting their patients. The first describes a case of what might be called romantic High Toryism, that of the upper-class young man who, with the traditional world in ruins about him, retreats into worship of the past. He becomes Co-Warden of the Badgeries. His duties?

> The stuffed, or token, boar-badger is inserted into a symbolic cage and then eased out with your official emblem, a symbolic gold spade. In this way, there is no need actually to disturb any living badger: the whole ceremony is performed quietly in London.

This case is in a sense local. The others are of much wider application. One is a case of sexual identity. 'Sometimes', its subject says, 'I soar above this humdrum and see myself as a rough prototype created hundreds of years too soon—product of some fantastic mating between an inverted man-girl and a perverted girl-man.' The third is that of a monk, a convert from international Communism who specializes in writing his confessions as a Communist spy. All three are presented in great detail; as parodies of genuine case-histories they are superb. Their relevance as satire on types and tendencies in the contemporary world is obvious. The readings of them are followed by a performance by the domestic staff of the Club of Shakespeare's play *The Prince of Antioch. Or a New Way to an Old Identity*; after which the house is visited by the police investigating a suspected murder. But by then the members of the Club have again changed their identities, and the novel ends with a duke displaying his ancestral home to tourists.

Cards of Identity is long and somewhat uneven. The machinery of the fable, to use the eighteenth-century phrase, is a little unwieldy, and the burlesque of early Shakespeare no more successful than such parodies generally are. It is the case-histories that form the hard core of the book and stick in the mind. But three things stand out in the novel, qualities indispensable to good satire: a serious subject, a hard-headed intellectuality of approach to it, and an exuberance of comic invention.

One of the best first novels of our time was Doris Lessing's *The Grass Is Singing* (1950). The story of a town girl married to a farmer in Africa, and of her behaviour towards her Negro servants, behaviour reflecting her own inner uncertainty and in the end with fatal conse-quences to herself, it satisfies both as a novel and as a parable on the nature of relations between black and white in Africa. It heralds one of Doris Lessing's two main themes, the relationship between the races in Africa. The other is the problem of being a woman in what is largely a man's world. Both themes come together in her work in progress, *Children of Violence*, of which so far *Martha Quest* (1952), *A Proper Marriage* (1954) and *A Ripple from the Storm* (1958) have appeared. The sequence traces the life of Martha Quest from her childhood and adolescence on a farm in what seems to be Rhodesia to the break-up of her marriage in the country's capital during the war and her involve-ment in left-wing political activities at the time. In these books Doris Lessing does for a young woman something very similar to what Bennett in *Clayhanger* and Lawrence in *Sons and Lovers* did for a young man, but the closer parallel is probably with George Eliot. In the passionate seriousness of her response to life Martha Quest is in the direct line of descent from Maggie Tulliver, and Doris Lessing shows her kinship to George Eliot both in her technique here and in her sober, unsentimental scrutiny of behaviour, motives and morals. As the work goes on, there is a deepening irony, so that one sees Martha with as it were a double vision, as she sees herself and as she is seen from the outside by a mature observer.

How the work will continue it is difficult to say. In *A Ripple from the Storm* Martha Quest seems no longer the channel through which the action flows. She has become smaller, overshadowed by the events described, lost in the minute political detail of the book, which relates the break-down during the war of a raw provincial society, in which the colour problem can still be seen in terms of crude white and black, under the impact of invasion from the outside, by Jewish refugees from Nazis and by class- and politically-conscious airmen of the

Royal Air Force. What had begun as a full-length portrait of a young woman has become a study of a society in a process of disintegration.

In her most recent novel, *The Golden Notebook* (1962), the African theme is subsidiary to that of being a woman in a man's world. The central character, Anna, is a 'free woman', who, having written one successful novel, is unable because of the difficulties of her personal life—among other things she is a disillusioned Communist—to write a second. The novel consists largely of the notebooks Anna keeps, so that we have something like a series of novels within a novel. As a work of art, *The Golden Notebook* seems to me to fail. The structure is clumsy, complicated rather than complex. But all the same it is most impressive in its honesty and integrity, and unique, it seems to me, as an exposition of the emotional problems that face an intelligent woman who wishes to live in the kind of freedom a man may take for granted. The comparison commonly made by English reviewers was with Simone de Beauvoir's *The Second Sex*: the comparison indicates its merit, the nature of its interest and also, perhaps, its limitations as a novel. Its main interest seems to be sociological; but that said, it must also be said that it is essential reading for anyone interested in our times and the response to them of a formidably intelligent and independent-minded woman.

John Lodwick died in early middle age in 1959, without having received the recognition he deserved. He was something of an odd-man-out in contemporary English fiction. His imagination was picaresque and romantic. His character Desmond Thornton, the hero of the two related novels, *Somewhere a Voice Is Calling* (1953) and *The Starless Night* (1955), which seem to me to show Lodwick at his best, says of himself, 'I was a stupid little boy, and I had just two gears: the tough and sentimental'. Lodwick had the same two gears, but also an extraordinarily sensitive understanding of the tough, of men like Thornton, a minor consular official in Spain who is always in trouble because violent action is his only means of expression. Thornton is a former Commando, and he emerges as a striking representation of a type common to all classes and cultural levels, the self-imprisoned man who can resolve the problems that beset him only through violence, the man for whom war is the ideal condition because in war his normally anti-social behaviour receives social sanction.

Lodwick portrays Thornton with great sympathy in a story of action and revenge that begins in Provence, moves to Barcelona and thence to Minorca, shifts to Valencia, goes back to Provence and returns to Spain, taking in on the way heroin-smuggling from Tangier and a quixotic bank-robbery by the Spanish underground movement. At the same time, Thornton has the art of starting up, like hares at his feet, vivid and amusing characters. But Lodwick's romantic quality comes out not only in his choice of hero, and what finally gives his work its distinction is his prose style. He writes with great *panache*, afraid neither of lyricism nor of the purple passage. His use of metaphor is especially skilful, and he uses it particularly to describe and reveal his characters and their behaviour, thereby opening them up, enlarging them, giving them at times something like universality. The final effect of these novels of action, mannered, sophisticated, lyrical as they are, is elegiac.

[6]

IN RETROSPECT, the years 1953 and 1954 seem to have a quite special significance in post-war fiction. In the autumn of 1953 John Wain's *Hurry on down* appeared, to be followed early in the new year by Amis's *Lucky Jim*. Iris Murdoch's *Under the Net* and William Golding's *Lord of the Flies* came out later in 1954. Golding was recognized as *sui generis* from the moment he appeared. Wain, Amis and Iris Murdoch were believed to have much more in common than seems possible today, now that they have gone their very divergent ways. But all of them aroused immediate interest because they were plainly striking new notes in fiction. In these years the new was being eagerly awaited, but the form it would take was not, of course, easily foreseeable. All one could say was that there was a new generation of writing age that had been brought up during the war years and in the years of social change that followed. It had not, as yet, spoken, or perhaps only in one novel, Thomas Hinde's *Mr Nicholas*, which was published in 1952. A study of the relationship between an eccentric, unpredictable father—an admirable comic figure—and his son, it was written in a manner reminiscent in its coolness, detachment and under-statement of the early Christopher Isherwood.

What gave it its particular strength was the exactness of the observation of one section of middle-class life in transition. Mr Nicholas is a retired man living in that part of the south of England that may be called, after its laureate, the Betjeman country, a corner of England that is largely the retiring place of the middle classes. Because he does not work, Mr Nicholas lives in a void that tennis parties and cocktail parties can never wholly fill and that leaves him at the mercy of his excessive, unharnessed energy. But, at the same time as he pursues the conventional social round of a man of his class and position, his wife, servantless, does her own cooking and housework, and though the elder son, an undergraduate, has been to Harrow, the younger is at the local grammar school. The full effect of *Mr Nicholas*, in other words, comes from the precise recording of a process of complex and typical social change mirrored within the confines of a single small family.

When *Hurry on down* appeared it seemed as though John Wain might be the satirist of this period of social change, but though he has written several novels since, he has produced nothing to equal it either in attack or in authority. *Hurry on down* is an exercise in the picaresque. Its hero Charles Lumley—it seems pointless to call him an anti-hero, since the anti-hero is as ancient in fiction as the hero and is indeed the other face of the hero—the possessor of a mediocre degree in history from Oxford and a driving obsession to avoid the phoney in life, becomes in turn a window-cleaner, a driver of motor cars for export, a dope smuggler, a hospital orderly, a chauffeur, a chucker-out in a night club and a gag-writer for radio shows. As he reflects:

> As ever, the serious point had emerged from the machinery of the ludicrous. His life was a dialogue, full of deep and tragic truths, expressed in hoarse shouts by red-nosed music-hall comics.

For Wain in *Hurry on down*, the picaresque is essentially the satiric; and in this novel Wain, in his grim and gritty and tough-minded way, is very funny indeed, with the true churlish, curmudgeonly denigrating attitude towards men and institutions of a Smollett, and something, too, of Smollett's frenetic speed in the building up and capping of comic situations.

Kingsley Amis's *Lucky Jim* is not picaresque or even satire. Its relation to *Hurry on down* is probably much less apparent now than it was when it first appeared, but there are affinities between the novels and between the heroes and their attitudes. Reviewing the book when it was published, I described this common attitude as follows:

A new hero has arisen among us. Is he the intellectual tough, or the tough intellectual? He is consciously, even conscientiously, graceless. His face, when not dead-pan, is set in a snarl of exasperation. He has one skin too few, but his is not the sensitiveness of the young man in earlier twentieth-century fiction: it is to the phoney that his nerve-ends are tremblingly exposed, and at the least suspicion of the phoney he goes tough. He is at odds with his conventional university education, though he comes generally from a famous university: he has seen through the academic racket as he sees through all the others. A racket is phoneyness organized, and in contact with phoneyness he turns red just as litmus paper does in contact with acid. In life he has been among us for some little time. One may speculate whence he derives. The Services, certainly, helped to make him; but George Orwell, Dr Leavis and the Logical Positivists—or, rather, the attitudes these represent—all contributed to his genesis. In fiction I think he first arrived last year, as the central character of Mr John Wain's novel *Hurry on down*. He turns up again in Mr Amis's *Lucky Jim*.

If I had to add to this now I should merely throw in, as a further illustration of attitude, Robert Graves's *Goodbye to All That* and perhaps point out that underlying all the illustrations is a belief in the virtues of English empirical common-sense.

Lucky Jim still seems to me the funniest first novel since *Decline and Fall*. Its immediate success was much more than a literary one. In the popular press Lucky Jim himself was very quickly being used as a readily understandable symbol, while among the young he became a figure to be identified with in much the same way, though admittedly to a less degree, as Holden Caulfield was for the young in the United States. As scores of first novels published in Britain since show, he was an archetypal figure, the hero of a generation in the everlasting battle between the generations.

Jim Dixon is in his first term as an assistant lecturer in history in a provincial university. Everything goes wrong with him; he has the gift of precipitating the most impossible situations, situations that cannot be explained away. On his first appearance in the university, it looks as though he has gratuitously assaulted the Professor of English.

Staying with his own Professor for a weekend, he quarrels with the Professor's son, gets drunk and sets his bed on fire with a forgotten cigarette. When he delivers the popular lecture that may reinstate him in the eyes of the Faculty and save him his job, he finds himself involuntarily parodying the manner first of the Principal and then of his Professor and finally embarks on a wild burlesque of all lectures on his theme, 'Merrie England', ending with a declaration of his own independence.

This may suggest that Dixon is a Chaplin-figure, the *naïf* who, by his very innocence, exposes the sham. He is nothing like it. In his anxious way, he too is playing the racket. If he were less anxious he would play it better. The impossible situations arise from the fact that he cannot quite persuade himself the racket is worth playing—and he has, besides, luck, which is a form of grace.

Lucky Jim strikes one now as very much a young man's novel. It is obviously not a realistic novel in any sense; it is much more the comic expression of a young man's fears of what he may find when he goes out into the relatively unknown world of work and of his sense of inadequacy in the face of that world. It scarcely prepared one for what was to come, for though at the centre of every Amis novel there is a young man recognizably akin to Lucky Jim, the Amis man as he might be called, he has been increasingly explored in depth. The clue to Amis is found, I think, in a passage in his third—and least good—novel, *I Like it Here*, the hero's apostrophe to Henry Fielding:

> Perhaps it was worth dying in your forties if two hundred years later you were the only non-contemporary novelist who could be read with unaffected and wholehearted interest, the only one who never had to be apologized for or excused on the grounds of changing taste. And how enviable to live in the world of his novels, where duty was plain, evil arose from malevolence and a starving wayfarer could be invited indoors without hesitation and without fear. Did that make it a simplified world? Perhaps, but that hardly mattered beside the existence of a moral seriousness that could be made apparent without the aid of evangelical puffing and blowing.

It was precisely the element of moral seriousness that one hadn't spotted in *Lucky Jim* and that is increasingly evident in the later novels. It is a moral seriousness much like Fielding's, especially in the treatment of the relations between the sexes. The Amis hero can be described as Fielding does Tom Jones: 'Though he did not always act rightly, yet he never did otherwise without feeling and suffering for it'; and like Tom Jones's, his life is 'a constant struggle between honour and inclination'. He is often weak and silly, and though he recognizes the higher, he must needs follow the lower—or rather, he would if woman, who is seen as better than man, more grown up, more sensible, more realistic, were not there to rescue him and protect him from himself. This seems to me very much a man's view of the relations between the sexes. Amis sketches it in *That Uncertain Feeling* (1955) and develops it in *Take a Girl Like You* (1960), bringing to it a generosity and chivalry that are again reminiscent of Fielding and suggesting that one day he may produce his equivalent of *Amelia*. Already, the subject he has made his own and his treatment of it make him one of the most interesting and attractive of contemporary novelists.

Amis's has been a straightforward development, Iris Murdoch's anything but that. Her gifts are such that, more than any other novelist of her generation, she seems to have it in her to become a great novelist, but her management of her gifts has been baffling. Her first novel, *Under the Net*, was picaresque set in Soho, and it was reasonable of reviewers, without benefit of hindsight, to link her with Wain and Amis. *The Flight from the Enchanter* (1956) was also picaresque, but containing disconcerting elements developed in her later fiction, in which she emerges as the leading symbolist novelist of the period. Ultimately, one's view of her novels will depend on one's view of the place of symbolism in fiction. My own belief is that symbolism only works when it is integrated into the action, characters and tone of the novel.

Believing this, I am bound to think her best novel is *The Bell* (1958). For me, her other fiction, the later novels especially, consist of dazzling passages set in opacity, at any rate where meaning is concerned, since she is not in the normal sense a difficult writer. *A Severed Head* (1961) will show what I mean. On the surface, it is an attempt at artificial comedy of the sort we associate with Restoration drama, in which the characters change their sexual partners in the manner of a highly formal and intricate dance. But this is not by any means the whole of it; the very presence in the novel of the mysterious, charismatic figure of Honor Klein is enough to show that we are not to take the novel simply as artificial comedy. Miss Murdoch has apparently said that in

A Severed Head she is creating myth, and there are passages of great poetic power that move one intensely even if obscurely, the description of Honor Klein cutting the silk with the Samurai sword, for example. But one is still left at a loss to disengage a meaning that satisfies. Miss Murdoch has denied that the novel is intended as a satire of psycho-analysis. It has been taken by some reviewers as a satire on the rationalistic values of Bloomsbury. It might equally well be taken, in its evocation of the luxury, comfort and connoisseurship attendant on the lives of the cultured upper middle-class, as a satire on the world described by Elizabeth Bowen in *The Death of the Heart*.

The Bell, however, difficult though it is, is something different. The difficulty stems in part from one's uncertainty about Iris Murdoch's intention, but much of it also arises naturally from its complexity, which is rooted largely in the complex motives of the main character, Michael Meade. He is the founder of a religious lay community linked remotely to a convent on the estate, which is the ancestral estate of the Meade family. Generally, the convent and the nuns in it play little part in the action of the novel, though on occasion they intervene decisively; and their presence is felt the whole time. What we observe in the novel is the disruption of Meade's community partly through flaws in his character revealed to himself by the presence of alien elements—intruders—in the community, and partly by the behaviour of the intruders themselves. Meade is as it were a failed priest. He has not become a priest because of his homosexual tendencies. The community is his compensation for his failure, and it is undone, partly at least, by his inability to resist temptation.

It seems clear that the novel is meant to be a dramatization of the nature of the religious life; but when this is said, it must be admitted that a good deal of it remains mysterious. How are we to take, for instance, the raising by Dora and Toby, the intruders, of the ancient convent bell buried in the lake? Then there is the general difficulty inseparable from novels of this kind of deciding what is symbolic and what is not. At the end, we learn that the house and grounds of the community are to be taken into the convent estate: I confess I do not know what conclusions are to be drawn from this.

Yet despite one's doubts and uncertainties, *The Bell* is an impressive and intellectually stimulating novel. The behaviour of the characters may strike one as sometimes arbitrary—though never as arbitrary as in the other novels—but the characters themselves are firmly and sharply there, admirably differentiated, existing in full complexity of motive and rendered with a shrewd, unsentimental charity. And what may be called the minor symbolism, the juxtaposition of character and image that somehow reveals character, is always successful. An example is the incident in which Dora, a young woman who seems to stand for the good-hearted sensual life, sitting in a crowded carriage in a railway train, rescues from the dusty floor under the seat opposite a Red Admiral butterfly. She scoops it up from beneath a man's feet, much embarrassed by what she is doing, and, not wishing to call attention to herself, holds it in her hand and forgets it. Then, when she alights at the station, she opens her hands and the butterfly emerges. 'It circled round them for a moment and then fluttered across the sunlit platform and flew away into the distance. There was a moment's surprised silence.'

The passage astonishes, enchants, liberates and enhances. It tells us, in the simple juxtaposition of Dora and butterfly, more about Dora than any amount of description or psychological analysis could; and what it tells us is something we could learn in no other way. Indeed, whenever I am moved by Iris Murdoch it is as by poetry. In *The Bell*, the poetry is as it were more completely integrated into the prose of fiction than elsewhere in her novels; and the rich, sensuous appreciation of nature, landscape and the seasons which is constant in this book is always in juxtaposition with her characters and so revelatory of them.

Long before he won international fame as the author of the *Alexandria Quartet—Justine* (1956), *Balthazar* (1958), *Mountolive* (1958), *Clea* (1960)—Lawrence Durrell was well known as a poet. In some ways the *Alexandria Quartet* seems a curious work to have been written by an English novelist in the fifties. It is an experimental novel possessing affinities both with Joyce and with Proust. Yet the experimental, technical interest of the work can easily be over-estimated, and I do not think Durrell has helped us with his talk about 'word-continuums' and forms 'based on the relativity proposition. Three sides of space and one of time constitute the soup-mix recipe of a continuum'. In fact, the whole work abounds in descriptions, even prescriptions, of the kind of novel the *Alexandria Quartet* is and, indeed, from one point of view its subject is precisely the writing of a novel. There are no less than three novelists among the characters: Darley, the narrator of the 'space' sections of the works, *Justine*, *Balthazar* and *Clea*, Pursewarden, whose opinions on art seem to be Durrell's own, and Arnauti, a writer dead before the action begins, whose novel about Justine is extensively quoted by Darley.

The simplest description of the work is probably contained in one of Pursewarden's many statements about life and art:

> We live lives based on selected fictions. Our view of reality is conditioned by our position in space and time—not by our personalities, as we like to think. Thus every interpretation is based upon a unique position. Two paces west and the whole picture is changed.

So the second novel, *Balthazar*, is as it were a gloss on the first, *Justine*, in the light of further and disconcerting information on the characters and events related there that has come to Darley from Balthazar, a doctor. The shift in point of view reveals the characters in a new pattern. The third part of the 'continuum' is a straightforward naturalistic novel in which Darley appears merely as a minor character; but it throws still further light on the characters of the work and arranges them in yet another pattern; as does the fourth, *Clea*, of which Darley is again the narrator.

A simple instance will show how it works—the suicide of Pursewarden. In *Balthazar* it is essentially mysterious. In *Mountolive* it appears as the resolution of intolerable conflict between his personal affection for Nassim, Justine's husband, the Coptic millionaire who is suddenly discovered to be leading a conspiracy against British power in the Near East, and his duty as a Foreign Office official. Then in *Clea* it is revealed that it is the consequence of his incestuous relation with his blind sister Liza, who is now in love with Mountolive, the British Ambassador in Cairo.

The four novels, then, may be seen as a series of partial pictures which come together as a complete canvas only when all four are held in the mind as it were simultaneously. In this respect it seems to me that the *Alexandria Quartet* does not differ radically from Joyce Cary's *Herself Surprised–The Horse's Mouth–To Be a Pilgrim* triptych, to which Pursewarden's notion, 'We live lives based on selected fictions', is not by any means foreign, and where, again, to see the action as a whole we have to hold all three novels in mind simultaneously. Nor, for that matter, are we so very remote from C. P. Snow's *Strangers and Brothers*, where there are, so to speak, simultaneous actions proceeding in the various parts of the sequence.

Yet there is obviously a fundamental difference between these works and Durrell's. It lies, I think, in this, that Cary's and Snow's refer to life outside their novels, to 'real life', whereas for Durrell life exists only in order to be transformed into art and has significance only when the transformation has been wrought. The ostensible subject of the *Alexandria Quartet* is love: the true subject is art, and one particular theory of art at that, the Symbolist. It is here that the real resemblance to Joyce and Proust occurs.

It is the penalty of Durrell's ambition that these names must be invoked when his work is discussed; it is his misfortune that he cannot stand comparison with them. There are minor faults which are often, one feels, the consequence of too rapid writing and of inadequate revision, lapses into an easy, florid romanticism, the exotic in Technicolor, as in this sentence from *Clea*, which seems to me the weakest section of the work in this respect: 'This Grecian world was already being invaded by the odours of the forgotten city—promontories where the sweating sea-captains had boozed and eaten until their intestines cracked, had drained their bodies, like kegs, of every lust, foundering in the embrace of black slaves with spaniels' eyes.' But the fundamental weakness seems to be intimately connected with its main source of strength, which is its loving evocation of Alexandria. This is superb: we are brought face to face with the living mystery of a specific place; and the characters are steeped through and through with the atmosphere and being of the fabulous city of many races and religions, with all its attributes of beauty, antiquity, decadence and perversity.

The effect of this, however, is very severely to limit the characters. They possess only Alexandrian attributes; they are inhabitants of a fairyland that seems, the more one examines it, the less related to life as commonly experienced anywhere in the world, irrespective of geography, religion or race. Darley, the narrator of the 'space' parts of the work, the young English novelist and language-teacher, has simultaneous affairs with Melissa and Justine and seems on occasion to live on the prostitution of the one and the bounty of the other. This strikes neither him nor any of the other characters of the novel as out of the ordinary. We are in a world so far outside morality as not even to make it possible to apply the word 'amoral' to it. Now to say this is not to be unduly puritanical; it is merely to point out that a very large part of our interest in men and women and in the literature about them, which is concerned with conduct and behaviour, with moral choices and discrimination, has no place in the *Alexandria Quartet*, and its characters are diminished thereby.

I like very much Professor Karl's comment in his *The Contemporary English Novel*: 'As an adherent to the ideas of Georg Groddeck, perhaps Durrell is equating Alexandria to Groddeck's "It": that is, the "It" as a container of all those forces which influence man and make him the mysterious creature he is.' This seems to me perceptive: but all the same, Groddeck's 'It' is not so very different from Freud's Id, the Unconscious, and if we are interpreting the novel in these terms, then comparison with Lawrence in *The Rainbow* and *Women in Love* is forced upon us, and again it is plain that Durrell cannot stand up to the comparison. Set against Ursula and Gudrun Brangwyn, Durrell's women are extraordinarily pale creatures. Justine, seen sometimes as the 'austere mindless primitive Aphrodite', sometimes as Cleopatra, sometimes as 'the girl-friend of the man whose head was presented on a charger', seems to me exactly the sort of romantic conception such invocations suggest; we are indeed with Justine very much in the realm of *fin-de-siècle* decadence. Professor Kermode notes, I think rightly, that the novel to which she gives her name 'has a faintly Huysmans-like atmosphere: neurasthenia, perversion, *femmes fatales*'. I find Clea even more shadowy.

For the most part, the characters exist on the surface only. They suffer from the lack of depth that comes from a lack of ascertainable roots. Pursewarden, for instance, the intellectual centre of the novel, is no more than the disembodied coiner of epigrams familiar in the early novels of Aldous Huxley; and as a motivation for incest, his isolated childhood spent with Liza seems altogether too convenient. It belongs if not to a fairytale world at least to the world of extremely romantic fiction. Much the solidest parts of the work are those describing the life in the desert of Nassim's family, especially Narouz, his younger brother. He is very fine indeed, and in his portrayal of him, particularly of his death, Durrell reaches his highest achievement. Narouz, the uncouth farmer with his whip of hippopotamus hide, is a striking figure of primitive power.

It is not difficult to account for the popularity of the *Alexandria Quartet*. It is full of colour; it is enacted in an exotic fairyland in which everything sensual is possible. And it has many fine things: the whole evocation of Alexandria, the descriptions of the life on Narouz's farm, and the superb scenes of duck-hunting and fish-drives. Even if what most impresses one on a second reading is the extraordinary skill with which Durrell keeps his pot boiling, it must be admired for the very boldness of its conception.

By comparison with Durrell's, the novels of William Golding strike one as strictly contemporary; they are rooted in the anguish and anxiety of their times. They pose many problems. There is the initial paradox expressed by Frank Kermode in his essay on Golding in *Puzzles and Epiphanies*, a sympathetic and persuasive essay, the best on its subject that I know and one impossible not to lean on, even though one is still not persuaded: 'Not since his first, *Lord of the Flies* (1954), has he enjoyed general acclaim; yet the opinion that he is the most important practising novelist in English has, over this period of five or six years, become almost commonplace.' Commonplace, perhaps one ought hastily to add, in English academic circles rather than generally; the unanimity of opinion is not as complete as Kermode suggests. Even so, Golding's reputation is formidable, and, as Kermode indicates, there is an intriguing gap between the initial critical receptions of his books and the critics' second thoughts.

The first thing to be said of Golding's novels is that they are self-contained wholes beneath whose surface action and realism are to be found much wider and, in a sense, cosmic meanings. Kermode notes that Golding has been called 'a writer of fables'—I have called him that myself—and adds Golding's comment on this: 'what I would regard as a tremendous compliment to myself would be if someone would substitute the word "myth" for "fable" . . . I do feel fable as being an invented thing on the surface whereas myth is something which comes out from the roots of things in the ancient sense of being the key to existence, the whole meaning of life, and experience as a whole.' Golding is here making a valid distinction; and all one can say is that his definition of the word 'fable' fits one's own feelings about his novels, whatever his intentions may be.

His first novel, *Lord of the Flies*, seems to me still his most successful. It is equally brilliant as invention and as narration. As Kermode shows —the value of his essay comes almost as much from the conversations he has had with Golding as from his own insights—it is in a way a gloss on R. M. Ballantyne's *The Coral Island*. First published in 1858, *The Coral Island* has been a boys' classic for the best part of a century, even though it may not be much read now. Kermode observes that *The Coral Island* 'could be used as a document in the history of ideas; it belongs inseparably to the period when boys were sent out of Arnoldish schools certified free of Original Sin'. It is indeed a document of British Victorian liberal optimism. In Ballantyne's book, Ralph, Jack and Peterkin are cast away on a desert island where they live busy, 'civilized, and civilizing lives'—the words are Kermode's—reforming the benighted natives, curing them of cannibalism and holding the fort, as it were, against the arrival of the missionaries. *The Coral Island* is a fable about imperialism in its beneficent aspect.

Golding, in *Lord of the Flies*, casts away a plane-load of small boys, English prep-school boys, on his desert island, which, unlike Ballantyne's, is uninhabited. They are, obscurely, casual victims of a nuclear war. Ralph, Jack, and Peterkin, now called Simon, are among them. What Golding shows, after the initial boy-scout and wolf-cub enthusiasm for a world empty of adults, is a degeneration into savagery and bestiality, a lapse into primitive religion dominated by blood and terror. At least one boy has the potentialities of responsible leadership; another, it seems to be Golding's intention, is to be taken as a saint; another, presented partly as a figure of fun, may be equated with the scientist. They are all these to no avail, killed or hunted down by the pack of savage boys under the 'war-lord' Jack. When the boys are finally rescued by a British warship, the officer says to Ralph, the born leader in a different kind of society, 'I should have thought that a pack of British boys . . . would have been able to put up a better show than that'; while 'with filthy body, matted hair, and unwiped nose, Ralph wept for the end of innocence, the darkness of man's heart, and the fall through the air of the true, wise friend called Piggy'.

The brilliance of *Lord of the Flies* can scarcely be exaggerated, and horrific as it is, it cannot be dismissed merely as a horror-comic of high literary merit, as a 'sick' comment on R. M. Ballantyne's nineteenth-century views on the nature of British boyhood. The fact is, its apprehension of evil is such that it touches the nerve of contemporary horror as no English novel of its time has done; it takes us, with the greatest dramatic power and through the most poignant symbolism, into a world of active, proliferating evil which is seen, one feels, as the natural condition of man and which is bound to remind the reader of the vilest manifestations of Nazi regression.

One sees what Golding is doing. He is showing us stripped man, man naked of all the sanctions of custom and civilization, man as he is alone and in his essence, or at any rate as he can be conceived to be in such a condition. But still the mind—mine, at least—boggles. One admires the shock-tactics that force the recognition but still questions their legitimacy, especially when the behaviour of the children is taken, as many of Golding's admirers seem to take it, as paradigmatic of general human behaviour in the absence of restraint. There can be no conceivable parallel at all, as would be plain if Golding had lowered the age-range of his boys from roughly five years old to twelve to, say, from one to seven. Golding's great literary skill enables him to pull off a considerable confidence-trick.

Further light is shown on Golding's view of man in his second novel, *The Inheritors* (1955). Again, it seems to have had its inception in Golding's reaction to an earlier book, in this instance Wells's *The Outline of History*. Golding's subject is the displacement of Neanderthal Man by *Homo sapiens*, but whereas Wells saw Neanderthal as brutish, cannibalistic, the source, perhaps, of the ogre in folk-lore, Golding imagines him as innocent and gentle, who lived in a universe that was essentially religious and was bound to his fellows in a *participation mystique* that made language unnecessary. No match for man the predator, whom we see through Neanderthal's eyes. We see, too, the last survivors of Neanderthal Man as it were corrupted by man's example, by his alcohol and by his attitude towards sex, which is, as witnessed by the not-quite-human creatures whose place he is taking, an act of cruelty rather than of love.

The Inheritors is a remarkable imaginative feat. The task Golding has set himself is the all-but impossible one of showing us Neanderthal Man in his own terms, in a language that is an approximation to his own thoughts, which are almost entirely non-verbal. Golding succeeds, well enough at least to give us a notion of Neanderthal Man that is at once plausible and moving. And through his innocent anthropoids he shows us man as cruel, as evil, as he is inventive. It is as though evil is equated with knowledge, indeed with being human.

Golding's two most recent novels, *Pincher Martin* (1956)—*The Two Deaths of Christopher Martin* in the United States—and *Free Fall* (1959) are, so to speak, individual applications of what in the earlier books are worked out in terms of groups, of generic beings. On a superficial reading, *Pincher Martin* relates a sailor's struggle for survival, as, after his ship has been torpedoed, he scrabbles for existence on an almost bare rock in mid Atlantic. It is all extraordinarily vivid, rendering in precise details the degradation to an animal level, or at least a level at which blind instinctual craving takes over completely. A more careful reading reveals that Martin is dead, drowned, before he is cast up on the rock, and that his sojourn on the rock, in which he lives through his past life, before he is finally reduced to a mass of cringing, beaten flesh, is a sojourn in purgatory. It represents a confrontation with the facts and consequences of his life of selfishness. The hero's very name is significant. All Martins in the Royal Navy are nicknamed 'Pincher' and the slang term 'to pinch' means to steal, to convert to one's own use what is another's. In a note on the novel, Golding has written: 'The greed for life which had been the mainspring of his nature forced him to refuse the selfless act of dying. He continued to exist separately in a world composed of his own murderous nature.'

Pincher Martin is an exceedingly powerful sermon, almost medieval in its author's remorseless insistence on the physical life of sin. In *Free Fall* Golding approaches his theme from another angle. This is a novel in the first person in which a successful painter, Sammy Mountjoy— the name is again emblematic—reviews his life in order to discover the point at which he fell from grace and lost his soul. He has 'mounted joy' to the exclusion of all other considerations, but, unlike Martin, has not wholly lost his moral nature: 'At the moment I was deciding that right and wrong were nominal and relative, I felt I saw the beauty of holiness and tasted evil in my mouth like the taste of vomit.' The two crucial experiences in Sammy's progress towards the recovery of his freedom are his interrogation by a German officer in a prisoner-of-war camp followed by a spell of solitary confinement, in which he has to face himself, and his confrontation in a mental hospital with Beatrice— again the name is significant—the girl he has seduced and abandoned: at sight of him she is reduced to sheer animal terror that manifests itself in micturition.

Powerful as they are, Golding's novels seem to me to have the weakness normal to and perhaps inevitable in allegorical fiction. At the same time, he is a genuinely religious novelist with a vision, based on the concept of original sin, of the horrifying thinness of civilization, of the fragile barriers that lie between man and regression into barbarism and chaos. He uses his great gifts of imagination and narrative to force us to accept, as part of the truth about man and his nature, the realities summed up in our time in the hysterical nastiness of Nazism and concentration camps. These, for many of us, remain the most baffling phenomena of our century, the brutally ugly fact it is impossible to be reconciled to but yet has to be faced. There is, however, a danger here: the acceptance of the evil displayed in the phenomena as being *the* fundamental truth about man. It is, it seems to me, a danger most carefully to be guarded against. I am bound to say that for me the general effect of Golding's novels suggests that he has not done so. The very intransigence of his work compels the protest against it.

WAR AND POST WAR:
AMERICAN

▲▼▲▼▲▼▲▼▲▼▲▼▲▼▲▼▲▼▲▼▲▼▲▼▲▼▲▼▲▼▲▼▲▼▲▼▲▼▲

[1]

IN THE United States, in contrast with what happened in Britain, the second world war let loose a flood of war novels, which was repeated more than ten years later after the Korean War. In memory these novels coalesce into a grey amorphous mass. In his analysis of them in *The Literary Situation* Malcolm Cowley describes their authors in these words:

> War novelists are not sociologists or historians, and neither are they average soldiers. The special training and talent of novelists lead them to express rather special moods. They are usually critical in temper and often they are self-critical to the point of being burdened with feelings of guilt. They are sensitive— about themselves in the beginning; but if they have imagination (and they need it) they learn to be sensitive for others, including the conquered peoples among whom American soldiers were forced to live. In military service many future writers were men of whom their comrades said that they were 'always goofing off by themselves'. They suffered more than others from the enforced promiscuity of Army and shipboard life. Most of them were rebels against discipline when they thought it was illogical —which they usually did—and rebels against the system that divides officers from enlisted men.

Their novels were written in what Gore Vidal, commenting on his own war story, *Williwaw* (1946), called 'the national manner . . . a simple calculated style, a bit simple-minded but useful in telling this sort of story', a style that is essentially a vulgarization of Hemingway.

Nevertheless, from this ruck of war fiction three or four novels stand out sharply and clearly as achievements in their own right, the earliest being *Williwaw* itself, written when Vidal was only nineteen. It seems now only tangentially a war novel, for in essence it is a sea story after

Typhoon and *In Hazard*. Williwaw is the Indian word for a kind of hurricane found among the Aleutian Islands; and the novel describes the successful negotiation of such a hurricane by a small vessel of the Army Transportation Corps, a vessel containing not only its small crew but three passengers, a senior Army officer, a younger officer and a Roman Catholic chaplain. The officers and men of the ship have lived for too long in the close and unnatural proximity forced upon them by war, and the tensions and irritations they endure as a result are vividly suggested. But the heart of the novel is the account of the williwaw, which is very well done indeed.

Vidal calls John Horne Burns's *The Gallery* (1947) the best of the war novels. One of the most interesting pieces of writing on the war produced by an American, its weakness is that it never quite succeeds in becoming a novel. The gallery of the title is the Galleria Umberto in Naples:

> . . . In August, 1944, everyone in Naples sooner or later found his way into this place and became like a picture on the wall of a museum.
>
> The Neapolitans came to the Galleria to watch the Americans, to pity them, and to prey upon them.
>
> The Americans came there to get drunk or to pick up something or to wrestle with the riddle. Everyone was aware of this riddle. It was the riddle of war, of human dignity, of life, of life itself. Some came closer than others to solving it. But all the people in the Galleria were human beings in the middle of a war. They struck attitudes. Some loved. Some tried to love.
>
> But they were all in the Galleria Umberto in August, 1944. They were all in Naples, where something in them got shaken up. They'd never be the same again—either dead or changed somehow. And these people who became living portraits in this Gallery were synecdoches for most of the people anywhere in the world.
>
> Outside the Galleria Umberto is the city of Naples. And Naples is on the bay, in the Tyrrhenian Sea, on the Mediterranean. This sea is a centre of human life and thought. Wonderful and sad things have come out of Italy. And they came back there in August, 1944. For they were dots in a circle that never stops.

That is the epilogue of the novel, and it sums up Burns's intention. *The Gallery* is at once a collection of portraits and the account of an American's discovery of Europe and the Mediterranean. The only unity the novel has is the galleria itself, in which all the characters eventually find themselves. There are nine chief characters in all, Americans and Italians. A chapter is devoted to each, and between chapters there is what Burns calls a 'promenade', an essay or soliloquy in which the author himself reflects upon the war, and upon his progress during its course from Casablanca to Naples. So the book resembles a many-layered sandwich, a sharp study of a character followed by a wedge of personal recollection followed by another character-study, and so on.

It certainly cannot be said that Burns writes in Vidal's 'national manner'. In his book two American traditions come together. Stylistically, Burns is reminiscent of Whitman and Wolfe. He is always in full spate, and one is carried along like a cork on its surface, by his turbulent, breathless, brilliantly coloured prose. And he submits himself to experience with Wolfe's abandon. The experience, however, is Jamesian, the American's submission to Europe; and Europe, or rather Italy, represents for Burns, though not for all his characters, liberty, a freer, more civilized atmosphere than is found in America, particularly in sexual matters. 'I remember', writes Burns in the Seventh Promenade, 'that I came to love the courtesy and the laughter and the simplicity of Italian life. The compliment I pay to most Italians who haven't too much of this world's goods is that they love life and love. I don't know what else there is, after all.' And the background of the novel, giving it its depth and solidity, is this sense of revelation, of a mode of living that exists in the sharpest possible contrast with, and therefore offers the sharpest possible criticism of, the American way of life. In *The Gallery* it is the Americans, their fundamental assumptions and their behaviour, that are found wanting.

The portraits in *The Gallery* vary greatly in merit. Those of the American woman welfare-worker ('Her permanent was always a wreck in Naples. It was hard to retain either her dignity or her crispness in the simple act of walking along Via Roma') and of the middle-aged military censor strike one as being merely smart, lacking in the sympathy that is normally one of Burns's outstanding qualities. The portrait of Momma, the keeper of a pansy bar, is brilliant in the extreme. The chapter 'Queen Penicillin', describing the U.S. Army's forty-eight-hour cure for syphilis, is quite horrible in its realism. The most moving portrait is certainly that of Giulia, the one girl in Naples, it seems, who kept her honour.

Fine achievement as it is, *The Gallery* is a bundle of impressions and character-sketches rather than a coherent whole; and I think that against its generous indignation on behalf of the Italians and its sustained and valuable criticism of American manners must be set a distorting element that runs through it, a too great preoccupation with homosexuality, which makes it difficult to believe that, even in wartime, the 'people who became living portraits in this Gallery were synecdoches for most of the people anywhere in the world'.

The best of these war novels remains Norman Mailer's *The Naked and the Dead* (1948). Despite its faults, it is a formidably impressive work. It belongs to a familiar pattern of American Radicalism and owes much technically to Dos Passos and Farrell. Mailer's own statement of his intentions in the novel seems to me just: 'I intended it to be a parable about the movement of man through history. I tried to explore the outrageous propositions of cause and effect, of effort and recompense, in a sick society. The book finds man corrupted, confused to the point of helplessness, but it also finds there are limits beyond which he cannot be pushed, and it finds that even in his corruption and sickness there are yearnings for a better world.'

The parable is executed remorselessly in terms of flesh and blood, of the capture of the island of Anopopei from the Japanese. The action takes place on two planes. There is the actual fighting of the reconnaissance platoon under Sergeant Croft, which gives us the experience of the combatant soldier, the worm's-eye view of war. Then there is, as it were, the grand strategy of the operation as conceived by General Cummings. Linking these is the upper middle-class liberal Lieutenant Hearn, who will not fall in with Cummings's Fascist beliefs, is humiliated by him, and is killed by the agency of Croft. But irony rules all: the island is captured, and its capture, the result not of Cummings's brilliant planning but of action by the incompetent Major Dalleson, serves no useful purpose. Throughout, we are in the realm of the Absurd, and what prevails in the end is the obstinacy of oppressed men who reach the point when they can be oppressed and pushed no further. The final irony is the way in which the men of the platoon turn. Driven by Croft almost to the summit of Mount Anaka, they blunder into a nest of hornets from whose stings they flee in terror down the mountainside, discarding their weapons and equipment as they go, for they suddenly realize that 'if they threw away enough possessions they would not be able to continue the patrol'.

What the novel conspicuously lacks is the sense of sympathy, of fellow-feeling, except in the most abstract theoretical way. It is very much an intellectual's novel. The eight men of the reconnaissance platoon are obviously intended to present a microcosm of America: a Texan, a Brooklyn Jew, a Chicago Pole, a Boston Irishman, a man from the Middle West, a Swede, a poor white from the Deep South, a Mexican. No doubt they suffer from having to be representative, but beyond this, as their backgrounds and pre-war lives are presented in the inter-chapters Mailer calls 'The Time-Machine', a device deriving from Dos Passos, they suffer from a wearisome similarity of conditioning marked by a complete spiritual impoverishment and by a reduction of experience to sex in its crudest terms. There is not merely not enough variety in their backgrounds, apart from the purely geographical; there is not nearly enough observation of what goes to make up the experience of ordinary people, which is much wider, much more diverse, than anything depicted here. The enlisted men of the platoon seem survivors from the proletarian novel of the thirties, conceived and drawn to a theory.

The characters that dominate the novel are the two men of power, General Cummings and Sergeant Croft, and they do so because they *are* men of power, men who can initiate action, whereas the others, Hearn included, are dumb oxen. Cummings and Croft are also the enemies in the novel, agents of destruction; and significantly both are officers, for though Croft is only a non-commissioned officer his power over the men of his platoon is much more direct than that of the General himself. In a sense, both men are isolated by their power; and it cannot be accidental that they are in many respects the counterparts of each other. Cummings is the intellectually convinced Fascist. 'The only morality of the future', he tells Hearn, 'is a power morality, and a man who cannot find his adjustment to it is doomed. There is one thing about power. It can flow only from the top down. When there are little surges of resistance at the middle levels, it merely calls for more power to be directed downward, to burn it out. . . . You can consider the Army as a preview of the future.' As a delineation of one kind of intellectual, the character of Cummings is masterly. But that of Croft, the natural Fascist, is as fine. He is the hunter and sadist who kills for the thrill of killing. And as with Cummings, war fits naturally into his pattern of life; it is a means of exercising domination and also, as in his fanatical determination to climb Mount Anaka, of measuring himself against natural forces that are the symbolic representations of the forces driving him from within. These two characters, Cummings and Croft, are poetic creations, Promethean if perverted idealists.They partake of myth.

They indicate the grandeur of Mailer's conception in this novel. Its purely sensational qualities are the least important thing about it. What is important is that Mailer has embodied his parable in the flesh and blood of an actual historical situation. The horror and bestiality of war have never been more terrifyingly realized than here; but its merit is that, grounded in war as it is, it is still more than simply a war novel.

It has, I think, been Mailer's misfortune that he found his great subject, the theme that more than any other would provide the material for the summation of his view of the human condition, at the outset of his career. Beside *The Naked and the Dead*, both his later novels, *Barbary Shore* and *The Deer Park*, appear small. Yet for me Mailer remains the most exciting American prose-writer of his generation. There are times when it seems he has ceased to be a novelist and has set himself up to be the voice of what might be called the permanent opposition in America. Essays like 'The White Negro' link him to writers rather younger than himself; and then one turns to the fragment of a novel in progress called *The Time of Her Time*, published in *Advertisements for Myself*, and it seems possible that what he did in fiction with the war in the Pacific he may be on the verge of doing with the war between the sexes.

There are some resemblances, mainly superficial, between *The Naked and the Dead* and James Jones's *From Here to Eternity* (1951). Jones's novel also belongs to the tradition of American Radical dissent. Again, as in Mailer, we have the difference, the almost unbridgeable gap, as between separate species, between officers and men. As an encyclopaedic account of life in the peace-time Army of the United States before Pearl Harbour, *From Here to Eternity* has a certain horrible fascination. Whether it is anything like an accurate account I have no means of knowing, but it must come very high among the most depressing novels ever written, as it is certainly one of the most brutal. Private Robert E. Lee Prewitt, the regular soldier from the coal mines of Harlan County, Kentucky, the boxer who refuses to box for his company, is an attempt at a tragic hero, but at so primitive a level as to be, in my view, almost without interest. I am bound to confess I find the novel almost unreadable, not so much because of what it says as because of the way it is said. Jones's second novel, *Some Came Running* (1957), one of the longest novels ever written, I find completely unreadable.

Gore Vidal has said that with the finishing of *Williwaw* his life as a writer began. It has proved to be rather different from what *Williwaw* might have seemed to indicate. He has made a reputation as a television playwright and has written a number of novels of which *The City and the Pillar* (1948) is typical. It was one of the first novels to bring into the open a subject latent in American fiction from its earliest days— homosexuality. The relationship between man and man, often idealized and never overtly sexual, but involving a virtual exclusion of woman, is a common theme in classic American fiction, so common, indeed, as to argue the existence of a strong homosexual strain, however repressed, in American experience. But the point is, it *was* repressed, and one has the feeling that the tabu on male homosexuality was much more binding, at any rate until very recently, in American society than in English. From Burns's *The Gallery* onwards, however, the open homosexual becomes increasingly frequent in the American novel, figuring, indeed, rather as the Negro and the Jew traditionally appear, as the representative of an unaccepted minority in American society and therefore of what might be called the self-outlawed, the nay-sayers to the notion of conformity that for good historical reasons has always been so compelling in the United States.

The City and the Pillar is a defiantly frank novel. Vidal's hero Jim Willard, drifting from place to place across America, from Hollywood to New York by way of Texas, and from homosexual encounter to homosexual encounter, is buoyed up throughout by the memory of his adolescent love for his friend Bod Ford. Heterosexual love is seen as 'devouring', again a common view of it in American fiction, where, as in *From Here to Eternity*, women appear as predatory enemies the price of whose love is the emasculation of the male. In fact, Vidal is unable to show that homosexual love is any more satisfactory, and the novel ends with Willard, having rediscovered his boyhood friend, murdering him because he has grown up normally into heterosexuality.

The fundamental criticism of Vidal's novel is that made by John W. Aldridge in *After the Lost Generation*: 'There is no vitality or significance in the view of life which has gone into it. It seems to have evolved out of an absolute spiritual nothingness in which all things suffer from the same poverty of content and in which the vitally important and the cheaply trivial are viewed alike.' This seems to me also true of the novels of Paul Bowles. If the word 'Gothic' still has any meaning when applied to fiction then Bowles's—*The Sheltering Sky* (1949), *Let it Come Down* (1952), *The Spider's House* (1955)—are Gothic novels and as such are related to horror comics. In a sense, they are indeed highbrow horror comics, and the isolation of the horrific or the beastly or the vilely incongruous is an essential part of Bowles's method. An example out of many from *The Sheltering Sky*. Kit Moresby is deserting her husband, who is dying of typhoid:

> Softly she laid her cheek on the pillow and stroked his hair. No tears flowed; it was a silent leave-taking. A strangely intense buzzing in front of her made her open her eyes. She watched fascinated while two flies made their brief, frantic love on his lower lip.

As a Gothic novelist, Bowles is a modern version of Poe. Like Poe's, his theme is the disintegration of the psyche; and his novels are works of symbolism in which the world described is really the interior world of his characters. It is projected with great brilliance: in his ability to suggest tropical heat and squalor, the seediness of the exotic, Bowles is not surpassed by Graham Greene. Bowles's scene is North Africa, and his first novel, *The Sheltering Sky*, may be taken as typical of his work. The central characters are Port and Kit Moresby, husband and wife, rich American expatriates, each bearing a burden of undefined guilt. Port is a man who, 'in order to avoid having to deal with relative values', had 'long since come to deny all purpose to the phenomena of existence—it was more expedient and comforting'. He is a man whose soul only 'silences and emptinesses' can touch; his soul aspires to the blankness of the desert and of the cloudless African sky. His attempts to make some sort of living contact with his wife are fumbling and abortive, tentative gestures only; and Kit's life is ruled by omens that she cannot decipher. Their wanderings in the interior of Algeria are described in every vivid detail of physical discomfort and dirt. Port dies meaninglessly of typhoid at a French military post ('His cry went on through the final image: the spots of raw bright blood on the earth. Blood on excrement. The supreme moment, high above the desert, when the two elements, blood and excrement, long kept apart, merge. A black star appears, a point of darkness in the night sky's clarity. Point of darkness and gateway to repose. Reach out, pierce the fine fabric of the sheltering sky, take repose.'), and Kit disappears alone into the desert to bum a lift on a camel caravan into the interior. She is raped repeatedly by the two Arabs whose caravan it is, and with one of them, who instals her in his harem, she sinks into a state of frantic sensual bliss and craving, a mindless abandonment to sexual subjugation, from which she escapes only to return to Algiers little better than an imbecile.

In these novels Bowles expresses the ultimate horror of nothingness. Yet, though the books affect one while reading almost as a series of physical assaults, one is scarcely moved by them, because Bowles scarcely tries to persuade us that his characters have value as human beings.

Truman Capote's novels may also be called Gothic, but here the Gothic has been turned all to favour and to prettiness. The nightmare has become the fairy-tale, which could be considered the censored form of nightmare. Any account of Capote's work is bound to appear depreciatory. He is in fact a delightful and highly original artist who does almost perfectly what he sets out to do, and, as one reads, the spell he exercises is irresistible. Admittedly, one's pleasure is in the surface of his exquisitely iridescent prose, in the subtlety and nuances of his rhythms and the wit and humour of his observation of detail. Analysis of content may appear to be as brutal as the bursting of a soap bubble; yet there is a very firm structure to his novels, as is shown in Aldridge's twenty-page dissection of *Other Voices, Other Rooms* in *After the Lost Generation*. It is very well done, yet its effect, as Malcolm Cowley has said, is to give one a new and more favourable impression of Capote's talent.

For the most part, Capote's fiction presents a self-contained world which refers to nothing outside itself, a world comparable in its magic and the fascination it exercises to those toy globes in which a twist of the hand produces a snowstorm swirling round an Alpine chalet. The comparison indicates the limitations of the novels: it is a toy world that is described; but all the same, the toys have a mysterious appeal to the imagination, and this also Capote's novels reproduce. The properties that Capote draws upon in the construction of his toy world are, of course, anything but Alpine: they are the familiar ingredients of the Deep South as found in Faulkner—decayed mansions, decayed families, degeneracy set in a landscape of swamps, forests and small isolated townships. This world, which has the fairy-tale illusion of existing outside time, is created in great detail; but it is not sinister, as in Faulkner. Or rather, it becomes sinister only when the dream—for dream is what it is—is analysed.

Other Voices, Other Rooms (1948) is the story of the journey of the boy Joel Knox from New Orleans to the sequestered town of Noon City to find his father at Skully's Landing. In the mysterious house there, which is sinking slowly into the swamp beneath it, he finds his father, helplessly paralysed, able to make his wants known only by jerking red tennis balls down the stairs. Joel repudiates him and turns, instead, to his cousin Randolph, a failed painter who is homosexual and a transvestite. Joel's attempt to break out into the adult world of normal relations fails because he is in a sense let down by his partner, Idabel Thompkins, whose tomboyishness is the counterpart of his own girlishness. At the end of the novel he seems committed to a homosexual existence with Randolph.

But this conveys nothing of the novel's essence and its ambience. It is clumsily to rationalize a poetic description of regression which is evoked in terms of mystery and ambiguity, as though the action were being seen through a medium like twilight or sea-water. For all its vividness, everything is ghostly and remote, invoking the nostalgia of a twilight kingdom. The style is everything:

> The gentle jog of John Brown's trot set ajar the brittle woods; sycamores released their spice-brown leaves in a ruin of October: like veins dappled trails veered through storms of showering yellow; perched on dying towers of jack-in-the-pulpit cranberry beetles sang of their approach, and tree-toads, no bigger than dewdrops, skipped and shrilled, relaying the news through the light that was dusk all day. They followed the remnants of a road down which once had spun the wheels of lacquered carriages carrying verbena-scented ladies who twittered like linnets in the shade of parasols, and leathery cotton-rich gentlemen gruffing at each other through a violet haze of Havana smoke, and their children, prim little girls with mint crushed in their handkerchiefs, and boys with mean blackberry eyes, little boys who sent their sisters screaming with tales of roaring tigers. Gusts of autumn, exhaling through the inheriting weeds, grieved for the cruel velvet children and their virile bearded fathers: Was, said the weeds, Gone, said the sky, Dead, said the woods, but the full laments of history were left to the Whip-poor-will.

Capote's is a world of freaks, reminiscent of Carson McCullers's. The difference is that Carson McCullers's novels have an immediate reference to the world outside them, the 'real world' of universal experience. Not that Capote's work does not show a crabwise progress in the direction of that 'real world'. In *The Grass Harp* (1951), though the central characters are as freakish as those of *Other Voices, Other Rooms* and as childish, whatever their physical maturity, and though the central situation is as bizarre, yet there is a direct reference to the external adult world in that the novel is presented as a grown-up's memories of an episode of his childhood. There is even a moral: 'A leaf, a handful of seed—begin with these, learn a little what it is to love', an explicit avowal that the world is a bad place, that 'no matter what passions compose them, all private worlds are good' and that the values of childhood are better than those of maturity. These conclusions do not seem to me contradicted by *Breakfast at Tiffany's* (1958), even though Capote seems to have broken out of his narcissistic universe into the strictly contemporary scene of Manhattan and even though his heroine, Holly Golightly, is very much a picaresque heroine. Her surname is plainly symbolic: she goes lightly through life; and for all her experience—married at fourteen, a Southern child-bride—she is still a child, with a child's values and a child's impossible dream of freedom. She has her affinities with Isherwood's Sally Bowles; and again comparison sets off Capote's limits and limitations. For the significance of Sally Bowles in Isherwood's story lies in the context in which she had her being—Berlin at the beginning of the Nazis' rise to power; she is symptomatic; and the power of the story comes from the tension Isherwood establishes between her and her background. There is nothing comparable to this in *Breakfast at Tiffany's*.

In Capote's fiction several strands in the contemporary American novel come together: the notion of the novel as a self-contained whole, which stems from James but in the twenties, through the practice of Joyce, became linked with the theory of symbolist poetry; the continuing preoccupation with the myth of the South; and the preoccupation with childhood as a state beyond which lie anticlimax and degeneration, with the child as the modern counterpart of the noble savage.

One version of the self-contained novel is Frederick Buechner's *A Long Day's Dying* (1949). It is based on the Philomela myth, but reference to Bulfinch will not throw much light on the novel, for the myth, shadowy as it is in the context, is presented in an extremely contorted form. The purpose of myth as the basis of a novel or a poem, as in *Ulysses* and *The Waste Land*, is, of course, to universalize and epitomize, to bring past and present together, to give the characters of the action, as Malcolm Cowley puts it, 'a sort of retrospective magnitude'. But, as he goes on to say of Buechner's novel, it may emphasize 'their smallness instead . . . as if the ancient story of lust and revenge were being re-enacted in a doll's house'.

The plot is as follows. Elizabeth Poor, a wealthy widow, visits the university where her son Leander is a student in order to hear a lecture by George Motley, a novelist who is in love with her. She meets Leander's friend, Steitler, an English instructor, and goes to bed with him. Motley guesses what has happened and reports his suspicions to Tristram Bone, an enormously fat, sad man who is also in love with her. After vast hesitations Bone reports his and Motley's suspicions to Elizabeth, who denies the charge and accuses Steitler of having homosexual relations with Leander. Her lie is obvious, but she is saved from its further consequences by the death of her mother, Maroo, who rushes up from the South to help her. But all the relationships between the characters have been broken, relationships of love, friendship and respect, the whole being symbolized by the suicide of Bone's pet monkey and as it were shadow image of himself, who cuts his throat in a parody of his master's gesture.

The style of the novel is highly mannered, charged in every sentence with ambiguities and ironies to produce the appearance of significance; as in the first paragraph:

> The mirror reflected what seemed at first a priest. A white robe, which fell from his thick shoulders in crescent folds, circumscribed with diminishing accuracy the ponderous art of his great head, and gave to his obesity the suggestion of vulnerability rather than strength as he sat face to face with the fact of himself. This effect was intensified by the resignation with which he suffered what might have been his acolyte, also dressed in white, either to anoint his flourishing, grey-brown hair as if in preparation for some imminent solemnity or to give it a tonsure.

Tristram Bone is at the barber's, having his hair cut. Admittedly, the passage establishes Bone's priestly presence, which broods over the novel. The style, as Ihab Hassan observes, 'attempts to mythicize Tristram by establishing connections between the sacred and profane, the priestly and lay qualities of existence'. But the connections seem to me stylistic only. The action narrated and the myth on which it is based neither mirror nor illuminate each other; and the moral intention of the book is rendered in terms so shadowy and bizarre as to make it impossible for it to be taken seriously. Indeed, the novel is at best where it is at its most fantastic, as in the suicide of the monkey, the grotesque pathos of which touches the nerve of horror and outrage as nothing else in the novel.

Bigger in every way is William Styron's *Lie down in Darkness* (1951), which exploits both the self-contained form and the preoccupation with the South. One of the major novels of the decade, it is saturated in the sense of actuality; witness the scenes at the university football game and in the fraternity house before it and the account of Peyton's wedding. But, beyond this, it is an attempt at what might be called Freudian tragedy made very nearly successful by the power of the poetry—descriptive, lyrical, elegiac—that clothes it; and it is also a formal achievement on a high plane of intention.

In this novel time flows on two levels. In actual clock-time, the action describes the progress of the hearse containing Peyton Loftis's corpse from its arrival at Port Warwick, in the Tidewater country of Virginia, to its destination at the cemetery. The progress is brilliantly rendered and often macabrely comic; but during it Styron reaches down and recreates whole stretches of time of much greater sweep, indeed, the lives of the principal characters, Peyton and her father and mother, Milton and Helen, and the recurring conflicts between them.

Styron's tragedy is Meredithean:

> In tragic life, God wot,
> No villain need be! Passions spin the plot:
> We are betrayed by what is false within.

As Milton reflects at the terrible, farcical wedding breakfast of his daughter:

> Not anything he had done or failed to do had made them hate each other. Not even Dolly. None of his actions, whether right or wrong, had caused this tragedy, so much as the pure fact of himself, his very existence, interposed weaponless and defenceless in a no-man's-land between two desperate, warring female machines. Now he had kissed Peyton, said the wrong words, and he had somehow hurt her. And the smile she wore concealed her

hurt—to everyone else, at least—just as Helen's smile, echoing Peyton's, concealed only the wild, envenomed jealousy which stirred in her breast. What had she done? Why had Helen deceived him like this? Those smiles. He was chilled with a sudden horror. Those smiles. They had fluttered across the web of his life like deceptive, lovely butterflies, always leading him on, always making him believe that, in spite of everything, these two women really did love each other. That, deep down, there was motherly, daughterly, affection. But no. Now he saw the smiles in a split second for what they were: women smiles— Great God, so treacherous, so false, displayed here—himself between them—like the hateful wings of bats.

There is no blame in Styron's novel. This is a tragedy of love, which, however contorted or perverted, is still love. One might say that the tragic situation arises from the incompatibility, the inability to achieve an adequate sexual relation, between Milton and Helen, but that is itself the consequence of their ancestors and their upbringing. And no matter how desperate their estrangement from each other, they still— Milton drunk and with Dolly, Helen in her wildest hysteria—strive as best they can to reach each other. There is always something between them. Alone, they may be lost, but they know that without the other they are doubly lost. They are, one can only think, distorted from the start. Helen's idea of love is utterly possessive, that of mother for helpless child, and no more; and it finds satisfaction in her love for her helpless crippled daughter Maudie. It is the perverted nature of this love that drives Milton into his latently incestuous relation with Peyton. The recognition of this drives Helen into her almost insane jealousy of Peyton. And it is Peyton's participation in this incestuous relation which leads to the failure of her marriage, her promiscuity, her compulsive drinking, which mirrors Milton's and which is at once a consequence and symbol of their relationship, and in the end her suicide.

The tragic plot is worked out with passion, pity and eloquence. Yet, impressive as it is, in the end one has one's reservations. They centre in the character of Milton Loftis, dipsomaniac, failed lawyer, failed husband, failed father—one might, recognizing his aspirations and self-knowledge, say failed good man. His aspirations we never lose sight of, as we never lose sight of his sufferings and his misery: the account of his behaviour at the fraternity house and the university football game is a terrifying revelation of anguish and degradation. He is pitiful. But he is never more than this. He never achieves the stature of the tragic figure, as the Consul does in Lowry's *Under the Volcano*. Or rather, he achieves it only if we read more into the narrative than is, I think, actually there.

This brings us to the Southern element in Styron's novel. The novel seems to be presented as the rendering of a situation that is specifically of the South, and Milton seems to be meant as in some way a representation of, so to say, the Southern man. There is an interesting comment on this in the novel itself, when the homosexual Berger says to Peyton at a party in New York: 'It is symptomatic of that society from which you emanate that it should produce the dissolving family: *ah, ah*, patience, my pretty, I know you say symptomatic not of that society, but of *our* society, the machine culture, yet so archetypal is this South with its cancerous religiosity, its exhausting need to put manners before morals, to negate all *ethos*—Call it a *husk* of a culture!' This surely suggests the Southern experience as being archetypal of American experience generally. Yet the Southern element in *Lie down in Darkness*, apart from its function as a setting of the action, seems scarcely made relevant, no more than stage properties that can be disposed of and rearranged more or less at will. The decayed gentleman who is Milton's father reminds me of literature: we have met him, with his orotund platitudinous wisdom, his rhetorical invocations of former glory, many times before, in Faulkner and in Tate. He is certainly not made new here. Neither are Styron's Negroes, who, as so often, serve as a kind of chorus to the action. They are very well done, and the description of the revival, with its mass baptisms, which ends the book is brilliant. Its symbolic function is obvious; but it all seems a little too pat, in some way a little too inflated, as though Styron is writing to a formula of Southern fiction. It is difficult not to think that the interpretation of the South in fiction is in great danger of becoming utterly conventional, a constant rearrangement of certain traditional and picturesque properties with fixed attributes. Looking at the work of lesser novelists than Styron—William Humphrey, Davis Grubb and Mary Lee Settle—one realizes it is now possible to talk of 'Southerns' as we talk of Westerns, and for similar reasons. If, as Flannery O'Connor has complained, most Southern writers are considered by the world outside 'to be unhappy combinations of Poe and Erskine Caldwell', they have, largely, only themselves to blame.

But that a new treatment of the South is possible in fiction Flannery
O'Connor herself demonstrates. She approaches the religious primitivism of the South, traditionally Protestant, from the standpoint of a
Roman Catholic, and her theme, if I understand it right, is the spiritual
distortions that are the consequence of Protestant primitivism. Her
characters are grotesque precisely because they are spiritually primitive
and afflicted both in mind and body. Their lives are like nightmares
that are both brutal and farcical, and this is because they are God-
intoxicated, one might say doomed to God. God is the sole reality in
their lives, and this is so even when they repudiate Him. In *Wise Blood*
(1952) Hazel Motes, descendant of a line of Fundamentalist preachers,
becomes, as a result of his war experiences, the founder of a new
religion:

> '. . . I preach the Church without Christ. I'm member and
> preacher to that church where the blind don't see and the lame
> don't walk and what's dead stays that way. Ask me about that
> church and I'll tell you it's the church that the blood of Jesus
> don't foul with redemption . . . Listen, you people, I'm going to
> take the truth with me wherever I go . . . I'm going to preach it to
> whoever'll listen at whatever place. I'm going to preach there was
> no Fall because there was nothing to fall from and no Redemp-
> tion because there was no Fall and no Judgement because there
> wasn't the first two. Nothing matters but that Jesus was a liar.'

An anti-saint, as it were, in the end he wears barbed wire next to the
skin and blinds himself with quicklime for anti-Jesus' sake. Flannery
O'Connor has said of her own work: 'It is literal in the same sense that
a child's drawing is literal. When a child draws he doesn't try to be
grotesque but to set down exactly what he sees, and as his gaze is
direct, he sees the lines that create motion. I am interested in the lines
that create spiritual motion.' And this is what she does in this raw,
extraordinarily powerful, savagely comic novel of spiritual emptiness
through which the God-intoxicated Hazel moves.

In *The Violent Bear It Away* the world outside the God-intoxicated
hardly exists at all, is almost without relevance to them. The novel
begins with the death of Francis Marion Tarwater's great-uncle on his
patch of ground in a forest almost entirely cut off from civilization.
Tarwater is a boy of fourteen:

> The old man, who said he was a prophet, had raised the boy
> to expect the Lord's call himself and to be prepared for the day

he would hear it. He had schooled him in the evils that befall prophets; in those that come from the world, which are trifling, and those that come from the Lord and burn the prophet clean; for he himself had been burned clean and burned clean again. He had learned by fire.

The boy rebels against the doom the old man has placed upon him and in a spirit of inquiry seeks out his cousin, a schoolteacher and an angry atheist, in the neighbouring town. Rayber, who has himself as a boy been under the old man's thrall and believes his life to have been ruined in consequence, welcomes Tarwater almost as a lost son. But the boy is suspicious and will not commit himself. The novel is a confrontation between religion and scepticism, though both in a non-intellectual sense, as ways of life; and it becomes apparent that Rayber, for all his furious repudiations of the old prophet, is as much his child as Tarwater is. In the end Tarwater goes back to the patch of cultivated land in the forest and hears his call: 'Go warn the children of God of the terrible speed of Mercy.' He takes up his burden and leaves: 'His singed eyes, black in their deep sockets, seemed already to envision the fate that awaited him but he moved steadily on, his face set toward the dark city, where the children of God lay sleeping.'

The circumstances of his environment and upbringing, to say nothing of his creator's original vision, set Tarwater apart as a special case. He is his great-uncle born again, and though he is a boy he is not to be confused with the child as Noble Savage, the human being uncorrupted by society. He has no kinship with Huckleberry Finn, in whose being the child as Noble Savage first makes his appearance in American fiction. Similarly, he has no kinship with Salinger's Holden Caulfield. Like *Huckleberry Finn*, *The Catcher in the Rye* (1951) has a significance that goes beyond literature. In some very important respects, it is *the* American novel of its generation, for in Holden Caulfield Salinger has created a myth-figure with which millions of young and youngish Americans have identified themselves.

As an accomplishment, its brilliance cannot be questioned. In Holden's monologue, for that is what the novel is, Salinger has created the dialect of a generation; it is a triumph of a special kind of vernacular writing, which has its roots partly in Ring Lardner's stories, partly in high-school and hipster slang. Its enormous success and the nature of that success already make it difficult for the critic to see the book clearly; and the difficulty has been increased by the problems raised by

Salinger's later work, the stories—'Franny', 'Zooey', 'Raise High the Roof Beam, Carpenter'—which, with others, compose the fragmentary saga of the Glass family. It is no longer possible to take it simply as a piece of naturalism, as the presentation, without comment, of an individual case. It contains—or seems, in the light of the Glass stories, to contain—a view of life that has to be scrutinized, however gladly one salutes Salinger's remarkable feat in getting inside the skin and the mind of a boy in early adolescence.

Like *Huckleberry Finn*, *The Catcher in the Rye* is a picaresque novel about initiation into manhood. But though Twain's—or Huck's—attitude towards initiation is ambiguous, at least Huck intervenes in the activities of the adult world and makes deliberate moral choices, for all that at the end he seems to repudiate the adult world. In *The Catcher*, however, the attitude towards initiation is not even ambiguous. It is rejected, for the novel ends with Holden's fugue into illness, though I suppose it could be maintained that Holden's actual writing of his book, under, one assumes, the influence of psychoanalytical treatment, represents a kind of facing of reality.

So, though *The Catcher* is extremely funny, it is also extremely sad, and it is difficult not to agree with Frank Kermode when he says that it has 'a built-in death wish'. Holden is fixated on memories of his dead younger brother and on his kid sister Phoebe, fixated on the notion of innocence, against which seems to be set the idea of sex as a dirty, sordid thing. Psychoanalytically, this seems to be implied in Holden's fantasy from which the novel gets its title.

The difficulty of assessing *The Catcher* can be put in another way, as Ihab Hassan does very well in *Radical Innocence*: 'The partial blindness of Holden, which has been correctly attributed to Holden's juvenile impatience with the reality of compromise, is made more serious by Salinger's failure to modify Holden's point of view by any other. In *Joseph Andrews*, for instance, the innocence of Adams is constantly criticized by the tone of the book and the nature of its comic incidents.' It is for the lack of such a check in the novel itself that one turns to Salinger's later work, and in its light it seems clear that Holden's sentimentality is Salinger's. *The Catcher* is as it were the negative counterpart of what in my view is the woozy religiosity of the Glass stories, a religiosity which strikingly manages to get the best of both worlds, God's and Mammon's.

As a self-portrait of a neurotic adolescent who flunks out of his prep school, runs off to New York where he spends a lost weekend in hotels, nightclubs, theatres and museums, fails to sleep with a prostitute and is beaten up by her ponce, wanders round Central Park, meets his kid sister and finds himself the objective of tentative homosexual advances from one of the few adults for whom he has any respect, *The Catcher in the Rye* can scarcely be faulted. But it doesn't seem possible to take it simply as this. Yet if it is more, we need to know more. We need to know more, for example, about Holden's parents, who are scarcely in the book at all. What are fascinating, of course, are Holden's moral judgments. While his kid sister Phoebe's accusation that he dislikes everything is not in fact true, it is true that the world in which he lives is populated to an overwhelming degree by phoney creeps. The whole adult world as he encounters it, except for the two nuns —and nuns are obviously not *of* the world—is phoney. Success is always phoney, and, as much as Hemingway, a writer he does not approve of, Holden is nauseated by the great abstractions. He is nauseated, indeed, by all those features of American society that make up the publicly approved face of America. Unluckier than Huck Finn, he has no Territory he can light out for: his only escape is into illness.

There are, it seems to me, two ways in which one can see Holden as Salinger presents him. One is that indicated by Kermode, who describes him as a hero 'in some ways inferior, and in others superior, to the reader'. The effect, Kermode adds, 'is comfortably compassionate'. This, I suspect, is how less-than-young readers of Salinger accept him: with the sentimental nostalgia of those who have acquired, have had forced upon them, tolerance and that ambiguous quality, a sense of humour. They can afford to be tolerant of Holden: if he grows up he too will acquire a sense of humour. Meanwhile, he is at once cute and reminiscent of their nobler, i.e. their earlier, less life-stained selves.

I doubt whether young readers see Holden in this way. I suspect there is a passionate identification with him, however temporary it may be, and particularly with him as the repudiator of the adult world and American values, which is tantamount to saying Western values in their secular aspect. And in this repudiation Salinger, through Holden Caulfield, links up with the beats and the hipsters. If one wished to be unkind, one might call Salinger the *New Yorker* version of the beats. Not that one would care to press the comparison between Salinger and the Beat novelists far in literary terms: Salinger is a

writer of great accomplishment, whereas Kerouac and the rest belong
to sociology rather than to literature. As such, they have their interest,
but the best of Jack Kerouac's *On the Road* (1957) is what is most
reminiscent of Whitman, the evocation of America as the cars tear
across the continent: "'It's an anywhere road for anybody anyhow.'"
But it is very much sub-Whitman: Dean Moriarty's behaviour springs
from a 'wild yea-saying overburst of American joy'; and it strikes one
as curiously innocent and naïve:

> 'The Bodhisattva women of Tibet and parts of ancient India,'
> said Japhy, 'were taken and used as holy concubines in temples
> and sometimes in ritual caves and would get to lay up a stock of
> merit and they meditated too. All of them, men and women,
> they'd meditate, fast, have balls like this, go back to eating,
> drinking, talking, hike around, live in viharas in the rainy season
> and outdoors in the dry, there was no question of what to do
> about sex which is what I always liked about Oriental religion.
> And what I always dug about the Indians in our country ... You
> know when I was a little kid in Oregon I didn't feel that I was an
> American at all, with all that suburban ideal and sex repression
> and general dreary newspaper grey censorship of all our real
> human values but when I discovered Buddhism and all I suddenly
> felt that I had lived in a previous lifetime innumerable ages ago
> and now because of faults and sins in that lifetime I was being
> degraded to a grievous domain of existence and my karma was to
> be born in America where nobody has any fun or believes in
> anything, especially freedom. That's why I was always sym-
> pathetic to freedom movements, too, like anarchism in the
> Northwest, the old-time heroes of Everett Massacre and all. ...' It
> ended up with long earnest discussions about all these subjects
> and finally Princess got dressed and went home with Japhy on
> their bicycles and Alvah and I sat facing each other in the dim red
> light.

This, from *The Dharma Bums* (1958), might be Huck Finn relating
a romantic notion newly propounded by Tom Sawyer. I think it
would not be difficult to see the beliefs of the Beats as the latest re-
hearsal of certain traditional American minority ideas, among them
some associated with Emerson and Thoreau as well with Whitman.
They have been better expressed before. But one's real complaint is
that, up till now, they have been expressed by the Beats in the most
superficial terms and the implications of them hardly examined. An

adequate expression would mean that these writers would be in competition not only with Whitman but with Dostoevsky; but of this the Beat writers themselves seem to have no inkling.

[3]

ONE ASPECT of contemporary American society from which both Holden Caulfield and the Beats flee in disgust is that presented in the novels of Edward Newhouse and Louis Auchincloss. Both deal with the very rich, the long-established 'responsible' rich who make up the American equivalent of the British aristocracy. Both are highly accomplished, eminently civilized craftsmen. Their subject and manner taken together no doubt account for the regularity with which reviewers in the presence of their novels murmur 'James' or 'Edith Wharton'. Attractive writers though they are, this is very much to overpraise. Auchincloss, it seems to me, has much more bite in his short stories than in his novels, of which *Venus in Sparta* (1958) may be taken as typical. Here his world is that of New York bankers who commute by seaplane between Wall Street and Long Island, his theme the man in the impossible situation, 'holder of one position, wrong for years'. At forty-five vice-president of the Hudson Trust Company, Michael Farish discovers more or less simultaneously that his wife is unfaithful to him, his son a nasty little Jew- and Negro-baiter, and that a professional error, made many years before, which could be construed as a piece of sharp practice, may lose him his reputation as a banker. Throughout his life Farish has been the complete conformist, the smooth fixer. With his career in ruins about him, he realizes that throughout his life he has believed in nothing, and, having seduced his ex-step-daughter, he drowns himself.

Auchincloss shows us, once again, American success turned sour in the American belly. Despite the elegance of his style, he does not seem to me to have anything new to say about it. He relies overmuch on his ability, which is great, to describe a social milieu. The milieu is so immediately convincing that one is almost persuaded that the characters within it are no less convincing. In fact, when Farish is abstracted from his setting all that remains is a pretty tenuous case-history. But successful characters in fiction are much more than their case-histories; which is why, with all his obvious talent, it is nonsense to talk about him in the same breath as James and Edith Wharton. He is a glossier O'Hara—and not the O'Hara of *Appointment in Samarra*.

Newhouse's theme in *The Temptation of Roger Heriott* (1955) is the responsibility of the responsible rich man. The temptations that assail the hero, who is secretary of a foundation in New York that awards scholarships to promising violinists, do not strike one as particularly perilous. The novel becomes a hymn of praise of the domestic life and the domestic virtues, but as this novel reveals quite uncritically, they merge at one end of their range into the world of Gracious Living, the world of the Wouks and the Sloan Wilsons and Richard Powells, the sagas of American middle-class life.

Fitzgerald's remark, 'The very rich are different from you and me', has echoed down the corridors of American fiction for forty years now. The most brilliant treatment of the theme during the past decade seems to me John Phillips's *The Second Happiest Day* (1953). Phillips is as aware of his generation as a war-generation—and perhaps as a pre-war generation—as Fitzgerald was of his; and like Fitzgerald, Phillips writes of the very rich from the point of view of one who, poor by origin, is accepted by them but in himself still remains outside them.

The Second Happiest Day records, slowly and relentlessly, the history of a revolt against the very rich or, rather, against what James called 'the black and merciless things behind great possessions'. The novel, which is long and worked out in massive detail, is essentially an extended character-study of George Warwick Marsh III. We see him entirely through the eyes of the narrator, Gus Taylor, his friend through boyhood and his betrayer. Marsh is isolated from life in the deepest sense by his wealth—there is a splendid scene of their first days together in the Army as enlisted men when Marsh attempts to pass himself off as a socially ordinary young man. Without a pattern to conform to, a duty to accept, a role to fulfil, he is lost; and his family background is unstable. His father committed suicide when drunk; his mother, called 'Baby' by everyone, is much married and much divorced: his parents are, in fact, characters from Fitzgerald's Jazz Age grown to middle age.

This is a novel about relationships, the relationship, among others, between Marsh and the poor boy Taylor whose mentor and arbiter he is. It recounts Taylor's break for freedom through his war-experiences after his vassalage at Emmanuel, the expensive prep school, and at Harvard; and it leaves him at the end of the novel faced with a similar situation, for he is then in love with Marsh's ex-fiancée Lila, and though she loves him, the relation between them, because of her background of wealth and position, can only be that of slave to master.

It is also a superb re-creation of a society at a specific time, roughly from 1939 to 1950, with the United States in and under the shadow of war. Indeed, the time is almost a character in the book, the outbreak of the Korean War representing the closing of the bracket, as it were, in which the novel is contained. During this time the society rendered is being constantly criticized through the person of Gus Taylor, the disillusioned, wry, self-sick man. This makes it a novel full of the most cruel perceptions. The criticisms are devastating, of relations between the sexes, between the young and the middle-aged, between the very rich and the rest of the community. Nor are individual institutions spared. One doesn't feel that Phillips's intentions are to expose in any crude sense; the institutions are important because they reveal the unconscious assumptions on which the characters base their lives. The expensive school, Emmanuel, for example, is beautifully shown up and the picture of wealthy Harvard is almost as good. *The Second Happiest Day* seems to me a most thorough and satisfying anatomy of one section of New York and New England society—witness the description of the wedding reception that takes up the first quarter of the novel. And throughout, the characters are shown remarkably in the round.

Great riches such as Marsh's turn their possessor almost into a sacrificial victim, as they seem sometimes to do in James's novels, particularly in the representation of Milly Theale in *The Wings of the Dove*. This doom the very rich young man carried with him, like the haemophilic strain borne by the males of some European royal families, is at the centre of Wright Morris's *The Huge Season* (1954), together with the magnetism exercised by the very rich on those less rich. Wright Morris is one of the liveliest talents in the American novel today, and of his dozen or so novels one could scarcely pick out any single one as absolutely typical of his work. But he is always a formidable technician, able to bring past and present together in a single moment of time, and a writer in whom the bizarre, the pathetic and the comic exist cheek by jowl. His most purely funny novel is *Love among the Cannibals* (1957). But when one has said that one must add that it is a formidable piece of social criticism, as is indicated by the quotations that appear in juxtaposition as the epigraph of the book, Sir Thomas Browne's 'Nay further, we are what we all abhor, *Anthropophagi* and Cannibals, devourers not only of men, but of ourselves; and that not in an allegory, but a positive truth', and James's 'The *manners*, the manners: where and what have they, and what have they to tell?'—significantly from *The American Scene*. This account of the adventures of the song-writing team of MacGregor and Horter ('The poor man's Rodgers and Hart') when they take two girls down from Malibu Bay to Acapulco, in Mexico, is a brilliant invention in which, it seems to me, Morris claims new territory for fiction, and it carries with it its own deadly irony, as in the progressive stripping down, until nothing is left to it, of Horter's car by the local Mexicans.

On the surface, *The Field of Vision* (1957) is even more grotesque. To a bull-fight in Mexico City Morris brings his apparently crazy collection of characters: a failed playwright, 'a dedicated no-man, one who had turned to failure as a field that offered real opportunity for success', a phoney psychiatrist with an attendant man-woman who is both patient and housekeeper, the failure's boyhood friends, an elderly couple from small-town Nebraska, their grandson, dressed in Davy Crockett costume, and his great-grandfather, an aged frontiersman and friend of Buffalo Bill, for whom life stopped at 1900. Yet, grotesque though the characters are, Wright Morris transmits through them a sure sense of the great empty plains, with their tiny towns, of the further Middle West and evokes the ardours and endurances of the covered-wagon days.

The Huge Season, however, seems to me his best novel to date. At the centre, either as a character or in memory, is the very rich young man Lawrence, who is not only heir to the barbed-wire millions but a tennis star in his own right. Again, the point of vantage from which we see him is that of the relatively poor Peter Foley, the son of a Middle West Latin teacher, who becomes a college professor himself. The novel is ingenious technically since it consists of chapters alternating between Foley's own account of his life at a college in California with Lawrence in 1929 and third-person reports of a day spent by Foley in New York City in 1952; the point being that it is not until this day in 1952 has ended that Foley is free of Lawrence's domination, for all that he has been dead twenty-three years.

The college scenes, in which Lawrence is shown as the focal point of a group of four young men, are extraordinarily well done; and so, too, are the scenes of American expatriate life in Paris in 1929. A remarkable quality of this novel is the way in which the feel of the twenties is captured and the way in which it dominates the characters into the fifties. Indeed, this side of the book is perhaps best summed up in the character of Montana Lou Baker, the girl Foley met in Paris and who remains, in her unfulfilled promise, almost a myth-figure of the twenties. One has the sense in this novel not only of the rich young man as sacrificial hero but also of the enacting of a ritual of exorcism to which all associated with the hero must submit.

[4]

NOTHING has been more striking in post-war American fiction than the shifting emphasis in the novel as written by Negroes. The seminal novel, as seminal for its time as Wright's *Native Son* was, is Ralph Ellison's *The Invisible Man* (1952). Ellison's only novel up to the present, it suggests in its beginnings the novel of Negro protest as Wright wrote it:

I am not ashamed of my grandparents for having been slaves. I am only ashamed of myself for having at one time been ashamed. About eighty-five years ago they were told that they were free, united with others of our country in everything pertaining to the common good, and, in everything social, separate like the fingers of the hand. And they believed it. They exulted in it. They stayed in their place, worked hard, and brought up my father to do the same. But my grandfather is the one. He was an odd old guy—my grandfather, and I'm told I take after him. It was he who caused the trouble. On his deathbed he called my father to him and said, 'Son, after I'm gone I want you to keep up the good fight. I never told you, but our life is a war and I have been a traitor all my born days, a spy in the enemy's country all my born days, ever since I give up my gun back in the Reconstruction. Live with your head in the lion's mouth. I want you to overcome 'em with yesses, undermine 'em with grins, agree 'em to death and destruction, let 'em swoller you till they vomit or bust wide open.' They thought the old man had gone out of his head. He had been the meekest of men. The younger children were rushed from the room, the shades drawn and the flame of the lamp turned so low that it sputtered on the wick like the old man's breathing. 'Learn it to the young 'un', he whispered fiercely. Then he died.

The boy's first experiences of living with his head in the lion's mouth are described, with great brilliance in terms of macabre comedy, in the first chapter:

The old man's words were like a curse. On my graduation day I delivered a paper in which I showed that humility was the secret, indeed, the very essence of progress. (Not that I believed this. How could I, remembering my grandfather? I only knew that it worked.) It was a great success. Everyone praised me and I was invited to give the speech before the town's leading white citizens. It was a triumph for our whole community.

As a reward, with a number of other Negro boys he is made to 'entertain' the white business men of the town at a smoking concert, is teased by the presence of a statuesque naked blonde, is forced, blindfolded and wearing boxing gloves, to fight with the other boys similarly blindfolded, compelled to pick up coins (they are counterfeit) from an electrified mat, is given five dollars, allowed to deliver his speech and then presented by the white community with a leather briefcase containing a document awarding him a scholarship at the state college for Negroes. That night in a dream he meets his grandfather, who orders him to open the briefcase and read aloud what is said in the document. '"To Whom It May Concern", I intoned. "Keep This Nigger-Boy Running". I awoke with the old man's laughter ringing in my ears.'

Reading this first chapter of *The Invisible Man* without knowledge of what is to follow, one would, I think, almost automatically assume that it was naturalistic; though the pace is, in fact, much swifter than one normally associates with naturalism, and it is impossible to ignore in the prose itself a note of subdued and controlled hysteria. Very soon it is evident that, whatever else it may be, *The Invisible Man* is not a piece of naturalism. It is a symbolic novel rendered in terms of the picaresque. The boy, whose name we never know, is expelled from college through no fault of his own. He goes North and finds a job in a white paint factory on Long Island, where he is injured through the malice of another Negro. He becomes the subject of experiments in the factory hospital. In Harlem, he is taken by the Community Party, which betrays him. The line has changed and the Party is now supporting a group of race-fanatics not unlike the Rastafarians of Jamaica.

By the end of the novel we have almost forgotten the hero is a Negro; certainly as a symbol of any specific Negro problem he has disappeared altogether. That this is intentional is plain from the incidental symbolism, as, for example, in the factory scenes of Negroes working underground to make a black liquid which, brought into the sunlight, turns paint white. Indeed, the hero is any man and every man; the real theme of the novel is stated in the prologue:

> I am an invisible man. No, I am not a spook like those who haunted Edgar Allan Poe; nor am I one of your Hollywood movie ectoplasms. I am a man of flesh and blood, fibre and liquids—and I might even be said to possess a mind. I am invisible, understand, simply because people refuse to see me. Like the bodiless heads you see sometimes in circus sideshows, it is as though I have been surrounded by mirrors of hard, distorting glass. When they approach me they see only my surroundings, themselves, or figments of their imagination—indeed, everything and anything except me.

And presumably the hero is nameless for the same reason as the central character in Kafka's *The Trial* is known only as K: to reinforce the suggestion not only of invisibility—an invisible man has no use for a name—but also of impersonality and universality. The nameless man contains, as it were, all men.

It is from Kafka that the novel in part derives. While the individual scenes that compose the book bear the immediate impression of actuality, they have the surrealistic vividness, the unnatural clarity as well as the convincing illogic, of dream rather than of real life, or, if of real life, then of life surrounded, to use Ellison's words, by mirrors of hard, distorting glass. Yet the final effect is not that of Kafka; the novel contains, as John McCormick notes in *Catastrophe and Imagination*, 'not the slightest suggestion of the Kafka-cult lament'; partly because, as Professor McCormick also points out, Kafka is not the only source of the novel. There is also Melville's *The Confidence Man*: Ellison has grafted European symbolism on to the native stock of symbolism.

Though *The Invisible Man* is the most impressive of contemporary Negro novels, there are others of great interest. One is James Baldwin's *Go Tell It on the Mountain* (1954), the clue to which is perhaps given in one of the essays in *Notes of a Native Son*:

> I began to see that one would have to hold in the mind forever two ideas which seemed to be in opposition. The first idea was acceptance, the acceptance, totally without rancour, of life as it is, and men as they are: in the light of this idea, it goes without saying, injustice is a commonplace. But this did not mean that one could be complacent, for the second idea was of equal power: that one must never, in one's own life, accept these injustices as commonplace but must fight them with all one's strength.

The novel deals with the Negro not as a social problem or as an oppressed minority, but concentrates almost exclusively on one aspect of him and his way of life—the religious, and the particular kind of religion he assumes. The kind it is grows out of his traditional situation in America and especially of his experience of slavery. This leads him to identify himself in his religion with the Children of Israel in bondage in Egypt. The language and action of the novel bring this out clearly and fascinatingly. And the novel is remarkably self-contained. We are never allowed to forget the central theme. The very language in which the book is written—lyrical, with strong echoes of the Old Testament—reinforces it. One gets the sense of the Bible as the one book known, just as it was very largely among the Methodists of the eighteenth century.

The novel covers two days, a Saturday and Sunday, in the life of the Grimeses, a family living in Harlem. The father, Gabriel, is a preacher in a sect called the Fire-Baptized. His elder son, John, is a clever boy who is fourteen on the Saturday, a boy destined, it has always been assumed, to become a preacher. There is a younger son, Roy. Both are in revolt against their sin-obsessed father, Roy actively, John much more passively, in a sense intellectually. His mother gives John money for his birthday and, conscious of sin, he goes into downtown New York to see a film. He returns to find his parents tending Roy, who has been stabbed in a gang fight between white and coloured boys.

There is a quarrel between Gabriel and his wife, the boys identifying themselves with their mother; and then the scene switches to the church and the service there, which begins on Saturday evening and continues into the small hours. James Baldwin renders the service with great skill. Through their prayers we learn the past lives of Gabriel, his wife and John in a series of flashbacks: a whole intricate dramatic pattern of sin and guilt and repentance underlying their lives is revealed. And the novel ends with John's experience of conversion, through the very pressure of the scene about him working on his own feelings of guilt, at his recent discovery of sex, at his hatred of his father, at his wish to break clean away from his background.

The characters in this novel, and the relationships between them, exist in depth; behind them, moulding them all the time, is a whole historical background, a conception of themselves born of the experience of slavery and injustice. This background is not so much stated as felt implicitly. *Go Tell It on the Mountain*, one feels, is an expression of the experience of a whole people, presented not as a problem or in terms of propaganda but as it truly is. It is this sense one has of the dignity of a great subject finely handled that makes Baldwin's second novel, *Giovanni's Room* (1959), about a tragic homosexual relation set in Paris, seem by comparison something of an anti-climax, admirable though it is.

[5]

OF RALPH ELLISON and some other novelists who seem to have something in common with him Malcolm Cowley has written:

> Since all these novelists end by affirming the value of separate persons in conflict with social forces, I have thought of calling them personalists . . . Each of the novelists seems to believe that the author himself should be a personality instead of a recording instrument, and therefore he keeps trying to find a personal approach and a personal manner of writing.

These words are a brave attempt to isolate and describe an element in contemporary American fiction that is almost incapable of definition though immediately recognizable and that, in my view, is the most significant single element in the American novel today. Besides

Ellison, Cowley numbers among his personalists Saul Bellow and Herbert Gold, and I feel pretty sure that if his book, *The Literary Situation*, were appearing now, he would add Bernard Malamud. It is not an accident, I think, that all three are Jews whose forbears came to the United States from eastern or central Europe not so very long ago; and it seems to me plain that they are bringing something quite new into American fiction.

Bellow was the first of them to appear; his first novel, *Dangling Man*, was published in 1944. Bellow has written: 'It's obvious to everyone that the stature of characters in modern novels is smaller than it once was, and this diminution powerfully concerns those who value existence. I do not believe that human capacity to feel or do can really have dwindled or that the quality of humanity has degenerated. I rather think that people appear smaller because society has become so immense.' This very well defines at least one aspect of his novels, though in some of them the emphasis seems to be on the immensity of society while in others it is on the individual human being who in a sense opposes it. This dichotomy is indeed so pronounced in his work that Bellow sometimes seems to be two writers, one introvert, the other extravert.

On the naturalistic level, *Dangling Man* and the novel that followed it, *The Victim* (1947), both describe what may be called personal nightmares, and the element of nightmare, of the characters' exacerbated hypersensitivity to the world about them, removes them from the naturalistic plane and strikes a note of affinity with Kafka. The hero of *Dangling Man*, which is presented in the form of a journal, is a man named Joseph—he has no surname—who is awaiting his call-up for the U.S. Army in the early days of the war. He feels that he is living in a void and has given up his job, ostensibly in order to study the philosophy of the Enlightenment but really to try to come to terms with himself and the society in which he lives, as is expressed in this passage towards the beginning of the book. He is looking out of the window at the New York scene:

> The sun had been covered up; snow was beginning to fall. It was sprinkled over the black pores of the gravel and was lying in thin slips on the slanting roofs. I could see a long way from this third-floor height. Not far off there were chimneys, their smoke a lighter grey than the grey of the sky; and, straight before me, ranges of poor dwellings, warehouses, billboards, culverts,

electric signs blankly burning, parked cars and moving cars, and the occasional bare plan of a tree. These I surveyed, pressing my forehead on the glass. It was my painful obligation to look and to submit to myself the invariable question: Where was there a particle of what, elsewhere, or in the past, had spoken in man's favour? There could be no doubt that these billboards, streets, tracks, houses, ugly and blind, were related to interior life. And yet, I told myself, there had to be a doubt. There were human lives organized around these ways and houses, and that they, the houses, say, were the analogue, that what men created they also were, through some transcendental means, I could not bring myself to concede. There must be a difference, a quality that eluded me, somehow a difference between things and persons and even between acts and persons. Otherwise the people who lived here were actually a reflection of the things they lived among. I had always striven to avoid blaming them. Was not that in effect behind my daily reading of the paper? In their business and politics, their taverns, movies, assaults, divorces, murders, I tried continually to find clear signs of their common humanity.

It was undeniably to my interest to do this. Because I was involved with them; because, whether I liked it or not, they were my generation, my society, my world. We were figures in the same plot, eternally fixed together. I was aware, also, that their existence, just as it was, made mine possible.

Joseph's problem is not resolved. Indeed, the very extremity of his bid for freedom intensifies it. He is not only a dangling man, he is man alone, putting questions to society that society cannot answer. The manner of his life is itself a question, one that alienates him from his wife, his friends, his family; and the novel ends with his writing to the draft board requesting to be taken into the armed services at the earliest possible moment:

> Hurray for regular hours!
> And for the supervision of the spirit!
> Long live regimentation!

Dangling Man in its implications is a metaphysical novel. One has the sense of a man wrestling with himself and with the reality of being a man. It is, too, in a strange way an exacerbatedly funny book; and though the angle from which it is seen may be an unusual one, the city life of New York in its day-to-day aspects is rendered in solid actuality. One feels it as an element permeating the characters.

One feels this, too, in *The Victim*: Bellow is a novelist of urban man, particularly of the American as urban man. *The Victim* is more complex than *Dangling Man*, though at its centre there is still the man alone, Asa Leventhal, alone because his wife is away on a visit. Leventhal, by profession a journalist on a trade paper, the son of Jewish immigrants who were never assimilated into American life, solitary and suspicious by temperament, his perpetual anxiety masked by dourness, is wrestling with the related problems of his Americanness and his Jewishness. One pole of the novel, perhaps, is to be found in his father's contemptuous words, which he has rejected: 'Call me Ikey, call me Moe, but give me the dough. What's it to me if you despise me? What do you think equality with you means to me? What do you have that I care about except the groschen?'

The novel is the narration of a haunting and a debate. Leventhal is as it were picked upon by Kirby Albee, a deadbeat, a drunk and an anti-Semite who is, ironically, a descendant of Governor Winthrop. Albee accuses Leventhal, to his bewilderment, of having once lost him his job—hence his present degradation—and then proceeds to live parasitically upon him in a relationship that becomes increasingly complex. It does not end until Leventhal realizes: 'Admittedly, like others, he had been in the wrong . . . Everybody committed errors and offences. But it was supremely plain to him that everything, without exception, took place as if within a single soul or person.'

From one point of view, Albee is Leventhal's *Doppelgänger*, his shadow, in Jungian terminology. His condition represents everything Leventhal fears he might fall into himself and about which he even in a way feels guilty for not having done so, for it is through Albee that he realizes a vision of having fallen into 'horror, evil, that he had kept himself from'. But there is more to it than this. Albee is not a phantom, a hallucination. As Fiedler says:

> Bourgeois and bohemian, secure citizen and self-torturing bum, Semite and Anglo-Saxon, recent immigrant and old American— they are bound together by their manifold contrasts. Nothing renders them more 'dependent for the food of spiritual life' upon each other than Albee's indecent need for Jews to define his existence by defining a difference, or Leventhal's secret hunger for a hatred that can mark off the boundaries of his identity.

The novel ends on a note of reconciliation and affirmation beyond that struck by *Dangling Man*. It rings out, for example, in the statement of the old Yiddish journalist Schlossberg:

'I am as sure about greatness and beauty as you are about black and white. If a human life is a great thing to me, it *is* a great thing. Do you know better? I'm entitled as much as you. And why be measly? Do you have to be? Is somebody holding you by the neck? Have dignity, you understand me? Choose dignity. Nobody knows enough to turn it down.'

Even so, it is much more explicit in *The Adventures of Augie March* (1953), Bellow's first extravert novel and a long, sustained exercise in the picaresque told by Augie himself. It is set for the most part in the Depression years in Chicago, but though the evils of the period are certainly not palliated or written down in any way and though Augie himself comes of a class considerably more depressed than Studs Lonigan, we are in a very different world from Farrell's, a world of immense vitality, the feeling of which is expressed, perhaps, by one of the gods of Augie's boyhood, Einhorn, a near-crooked business man, when he tells Augie:

'There is some kind of advantage in the roughness of a place like Chicago, of not having any illusions either. Whereas in all the great capitals of the world there's some reason to think humanity is very different. All that ancient culture and those beautiful works of art right out in public, by Michelangelo and Christopher Wren, and those ceremonies, like trooping the colour at the Horse Guards' parade and burying a great man in the Panthéon over in Paris. You see those marvellous things and you think that everything savage belongs to the past. So you think. And then you have another think, and you see that after they rescued women from the coal mines, or pulled down the Bastille and got rid of Star Chambers and *lettres de cachet*, ran out the Jesuits, increased education, and built hospitals and spread courtesy and politeness, they have five or six years of war and revolutions and kill off twenty million people. And do they think there's less danger to life than here? That's a riot. Let them rather say that they blast better specimens, but not try to put it over that the only human beings who live by blood are away down on the Orinoco where they hunt heads, or out in Cicero.'

The passage is interesting, too, for another reason, also making for an enhanced vitality. The book is narrated by Augie in a consciousness of world history. Parallels for the characters are constantly being found with the heroic figures of the past. For example, within five lines of Einhorn's being introduced to the reader, Augie is invoking as implied comparisons Caesar, Machiavelli and Ulysses, and a few pages on Einhorn is seen as Pope Alexander VI. Throughout the novel there seems a conscious aggrandization almost to the point of mythicization on Bellow's part of the scene and characters. For myself I find this removes the novel somewhat away from reality, especially if one discounts the exuberance with which it is written. There is, in fact, a problem with Augie himself: he is a little too good, a little too literary, to be true, especially when he is reflecting upon rather than recounting his adventures. He appears then as it were the mouthpiece of Bellow's ventriloquism.

The adventures, though, are another matter. Augie is the second of three bastard sons of a poor half-blind Jewish woman. The youngest is feeble-minded, the eldest, Simon, whose story Augie relates in counterpart to his own, is brilliant, ambitious, unscrupulous and bent on getting rich as quickly as possible, which he does. Augie is rather different. At the core of him is an obstinate, almost unadmitted passion for freedom. As Einhorn tells him early on: 'You've got *opposition* in you. You don't slide through everything. You just make it look so.' It is his saving grace, the inner check to his handsomeness and his willingness to please. It keeps him perpetually open to experience; and his experiences are many. He helps to rob a store and associates with gangsters. He supports himself at the University of Chicago by stealing books. For a time he is a demonstrator at a sports outfitter's shop. He is chauffeur to a 'dogs' club'—an expensive kennel where dogs are boarded out. He becomes a union organizer in a Chicago hotel and later secretary-ghost-writer to an eccentric millionaire. As her lover, he accompanies a rich young woman to Mexico to hunt iguanas with eagles. He becomes purser during the war in a merchant ship which is torpedoed.

New characters come into the novel with each episode. Vigorous, eccentric, possessed of enormous vitality, they seem a little larger than life, as though distorted in the mirror of Augie's open-eyed receptivity to experience. He responds to each of them in turn. That is his function; he is in his way the indomitable saluting and rejoicing in the indomitable, as the last lines of the novel show:

Look at me, going everywhere! Why, I am a sort of Columbus of those near-at-hand and believe you can come to them in this immediate *terra incognita* that spreads out in every gaze. I may well be a flop at this line of endeavour. Columbus too thought he was a flop, probably, when they sent him back in chains. Which didn't prove there was no America.

Seize the Day (1956) is a return to Bellow's introverted novel; a wry, affectionate comedy of exasperated urban man, it has the same acceptance of the contemporary world. Tommy Wilhelm, a failed film actor, failed salesman, separated from his wife and children, jobless, lives in a hotel near Columbia University inhabited mainly by the aged and retired. As the novel opens, he has just handed over all his remaining money to a phoney psychiatrist who has promised him an income from gambling with it on the stock exchange. He loses it, as he knew he would, for he has decided:

Maybe the making of mistakes expressed the very purpose of his life and the essence of his being here. Maybe he was supposed to make them and suffer from them on this earth.

There is a case to be made against Bellow—and in *Seize the Day* Bellow is at his most assailable. The resolution of the novel seems to me altogether too easy; but what saves the book as a whole is the energy and firmness of the prose and the astonishing eye for externals; and there are two splendid comic characters, Tommy's father, the old doctor clinging desperately to his life and his money and finding his son only an embarrassment, and Dr Tamkin, the phoney poet-psychiatrist who is yet the centre of wisdom in the novel.

There is in *Seize the Day*, compared with *Dangling Man* and *The Victim*, a suspicion of the soft centre, as though acceptance, formerly difficult and the fruit of moral struggle, has become almost masochism. By contrast, the exuberance and expansiveness of *Henderson the Rain King* (1959) are such as to suggest over-compensation. Henderson, who is not a Jew, is big in every way, of great physical strength, many times a millionaire. He tells his story with comparable vigour; the novel begins:

When I think of my condition at the age of fifty-five when I bought the ticket, all is grief. The facts begin to crowd me and soon I get a pressure in the chest. A disorderly rush begins—my parents, my wives, my girls, my children, my farm, my animals, my habits, my money, my music lessons, my drunkenness, my prejudices, my brutality, my teeth, my face, my soul! I have to cry, 'no, no, get back, curse you, let me alone!' But how can they let me alone? They belong to me. They are mine. And they pile into me from all sides. It turns into chaos.

Henderson the Rain King is a myth of rebirth expressed in extremely romantic terms, something like a pantomime, Ihab Hassan suggests, 'co-authored by Rider Haggard and Dostoyevsky'. Henderson, at odds with his wife, his father, his children, his friends, goes to Africa, which is not so much a place as a state, the Jungian unconscious perhaps, where he undergoes a series of symbolic actions, submits to a series of initiation rites which, in the end, make him a new man; so that he returns to the United States to become, at the age of fifty-five, a medical student.

Striking as it is, *Henderson the Rain King* is not, I think, as successful as *Augie March*. We are in the presence the whole time of a continuous blast of energy in the form and voice of Henderson. It is a wonderful performance, but also an exhausting one for the reader, as though he is being physically borne down by it. And there is a monotony about Henderson which stems from an extremely narrow range of emotion and expression. It seems as though the novel has been written on the one single unwavering note. And though Bellow's invention is continuous and unflagging, it still seems curiously schematic, composed to an intellectual formula. This makes for a sense of thinness both of texture and of experience; Bellow's Africa, for instance, convinces neither as Africa nor as a representation of a psychic state, as is immediately apparent when compared with New York as suffered by Joseph in *Dangling Man* and Leventhal in *The Victim*.

Bellow is certainly one of the richest and most exciting talents in contemporary writing. He has, it seems, yet to heal the division within himself, and up to now he has been at his best in his more sombre, introverted mood, in *Dangling Man* and, especially, *The Victim*. The energy, overwhelmingly impressive as it is, of *Augie March* and *Henderson* does not compensate for the absence of the qualities of the earlier novels. Affirmation is not necessarily the more convincing for being made in a stentorian voice.

The novels of Herbert Gold have close affinities with those of Bellow in his exuberant, loudly-yea-saying manifestations. Their attitude is shown in the titles of the novels themselves: *Birth of a Hero*

(1951), *The Prospect before Us* (1954), *The Man Who Was Not with It* (1956), *The Optimist* (1959) and *Therefore Be Bold* (1960). Gold has said: 'What the novelist seems to be doing at his philosophical best is to explore possibility'; and the words describe his own novels. To assert possibility, however, is not thereby automatically to prove it; and Gold, who is an uneven writer, can be slick and facile. Indeed, I think the criticism one has to make of Gold as an existentialist novelist is that his characters are insufficiently tested; the fires they submit themselves to scarcely strike one as being real, at any rate by comparison with the tests of circumstance imposed upon their characters by European existentialists.

Gold's most ambitious novel is *The Optimist*. His best seems to me *Therefore Be Bold*, perhaps because there he is dealing with a stage of life of whose being possibility is an essential condition—adolescence. The novel, which is told in retrospect by a young Jew, Dan Berman, the only Jew among the characters, relates two or three years in the high-school life of a group of friends in a town in Ohio in the late thirties. It captures beautifully the aspirations and confusions of intelligent adolescents; it is funny and affectionate and never patronizing. The hard core of the novel is the depiction of the relationship between Dan and Mr Masters, the father of his girl friend. Masters is presented as a monster, a monster of a kind quite unfamiliar to the boy but one that hints at possibilities by no means optimistic. Masters hates the boy:

> This impressed me, that Euclid Masters would hate me without caring about me, that I should have so little to do with it; it brought into the springtime of that year some of the awe of congregations for useless miracles. The clock ran without a monkey, or imported a monkey only because the specifications called for rubies, radium paint, and ring-tailed grinners; Euclid Masters put me in his clock without a reason, and along the shale and shore of Lake Erie I wandered to know why. I climbed the hill to Homewood Drive. I found a soggy tennis ball on the playground of Taft School and heaved it up to Clifton Boulevard.
>
> In Europe the death agony of six million Jews had begun. A boy my age named Herschel Greenzpan had shot a Nazi third secretary in Paris. Before the Greenzpan boy disappeared into history, he helped me begin to define myself. But what—as my father said—did we know in Lakewood? Depression, recovery, newspapers; school, ambition, habits, hopes; Juicer, Tom, Red

and girls; our change of life—our public yearnings into philosophy and the suspicion that *others exist.*

I loved ice cream. I loved Eva. I loved the truth. As through a
glass darkly, as through a suburb protectedly, I began, just
began, to see that actual Herschel Greenzpan and living, breathing Euclid Masters were also a part of my Truth. In fact, the
Truth was really a sum of such parts, terrible and sweet.

The Truth—*All*—was what I lusted after . . .

The juxtapositions of Greenzpan and Masters, of ice cream and high
school and anti-semitism four thousand miles away in Europe, make
their own point; and they do so in what might be called a large area of
acceptance and charity, the field in which the notion of possibility has
its being.

It is within this area of acceptance and charity that the novels and
stories of Bernard Malamud exist. Malamud, together with Bellow,
seems to me the best and most remarkable of the younger American
novelists. Of his three novels, *The Natural* (1952), *The Assistant*
(1957) and *A New Life* (1961), *The Assistant* is the most successful, a
work of great subtlety and moral beauty. The theme, if one regards
Frank Alpine as the centre of the novel, is the struggle for moral
excellence, the wish to be good, though this is probably to over-
simplify, for Malamud's characters are seen in a Chekhovian irony.
Set in a slum district of Manhattan inhabited largely by poor Jews, the
main scene of the novel is Morris Bober's grocer's shop. Bober is an
unsuccessful Russian-Jewish immigrant dogged all his life by ill-luck.
He still mourns the death of his son in childhood, and he has to see his
daughter Helen, a girl in love with excellence, give up her aspirations
to a college education in order to help support the family. 'He had
hoped for much in America and got little. And because of him Helen
and Ida had less. He had defrauded them, he and the blood-sucking
store.' But he is a good man; he rises each morning before dawn in
order to sell a three-cent roll to a Polish woman on her way to work.
Malamud persuades us of his goodness without sentimentality: he is, I
think, more successful here than Bellow. For Morris is not a tragic
character; he is comic, as the figure repeatedly knocked down by fate
can hardly help being.

The novel hinges on the relationship to the Bobers of a young
Italian-American, Frank Alpine, who arrives as it were out of nowhere,
down and out, and whom Morris befriends. He disappears, and shortly

afterwards Morris is beaten up in his shop by a couple of gangsters. Frank returns and, without being asked, runs the shop while Morris is ill and stays on afterwards as the assistant, for practically no wages. He seems to bring them luck; the shop prospers, at any rate relatively, even though from time to time he fiddles a dollar or two from the till. He is, in fact, one of the two gangsters who held up Morris. Now he is stricken by remorse but unable to confess his guilt to Morris, as he wants to, through simple ignorance of how to do so.

Morris's wife regards him with intense suspicion as a *Goy*; she is fearful that he will attempt to seduce Helen. And indeed he falls in love with her. After a time she is attracted to him, partly by his confused goodness, his almost inarticulate aspirations. He is puzzled by himself and by her; Jews are as alien to him as he is to Mrs Bober. But though Helen is not a virgin she will not give herself to him because she now repudiates sex without love and is uncertain whether she loves him. To his own surprise, he finds himself responding to this; it is as though he is exhilarated by the entirely novel notion of self-control.

Morris is taken ill again, and Frank takes over the shop; and to keep it going works at night as a cook in a short-order joint, slipping the money he earns there into the till in the shop. He seems to have lost Helen, who is unwilling to live her life in a struggling grocery store. Then one night a drunken hoodlum, Frank's partner in the hold-up, tries to rape her. Frank rescues her, and she turns to him in gratitude; misunderstanding her, he rapes her himself. 'Dog! Uncircumcized dog!' she cries.

Frank is sacked from the shop for pilfering, but when Morris can no longer look after it because of illness, he returns, unasked and unwanted. Helen will have nothing to do with him, despising him. With Morris dead, but not before Frank has confessed his guilt to him, which has already been guessed, Frank expands the business. It is now his ambition, as a form of recompense to her, to see Helen through college. She still hates him; until by chance one night she catches a glimpse of him asleep in the short-order joint, realizes all he has done for her and her family, realizes, too, the confused nature of good and evil, and thanks him. Next night he overhears her refusing a comparatively wealthy suitor. He stays on in the grocer's shop and a few months later has himself circumcized and becomes a Jew.

The milieu of *The Assistant* is depressing enough and the story, on the material level, one of defeat. But the final effect is of moral beauty.

It comes from several sources. There is the intensity of the observation of life in what in effect is one very short street in Manhattan, a street crowded with characters freshly and sharply perceived. There is, too, Malamud's mastery of the speech-rhythms of Yiddish in his dialogue. The invention is continuous and fascinating in its detail. One feels that nothing, either in the setting or the characters, is shirked; all, setting and characters, good and bad, are invested with a wonderfully luminous charity, as though the author sees all around them and beyond them.

And what is fundamental to the novel, of course, is the theme of purgation through the acceptance of the burden of others' suffering. This, or something very close to it, seems to be the theme also of *A New Life*. This novel lacks the concentration of *The Assistant*, and one wants to know much more than one is ever told about the hero, Levin, 'formerly a drunkard', who begins a new life by joining the staff of the English department of a small agricultural college in a north-west state. It is much more episodic, with the result that interest dissipates in too many directions. At the same time, with its much broader comedy and with its response to natural beauty—Levin is a New Yorker in the Rockies—it gives evidence of an expansion of talents not foreshadowed in Malamud's earlier work at the same time as it reinforces the impression made by them that the future is still his.

Bellow and Malamud have brought a new note into the American novel. It is Jewish certainly but also, one feels, partly Russian. It is not English. Whether it will endure to become a significant conditioning factor in American fiction remains to be seen. But its emergence, after a hundred years of the American novel, shows that that fiction is still a new fiction, capable of drawing upon the traditional values and habits of feeling of the various racial and religious stocks that make up the population of the United States, and capable of sudden growth, development and expansion in directions scarcely predictable.

AFTERWORD

This book was first published in 1964. Its author was a congenital reviewer of new fiction whose enthusiasm for his craft had been sparked off by his own dreams as a novelist, for he believed himself to be one of those who, if small may be compared with the greatest, 'was born,' in Henry James's words, 'a novelist, grew up, lived, died a novelist, breathing, feeling, thinking, speaking, performing every action of his life, only as that votary'. Roughly, the book covered the years from 1920 to 1955.

Well, much has happened in more than twenty years. New generations of novelists have come into being and very different fashions and theories of criticism have largely taken over. Moreover, the author has changed. Inevitably, the book must seem a period-piece. Whether it is more than this is for others to say. Its reissue now cannot help making me reflect in this Afterword on how my perceptions of the novel have changed; how I might alter the book, with hindsight, and how I could briefly chart a few of the landmarks on the road from its first publication to the present.

I had always seen the novel as broadly realistic and had been puzzled by earlier historians of the form who declared it had developed by a process of evolution out of something called the romance, something which, when I came to read it, seemed to me to have nothing to do with the novel. It was as though, I thought, an historian of the internal combustion engine should begin his thesis with an exhaustive study of the ox-cart. So I took the line that what was called the romance belonged to pre-history and I accounted for its virtual disappearance by invoking the development of the scientific spirit, which seemed to be roughly contemporary with the rise of the novel.

I was horribly mistaken, of course, and reluctantly I began

to realise that we were still surrounded on all sides by manifestations of romance, not merely in the popular fiction of romantic love, but in the visions of science fiction and the fantasies of Tolkien. When I was lecturing in American universities in the Sixties, it seemed as though the Hobbits and their world were as real to undergraduates as those of Paul Morel and the Brangwyn sisters had been to me at their age, and I was faced again with the question of what the connection between the novel as I conceived it and the romance was. I remembered that Hawthorne had produced fictions for which he specifically disclaimed the title of novels. This had not bothered me, for to my mind *The Scarlet Letter* was without any question a novel. The most I would concede was that it was an *American* novel, for I had been enlightened by the seminal work, Richard Chase's *The American Novel and Its Tradition*.

In his first pages, Chase notes that in *The Great Tradition* Leavis had seen *Wuthering Heights* as a freak. If this is so, then many of the greatest American novels are freaks in that they are 'eccentric, in their differing ways, to a tradition of which, let us say, *Middlemarch* is a standard representative'. For me, this was very much the nub of the matter, for *Middlemarch* was one of my touchstones for determining what a novel was. And how did you square *Middlemarch* with the romance?

Convinced that the rise of the novel must have had something to do with the rise of science, I recalled that the seminal novelists, from Cervantes, Fielding, Jane Austen and the Naturalists, seemed always to have seen the novel as the enemy of the romance. Naively, in other words, I had equated the latter with falsity and the former with the search for truth, or at least with freedom from illusion.

A reading of Northrop Frye's *Anatomy of Criticism* forced me to give up my notion that one form had been superseded by the other and offered a new perspective. Frye defines the romance as 'a fictional mode in which the chief characters live in a world of marvels (naive romance) or in which the mode is elegiac and hence less subject to social criticism than the mimetic modes'. Which throws light, for instance, on Hardy's statement that 'a story must be exceptional enough to justify its telling'. Hardy goes on: 'Therein lies the problem – to reconcile the average with that uncommonness which alone makes it natural that a tale or experience would dwell in the memory and induce repetition.'

It dawned upon me that it was the elements of the romance in it that gave even the most realistic of novels its memorability and that a suggestion of the essentially strange, the magical, the fairy tale, however disguised or submerged, is a necessary ingredient of nearly all good fiction. I saw, moreover, that it was precisely these ingredients which gave novels their enduring quality, and placed them in the dimension of the mythical.

It seems to me now that the abiding strength of the form lies in the vastness of the heritage it draws upon. We can see this even in the names novelists choose for their characters. No doubt the names that the authors of the old comedy of manners gave their characters – Sir Epicure Mammon and the like – have disappeared, although they survived in modified ways until well into the eighteenth century, as Fielding's Squire Allworthy shows, and we may remember from a century later Trollope's poor curate, Mr Quiverful. The point is that something akin to the old practice lingers on even among the avowedly realistic: isn't the name Clayhanger, with its dual suggestion of earthiness and tenacity, of hanging on, and of precariousness, an apt choice for a character from the Potteries?

One can't think that Faulkner's characters in *Light in August*, Hightower and Joe Christmas, have their names other than by conscious design. Or even Jack Burden in Robert Penn Warren's *All the King's Men*, at once the narrator and the chorus and the man who delivers judgement. Faced with the name, can we be expected not to think of tags like the burden of responsibility, the burden of knowledge, the burden of guilt?

Another instance is the heroine of Doris Lessing's *bildungsroman, Children of Violence*. For the greater part, it is a work of George Eliot-like realism and sobriety. The name Martha Quest is apt, but then the question of probability arises. Quest isn't one of the more common English surnames; indeed, a glance at the London telephone directory shows that there are precisely three Quests in the metropolitan area.

And so even within the realms of the broadly realistic novel, what Chase calls 'the massive, temperate, moralistic rendering of life and thought we associate with Mr Leavis's "great tradition"', the atavistic may still lurk, and the great fault of *Tradition and Dream*, I now think, was its failure to recognise how inextricably the novel is bound up with the other, more symbolic genres. I don't recall that anyone remarked on this when it was published, and I was lucky, I can only conclude, in my cut-off date. John Barth, for instance, with his brilliant invention and parodic gifts had not appeared, nor had the British novelists of 'magical realism'.

I was aware of course of omissions when *Tradition and Dream* first came out. Some were deliberate, some the result of ignorance, some due to the design of the book, for I did not wish to fall into the trap of finding at the end that I had done no more than compile a catalogue. And I was conscious all the time of the limitations that the prescribed length imposed on me. Then, as I explained in my prefatory note, the book was in some sense a sequel to my earlier *The English Novel: A Short Critical History*. That had ended with a consideration of Dorothy Richardson, Joyce, Lawrence and Woolf. Other writers discussed in *The English Novel* included Maugham. I left him out of the new book along with J. D. Beresford, Walpole *et al*, for it did not seem to me that what they had published after 1920 in any way affected my earlier comments.

Whom do I wish now I had included? Jean Rhys for a certainty. However, *Wide Sargasso Sea*, which I believe changed everyone's perception of this author, had yet to appear. And, in the event, I found myself having to exclude other novelists of the period between the wars whom I had read with delight, among them Sarah Salt, who seems totally forgotten today, Hester Chapman and Julia Strachey. I suspect I should have taken a much harder look at R. C. Hutchinson and, of the Americans, I ought to have made room for Mary McCarthy. I regret not having chanced my arm and included Brian Moore. He had published one novel, *Judith Hearne*, which I had reviewed and been much impressed by. Paul Scott had published a couple of novels by my crucial date, but they give little indication of his later achievement in *The Raj Quartet* and *Staying On*.

Of the novelists I did deal with some are still in full spate, and in most instances they do not seem to me to have developed in wholly unexpected ways. One who has is Doris Lessing. I certainly could not have foreseen after either the Martha Quest sequence or *The Golden Notebook* the books that followed, which have taken her into the field of science fiction.

Four *roman-fleuves* were under way when I finished *Tradition and Dream*, and the one I believed would prove the most notable was unfinished at its author's death. This was Richard Hughes's *The Human Predicament*. I recall he assured me in 1969 that he would have to live until he was a hundred and twenty to bring it to an end, for he was the slowest of writers and a perfectionist. He was a most fastidious craftsman and as conscious a novelist as any in our century; he seemed, as it were, self-begotten. He had affinities but no obvious forebears: *A High Wind in Jamaica* seems to me unique, a wholly original novel, and *In Hazard* is no less remarkable. *The Human Predicament* was to have covered the period from the rise of Nazism until Hitler's defeat, and the action was to have been played out variously in Britain, the United States, Germany and the Spain of the Civil War, the central character being a Welsh squire, Augustine Penry-Herbert. Of this vast work, which was to be, Hughes said, an 'historical novel of my own times', two volumes appeared, *The Fox in the Attic* and *The Wooden Shepherdess*. What we have, in other words, is the most tantalising of torsos and a working that is likely to remain of permanent fascination, so beautifully is it written and so vividly and unconventionally are presented the historic figures it illuminates, Hitler among them.

Olivia Manning brought *The Balkan Trilogy* to a conclusion with *Friends and Heroes* and then went on to write a further group of novels, *The Levant Trilogy*. *The Balkan Trilogy* remains a strikingly vivid evocation of an eastern European country writhing under and succumbing to the blandishments and threats of the Nazis. It is also a most perceptive study of a marriage, and the rendering of Guy Pringle, the narrator Harriet's husband, maddening, impossible, much loved, a man for whom the welfare of his fellows takes precedence over everything else, seems to me one of the triumphs of character-creation in the fiction of our time. *The Levant Trilogy* (*The Danger Tree*, *The Battle Lost and Won* and *The Sum of Things*) continues the story of Harriet's life as she and Guy are forced to flee from Romania before the German invasion by way of Greece, until they reach a precarious safety in Egypt, where they are terribly close to the war being fought in the Western Desert. In these novels, by comparison with the first trilogy, the lives of Harriet and Guy are overshadowed, dwarfed, robbed of significance, by the ebb and flow of the war being fought so near them. But this is not at all to deny that *The Levant Trilogy* is a *tour de force* of a very high order in which we see the novelist's imagination responding greatly to great historic events, as for instance the depiction of the Battle of El Alamein as experienced by the young British officer Simon Boulderstone, a relatively peripheral character.

C. P. Snow brought his eleven-volume sequence *Strangers and Brothers* to an end with *Last Things* in 1970. I am bound to admit that I find the whole work considerably less interesting than I did while reading the separate contributory novels as they appeared, and why this should be so I find fascinating to analyse.

For one thing, the individual novels vary greatly in quality. More important, they suffer – the later volumes particularly, I cannot help thinking – from the similarity between the narrator Lewis Eliot and Snow himself, as we know him from the publicly recorded facts of his own life. In the end, Eliot and Snow seem all but identical, and it is difficult not to feel that the novelist is all too blatantly turning his actual life into copy. This seems to me to display a fatal lack of literary tact, which is not a charge we can make against Anthony Powell, whose sequence *A Dance to the Music of Time* was brought to a conclusion in 1975 with *Hearing Secret Harmonies*. We are never in any danger of confusing Powell with Nicholas Jenkins, his narrator. By contrast, too, with Snow's, Powell's work gains immeasurably from its architecture; it is a *designed* work, as Snow's scarcely is. In consequence, Powell's novels make up a magnificent panorama of our times, presenting, one is tempted to say, an acceptable alternative to what actually happened.

There is something else. Powell's prose is much richer and more subtle than Snow's, and Snow, I would guess, viewed with something like Puritan distaste those resources of language that Powell, along with most significant novelists, draws upon as being adventitious aids the honest writer had best eschew.   Snow had thought seriously about fiction and was impressively well read in the novel, the English and the European alike. His hero, indeed, was Proust, and he saw himself as a Proustian novelist. At the same time, he grossly underrated Henry James and had little use for Joyce. Perhaps he feared them, for they threatened his position; if their practice was right, then his own allegiance to the plain style, the hallmark of British prose since the seventeenth century, was wrong.

There are some things he did admirably: worldly ambition in the male of the species obviously, male self-regard and the obsessive, tortuous pursuit of power, and the strangled feelings of affection between siblings. But where anything approaching poetry is called for he is almost ludicrously inadequate.

How far the new modes of criticism that have emerged in the last twenty years have affected or are likely to affect our judgement of novels I cannot say, for the most I can achieve is a transient and intermittent feeling that I may be on the verge of seeing through a glass, darkly. As a matter of fact, it was round about 1970 that I was first made aware that something unsuspected by me was happening when, belatedly, I read David Lodge's *The Language of Fiction*. The effect on me was startling – and chastening; I found myself obliged to let my students know next day that I had presented them with a wrong and over-simplistic interpretation of Wells's *Tono-Bungay*.

I caught up with David Lodge the novelist a little later and recognised *The British Museum Is Falling Down* as the funniest and most original comic novel since *Lucky Jim*. He has done much more since then and in *How Far Can You Go?* and *Small World* has shown himself our most brilliant comic dramatist of ideas in today's fiction, rivalled only by Malcolm Bradbury.

Pride of place, though, in any sequel to *Tradition and Dream* would go to Anthony Burgess, as the boldest, most variously gifted and ambitious of our contemporaries, as demonstrated by the freshness and linguistic inventiveness of *The Malayan Trilogy, A Clockwork Orange*, the Enderby series and *Earthly Powers*. And William Golding and John Fowles would also rank high, as would Muriel Spark, especially on the strength of her earlier novels, such as *Memento Mori, The Bachelors* and *The Prime of Miss Jean Brodie*. Her novels brought a new *frisson* into our fiction and, behind the wit, gave disturbing and salutary insights into the human condition, qualities that in our time often seem to be the prerogative of the Roman Catholic writer.

In this personal overview I am satisfied of one further thing: that English writing suffered a tremendous loss with the death of J. G. Farrell in 1979. He had learnt, I think, from Richard Hughes's *The Human Predicament* but made himself a most formidable historical novelist of a new kind in his own right. *Troubles, The Siege of Krishnapur* and *The Singapore Grip* are deeply satisfying imaginative reconstructions, superbly researched, of crucial events in British imperial history of the last century and a half, and much of their power comes from the sense we have that they are also symbolic statements of British assumptions and preoccupations at the times the events took place.

In the last pages of my introduction to *Tradition and Dream* I managed to record the emergence of a new wave of what could fairly be called working-class fiction with Keith Waterhouse in 1957 and Alan Sillitoe and David Storey a year or two later. Something not unlike this has occurred during the past fifteen years in the rise of a new generation of women novelists significantly different from those who had gone before, though it had its precursors in Doris Lessing and perhaps also in the wry, half-regretful novels of Barbara Pym. The first of these new women writers I was aware of was Margaret Drabble, whose *A Summer Bird-Cage* came out in 1964. The post-1960 women novelists in Britain have been distinguished in many ways: A. S. Byatt, Edna O'Brien, Anita Brookner, Fay Weldon, Angela Carter. It is difficult not to feel that they are differently orientated from a representative novelist of an earlier generation like Rosamond Lehmann. With her, Byron's lines, 'Man's love is of man's life a thing apart/'Tis woman's whole existence', still seem apposite since her theme is invariably, despite the note of protest and resentment, the relation of the woman to the man. Women's fiction is still largely concerned with their status as relative beings, but the novels of many recent writers seem rooted not in their experience as women so much as in their being women who have made their way in education and career as independent human beings in more direct and close competition with the other sex; still another group have re-defined female experience and sought to create a different type of women's fiction in the aftermath of the feminist debates of the 1970s.

The extraordinary breadth and variety of the American novel in the last two decades (in addition to the continuing work of authors like Vidal, Bellow or Mailer) is illustrated by the handful of names I would pick from my own reading – Updike, Cheever, Philip Roth, Flannery O'Connor, Vonnegut, Joyce Carol Oates and Alison Lurie, the last not least because she is a practitioner of the novel as comedy of manners, always a rare genre in American writing.

Even at the risk of having to decimate my English and Americans, I would now find room for novelists from other English-speaking peoples, specifically Narayan, Patrick White, Nadine Gordimer, Mordecai Richler, V. S. Naipaul, George Lamming and other Commonwealth writers.

Finally I would want to do more adequate justice than was possible in *Tradition and Dream* to one man: Graham Greene. True, I had noted the existence of *The Quiet American* (1955), *Our Man in Havana* (1958) and *A Burnt-out Case* (1961), but it was scarcely possible to know that these novels marked a new phase in Greene's progress. They seemed merely to highlight the indefatigable journalist in Greene, admittedly an important element in his equipment as a novelist, rather than emphasise a shift in his vision, for the emphasis on the political is now as strong as the emphasis on the religious. This, of course, is grossly to oversimplify, for Greene the novelist has never made a hard distinction between the two. After all, aren't the priest and the police lieutenant in *The Power and the Glory* in a real sense each other's alter ego? Greene, it seems to me, makes his position explicit in *The Comedians* (1966), where in the last pages of the novel the Communist Dr Magiot writes to Brown, the narrator:

Communism, my friend, is more than Marxism, just as Catholicism – remember I was born a Catholic too – is more than the Roman Curia. There is a *mystique* as well as a *politique* . . . Communists have committed great crimes, but at least they have not stood aside, like an established society, and been indifferent. I implore you – a knock on the door may not allow me to finish this sentence, so take it as a last request of a dying man – if you have abandoned one faith, do not abandon all faith. There is always an alternative to the faith we lose. Or is it the same faith under another mask?

Such has been the belief that has sustained Greene throughout his fifty-seven-year-long career as a novelist. It is dramatised most starkly in his later fiction, perhaps, in *A Burnt-out Case*, but it is examined in a greater variety of contexts and against a whole range of backgrounds in a score of novels all brilliantly told. The seriousness of his subject and the virtuosity with which he has rendered it suggest that the place of his novels on the bookshelves is with those of his kinsman Stevenson and his exemplar Conrad.

In this retrospective essay I have picked up some of the threads of *Tradition and Dream*. But since the Sixties other commitments have occupied my time and I have turned to other loves, to poetry and, especially perhaps, American poetry. Willy-nilly, I feel myself more than ever overwhelmed by the enormous variety of the novel, even though I know that is its greatest glory.

All the same, I'd like to think this book, imperfect as it may be, says something for the value and importance of the craft of the literary journalist, the book reviewer, the first person to make public judgement on new books, and that necessarily in haste. The critics proper follow later.

Walter Allen, London 1985

INDEX

345

THE HOGARTH PRESS

This is a paperback list for today's readers – but it holds to a tradition of adventurous and original publishing set by Leonard and Virginia Woolf when they founded The Hogarth Press in 1917 and started their first paperback series in 1924.

Some of the books are light-hearted, some serious, and include Fiction, Lives and Letters, Travel, Critics, Poetry, History and Hogarth Crime and Gaslight Crime.

A list of our books already published, together with some of our forthcoming titles, follows. If you would like more information about Hogarth Press books, write to us for a catalogue:

40 William IV Street, London WC2N 4DF

Please send a large stamped addressed envelope

HOGARTH CRITICS

Tradition and Dream: The English and American Novel from the Twenties to Our Time by Walter Allen
New Afterword by the Author

The Condemned Playground: Essays 1927-1944 by Cyril Connolly
New Introduction by Philip Larkin

Seven Types of Ambiguity by William Empson
Some Versions of Pastoral by William Empson
The Structure of Complex Words by William Empson

Music Ho!: A Study of Music in Decline by Constant Lambert
New Introduction by Angus Morrison

The Common Pursuit by F.R. Leavis

England, Half English by Colin MacInnes
New Foreword by Paul Weller

By Way of Sainte-Beuve by Marcel Proust
Translated by Sylvia Townsend Warner
New Introduction by Terence Kilmartin

The Country and the City by Raymond Williams
The English Novel from Dickens to Lawrence by Raymond Williams

The Common Reader 1 by Virginia Woolf
The Common Reader 2 by Virginia Woolf
Edited and Introduced by Andrew McNeillie
Three Guineas by Virginia Woolf
New Introduction by Hermione Lee

Walter Allen
All in a Lifetime

New Introduction by Alan Sillitoe

'One of the most magnificent literary portraits achieved by any modern novelist' – *Daily Telegraph*

A classic of working-class fiction, *All in a Lifetime* is a history of a life, but also history as it is lived, in all its strangeness and magical ordinariness. The story of a retired silversmith, born in 1875, this novel is not concerned with world events, but with personal struggles and triumphs in friendship, marriage and political convictions – a moving, powerful testament to a whole way of living in this century.

F. R. Leavis
The Common Pursuit

A critic's perceptions are 'his, or they are nothing', but they are still part of a collaborative effort, 'the common pursuit of true judgement'. In these penetrating and forthright essays Leavis demonstrates his refusal to 'rest inertly on a conventional consensus', subjecting individual authors, literary schools and critical attitudes to a personal yet deliberately disinterested scrutiny. From Milton to Hopkins, Bunyan to T. S. Eliot, *The Common Pursuit* is one of the most important of F. R. Leavis's great critical works.

Cyril Connolly

The Condemned Playground

Essays 1927-1944

New Introduction by Philip Larkin

The playground is the literary scene of the Thirties, with its ebullience, mediocrity, frivolity and talent. It is the leafy streets of Chelsea in which Connolly worked and wandered, and it is the world of art itself where men try to make 'mudpies that endure'. It has room for Joyce and Swift, Horace and Housman, for anarchists from Barcelona and revolutionary students from Greece, for conversations in Berlin and meditations in the Midi. With its wicked parodies, elegant criticism and elegiac autobiography this is a book to linger over – Connolly at his inimitable best.